HEADING
EAST

BY DAWN EAST

Heading East by Dawn East

www.headingeast33.wordpress.com/

© 2020 Dawn East

Cover by Dawn East

HEADING
EAST

This book is dedicated to my wonderful friend, Gail Podevin, one of my biggest supporters throughout my journey and who helped me to get this book off the ground.

Thank you x

Contents

The Power of a Dozen Words

"I've not been on a proper holiday since I bought the house."

These twelve words, said innocently over post-run drinks, stuck an icy dagger of fear into the very heart of me. Up until that moment, I'd been planning on buying a flat but while Martine told me about the expense of living alone, I started having *very* different ideas...

Since beginning my teaching career in September of 2010, travel had become an integral part of my life. I'd island-hopped the Hawaiian Islands; spent four days in the Amazon Jungle; seen the mystical Northern Lights in Lapland; trekked across the Wadi Rum desert in Jordan; and travelled New Zealand, sky-diving and hang-gliding along the way. To me, nothing could replace the simple joy of discovering new places and photographing them. I'd been away numerous times a year, sometimes travelling with friends, sometimes with my eldest niece (Kerry-Anne), occasionally joining organised group tours, and frequently travelling alone.

However, after my New Zealand trip, at the age of thirty-seven, I decided that my more extravagant travels had to come to an end: it was time to be a grown-up and start saving. Once I had enough money, I would finally move out of my mum's house and buy a place of my own before I hit the terrifying age of forty. I can't pretend I was excited by the prospect of home ownership; it was something I felt I *should* do rather than *wanted* to do. I had no desire to follow the well-trodden 'marriage and kids' path through life but I needed somewhere to live. After all, mum wouldn't be around forever to put me up - or to put up with me.

Over the next two years, I surprised myself by saving sixteen thousand pounds while still managing to take regular short holidays. I was telling this to Martine on the first Friday of September in 2017 as we sat at the pub, recovering from a run around Windsor Great Park. It was then that she uttered those powerful words, the words that would instantaneously change my plans.

While driving home that bright summer's afternoon, the tendrils of an idea crept into my mind: I could take my savings and use them to see the world. The thought ignited a passion in me that buying a flat never had and for the first time in a while, I felt giddy with excitement. By the time I pulled up outside my house, my mind was made up. I didn't know where I would go or how I would do it, but I was going to hand in my notice at school and go travelling for as long as my money would allow, years maybe. When I told my mum, she didn't seem particularly shocked.

That weekend, I researched ways to make money while I travelled. The most viable options seemed to be teaching English as a second language or learning to create websites, effectively becoming a digital nomad. However, neither appealed to me and both would require retraining. I soon decided against working at all; instead, I would travel until my money ran out and see where I ended up. Maybe I would be inspired by a new career, meet my ideal man, or fall in love with a country and want to stay there – the possibilities were endless. However, travelling without working would require more funding so I decided to keep saving until the end of the school year, which would give me ample time to plan things out, and depart in August 2018.

When I arrived at school on Monday, I eagerly informed my head teacher that I was planning to hand in my notice: it suddenly made everything very real. As the autumn term progressed, and I was reluctantly plunged into my forties, doubt began creeping in: so much so that within a few weeks, I found myself requesting, and receiving, the safety net of a sabbatical. Even though I considered it a cop out from my original plan, a year of travelling seemed far less daunting and I felt more secure knowing that I would have a job to come back to.

Over the next few months, nearly every spare moment was spent researching, planning, making bookings and fretting. As a worrier, I had a long list of questions (in case you're planning your own travels, I answer all of these at the back of the book):

What kind of luggage should I buy?
What travel insurance should I get?
How will I prevent theft of my belongings?
What credit and debit cards should I take to avoid international fees?
How will I manage my budget?
What visas will I need in advance?
Will I get homesick or lonely?
How will I chat to friends and family?
As a fussy eater, what will I eat?
Will I get food poisoning?
Will I get a horrible parasite or disease?
What immunisations will I need and how will I prevent malaria?
Will I lose my running ability and how will I track my runs?
Should I take my heavy Canon camera or buy something smaller?
How will I edit and back up my photos?
How about toiletries and sanitary products?
How will I do my washing?
What will I do about my mobile phone?
What will happen to my car?
What should I pack?

Sometimes I'd read something that would send me spiraling into panic mode. For example, it was mentioned online that in Vietnam's major cities, bag snatching by criminals on motorbikes was common. The next six hours were then spent frantically researching what kind of bag to take for sightseeing – should I buy a strong, secure bag or something more modest, like a canvas tote, that wouldn't attract much attention? Even though I already had a perfectly sufficient neck pouch, by the end of the day, I'd bought a money pouch to attach to my bra and a slim money belt. I'd also purchased some RFID pockets to protect my contactless cards and had added anti-theft knickers with secure pockets (I hadn't even known that such a thing existed) and an expensive slashproof bag to my online wishlist. The last two items never made it into my basket and the bra purse was sent home with a friend early on. Looking back, I can honestly say that it's often not fancy bags that protect you from theft, but a healthy dose of common sense and a pinch of good luck.

Safety issues aside, I had one key question: 'Where should I go?' A few months before, someone had told me about her experience on the Transiberian Express. It was something I was eager to do, which would lead me east, to where I could explore South-East Asia and Australia. The train journey ended up being the most expensive part of the whole trip. I wasn't confident about travelling solo across Russia, Mongolia and China so I used a tour company, *The Real Russia*, to arrange everything for me. I didn't want to share a small cabin with a complete stranger so I bought two first class train tickets. Including train travel, hotels, visas and transfers, it cost close to three thousand pounds for the sixteen day trip, not even including the flight to Moscow. It would be worth it though.

Using relevant visa and climate information, an itinerary began to formulate for the first seven months of travelling: I knew where I wanted to go, when was best to visit each place and how long I could stay in each country. Gradually, friends began showing an interest in joining me for different legs of the trip and kind offers came in to meet up with, and even stay with, a couple of international friends that I'd met on my previous adventures.

By the time summer term came around, I had most things organised: key flights, tours and accommodation had been booked; I'd paid for travel insurance; I'd bought my rucksack and essential electronics; I'd had all my jabs and had applied for new credit and debit cards. The complicated visa applications had also been submitted and all I had left to do was visit the Russian Embassy in London so they could take my fingerprints.

Typically, it was around this time that I started to develop feelings for someone. His name was Tom (it wasn't actually but I've changed it for the book). We'd been friends since the start of the year but the more time we'd spent together, the closer we'd become. It wasn't good timing for either of us. I couldn't believe it; after thirteen years of being single, I had to meet someone *just* as I was preparing to leave the country for a year. I tried not to let it negate the excitement of my upcoming trip but I can't pretend it didn't; with every passing week, my sadness about our upcoming separation grew.

Before I knew it, the academic year was over and it was time to say goodbye to my eighth Year 6 class as they moved on to secondary school. As I emptied my classroom and packed my car, I felt relieved that I wouldn't be back for thirteen months - I enjoyed teaching but it was stressful and I was eager to escape it. Over the next few days, I slowly said goodbye to my friends, some individually, but mostly at my leaving party by the river in Richmond. I would miss my friends and family but I was grateful that so many people would be coming out to see me and I could use social media to stay in touch.

After much procrastination, I reluctantly packed my green Osprey backpack (a packing list is included at the back of the book) a couple of days before I was due to leave. Thanks to packing cubes, everything fit. However, although the cubes made my luggage more compact, they did not have the magical ability to make it lighter, so I could barely lift, let alone carry, what I called the 'Green Turtle'.

As my departure date loomed, sadness and anxiety began to get the better of me. I often felt sick but never excited. It felt like I was being thrust from my well-ordered routine into chaos and it was hard to see the sun through the dark clouds of fear. Bidding an emotional farewell to Tom didn't improve my mood as I wasn't sure where we stood with each other or what the future might hold for us. When we said goodbye, it felt like my heart would break. I would miss him so much and I worried that my feelings for him would hinder my enjoyment of the trip.

The day before I left, I went to the Hazelwood parkrun with my friend Alex, who paced me to achieve a personal best of five kilometres in under twenty-five minutes. I'd started running a couple of years before and had completed two marathons and a fifty kilometre ultra-marathon since deciding to travel for a year. I knew I wouldn't be able to sustain the intense level of training I'd been doing while I was home but I was determined to at least run twice a week while I was away.

Once I'd showered and changed, I went to the wedding of my friend Frances. Despite already missing Tom, and wishing he were there with me, it was a wonderful day and my good friends Charley and Gareth, also guests, were the perfect distraction from the myriad of strong feelings threatening to overwhelm me.

Finally, the morning of Sunday 12th August arrived. Putting on a brave face, I hugged my mum goodbye and then my friend Paul drove me towards Heathrow. As we neared the airport, I suddenly changed my mind - I didn't want to go anymore. I screamed at Paul to turn around and take me home. The tyres of his little red car screeched as we spun dramatically on the A30 and then sped back in the direction of Shepperton, to where I would hide in the safety of my bedroom for a year. From there, I would copy and paste myself into photos of the places I'd wanted to travel to and save myself the discomfort of actually visiting them.

Of course, this scenario only happened in my head. In reality, I kept quiet until we reached the drop-off zone, and then tried not to cry when I hugged Paul goodbye. Standing at the busy entrance to the airport with the Green Turtle, I felt very alone and very anxious. But as my friend Gail had told me, I could come back *whenever* I wanted:

home was rarely more than twenty-four hours away and there was no shame in returning early. Taking a deep breath and wiping away my tears, I picked up the Green Turtle and stepped through the doors...

The Blog

"I think I'm quite ready for another adventure." (Bilbo Baggins)

Before I left, I decided to write a blog (www.headingeast33.wordpress.com) so my close friends and family could track my travels and see how I was getting on. I surprised myself with how much I loved the act of writing and the blog soon became my main focus. I spent hours on it each week, writing, editing and choosing photos for it, and every word was painstakingly typed out on my phone. As situations and scenarios unfolded, I would imagine how I would write about them in an entertaining way: it helped me to appreciate even the negative aspects of my travels. The main bulk of this book is based on my original blog posts and there is generally one for each city I visited, in chronological order. Check it out if you want to see the numerous photos of my trip.

Now is probably a good time to tell you that I am not Bill Bryson or Jack Kerouac so you might not find much in the way of poetically descriptive prose. I'm more like Karl Pilkington. Our tastes are similar, both with crisps (we both love Monster Munch) and travel destinations (though I tend to be more easily impressed than Karl) and we get annoyed by some of the same things. In the past, his television show inspired me to visit both Peru and Jordan. He'd enjoyed Petra (Jordan) and so did I; he'd liked Machu Picchu (Peru) and so did I. He was less impressed with China so I had a feeling I might feel the same way.

As you start reading, you may have many questions. Would I last the year? Would I have any disasters? Would I love somewhere so much that I wouldn't leave? Well, I hope you enjoy following my journey and finding out...

England: Heathrow Airport - Taking Off

My blog, as written on the day:

I'm finally here at the airport - I'm a bag of nerves and still can't quite feel the excitement. Anyone would think that I'm getting ready for my own public hanging rather than going off to explore the world. Maybe I'd feel better if I weren't alone? I'm jealous of the people around me who have company but my friend Andy is coming out to see me in only two weeks so that cheers me up.

The thought of entering Russia is rather daunting: for some reason, I'm expecting to be strip-searched and interrogated as soon as I step off the plane. I've heard from friends that Moscow is a great city so I'm sure I have little to worry about. I just hope the driver is there at the airport, ready to take me to the hotel. What if my name is written in Russian on his little board though? I'll be there all day...

I suppose there isn't much left to say. Soon I will board the plane and start my journey east through Russia, Mongolia and China. All of my hotels should have WiFi so I will keep you updated. I have already planned a riverside run for Moscow and have booked a free walking tour, where hopefully I'll get to meet some fellow travelers and not feel so alone.

I'm scared but as someone recently told me, I can always come home if I'm unhappy. For now, I will try to dig out my excited face and start my journey...

Russia: Moscow -
The Thing About Pigeons...

12TH - 14TH AUGUST 2018

The thing about pigeons is that they are universal; therefore I don't understand why so many tourists become enthralled by them. It wasn't the actual pigeons that irritated me, it was the *other* tourists (as much as I hated the fact, I was aware that I was equally cluttering up the streets of Moscow), who would try to take selfies with the pigeons, even putting food on their shoulder so the birds would climb up onto them. Moscow wasn't alone in being filled with selfie-obsessed tourists but it was where I first understood how bloated the selfie-monster had become and how much I disliked it.

Upon entering Russia, there was no grueling interrogation. Much to my relief, it was entirely painless: an officer checked my visa, robotically stamped my passport and waved me through. The Green Turtle and I were reunited at baggage claim and we made our way to the arrivals hall. Despite my fears, a driver was waiting for me, holding up an IPad showing my name in a big, bold font. He didn't speak much English but he greeted me politely and led me to a fancy private car featuring WiFi, music and free drinks.

After a speedy journey, I was dropped off at the four-star Arbat House Hotel. Considering I'd paid for the *budget* tour package, I was pleasantly surprised by the high quality of the hotel and I loved the views of the city from the window of my sixth-floor room. As I sat alone on my bed, I was overcome by a dark wave of loneliness. A year away from home suddenly felt like a lifetime and I wondered if I would be able to manage it. I wanted to hug Tom and have him tell me that it would all be ok, but of course, that wasn't going to happen.

To distract my anxious mind, I ventured out into the city. I meandered through the crowds: most, like me, were walking, some were on electric scooters and a few were on horseback, carrying swords and pistols. Now, as a general rule, Russians don't go around carrying large weapons in the streets, there just happened to be a military fair on. I couldn't read any of the information (it was all in Russian of course) but it was interesting seeing people dressed in military costumes marching and preparing for battle.

As I weaved through the masses of people, it suddenly hit me - this was now my life. I didn't have a real purpose anymore, except to wander, wonder, look and listen. It also hit me, as I walked past some *very* inviting restaurants, that dinner from the supermarket was my new reality. I'd never been great at being thrifty, as within reason, I tended to buy things when I wanted them. But if I was going to travel long-term, I would have to stick to a tight budget and that would mean limited visits to restaurants.

The following morning, I joined a free walking tour. It was interesting but the experience was marred by one annoying woman, who repeatedly asked questions the guide had already answered; it led to a lot of eye-rolling amongst the rest of us. As the only Brit, I was verbally bashed by the tour guide but I gave as good as I got and he didn't offend me. Moscow was beautiful. Before I'd arrived, I'd had images of a grey, grimy city filled with miserable people, all wrapped up in big fur coats, but in reality, it was colourful, clean and modern. I'd like to say I was wrong about the people but I honestly don't think one person smiled at me the whole time I was there. Rather than label them as unfriendly, I prefer to liken Russians to scary teachers - terrifying until you get to know them and then they reveal a softer side.

The fortified complex of the Kremlin was a little underwhelming. I didn't see Putin, just his helipad, but there were some pretty cathedrals (most notably St. Basil's) to admire. Too lazy to queue to get into any of them, I chose to sit in the square, people-watching. I noticed that the guards blew whistles *a lot* - if anyone walked or sat in the wrong place, a whistle would soon be blown aggressively. I enjoyed playing 'spot the wrong-doer'. As a teacher, I greatly approved - rules pleased me; I didn't always follow them but I liked other people to.

As well as whistle-blowers, the square was home to pigeons. Wherever I'd been in the world, I'd seen pigeons yet the tourists in Moscow seemed to love them, as if they were a rare sight. I watched French and Spanish people taking countless selfies with the mangy birds. I'd been to both countries and seen pigeons in both, so why were they so excited by *Russian* pigeons? They all looked the same to me.

On my final day in Moscow, I ran ten miles, mostly along the scenic riverside, and then visited the gorgeous Gorky Park and a Banksy exhibition. I also came across some old Soviet Union statues and monuments in a different park. I packed in as much as possible and then returned to the hotel to pack.

At 10pm, a taxi arrived to take me to Yaroslavsky Train Station. As I stepped out of the car, I felt nervous. I'd been lonely in Moscow and really hoped to meet at least one friendly person on the train. I'd read that unless I wanted to get completely wasted, I needed to avoid any vodka-wielding Russians. Apparently it's rude in Russia to decline an invitation of drinking vodka and once you begin drinking, you can't leave until the bottle is completely drained. I'd had some bad experiences with vodka in my youth and I wasn't eager to have them repeated, so I would have to be vigilant.

Inside the station, I sat on a bench, waiting for my platform number to be displayed. Unexpectedly, there was free WiFi, so I used this to talk to Tom. It was a fraught yet stilted conversation and I wanted to go home and talk to him properly – I didn't like how we'd left things between us. I found myself wishing I'd never met him, that I didn't feel pulled in half when I was supposed to be enjoying the trip of a lifetime. I asked him an important question just as my platform came up and I had to leave. With each step I took, the WiFi signal grew weaker until it disappeared altogether. I could see he'd been typing an answer but I would have to wait to find out what it was.

With tears running down my face, I tried to navigate my way through the busy station whilst lugging the Green Turtle, a smaller yet heavy rucksack and a large bag of food. I only had a few minutes before my train, number 004, departed but I couldn't find the platform. None of the staff were informative and one older worker was particularly rude when I desperately asked for help. Just when I thought the situation was hopeless, a young Australian couple pointed me in the right direction. With only four minutes to spare, I made it onto the train and into the safety of my cabin. The 4735 mile train journey to Beijing was about to begin...

Trans-Mongolian Train:
Moscow to Ulan Bator - Sliding Doors

14TH - 19TH AUGUST 2018

"It's mental how long this is - mental. They said it's the greatest - it's not. It's the longest. They've sold it on the worst thing about it."
(Karl Pilkington on the Transiberian train journey)

I'd have to disagree with this as I absolutely *loved* the train journey. Maybe this was because I could liken it to another love of mine - camping. Here are my reasons:

1. You have to fetch your own water. You can get boiling water from the samovar (an urn). If you need cold water you'll unfortunately need to wait for your hot water to cool down.

2. You need to prepare your own food (although there is a dining cart if you're feeling fancy). Below is a sample menu:

   o Breakfast: Porridge
   o Lunch: Bread with cherry jam
   o Dinner: Noodles or rice from a plastic pot, mixed with boiling water
   o Snacks & Drinks: Fruit, cereal bars, biscuits, peppermint tea, hot chocolate and cartons of orange juice

3. The toilet facilities aren't ideal. When you 'flush', your waste goes down the hole, straight onto the train tracks. It's a good job the movie *Stand By Me* wasn't set in Russia, otherwise those kids would've had a lot more to deal with than a dead body and a few hungry leeches.

4. You make small talk with your neighbours. Topics up for discussion include how you slept, the timing of the next stop,

whether the cabin plug sockets are currently working (rarely), which food to buy from the kiosks at the stations, and of course, the weather.

5. Your bed is somewhat uncomfortable. Well it would've been but a friend recommended that I take a cheap, inflatable lilo with me. I'm glad I did as the so-called 'soft' beds were actually very firm. The blind pulled down at night and made the cabin pitch black so I slept really well. It was a bit weird being bumped around as the train moved but it actually lulled me to sleep.

6. You make your own entertainment. I thought I'd get bored but it didn't happen. As long as the train was moving, I felt occupied. I read a little, did sudoku puzzles, ate, napped and chatted my way through the four and a half days.

7. The time doesn't matter much. To be fair, half of the time you don't *know* what the time is as you're always crossing time zones (Russia is *big*). One night, at about 8pm, I was wondering how to spend my evening. I looked again at my phone and it was suddenly two hours ahead: problem solved - it was time for bed.

8. Washing can be tricky. In first class, there is a small shower room between every two cabins, which you can enter from either side. There is a showerhead where you can hose yourself down with the pathetic dribble of water that comes out.

Camping comparisons over, I must say I felt safe and relaxed on the train from the moment I boarded. The Chinese guards were helpful and the people in my carriage were all polite, quiet European couples - there were certainly no fun parties at *our* end of the train. The journey itself was very pleasant; I loved to sit in my cosy cabin and watch the sunlit fields and silver birch blur past.

A couple of days into the journey, I turned on my data so I could check my messages. Tom's message didn't clear up anything for me and he seemed a little cold. Looking back, he was probably trying to distance himself from me but it didn't hurt any less. Not for the last time, I wished I hadn't met him. I wanted to enjoy my trip and not feel sad, but I couldn't pick and choose what life threw in my path – I would have to make the best of things and hope it got easier.

"It's a dangerous business, Frodo, going out your door. You step onto the road, and if you don't keep your feet, there's no knowing where you might be swept off to." (Bilbo Baggins)

I recalled this quote as I stepped out of Carriage 10 for the first time. I'd spent the first day hiding away in my cabin, just chatting briefly with my neighbours, but on Thursday, feeling in need of a change of scenery, I bravely ventured out to the dining car. When I arrived, only one table was occupied, by a small group of Australians. Too shy to join them, I sat alone and ordered some fried potatoes, the cheapest option on the menu.

At the same time my lunch arrived, so did *Alexander*, a moustached, middle-aged Russian. Grabbing my plate of food, he slammed it onto his table and insisted that I join him. Too polite to make a fuss, I reluctantly did as I was told. Naturally, a fresh bottle of vodka was in front of him. Judging by his bloodshot eyes, it clearly wasn't his first of the day.

Once he'd obtained two shot glasses, Alex began pouring neat vodka. Hating the taste, I washed it down with big gulps of lemonade. Alex knew slightly more English than I did Russian but communication between us was somewhat challenging. It didn't stop him from talking *at* me a lot though. He seemed to think that if he repeated himself enough, I'd eventually understand him. Actions were sometimes *more* helpful, as from these I learned that he was, or possibly had been, a helicopter pilot. Throughout our time together, Alex grabbed and kissed my hand frequently - it was somewhat awkward. I could see the Australians laughing at my predicament but they didn't attempt to rescue me. Instead, my saviour was a young, Swedish man, Jon, who having sat at the table next to us, started laughing as I tried to explain my profession. I was attempting to get across that I *taught* thirty children but Alex thought I was saying that I *had* thirty children.

Eager to have the vodka split between three instead of two, I invited Jon to join us. As he understood some Russian, the men were able to communicate more easily and Jon translated where possible. Apparently, Alex mostly talked about my *beautiful* smile and his love for me (or perhaps for flying helicopters - it wasn't entirely clear). There were moments when Jon awkwardly explained that the Russian was being 'inappropriate'. It wasn't a surprise - Alex's leering expression made his intentions pretty clear. Once the bottle of vodka was empty and we'd washed it down with some black coffee (I hated coffee and vodka equally), I pretended that I needed the toilet, whispered my cabin number to Jon and escaped to the safety of Carriage 10. Jon later told me that Alex had soon disappeared to sleep off the booze.

The vodka had made me brave so instead of going back to my own cabin, I went to sit with the Danish couple next door. Jon soon joined us, and as we all talked, I finally felt more content, a little less anxious. I still felt intimidated by the idea of being away for so long but I hoped the feeling would pass as I adjusted to life on the move. Jon became my train companion and would often come to my cabin: it gave me a chance to practice my Swedish and it was great to have company.

The next day, I met Josh, a relaxed Australian who'd been travelling around Europe by motorbike. Funnily enough, he'd been one of the Australians in the dining car when I'd been accosted. He offered to accompany me to the dining car (as protection) when I explained I'd been avoiding a repeat visit, in case Alex and a fresh bottle of vodka were waiting. Josh met me for lunch on Friday and luckily, Alex was nowhere to be seen. It was nice to chat about our lives and travels.

Apart from the vodka shenanigans, the only other trouble I had was with the sliding door: *my* sliding door. From the moment I boarded, the door to Cabin 3 had something against me and wouldn't open or close without a fight. Nobody else had a problem with *their* door; they all slid in the appropriate manner. I was once trapped in my cabin for fifteen minutes, desperate for the toilet. I must've yanked it fifty times. Just as panic was setting in, it gave up and slid open, as if it had had its fun. The guards saw me flailing with the door a few times and always came to my aid. *They* were always able to open it straight away and probably mocked me when they returned to their cabin. I felt perpetually embarrassed by my inability to open a door.

On Saturday night, the train crossed the border into Mongolia. It took two hours to exit Russia: the intimidating immigration officials came to check everyone's documents and we had to step out of our cabins while they were searched. Once the customs checks were complete, we had a brief train ride to enter Mongolia, where the whole process was repeated. The Mongolian officials were much more polite though; the passport officer even saluted when he entered my cabin. I saluted him back for some mortifying reason.

After five hours of sleep, I prepared to exit the train. I couldn't believe the journey was over. It had been a real adventure and I would really miss Jon and Josh, who were off to spend some time in the Mongolian countryside. I was nervous about being in Mongolia alone as I didn't know much about the country or its capital, Ulan Bator. Peering out of the window, the city looked very different to Moscow but I was sure I'd be fine. As the train pulled to a stop, the Green Turtle and I stepped onto the platform, where I waved goodbye to my friends and waited to be collected.

If you're thinking of following in my tracks on the Trans-Mongolian or the Trans-Siberian train, here are some tips:

- Bring an inflatable lilo to improve your sleeping comfort.
- Bring plenty of snacks (although some are available on the platform kiosks).
- Bring a metal cup and cutlery.
- Bring toilet paper (there was none on the train).
- Bring squash (the water can taste a bit weird).
- Ask the guard for the timetable so you know exactly how long you'll be at each stop - after all, you don't want to be left behind (you may have trouble reading it though as all times are in 'Moscow time' and are written in Russian).
- Bring things to do: books, puzzles, games etc.
- If you're a phone addict, you can get a decent signal along some of the route. My data plan allowed me to use it in Russia for six pounds a day. I did it for two of the days and the signal came and went but it was always better nearer to the major towns.
- Learn a little Russian - even 'please' and 'thank you' are well received

Mongolia: Ulan Bator - Milking a Horse

19TH - 23RD AUGUST 2018

After being picked up by a female guide at the train station, I was taken to the Hotel Nine. In the elevator up to reception, we agreed that she'd take me to the Chinggis Khan statue later in the week. As we parted, she warned me to be *very* careful with my bag in the city. It wouldn't be my first warning: the receptionist told me the same thing a few minutes later. *The Real Russia* had organised an early check-in, so after a free breakfast, I was shown to my room, where I indulged myself with a long nap.

"My brain is always against me. My brain is never on my side. The brain will make me panic. It'll be going, what are you doing? You could die here." (Karl Pilkington)

Karl Pilkington said this about being buried alive in Russia but I feel his pain because my brain is also a panic-merchant. Once I was fully awake, I started reading up on Ulan Bator. I didn't like what I read. The city was described as being *quite dangerous*. Despite the strong urge to hide in my hotel room for the next four days, I decided to risk venturing out to a nearby shopping centre. Thankfully, I didn't get attacked as soon as I stepped out of the hotel. Just to be on the safe side, I wore my small rucksack on my front. I safely purchased some nail files and a pumice stone (essentials that I had forgotten) and then found the city centre. The city square was surprisingly impressive and as there was a handful of other tourists around, I felt brave enough to pull Mr. Canon out of my bag. As I began taking photos, I noticed that lots of people were wandering around with their phones out - maybe Ulan Bator wasn't *quite* as dangerous as the internet had portrayed.

After five days of train travel, I was feeling the urge to run. The city's footpaths weren't great for running on so I decided to visit the National Recreation Park. It was a couple of miles away and as I wanted to be back by sunset, I thought it would be safer to take a taxi. How wrong I was...

The taxi driver appeared to be a sweet old man who smiled innocuously as I closed the car door. For a few seconds, I relaxed, but it didn't last long. I went to put the seatbelt on and realised there *was* no seatbelt. The elderly driver then proceeded to drive like a maniac. I'd read online about the terrible driving in Mongolia but I'd never seen anything like it. At home, I wasn't known for my patient driving, but the Mongolians made me seem like Mary Poppins. Cars almost rammed into each other; there was a constant stream of horns beeping; and cars weaved in and out of lanes randomly like drunks. Whenever my driver did something particularly dangerous, he would turn and grin at me, as if to say 'that was close'. I can honestly say it was the longest two miles of my life.

When we finally arrived at the park, I almost leapt out and kissed the ground in gratitude. I was left wondering whether people were failed for being too polite during Mongolian driving tests. "You could have pushed in there - that's a fail! You should never wait patiently - just go!" Or, "You only used your horn twenty times in an hour - that's a fail. You must beep continuously!" Driving in the Mongolian countryside was no better than in the city. There were fewer cars to contend with but there were many more potholes. Still, the roads in Mongolia had fewer potholes than back home in Surrey.

The recreation park was very pleasant and I enjoyed the beautiful backdrop of mountains and greenery. The paths were full of humans on scooters, bicycles and tiny cars (for kids). Luckily, apart from a few walkers, the sports track was very quiet so I had plenty of space to myself while I ran. I just wished it was a little closer to my hotel. When I was done, I jogged home. The air was full of dust and pollution from the traffic and the pavements were uneven and broken up - slow and steady was the only way to go. To avoid looking like an easy target, I strapped my resting bitch face on and moved purposefully, like I knew where I was going. *Everyone* always stared at me though, not because of my good looks but because I had one of the only Caucasian faces in the city. I drew even more attention when I was in my sweaty running gear - runners were clearly a rarity in Ulan Bator.

Bright and early on Monday morning, I was ready at reception for a tour to Terelj National Park. Aaltaa (a teacher as well as a tour guide) met me and introduced me to Tumee, our driver. He was a really sweet guy, who pointed out interesting sights and stopped the car whenever he thought I might want to take a photo. I enjoyed listening to his quiet singing as he drove (not nearly as manically as the taxi driver had and his car also had seatbelts which gave him bonus points).

As we entered the national park, I let go of the breath I'd been holding since I'd left home. I immediately felt calmer: I prefer nature to cities so it made sense. We drove around the park and visited 'Turtle Rock' (which from one angle looked more phallic than turtle-shaped). We then walked up to the Aryapala Buddhist Temple through some beautiful grounds. The mountain views were spectacular and I wished I could've sat alone there to meditate for a while (it didn't even occur to me to ask). I loved the silence. There were no planes, trains or cars to disturb the peace.

Eventually, it was time for lunch. I'd been dreading it all day. Instead of going to one of the park's restaurants, we would dine with a nomadic family, eating inside a traditional yurt. As we took our seats in the homely tent, I nervously bit my lip, wondering what was about to be served. I was the only tourist so it wasn't like I could hide in a crowd, I would *have* to eat what was put in front of me. First, I was provided with a cup of fermented horse milk. I hadn't even realised that horses *could* be milked - they seemed too dignified to allow such a thing. It tasted disgusting and I could only manage a few sips before my gag reflexes kicked in. Aaltaa laughingly told me that I wasn't expected to finish it as the family knew it was an *acquired* taste. Washing the sour taste away with water, I wondered if there would be unpleasant repercussions in the bathroom later on. The rest of the meal was a little better: I ate fermented cheese, lots of mini doughnut balls and a deep-fried, beef pancake pocket. The beef dish was particularly greasy so I could only manage one of the *ten* I was given. Aaltaa herself only ate two, mostly because she was too busy taking photos of us on her phone.

After lunch, it was time to go horse riding. Aaltaa and I clambered onto our trusty steeds and took hold of the reigns. Mongolian horses are notoriously short so we weren't too high up. My horse was chilled. A bit *too* chilled in fact. It walked for a bit and then stopped to eat, indicating it wasn't in the mood and wanted to relax with the other horses. Even the fourteen-year-old boy leading us shook his head at it. The animal always walked on eventually (after a lot of tugging and exasperated groans from us) but it wasn't happy. Maybe it had an issue with me as a person. It seemed to have a flatulence problem too - I was worried Aaltaa would think it was me trumping with such gusto. Once my lazy horse realised it was heading home, it picked up the pace. I think we were equally relieved when the trip was over. The views of the countryside had been worth it though and it had been less eventful than my previous horse-riding experience in New Zealand, where the creature had galloped off after being spooked by a sheep and had leapt over a wide stream with me holding on for dear life.

Before we drove back to the city, Aaltaa and I sat on a hill and watched the nomadic family go about their lives. A large amount of Mongolia's people are still nomadic and horses are in their blood. This was clear from watching a five-year-old boy ride a horse while also leading a bactrian camel - he was fearless and skilled at riding. The camel looked a little sulky; I hoped his day improved.

By Tuesday, I felt more confident, so I downgraded my security level from Red to Amber. This meant my rucksack returned to my back (the important stuff was in my neck pouch, hidden). It was while I was thinking how much safer I felt in Ulan Bator, that I encountered a Mongolian penis. I was cutting through some public gardens and there it was, being waved at me by a smiling, overweight man in his fifties. Maybe he'd been shaking it after peeing but he made no attempt to put it away and his trousers and pants were bunched around his feet, which was unusual for someone having a quick wee. The whole incident only lasted a few seconds but it felt like longer. I walked along the road from then on.

That afternoon, I visited a forty-metre steel statue of Chinggis (aka Ghengis) Khan, which was located fifty-five kilometres from Ulan Bator. This involved yet another scary car journey, this time with the tour guide (and her daughter), who'd picked me up from the train station. Her car had no seat belts in the back and the rear-view mirror had been replaced by a television screen. There were a few hairy moments but we arrived at our destination in one piece. The statue was big and shiny, as you'd expect from a huge steel statue but the surrounding area seemed poorly-maintained. Some of the outside steps were broken and well-established weeds forced their way between the cracks. Underneath the monument was a small museum which included some mock-ups of traditional Mongolian dwellings. I dressed myself in the provided furs and had some photos taken - I looked quite at home.

After an hour, we returned to the city. The guide recommended that I visit Tumen Ekh, a Mongolian song and dance ensemble, so I had her drop me there. It was really enjoyable - the dancing was very energetic and I loved the vibrant costumes. The contortionist's abilities were truly shocking: I didn't know the human body could move in such a way (I'm not even sure she was human). What surprised me during the show was that I developed a soft spot for the Mongolian throat singer: he was very talented, with great stage presence, and he produced some haunting, inhuman sounds. My friend Charley fancies morris dancers so I wasn't alone in my weird crush.

The next morning, I unexpectedly bumped into Josh. He'd returned from his stay in a yurt and was now at the same hotel as me. We had a long catch-up over breakfast and arranged to meet for dinner that evening. Feeling happy to have someone to eat with, I visited the National Museum of Mongolia to learn about the country's history.

That afternoon, I came across a funfair. It was hard to tell if it was open or not, as it was overgrown with rusty fencing and long grass crept through cracks in the pavement. It summed up Ulan Bator for me: there were lots of grand projects but once they were finished, they were left to deteriorate - maintenance wasn't a priority. Maybe it was part of the nomadic mindset, to keep moving on.

Feeling fed up, I decided I was done with the city. I was tired of almost being mowed down by bad drivers or having to walk on crumbling pavements next to dusty building sites. If Ulan Bator were a dinner date, I'd have escaped out of the toilet window before the main course: we weren't compatible. Mongolia's countryside was where the *real* romance was for me and I found myself wishing I'd spent more time in the national park, where I would've been happier (although the thought of having to drink more fermented horse milk was less appealing).

I met Josh at reception that evening. Walking around the city with him, I felt safe and relaxed. Nothing seemed to faze him as he chatted to locals and bartered happily with street vendors. I wished I had his confidence. From what Josh told me about himself, he sounded like a modern-day Crocodile Dundee, living alone in a house in the middle of nowhere, able to catch and kill his own food when it was required. He invited me to stay with him when I reached Australia but sadly I couldn't fit it into my tight schedule. For dinner, we settled on a quiet little restaurant and ordered chicken, rice and drinks. It was my first proper meal since I'd left home and it was therefore delicious. The evening flew as we talked but it was soon time to return to the hotel - I had a 6:30am train to catch the next morning. It was a shame to say goodbye to Josh but I wasn't sad about leaving Mongolia. I was ready to discover China.

Trans-Mongolian Train: Ulan Bator to Beijing - Screaming Like a Banshee

23RD - 24TH AUGUST 2018

On Thursday morning, I stepped onto the No.24 train and was greeted by a well-dressed train guard. As I entered my cabin in carriage 7, I was impressed: it was more modern than the previous train. There was a proper bathroom, with both a toilet and shower, between each two first class cabins and toilet paper was even provided. I felt excited for the journey ahead but my happiness wasn't set to last as two demonic children boarded. The *banshees* had two modes: crying or screaming. I wasn't sure what a banshee actually was. I would've looked it up on Google but there *was* no Google thanks to the Great Firewall of China. There was also no Facebook, WhatsApp, Instagram or Twitter.

When the din first began, I was certain it would soon cease but the children had the capacity to surprise me: they never stopped. I thought (rather naively) that as they were a few cabins down, I might not hear them, but their mother was happy for them to spend the entire journey running up and down the corridor. I had to close my cabin door; otherwise they would waltz in and stand staring at me. Not even my fiercest teacher glare could frighten them off. I tried *shooing* them but that only riled them up and they'd start laughing, thinking I was playing a game. The little monsters wouldn't leave me alone. They were like cats and headed straight for the person who liked them least. However, when they were quiet, they were actually sweet and I even found it hard not to smile back when they would enter my personal space and say, "Hello!" with a strong Chinese accent.

I gave in to my fate and allowed the screaming to wash over me while I thought about more pressing issues, like food. I'd spent most of my Mongolian money so I wouldn't be eating much on the train. I had one packet of porridge, some peanut butter, two slices of bread, a cereal bar and an apple to last me thirty-odd hours. Luckily my appetite had been negligible so I wasn't too worried by my predicament.

At 7pm, we reached the Mongolian border. Checks were completed on board and we were merrily on our way into China by 8:30pm. However, we were then told we would no longer be able to stay on the train when we reached China due to new security procedures. So, at 9pm, I was at the back of a long queue (with all my luggage that I'd quickly had to pack up and lug off the train) to get my passport checked at the security hall in the train station. While this was happening, the train's 'wheels' were changed (the tracks are a slightly different size in China). I happened to line up next to an older British couple from Wiltshire, whose names were Jane and Paul. We stuck together as we lined up to give our fingerprints, have our photos taken and our passports stamped. I smiled as Jane and Paul bickered over which forms were needed and which queue to join. It took well over an hour. We then had the pleasure of waiting in a large room, with minimal seating, for a few hours. Welcome to China!

I was thankful I'd met Jane and Paul. The hours passed relatively quickly while we chatted about our travels (they were just finishing the final part of a world trip, completed in one-month chunks over a few years) and tried to avoid the many cockroaches that called the station home. Paul bought us each a Snickers bar and Jane gave me some apples and leftover crisps. I think they felt sorry for me for having eaten so little. To our relief, at 12:30am, we were told to re-board. This was much better than the estimated 2am. I said goodbye to Jane and Paul, returned to my cabin and climbed up to bed.

The next morning, I was wide awake by 6:30am so I climbed down from my bed, eager to see what views waited behind the blind: lush green fields, snow-capped mountains or thriving forests? No - a rubbish dump. I closed the blind. A few minutes later, I tried again, hoping for an improvement and was greeted by a row of utilitarian tower blocks. That was when an ear-piercing cry echoed down the corridor. The banshees, who had been uncharacteristically quiet, had woken from their slumber.

Thus far, I hadn't been impressed by China but as I tucked into my porridge, the city's buildings gradually disappeared and gave way to gorgeous countryside and mountains. I decided China deserved a second chance. The scenery definitely improved throughout the morning, distracting me from my sudukos and I found myself wishing I would have longer to explore China's countryside.

As I prepared to exit the train in Beijing, I felt more excited about the future, about the places I was going to visit. The pull of home was slowly releasing its grip. It was only two weeks since I'd left but it seemed *much* longer. I didn't know how long it would be before I'd had enough and would want to return to Shepperton but I thought I'd be fine until at least March, when my rough itinerary ran out. I was glad that I was starting to feel more like myself, as I'd been worried that I was going to waste too much time feeling sad or regretful. In the grand scheme of things, a year wasn't *that* long, so I told myself to stop being a baby. After all, whiners are wieners. I was sure the trip would be an emotional roller coaster (a cliché I know) but I finally felt ready to strap myself in and enjoy the ride.

China: Beijing - Rules & Regulations

24TH - 27TH AUGUST 2018

Upon my arrival in Beijing, I made my way through the confusing train station to locate my taxi. Sure enough, a sign with my name on was being waved at me by a smiling young man. I'd been able to carry the Green Turtle for about ten minutes between the platform and the station exit but the poor driver couldn't manage it for even twenty seconds, and had to ask his mate to help him. I offered to carry it myself but not wanting their male pride dented, they refused.

Once I'd checked in at the Dong Fang Hotel, I went for a walk. I felt safe, and although busy, the roads weren't nearly as crazy as in Mongolia. As it was late afternoon, I decided it was time to eat. It was difficult to choose a restaurant as none of the menus had been translated into English so I wandered the streets for ages, clueless. Eventually, I found a restaurant where the menu had helpful pictures. Some of the dishes looked like chicken so I thought it was a safe bet. Self-consciously, I sat at a table, while waiters and other diners openly stared at me, and ordered what I hoped would be sweet and sour chicken. Unfortunately, it turned out to be more *spicy* than sweet or sour and it made my eyes water. I struggled through a quarter of it and then hid some in a tissue (to throw away later) so it looked like I'd eaten more than I had. I'm sorry to say it but I found a McDonalds, where I ate fries and a pineapple pie.

After eating, I found some bustling but interesting side streets with lots of shops to explore. It was hard to tell what anything was but I bought a few things I recognised, such as oranges, bananas and small cake bars that I could eat for lunch over the weekend. I was surprised that it was dark by 7:30pm - the sunsets were getting earlier and earlier as I headed east. But in Beijing, it didn't feel dangerous being out after dark so I wasn't in a hurry to get back to my lonely hotel room.

Early on Saturday, I was awoken by an urgent need to go to the bathroom. It was the first of many visits that morning - apparently the spicy chicken was neither appreciated by my taste buds nor by my digestive system. By late morning, my tummy had settled so I decided to stick to my original plan of running at the Olympic Forest Park. I took some Imodium to bung myself up and walked to the nearest station. Using the underground system was surprisingly easy: the self-service machines had an English option so I simply chose the station I wanted and paid for my ticket. Annoyingly, I had to go through a security scanner at every station entrance and exit but the staff didn't do anything even when the alarms sounded - it seemed to be a box-ticking exercise.

As the train moved through the stations, I noticed two things: *everyone* was staring at phones and the small subway TV screens were keen to teach the *rules*. Firstly, the phones - there must've been fifty people on my carriage and I could not find a single person without a phone in their hand. People's phones were an extension of themselves - they were *never* put away. Secondly, China loves rules: they were *everywhere* and police were placed on almost every street corner to enforce them. I tried to stay away from the police and be as polite as possible - I didn't want to get into trouble.

To show the value of obeying the rules, the screens on the subway showed a white cartoon bunny in various scenarios - each one ended in his untimely demise. Sometimes his pals died with him if he'd been particularly naughty. If he jumped in an elevator, everyone died when it plummeted. If he played with the escalator buttons, everyone on it died. If he jumped over a barrier into a road, he died. If he forced the lift doors open, he plummeted down the shaft and died. You get the idea. It was rather macabre, and a little wasted, as the target audience was too distracted by their phones to pay attention.

Exiting the station, I entered the Olympic Forest Park, which was bigger than I'd expected. I liked the futuristic, plant-like building which looked like it would have been more at home on an alien planet. Within the large park, there was a clearly-marked sports track with frequent running stations (in case drinks were required) and sports shops dotted along it. Despite my gurgling bowels, I completed ten and a half kilometres without any unpleasant incidents. It was a relief to finally find some fellow runners, even if I outran nearly all of them (nobody was moving very fast, probably due to the heat).

Later that afternoon, I did some sightseeing in the main city, including walking around the lake and buildings at the pretty Beihei Park. I'd been on my feet *a lot* that day and my legs hurt. I'd brought a few too many Chinese Yuan with me for only two and a half days so I thought I'd treat myself to a foot massage in a nearby spa. When I arrived, a petite woman showed me to a private room and sat me in a reclining chair. I was given hot, sweet lemon tea and a bowl of warm, scented water to put my aching feet into. Smiling, she stepped out of the room, I assumed to get some oil. I was therefore surprised when a stocky, muscled Chinese man entered. He ignored my confusion and asked, "OK?" When I nodded, he began massaging my neck and shoulders.

After a few minutes, he took the bowl of water away and started on my feet and legs. It was a bit uncomfortable as we were facing each other but couldn't make conversation. He was good at his job though: he had huge, strong hands which he used to knead, pummel and slap my feet and legs. Sometimes he'd use his fists and drum them on my legs - he seemed to enjoy creating a musical beat. When he hooked my legs around *his* legs, so our groins were only inches apart, the awkwardness stepped up a gear. He then proceeded to use his fists on my thighs and press on the tight areas near my groin - I didn't know where to look! Despite my embarrassment, I enjoyed the massage and smiled about it all the way home. When I got back to the hotel, I used a VPN (Virtual Private Network) to log on to Facebook but it was so slow and painful that I gave up. I sent Tom an e-mail but he wasn't very chatty. I started to wonder if it would be best if I cut off all contact with him.

On Sunday morning, I awoke feeling positive, excited about embarking on a guided tour of Beijing. After a buffet breakfast, I was picked up at reception. Two others were on the tour, Aiman and Lisa, who were both American. We hit it off straight away and had a lot of fun throughout the day. First we went to the Forbidden City and Tiananmen Square. I would like to say something good about them but the sites were so overcrowded that I never got a true feel for them. I'd been reading a lot about over-tourism, where too many tourists were visiting popular tourist spots and sometimes ruining famous landmarks. It was definitely true in Beijing. It wasn't all bad though. We had fun trying not to lose each other and our guide, Gale, insisted on taking lots of photos of us in silly poses.

'I've seen the Great Wall of China, which being honest with you, is not the Great Wall, it's an 'Alright Wall' – it's the 'Alright Wall of China.''
(Karl Pilkington)

In the afternoon, we went to the Great Wall of China, which snaked lazily around the mountains. We were asked which part we'd prefer to visit and chose the quieter option. It was amazing to see the wall in person and I felt overwhelmed for a couple of minutes (unlike Karl Pilkington). After Gale took some photos, we were left to climb the wall by ourselves. We decided to take on the steepest and highest section. The steps were never-ending and it wasn't long before we were drenched in sweat. We were *so* moist that the flies, which hung around in large clusters, stuck to our skin. It was pretty grim. When we reached one of the fortresses, we bought ice-cold drinks and took a break. Lisa had had enough by that point but Aiman and I continued up to Fortress 12, where a gate thankfully prevented us from going any further. After a few more photos, we made our way back down, collecting Lisa on the way. The whole experience was one of the highlights of my trip.

On the way back to the city, we were taken to an expensive jade factory, a tea-tasting demonstration and a silk factory. The information was always interesting but each place attempted to coerce us into spending money. I couldn't afford to buy anything so it was a little depressing. Back in the car, we discussed our views on Beijing and laughed at how the men would roll up their t-shirts to show off their bellies (I dubbed it the Chinese Crop Top). Sometimes they would rub and pat them lovingly. Still, it was better than men taking off their shirts entirely, like in England, as it was rarely a welcome sight.

At the end of our long day, we were dropped back at our respective hotels. I decided that I liked Beijing. It was my favourite of the three capital cities I'd visited. I could've lived without hearing people cough up and spit phlegm on the street though - it made me feel sick whenever it happened. Apparently, the government had tried to discourage such behavior before the 2008 Olympic Games by sending out enforcers to make people clean up after themselves. I don't think it had a lasting impact but at least they'd tried.

On Monday morning, a taxi took me to the airport for my flight to South Korea. My *Real Russia* organised tour was therefore over. From then on, I would be on my own (in terms of organisation at least). I was looking forward to seeing Seoul and being able to freely use social media again, but more pressingly, I was eager to meet up with my old friend Andy, who would travel with me for two weeks.

South Korea: Seoul - Closed on Tuesdays

My plane touched down in Seoul on Monday afternoon. I collected the Green Turtle from the carousel and for the first time, properly wore it on my back: at just under thirteen kilograms, it was uncomfortable but manageable (though if anyone had nudged me, I would've toppled over). I used the metro to reach the Hotel Aventree, where I met up with Andy. It was exciting but strange to see my friend again. To him, it felt like only a couple of weeks had passed since we'd last seen each other but to me it felt like months.

After showering, we headed into the city. There was a stunning temple over the road with vibrant colours everywhere we looked. I enjoyed listening to the peaceful chanting and noticed that people seemed politer than in China and Mongolia. I also didn't feel like anyone was staring at me for being *different*. In the area of Insadong, where we were staying, there were hundreds of narrow alleys, lined with both traditional, and modern, shops and restaurants. Lights and neon signs lit up the small streets, vying for consumers' attention and cash. We found a restaurant, where it looked like we could avoid being served intestines (a popular Korean snack), and enjoyed a simple but tasty meal of chicken and rice. The meal was accompanied by lots of little bowls of vegetables and sauces. Mine were all passed to Andy due to my resistance to eating anything too exotic (I've been told I eat with my eyes).

As soon we returned to the room, I hurried to the bathroom - not because of an upset stomach but since the toilet itself was such an amusing source of entertainment. I experimented with washing my undercarriage in numerous ways. Using the control pad, I adjusted the temperature of the seat and the water, the angle of the spray and the pressure of the water. I even gave myself a blow dry. I wanted one at home! Feeling brave, I braced myself and pressed the 'enema' button, which Andy had warned me against. Personally, I found it underwhelming: it didn't live up to my expectations at all.

On Tuesday morning, we tried to visit a palace but it was closed. We then tried a museum, which was also closed. So was the art gallery we'd wanted to see. Apparently tourist attractions in Seoul were closed on Tuesdays. We looked at lots of other attractions but they were also closed on Tuesdays. We started to worry that we wouldn't find anything to do. However, we tried our luck at Changedeokgung Palace and to our relief, it was open.

Shortly after our arrival, rain began to fall with increasing intensity. Some young Korean girls, who had hired traditional hambok dresses for selfie purposes, were sheltering under the roof of one of the buildings. Andy's compact umbrella wasn't big enough for the both of us, so we joined them. It was entertaining watching the giggling teens snap away. As we sat there, with mosquitoes nipping our ankles, more young girls in striking hamboks scampered backwards and forwards, huddled under their umbrellas: it certainly made for some colourful photographs.

After the palace, we visited Yongma Land, which was once a small theme park. Due to dwindling visitor numbers it had closed its doors to the public in 2011. The site was abandoned and soon became popular with *urbexers* (people who enjoy exploring derelict sites). I'd been a fan of visiting abandoned places for a long time: Andy and I had even been on holiday to Chernobyl in 2015. Since my childhood, I'd had an appreciation for anything unusual and creepy, and I liked the feeling of being somewhere I shouldn't. However, we *were* allowed to be at this place as we'd paid a shifty 'security guard'.

As we explored the park, we took photos of the decaying rides and the crumbling buildings. The steps up to the rides were rusty and as there was broken glass scattered everywhere, we had to be careful where we stepped. Eventually, we made our way up some concrete stairs to a graveyard of broken ride cars. That was when the heavens opened once again. We hid under Andy's umbrella but it wasn't long until we needed to take cover somewhere more substantial. We chose a concrete shelter full of old televisions, cables and other broken technology, guarded by a grumpy, life-size alien and some cheerful, pastel-coloured elephants. Rain hammered down heavily. We couldn't wait all day and needed to make a break for it. We ran down the steps and hid in a makeshift café with a few others. To save ourselves from a complete drenching, we took a taxi back to the metro station with two teenage girls and returned to the hotel to dry off.

The downpour continued into Wednesday, when we went on a tour of the border of North Korea. I'd never seen rain like it - it was relentless and the roads were becoming severely flooded. As we drove, our guide informed us that the border (known as the demilitarized zone (or the DMZ)) consists of a two-kilometre zone, where *no one* can enter. This is to prevent *any* interaction between the two sides which may reignite the war. According to a video we watched, animals and wildlife thrive in the zone. However, the area is littered with land mines so I couldn't help but wonder how many animals had been blown up as they sprinted gaily through the 'peaceful' DMZ.

Once our passports were checked, we visited the Freedom Bridge, where prisoners of war had been released after the ceasefire was agreed. Colourful ribbons hung in their thousands from the fences, representing families separated when Korea was divided - it was a poignant sight. Afterwards, we were taken into a tunnel, which we were told was created by North Korea, wanting to invade South Korea. There are four such known tunnels but apparently there are around twenty more that are so far undiscovered (according to information received from captured/escaped North Korean military personnel). Finally, we visited Dorasan train station. It is planned that the

Transiberian/Mongolian trains will one day pass through North Korea, via Dorasan. This would mean it would be possible to take a train from Paris into the south of South Korea. I wondered if it would ever actually happen. I wasn't sure I'd be up for passing through North Korea on my holidays. It didn't sound particularly relaxing.

When we returned to Seoul, the rain was still pouring so we took shelter in one of the popular barbeque restaurants, where we cooked our own meat at the table. I had pork belly and Andy had steak. It was delicious and barbequing it ourselves was fun. As usual, Andy ate all the *weird* side dishes and I just ate meat and rice. I was ashamed of my fear of new foods but I could never bring myself to eat something I didn't like the look of. It was the bane of my life.

I woke up early on Thursday to check the weather and discovered it was *not* raining. I pulled on my running gear and snuck out of the room, trying not to wake Andy. I took the metro to the river and ran along the bank. Some of it was pretty but there was a lot of flooding due to the rain so the path was wet, muddy and sometimes impassable. I didn't see many other runners but lots of Koreans were using the outdoor gyms that were scattered along the riverside. When my nine miles were complete, I returned to the hotel by metro. All the commuters avoided me. I couldn't blame them as I was dripping with sweat.

Later in the day, Andy and I visited Gyeongbokgung Palace, which looked similar to the other palace we'd been to. We enjoyed watching the changing of the guards - their colourful uniforms were very striking. Selfie-taking tourists swarmed them as they stood silent and serious. I felt a bit sorry for them: some people really needed a lesson in personal space.

Next, we visited some markets and then climbed to the top of Namsan Mountain (which involved *a lot* of steps). The views of the city were spectacular so it was well worth it. By the time we returned to the hotel, I'd done almost fifty-thousand steps (twenty-four miles) and my feet hurt. Needless, to say, I was grateful to shower and slip into bed.

On Friday, we had an early start to reach Bukhansan National Park. We wanted to climb Baegundae Peak. We'd heard it was quite easy initially but then became tougher, with ropes needed towards the summit (the ropes were embedded into the rock face). When we arrived, we followed two English-speaking men, who seemed to know their way. We got chatting at the shop and introduced ourselves. Hong Sik (a local) and Yousif (from Egypt), kindly offered to show us to Uisangbong Peak, where there would be fewer people. They promised it would be a nice route through the forest. When they said *nice*, I assumed they meant gentle and beautiful, but I should never assume anything. 'Nice' in Korea clearly meant terrifying and treacherous. The path was steep, up bare rock face and Yousif had to pull me up the parts where there were no footholds as my trainers didn't have enough grip.

After a grueling climb, we reached some metal steps. At the top, I stopped. The path over the rock face was too vertical for my liking and my fear of falling took over. I told the others to go ahead and waited patiently on the steps, enjoying the view of lush green trees carpeting the landscape while I ate a snack and took photos. It was a pleasant spot to relax and within thirty minutes, the men were back. Andy informed me that the path had become even more grueling and dangerous. I was therefore satisfied that I'd made a good decision to stay behind. We took a few group photos, and then Yousif and Hong Sik escorted us down the most precarious of the descents. Once we were in the safe zone, they returned the way they'd come, to hike a different peak.

Andy and I decided to go back to our original plan and climb Baegundae. The four kilometre path started well: we followed it along a stream and then up some wooden steps. But as we continued, the steps disappeared and we had to climb on the rocks. We had to watch our footing as they were slippery and it would've been very easy to fall. The path gradually became steeper and I began to feel nervous about going back down again. Finally, we reached what I thought was the top, but Andy pointed out the peak above us - it was still half a kilometre away. It was a scorching, sunny day so our clothes were soaked with perspiration. I felt exhausted and lightheaded: either from the elevation or from dehydration. I made it to two hundred metres from the top but the path became too much for me and I stopped.

Making myself comfortable on a large rock, I left Andy to continue to the peak alone - *again*. It was very peaceful looking down on the world, but I felt worry gnawing away about the return journey: I therefore began a slow descent. It wasn't long before Andy caught me up and we continued down together. With aching knees and tired legs, we found a nice spot to sit by the stream. We took off our sweaty shoes and socks, and bathed our feet in the cool water - it seemed to wash away some of the day's stress.

Eventually, we made it back to ground-level, where we celebrated with well-deserved ice cream. Funnily enough, just as we were leaving the 7-11 to catch the bus, we bumped into Hong Sik and Yousif. I was glad we'd met again. We travelled back to Seoul together and said our goodbyes on the metro.

We woke up late on Saturday. My legs really ached. It wasn't a shock, as although we'd only walked seven miles the previous day, we'd *ascended* 3122 feet. After breakfast, we spent rest of the day shopping. Well Andy did. It was difficult for me because I loved all the fun stationery and could have spent a fortune if I'd had the money. The lack of funds was getting me down. Although I loved having Andy with me, life felt simpler when I was alone, when I could skip meals to save money and only do *free* activities. I couldn't expect my visitors to live like that on their holiday though, as they'd want to enjoy their time away to the full. The guilt was something I'd struggle with whenever anyone came to see me. It wasn't their fault. It was mine. My guilt was a figment of my own creation.

Checking my budget consumed much of my time but after some careful calculations, I worked out that I had a budget of roughly forty pounds a day. It wasn't a lot considering that it would have to include accommodation. Andy had been very kind though and had paid for all the hotels in Korea and Japan so that gave me more money to play with. I was coming to learn that budget travel could be challenging and unglamorous: I spent a lot of time washing my knickers in the sink and eating from the 7-11.

After shopping, we returned to the hotel and Andy squeezed his new purchases into his luggage. We then left to catch our 10:30pm flight to Tokyo. I was sad to leave South Korea as I'd found it to be a vibrant country where modern life blended well with tradition. However, I was *very* disappointed that I hadn't been able to visit the amusing Penis Park (a place full of penis statues) - I would've loved it!

Japan: Tokyo - The Rock

The journeys both *to* and *out of* Tokyo, did *not* run smoothly. I blamed Andy and the small rock he kidnapped from Seoul. In Hawaii, legend has it that people who steal volcanic rock will be cursed by the goddess Pele. Apparently, every year, hundreds of tourists send rocks back to Hawaii as they try to halt the bad luck that they believe has plagued them since returning home. Andy's rock wasn't volcanic but it was cursed nonetheless. He'd picked it up at the foot of the mountain in Seoul, wanting to leave it at the peak, but he'd forgotten and ever since, we'd been inundated with bad luck.

Just after 6pm on Saturday, we took the metro to Incheon station. After ninety minutes on the subway, we reached what we thought was the airport. Stepping out of the train, we soon realised that Incheon station was nowhere near the airport. We'd messed up. The airport was actually on an island, over thirty kilometres away. It was almost 8pm and our flight was at 10:30pm. The station guard told us it would take ninety minutes to reach the airport by metro. We didn't have time: we needed an alternate plan.

After a lot of arm waving on the quiet Incheon streets, we managed to flag down a taxi and were soon on our way to the airport. However, traffic lights stopped us every two hundred metres so it took twenty minutes to travel just two kilometers. Just as I was starting to panic, we reached the highway and began to make more satisfactory progress. Feeling frazzled, we arrived at the airport at 8:40pm, where we were told that our flight had been delayed – bloody typical.

At midnight, we boarded the plane and settled down in our seats, hoping for a peaceful journey. Just as we were about to take off, the captain announced that he was expecting turbulence and that we should use the provided sick bags if we needed to vomit. This didn't fill us with hope. As it turned out, it was just a little bumpy and I slept through most of the flight. We landed at 2:16am. We therefore had four minutes to catch the last airport bus into Tokyo. The delay would be costly because as at that time in the morning, our only option was to take a taxi (for which Andy very kindly footed the bill).

We reached the Hotel Sunroute Plaza Shinjuku at 4am, where I changed into the provided nightwear: a long, white, buttoned nightshirt made of thick cotton. It wasn't very attractive but I put it on anyway and wearily climbed into the double bed, next to Andy. I was exhausted but after all the excitement, I couldn't sleep. Andy on the other hand, was snoring loudly within minutes. When I finally did sleep, I had a vivid dream about going home and seeing my mum. I woke up missing her...at 11am. Oops. We only had two days in Tokyo and we'd slept almost half a day away!

By lunchtime, we were out exploring the city. It had a very different feel to Seoul: everything was shiny and new, without a trace of tradition. Andy loved it but I preferred Seoul. Seoul had *soul,* while to me, Tokyo seemed soulless, just a pretty face. Tokyo, a consumer-driven city, was crammed with multi-level shops and the prices were very steep. The streets were teeming with shoppers and tourists. We stopped in a few stores but I managed to restrain myself from overspending and only bought a canvas bag featuring a picture of Gizmo (from the movie *Gremlins)*. Andy didn't though - he shopped merrily, buying numerous gifts and retro t-shirts.

Once we'd had our fill of consumerism, we walked to the famous Shibuya crossing, where all the pedestrian lights turn green simultaneously and people stream across the huge intersection in all directions. It was crazy how busy it was. It was a good place for people-watching though – the Japanese had very unique, individual styles and there was a bigger mix of cultures compared to the other

Asian cities I'd visited. We also noticed that Japanese people were very polite. If someone made an error, even a small one, it was hard for them to stop apologising.

After a lot of walking, it was time for dinner. We found a popular restaurant which had plastic meals in the window, showing the array of available dishes. The display made the job of choosing a meal much easier. As usual, I chose a simple rice and chicken meal. We were both satisfied with our choices and once we'd finished eating, we returned to the hotel, ready for an early night.

Andy and I agreed to go our separate ways on Monday: I would go running and *lose* the crowds, and he would *find* the crowds and go shopping for retro toys. I set off early and found a peaceful park to run around. There were some beautiful trees, adorned with pink flowers and the whole area sounded like the rainforest with insects and birds chirping and singing loudly. It was just what I needed. When it started to rain, I made my way back to the hotel. It was difficult trying to weave through the sea of umbrellas, as under one each was a person staring down at their phone. Nobody looked where they were going and it drove me mad. I managed to avoid any collisions and returned to the hotel in one, albeit very soggy, piece. I was lazy for the rest of the morning. I needed a break. I'd been so busy in the three weeks since I'd left home that my body just wanted some rest. I stopped at the 7-11 for food, showered and then curled up in bed to relax.

Later in the day, I became restless. I therefore visited the free observatory at the Tokyo Metropolitan Government building, from which Mount Fuji could sometimes be seen. I rode the elevator to the 45th floor and entered a large, busy room, surrounded by large windows. As the sun had come out, the views of Tokyo were spectacular. However, the elusive Mount Fuji remained shrouded in the haze and I never even caught a glimpse of it.

That evening, Andy and I went to a quirky restaurant close to the train station. We placed our orders and by ordering a particular dish, I won the chance to play a game. I competed against the waitress at Pokapon (where we repeatedly pressed a button to make two plastic figures bash each other on the head) and somehow won, earning myself a free cocktail.

After dinner, we had a few drinks (kindly funded by Andy) in an area where lots of tiny bars were crowded into narrow alleys. We chose an empty one, with foreign bank notes stuck all over the walls, that was marginally cheaper than some of the others, and ordered drinks from the cheerful barman. We were soon joined by a very crazy, and slightly famous (in Japan) samurai model and actor, who loved pretending to steal things. A few minutes later, a father and son from London sat down, and then Yousif from Saudi Arabia, who told us he was an army captain.

In such a small establishment, we had no choice but to make conversation. It certainly made for an interesting evening. Yousif told us about his life as a sniper in the army. He'd apparently killed twenty-seven people and saw their faces all the time. I didn't know what to do with that information: he seemed like a genuinely nice guy, not a killer. He had a few scars (supposedly from bullets) and an air of sadness about him so I believed his story to be true. He explained that his twin brother had been shot and killed in the army and that his life no longer had purpose. At around midnight, we were joined by four Austrians and we felt that we could leave Yousif with some new drinking buddies to talk to.

On Tuesday morning, we checked out of the hotel and went to the station to take the train to Kyoto. We'd both bought Japan Rail Passes before leaving the UK and had validated them on our first day in the city. With these, we were able to travel on almost any train in Japan. They hadn't been cheap (mine had cost around three-hundred pounds for a two-week pass) but they were more cost effective than buying individual tickets. As we waited for our 1:03pm train, we read about Typhoon Jebi, a weather system that had hit Osaka, but in Tokyo the weather was dry and calm, so we weren't overly concerned. However, Andy's rock was to strike its second blow: as of 1pm, the trains to Kyoto were suspended. Unsure of what to do, I went to customer services and rebooked us onto the 4:03pm train.

We sat around on the station floor with hundreds of other people, watching the unhelpful departure screens as time ticked past. Using the station WiFi, we discovered that Jebi was the worst typhoon to hit Japan in twenty-five years. It didn't look good for our travel plans. 4pm came and went and we rebooked onto the 6:03pm train, but by 6pm, it was clear that we weren't going anywhere. After six hours of waiting, we gave up and rebooked tickets for the following morning. Andy booked us into a nearby hotel and we left the station, keeping our fingers crossed that the weather would improve by morning.

Japan: Kyoto & Hiroshima - Fight Night

Typhoon number 21, or *Typhoon Jebi*, didn't affect us too much in Tokyo. We'd been annoyed that our train had been cancelled but in retrospect, it was good that we were out of Kyoto when the typhoon had hit. Maybe Andy's rock had protected us after all? We ditched it nevertheless. We found a nearby Buddhist shrine and left it there. I half-expected the rock to be on Andy's bed when we got back to the hotel - I was *that* certain it was a source of evil. I laughed that I should've secretly gone back for the rock and put it in Andy's house at some point in the future, just to freak him out.

Having exorcised the malevolent rock, we grabbed some Japanese food at an American-style restaurant and then explored a new part of Tokyo. When we got back to the hotel, I casually snuck a few more Shiseido sachets from reception into my bag (there was a wide range of complimentary beauty products available - I'd already taken some when we'd first checked in but I couldn't resist grabbing more). I counted my haul when we got back to my room and I had well over forty sachets. I wasn't proud of it.

That night, as I lay wide awake in our room that stank of cigarette smoke, I worried about our predicament. I hoped that my travels around Japan wouldn't be *too* disrupted. What if the trains were suspended for a few *days*? I didn't know how bad the damage was so it was difficult to judge what would happen. I had to put my trust into the famous Japanese rail efficiency.

We woke early on Wednesday morning, not feeling particularly hopeful. However, when we arrived at the station, people were going through the gates as normal. Excitedly, we boarded the bullet train.

The three hour journey was swift and comfortable, and we soon arrived in sunny Kyoto. The city was much drier than we'd expected - the only evidence that a typhoon had hit was a lot of fallen trees and scattered debris. We checked into the fancy Kyoto Hotel Okura. *Many* staff members welcomed us and they were all so polite: each person bowed, welcomed us and then wished us a good day. With the excessive swapping of pleasantries, it was exhausting just trying to reach the elevator. Customer service was obviously their top priority, as the young lady who showed us to our room was horrified when we tried to carry our own luggage, even though she could barely lift the Green Turtle.

Inside our spacious room, there was a selection of free toiletries, including a brand new hair brush (this was handy as mine had recently broken in two) and a nail kit. As usual, I took everything on offer. Each item was wrapped in plastic and put inside a box. I noted that Japan was somewhat behind in the eco-friendly stakes because *everything* seemed to be covered in plastic, including every individual banana in the 7-11. If only bananas had a protective outer layer...

Once we'd admired the view from our fourteenth floor room and checked out the toilet (the enema option certainly lived up to its name), we walked into town. We soon found ourselves in a large market, containing numerous stalls and shops, and a few higher-end stores. Andy mentally spent a lot of money and vowed to return the next day with his shopping list. I was excited to find the Japanese equivalent of Poundland: the 100 Yen store, where I wasted money on things I didn't need, including Hello Kitty sandwich bags. We then found a three-floor erotic shop - I'd never seen so much adult 'merchandise' in one place. The 'love doll' showroom was particularly creepy.

At lunchtime, we passed back through the food market. I couldn't tell what half of the *food* was, let alone want to eat any of it, so I stuck with some chicken from the 7-11 (much to Andy's disgust). My stomach turned as we perused the market's aisles. There was a lot of unspecified meat on sticks and food with tentacles. Anyone who knows me well is aware that I love octopuses, so seeing whole baby ones stuck on the end of a stick upset me. RIP my tiny, tentacled friends.

Recovering from my trauma in the market, we tried going to the castle and the palace but both were closed for repairs after the typhoon. Instead, we walked a few miles to a shrine we'd read about. The place was full of tourists and seemed open as usual, so we began trekking up the mountain, through the orange gateways. However, a fifth of the way up, a sign informed us that the remaining path was closed (also due to the typhoon). Well, it had been nice while it lasted.

Back in town, we found a small but popular restaurant where we sat at a bar and watched the chefs cook our food - they handed it straight to us. It was *so* good. We stuffed our faces with grilled chicken, teriyaki chicken, fried chicken, rice balls and more. It was the best meal I'd had in weeks! Sadly it was also the last evening meal Andy and I would share in Japan. I was thankful to him for coming to meet me. He had generously paid for the hotels, taxis and several meals. I owed him a slap-up meal at Harvester when I got home.

The following morning, after a four-mile run and some shopping, we sat at reception, waiting for a taxi to the train station. That was when I received an email from Tom. He hadn't been in contact for a few days so I was surprised and a little nervous - would he be cold and distant or would he say something positive? I knew he hadn't been totally happy that I'd been sharing a room (and sometimes a bed) with Andy, so I didn't know what to expect. Thankfully, it was the latter. Having heard about the storm, he was worried about me and wanted to check I was safe. Fighting against my childish urge to ignore his message, I immediately informed him that I was ok.

A few minutes later, our taxi arrived. At the station, Andy and I said our goodbyes. He then boarded the train to Tokyo and I took a train to Hiroshima. It was strange to be alone again, although I wouldn't miss Andy's snoring. From the station, I took a public bus to the Hostel Mallika. My *room* was basically a small but comfortable hole with a little door at the foot of the bed. I felt like a hobbit, or a mouse. To be honest, it was perfectly fine and featured a light, a shelf and a plug socket - what more could I have asked for?

After exploring the hostel's facilities, I went to the nearby Hiroshima Peace Memorial Park. I visited the Hiroshima museum, which was incredibly moving, and shed some tears at the photos of the burned victims, their ruined belongings and their terrible stories. The museum promotes a message of peace, in the hope that no more nuclear weapons will be used in the future. Looking at the destruction, it's a hope I shared whole-heartedly.

Next, I walked to a place marked as the hypo-centre of the blast. It was sobering looking up and imagining the enormous mushroom cloud, which I'd seen so many times in photos, right above where I stood. The ruined shell of the old promotion hall was interesting and serves as a memorial to the seventy-thousand people who were killed instantly, and the further seventy-thousand who suffered fatal radiation injuries.

On the way back to the hostel, I ate 'dinner' at the 7-11. I felt depressed sitting alone, on a small plastic chair. Living on a budget was not fun. However, when I got back to the hostel, I didn't feel like such a loser as *everyone* was eating supermarket meals and snacks. I decided that in the future, I would eat my food in the hostel's kitchen with everyone else. While I was in the kitchen, I heard an earthquake had just struck Northern Japan. The country was not having an easy time in 2018, being plagued by earthquakes, floods, deadly heat waves and landslides. I read that a large percentage of the world's earthquakes happen in Japan - it made me wonder if I would get out of the country in one piece.

On Friday morning, I popped out of my hobbit hole and into the kitchen. The hostel offered a free breakfast (if you call toast breakfast) and the hospitable lady who ran it even bought it to my table with a range of jams. Loaded up on carbs, I took the train and a ferry to Miyajima Island. I was struck by the island's beauty as soon as I arrived. Trees peppered the mountains and deer roamed freely, probably a bit *too* freely, as they kept bothering tourists for snacks. I even caught one munching the bag on my back while I was trying to have a moment of quiet introspection.

As I explored the seafront, some young school children approached me to ask a few questions about my favourite foods. It was a clever way for them to practice their English. When they were finished with me, I noticed four older school children gesturing shyly at me. They seemed to be daring each other to be the first to talk to me. I smiled and went over to say hello. The children had a longer set of questions, which required me to speak rather than point at pictures. They were very sweet, and afterwards, they took some selfies with me.

Next, I headed towards the bright orange O-Torii Gate (the colour is said to keep evil away), which stands at 16.6 metres tall. At low tide, people can walk through it. It's not fixed to the ground but cleverly stands under its own vast weight: the present gate was erected in 1875 so it's lasted well.

It wasn't long before my eyes landed on the forested peak of Mount Misen. After Seoul, I'd told myself that I was done with mountains but when one was right in front of me, I wanted to climb it. I appeared to be the only person to do so as everyone else favoured the cable car. This left the lazy buggers less than half a mile to climb to the peak on their own two feet - most clearly didn't bother as I only saw two people at the summit. Smothered in DEET (to keep the mosquitoes away), I began ascending the mountain path, a never-ending set of steep, narrow steps through gloomy woodland. As I lost a quarter of my body weight in perspiration, I started cursing my decision to climb the mountain: I was growing impatient with the numerous mosquitoes buzzing around my head (the only bit of me without DEET).

Despite the mossies and the steps, I enjoyed the quiet solitude of being alone on the path. It didn't last though as I soon discovered I was being hunted by a mountain lion. Not really. It was Bambi. Usually, if I see a deer and try to take its photo, it runs away. However, the deer on Miyajima Island *stalk* people. They are beyond tame and are *always* hungry. This one was barking up the wrong tree with me though because I didn't have food for myself let alone food for hungry wildlife. Bambi crept behind me for a while and would suddenly stop whenever I turned to narrow my eyes at it. Eventually, it figured out I had no food and wandered off, or perhaps it just hated the steep steps.

Unlike in South Korea, I did myself proud and reached the peak, where I stopped for a rest. Although it had been quite bright when I'd started hiking, storm clouds now loomed on the horizon and mist blocked the views. I thought I better get down quickly, before rain made the rocky steps too treacherous. I was about to start my descent, using an easier path, when a warning sign (the first of many) about vipers caught my attention. Great: something else to worry about. In my imagination, every fallen branch was a viper, ready to attack. In reality, the only thing I was bothered by was a group of loud Germans, who were shouting at each other like they were in a nightclub. After reaching the foot of the mountain, I explored a few more of the island's sights and then took the ferry back to the mainland. Hiroshima had disappeared into a grey raincloud. It wasn't long before the heavens opened and the light rain gave way to *torrential* rain - it had waited until I was off the mountain at least.

Friday evening was ever so exciting. Some youngsters from the dorm asked if I wanted to go out drinking with them but I chose to stay in and do some *proper* laundry (i.e. not in the sink) for the first time. Once that was done, I stayed in my hobbit hole, charging my electrical equipment and writing my blog. By 11pm, I was tucked up in bed. Within seconds of turning out the light, I heard screaming, banging and shaking, and what sounded like plaster falling - I thought it was an earthquake. The banging stopped quickly but the screaming did not. Despite feeling like I should hide, I decided to investigate as I was worried someone was being attacked. I crept up the outdoor stairs to the third floor and found the kitchen in a mess. Tables and chairs were strewn about and a young woman was crying on the floor. A young couple ran into the bathroom, locking the door, and a tall, wild-looking blonde man ran past me.

A German couple and an American girl explained that there had been a fight and the blonde man had tried to strangle the man who was now hiding in the bathroom. He'd also punched his own girlfriend in the face (the woman on the floor). We later discovered that the argument had started because the hiding couple had said they didn't want children. The blonde man had taken great offence to this and after a heated debate, had tried to strangle the other man. It seemed an odd thing to fight about. Shamefully, both (completely intoxicated) couples were English so I felt the need to apologise on behalf of my country. There was a bit of drama still going on from the Brits but I sat and drank tea with the others, talking about our travels while we tried to act like everything was normal. The police turned up a bit later but they didn't stay long and none of us were questioned.

By 1am, all was quiet, so I said goodnight to the others and returned to my dorm. The woman who'd been punched was packing her things. I didn't feel I could ignore her while she was in floods of tears so I asked if she needed anything. I then listened to her drunken babble for twenty minutes. She told me how he'd never hit her before, even when *she'd* hit *him* (it was clearly a very healthy relationship). Apparently her boyfriend had done a runner with their shared money and credit cards. She didn't know what to do and apart from suggesting she call her parents, I didn't know how to help her. Luckily, she received a phone call from her family so I escaped to bed.

Upstairs, the others had joked that the crazy blonde man was probably sleeping next to them on the fourth floor. They needn't have worried; he'd actually been staying in the bed right next to mine - typical. With fights, floods, typhoons and earthquakes, I was looking forward to leaving Japan. I needed somewhere a little *less* exciting.

Japan: Osaka - At It Like Rabbits

Just after 3pm on Saturday, I arrived at the Osaka Guesthouse U-En, which was situated in an old, traditional Japanese building. I was warned that due to its advanced years, the walls were *very* thin. They weren't wrong. Ear plugs were required and provided but they only partially blocked out the noise. Despite the thin walls, I liked the place immediately as it felt homely. I'd had a busy few weeks, so I was happy to sit in the kitchen, chatting to a young Japanese woman, Hiroko, who worked there.

Hiroko offered to take me to a supermarket. I finally had someone to ask what all the strange food was. I sometimes wished I hadn't asked, but I knew that next time I went, I'd be able to make more informed meal choices. Hiroko recommended some sweet wine so we went back to the guesthouse and sat drinking and chatting until after midnight. It was good to relax. I decided that while I was in Osaka, I wouldn't rush about trying to see everything: I'd take it easy.

On Sunday morning, I woke up to the sound of rain. My idea of a run went out of the window. However, I soon realised the sound was actually the air conditioning, so I pulled on my running gear and ran to the river. The riverside running route I'd mapped out was trickier than I'd expected, as fallen trees and large puddles (from the typhoon) littered the footpath. I wasn't the only runner there though. It was a well trodden route - by men at least (I didn't see a single solo, female runner). The men seemed to glare at me, as if I was an unwanted presence. Maybe it was because I was able to run faster than them.

"There's a woman with an axe! No matter where you live, there's always a nutter, whether it's London or the jungle." (Karl Pilkington)

Luckily, the path became easier but although there were fewer fallen trees, there were *more* nutters (without axes thankfully). I couldn't escape them as a tall fence had me trapped on the river bank. One lady was gently waving a small bag of food at nothing and making cooing noises, as if trying to entice a shy yet invisible pet from its hiding place. Shortly after, I passed a second elderly woman, shuffling backwards up a hill and cackling madly at herself. A few metres on was an old man shouting at pigeons. Even when they flew away, he would still yell at them in the sky. It was entertaining but I wasn't sure any of them should have been out alone.

After six and a half sweaty miles, I returned to the guesthouse and made poached eggs on toast. It was so good to have my favourite post-run meal again. Apart from Hiroko, the place was empty so I sat in my favourite swing-chair to decide on my plans for the day. I settled on Osaka Castle. To me, the castle itself wasn't anything particularly special - my interest was more piqued by the upbeat music coming from the courtyard. I followed my ears and soon discovered a dance performance. I'd happened upon some kind of Japanese High School Musical. Dance troops performed one after another, all wearing brightly-coloured costumes. Throughout the routine, dancers would repeatedly shrug layers off to reveal new outfits underneath, like dancing onions. I sat on the damp floor with lots of others and allowed myself be entertained for an hour.

Once the dancing was over, I left the castle grounds. A well-known shopping haven, I thought I'd discover what was on offer in one of Osaka's shopping centres. I soon regretted it as it was heaving with people. I was also drenched by yet another downpour. If there was one thing I hated more than people, it was *crowds* of people and I hated crowds of people in the rain even more. I only lasted ten minutes before escaping down a quiet side street, flanked on both sides by yet more shops.

Fed up with trudging about in sodden shoes, I left the luminosity of the shopping district and made my way along the river, back to the guesthouse. It took an age because the traffic lights at each intersection were so slow. I always looked ahead at the lights. If they were green, I had to quickly decide whether to make a run for it or give up three minutes of my life waiting. Much to the horror of the locals, I usually ran. I designated it the 'Green Man Dash'. I wasn't sure if it was illegal or just frowned upon, but if it was illegal, I was a repeat offender.

On Monday morning, while I was wondering what to do with my day, a picture of a cute bunny caught my eye. It was directions of how to get to *Rabbit Island*. My friend Natasha (a self-confessed bunny addict) had suggested I go a couple of days before, promising it would make me smile. I located the island on Google maps - it was all the way back down by Hiroshima and would require a rather complicated journey:

Train to Osaka Station (5 minutes)
Train to Shin-Osaka Station (5 minutes)
Train to Mihara Station (2 hours and 15 minutes)
Bus to Tadanoumi Port (45 minutes)
Ferry to Rabbit Island (20 minutes)

Feeling up for an adventure, I grabbed my bag and ran out of the door. At 2pm, without incident, I reached the small harbour. I purchased a ticket, a postcard for Natasha and some bunny food, and then waited for the next ferry. From the window of the terminal, I noticed a strange orange sphere glowing in the sky; by escaping Osaka, I'd found sunshine.

Upon reaching the island, a small rabbit hopped towards me. Five of his friends then joined him, all standing on their hind legs and begging for food. When I pulled out my bag of pellets, they went wild, fighting each other to get to them. Happily, I wandered around the island, feeding every little critter I could find. I always fed the diseased-looking bunnies as I felt sorry for them but sometimes I fed the cutest ones, unable to resist their adorable twitchy noses. The bunnies did their job, and by the time I left, a couple of hours later, I had a smile on my face. Not even the thought of the long return journey could make me frown.

At Shin-Osaka station, I noticed that the train on the opposite platform had a 'female only' carriage - it was packed. The other carriages were predominantly full of men. It was just like a Year 6 school disco, where boys and girls rarely mixed. Hiroko said the segregation idea had been implemented partly due to men touching women's bottoms. I thought it was a clever idea if it made women safer.

I woke up late on Tuesday. My original plan had been to take the train to Nara but when I'd researched it, Nara was just another city full of shrines and temples. I was bored of shrines and temples. They were all starting to look the same. It reminded me of when I'd been on a group tour in the Amazon and they took us to see the giant river otters. On the first day, we were amazed. On the second day, we were mildly impressed. By the third day, we were asking: "Do we *have* to get up at 4am to see bloody otters AGAIN?"

I went for a run instead. I hated it. The route was ugly: trucks, warehouses, road-works, building sites and power stations lined my path and there was nothing pretty to see. As was becoming usual in Japan, I ran out of energy quickly. I didn't think it was the humidity as I was used to that in England after the heat wave. I think it was a mix of running alone and not fuelling well. I missed my running buddies, my hydration tablets, my jelly babies and my chocolate milk. I'd not been eating much in Japan as food was so expensive, which is probably why my shorts were getting loose. Before I'd left, I'd been worried I'd put weight *on* when I travelled but it seemed to be having the opposite effect. While I ran, I thought about home. I didn't miss work or anything silly like that but I missed regular food, my friends and my routines. I wasn't depressed about it, if anything it was good, as it made me realise that I didn't want to live abroad permanently. I was discovering that I preferred short-term travel.

On Tuesday afternoon, I wandered aimlessly. I found myself getting annoyed for several reasons: people on bikes cycled wherever they fancied and were a menace to pedestrians; hardly anyone smiled; and nobody ever looked up from their phones, not even quickly, to check if they were about to walk into someone. At least it wasn't raining, as people with umbrellas were even more likely to barge into me. I decided to return to the quiet of the guesthouse before I grumbled at someone out loud. As my agitation grew, I began to wonder why I wasn't enjoying my trip more. I'd liked bits of it but I couldn't say I'd loved it as a whole. I considered why I'd wanted to travel in the first place and came up with three reasons:

1. Seeing beautiful landscapes and beaches
2. Meeting new people
3. Possibilities/the unexpected

It was obvious. My number one reason was to see natural beauty and I'd booked weeks of travel in cities. I was a cretin. I didn't even like cities. I mean, I like *some* cities but only for a few days at a time. No wonder I was feeling so grumpy: even more than a few hours in London did my head in. Luckily I would soon be going to Australia and even though I'd visit more cities, I'd also see amazing beaches and the rugged landscapes of the west coast. Things would get better in Australia, I was sure of it.

Japan: Kanazawa & Tokyo - Cold Dead Eyes

12TH - 14TH SEPTEMBER 2018

"I've found out that Malakula was named by Captain James Cook. It comes from the French 'mal au cul' which means 'pain in the arse', after Cook found it difficult to deal with cannibals, volcanoes and other annoying features. It's good to know proper explorers sometimes share the feelings I have on my travels." (Karl Pilkington)

Reading this quote made me smile. After my time in Osaka, it was a relief to know I wasn't alone in finding travel a bit difficult at times...

At 9:12am on Wednesday, I boarded the *Thunderbird 11* train and sped towards Kanazawa. The scenery was very soothing: mountains were touched by wisps of cloud and lush green fields flanked the tracks on either side. I was surprised to see about fifty white cranes (my ornithology is pretty poor so they could well have been herons) all sitting in the trees. As my train pulled into the station, I was disappointed. I'd been expecting a small town but Kanazawa looked suspiciously like another big city. With the Green Turtle under my arm (my preferred method of carrying it), I trudged to the Guesthouse Nagonde. People were noticeably chilled and it was quiet. No bicycles tried to mow me down and an elderly man even bowed his head at me to say hello. It was a vast improvement.

The person who checked me into the guesthouse was very welcoming and gave me a map and some ideas of where to go. I first visited the castle but I didn't find it particularly enthralling. The Kenrokuen Garden however was *very* pretty (it's said to be the best in Japan) and I enjoyed myself a lot, despite feeling nauseated all afternoon. An hour after I arrived, I noticed the all-too-familiar sound of rain. It seemed that the weather liked to tease me with the odd bit of sunshine, but would then go back to its default mode again. The downpour got heavier and heavier, as did my mood.

I tried to think positively - I bet the trees loved a bit of rain - but I couldn't sustain it. Mr. Canon and I were getting wet and a useful (but not entirely necessary) part had fallen off him. I hate losing things: it drives me mad. I always imagine the lost items waving at me, desperately wanting to be found. I therefore spent an hour retracing my steps, over and over again, continuously scanning the ground like a crazy person. I wondered how many times I'd already passed it, so close but yet so far. My mission was made more difficult by the rain, which eventually led me to give up. I couldn't find the stupid thing and would have to fashion some way of covering up the gap from the missing bit of my camera dial so dust didn't get into it (a small circular plaster did the trick). I hoped Mr. Canon would last until I came home at the end of July as he was starting to look a bit weathered and worn.

When I reached the guesthouse, I sat in the kitchen with some other guests. There were four young Japanese men, a Spanish woman and a Swiss girl; we females chatted amongst ourselves for a bit but then they revealed they could both speak Japanese. They asked *me* how much Japanese *I* knew. It was mortifying as I could only say hello and thank you (bloody Europeans, showing me up with their clever language skills). They were a friendly bunch but after a while, I left them all to have their conversations in Japanese and entertained myself by booking flights for later in my travels.

I wanted to fill the gap between Bali and Malaysia quickly, before I chickened out and booked a 'holiday' back to Shepperton. Despite one or two good reasons to go home, I wouldn't really want to spend mid-November to mid-December in England: it would be cold, dark and even worse, Christmassy. No, I would stick with the travelling malarkey, no matter what. I wasn't allowed home before March (when my plans became vague) and then *only* if I had dysentery, had been infected by a horrible parasite or the final season of Game of Thrones started.

On Thursday morning, I stepped out of the door and into bright, glaring sunshine. I've always said I'm solar-powered, so I immediately felt that the world was a better place. I decided to revisit the garden, as I wanted to experience it in more flattering conditions. Sunlight enhanced the place considerably and everything seemed much more beautiful. I noticed things I'd missed the day before: large koi carp swimming lazily in the pond and the subtle beginnings of autumn touching some of the leaves.

Bidding the tranquility of the trees and ponds farewell, I visited a chaya district, where traditional Japanese streets and houses could be found. It was peaceful walking through the narrow paths and I loved the wooden exteriors of the buildings. People often greeted me with nods and smiles and because of this, Kanazawa became my favourite Japanese city.

On the way back to the guesthouse, I accidentally took a wrong turn and ended up passing through what looked like an aquarium gone wrong: crabs, lobsters, shrimp, squid and a huge range of fish were there to be admired, but not in a good way. I'd entered the macabre, odious halls of the fish market. It was horrible seeing their limp bodies and cold dead eyes - it made me think of Fat Fred, my beloved goldfish, which had died four years before at the grand old age of twenty-two (just to be clear, I hadn't eaten him, the connection was his fishiness and his deadness - and before you ask, no, he hadn't died and been replaced by my mum).

Feeling saddened, and disgusted by the smell of fish, I left the market and returned to the guesthouse, where I packed up the Green Turtle. One of the workers made me some matcha green tea and shared some sweet potato with me. It wasn't actual *sweet potato* though. It was a regular, pedestrian potato covered in sugar. It was unusual but strangely tasty.

In the late afternoon, I boarded a bullet train for the last time and returned to the chaos of Tokyo for one final night. I checked into the Tokyo Nihonbashi Bay Hotel. I hadn't treated myself to anything fancy: it was a small but modern capsule hotel. I was provided with towels, slippers and bed clothes, which after dinner, I dutifully donned. With everyone in their orange night clothes, it looked like we were all in prison. I didn't sleep well, due to the thin mattress, but I was excited when I woke up as I was going to fly to Australia!

Australia: Brisbane - Going Down Under

I arrived at the airport early and had a sneaky McDonalds. I then walked towards the gate. I couldn't help laughing when a young Japanese man lost grip of his wheelie case, which slid all the way down a long escalator with its handle sticking out, almost taking out a dozen passengers. While waiting for my flight, a young Australian woman carrying a fluffy, rainbow-coloured rucksack sat next to me. I should've moved immediately. She didn't draw a breath and within fifteen minutes, I knew *everything* about her. She then proceeded to babble on about anime and manga while my eyes glazed over. When she occasionally asked *me* a question, her response was always, "How boring!" An older couple sitting opposite rolled their eyes sympathetically at me.

Just as I was about to escape (by pretending to need the toilet), she started listing the dangers of Australia. I thought it might be worth listening. The list was exhaustive and included jellyfish, a range of spiders and snakes, drop-bears (which I knew was a fake story told to tourists) and *teenagers*. Apparently, whatever happened, I *had* to be home before 10pm, before teenagers killed me. I sarcastically asked if homicidal teens were all over Australia and she confirmed that they were. At this point, I stopped feigning interest and suddenly became very distracted by my phone. Luckily she took the hint and moved away. I'd probably be killed by teenagers at 10pm the next evening.

When I finally boarded, I was relieved to be sat nowhere near Miss Chatty. I even had a seat right at the front of the economy section, so I had nobody reclining in front of me and squashing me. Things were looking up. The flight passed quickly and I was pleased when nobody clapped as we landed, like they had in Moscow. It always annoyed me.

Nobody ever claps train drivers when they make it into Waterloo or bus drivers when they pull into Staines. The only time I'd ever clap on a plane is if the flight had been so terrifying that I'd truly thought I was going to die.

We landed at the expected time of 6am. Passing through customs was surprisingly easy - I just had to have my bag sniffed by a cute dog. Thankfully, it didn't find anything incriminating so I was allowed through to catch my bus. It was a relief to see English signage everywhere and the weather felt more temperate than in Japan. I was certain I'd love Australia.

I checked into the Breeze Lodge Hostel and then went for a ten-mile run. I'd wanted to do a nearby parkrun but I hadn't realised they started at *7am* in Australia - crazy! Whilst running, I enjoyed how normal everything was, but yet how *unusual*. It was normal in that it was similar to England. For example, I had to push a button for the green man at traffic lights; people drove on the left side of the road; and lots of women ran alone in shorts and vests (I was no longer an oddity).

However, the nature was strange. I was surrounded by unusual plants, trees and creatures, including a pesky lizard that kept trying to hide in the shade of my foot every time I took a step (which could've ended *really* badly). Looking around, I was confused by the seasons. People kept telling me that it was winter but it didn't *feel* like winter. It was hot and sunny, yet there were *some* bare trees. There were also trees which looked autumnal. Some were in bloom, like in spring, and others were green and vibrant, like in summer. It seemed as if all four seasons were occurring simultaneously and I had no clue which it was.

Once I'd showered, I retraced my running route on the river's south bank. Brisbane was a vibrant city and I loved its energy. There were some great markets, many restaurants, Japanese-style gardens and even a 'beach', complete with lifeguards. A festival was taking place along the riverbank so I sat on a deckchair for a couple of hours, watching the world go by. Well sort of. I couldn't keep my eyes open so I ended up sleeping.

Deciding I was better off on the move, I walked to Kangaroo Point Park, intending to watch the sunset. I felt lonely when I got there, as everyone seemed to be having fun with friends or partners. It would be an ongoing internal battle while I was away because although I liked the autonomy and freedom of travelling alone, I didn't always enjoy actually *being* alone. I sat on the grass, watching people climb the rock walls, until I noticed a free bench. As I stalked towards it, another woman sat down, so I joined her. After a few seconds, she asked if I was alone. I said I was and we started chatting.

Her name was Joelle and she was a French au pair. We got on really well and ended up seeing the light show (part of the Brisbane festival) together. It was fun to watch and we laughed a lot. Afterwards, Joelle had to catch a bus so we said goodbye, promising to keep in touch (which we have), and I returned to the hostel. A young English woman, Maddy, was already in the room. She'd been travelling for a long time so she was able to advise me about where to go in Asia and how to get around. She would be travelling to Byron Bay on Tuesday so we arranged to meet up.

Early on Sunday, I began walking to the bus station, where I would be picked up for my trip to Tamborine National Park. However, a sign informed me that the road I needed to use was closed so I'd have to use a different (longer) route. I had to run but I arrived just in time (after a manic hunt for the correct bus stop). I was a sweaty mess so I don't think I made the best first impression on the rest of the group.

Twelve people were on the tour and everyone seemed friendly. There was a mix of Japanese, Koreans, Canadians and Brits. Brian (our tour guide) picked us up at 7:45am and I sat up front with him, talking about Australia. Later on, I got talking to the only other solo traveller -

a tall, handsome Syrian. Ahmad had been working in the finance industry in London for a few years. He'd been in Australia for three months but was due to return to London in two weeks. He became my buddy for the day.

First, we went to Natural Bridge, where there was a small but pretty waterfall in the rainforest. We then visited a small town where a scarecrow competition was being held. Lots of people had them outside of their houses and some entries, like a cyclist who'd crashed into a haystack, were quite amusing. There was even a Harry Potter scene, complete with a London double-decker bus.

Next, we stopped at a nearby glow-worm cave. The numerous residents created pretty lights on the ceiling, recreating the night sky. However, being a lover of lizards, I was more impressed by the large water dragon that was hanging about just outside of the cave. He was probably hoping to sneak in and have himself an all-you-can-eat buffet of the bioluminescent variety.

After lunch, we returned to the scarecrow town, where we were told we had an hour to explore the quaint shops. Ahmad and I, not interested in shopping, bought ice cream and left the main street. We spent the rest of the time talking intensely about life and love on a park bench - the conversation flowed so easily that I felt like we'd known each other for years.

On our way back to Brisbane, Brian took us to see native birds at a zoo. Some beautiful rainbow lorikeets had just been fed something that looked like porridge and it was smeared all over their beaks: they were very messy eaters. We were lucky enough to also see a kookaburra but it was so high up in a tree that I had to squint.

Brian dropped us off in Brisbane at 4:30pm. Ahmad and I wandered around the city for a while and bought some delicious frozen yoghurt. While we ate, he told me about the riverside apartment his company had put him up in and invited me up to see the great views.

The building's interior was rather classy. As we passed through a gathering of the Resident's Association being held in the lobby, I felt out of place in my casual hoodie. I was therefore glad to get into the lift. Ahmad wasn't wrong about the views and they were even better once the sun set and lights illuminated the city. As it was dark, Ahmad kindly invited me to stay over. We then sat on his ninth-floor balcony for hours, chatting and eating pizza. Just before midnight, Ahmad wished me goodnight and I curled up on his comfortable sofa. Ahmad's living room was quieter than the hostel had been so I slept really well.

The next morning, I needed to get back to do my washing and check out, so Ahmad walked me outside and pointed me in the right direction. He was a great guy and it had been a real pleasure to meet him. Australia was already providing me with friends, making me feel happier and more relaxed. After doing my laundry, packing and chatting to Maddy, I boarded the City Hopper ferry for a free two-hour river cruise. I then took the Stray bus to Byron Bay.

Australia: Byron Bay - A Whale of a Time

17TH - 20TH SEPTEMBER 2018

When I arrived at Discovery Parks Byron Bay (a holiday home and caravan site), I was delighted to be upgraded to a luxury cabin: it was brand new and very spacious. The only issue arose after sunset. The site was deserted and poorly lit, so it was creepy when I ventured outside after dark (usually to hunt for traces of the park's *very* weak WiFi signal). Even when I was safely locked inside my cabin, I would jump at every sound. I kept the blinds closed in case any local serial killers could see inside and begin plotting my demise.

On Tuesday morning, having survived the night, I went running. The beach was over a mile away so it took me a few minutes to reach it. I was amazed by how stunning it was: the turquoise water was crystal clear and golden sand stretched on endlessly. I made up my mind about one thing: I *loved* Australia. After running on the beach for a while, I took an uphill path towards the lighthouse. The trails weren't particularly runner-friendly as they were steep with lots of steps. It didn't matter though as I wasn't in a hurry. From my new perspective, I could see whales and dolphins swimming: it was fantastic.

Once I returned to the cabin, I showered and then picked up a bicycle from reception. They let me have one for free as my cabin's lock had broke the previous day. The bike was a rusty relic and had the style of brakes that were activated by pedaling backwards. In other words, it was a death trap. I safely made it into town but there were too many interesting shops. I didn't buy anything but I really wanted a t-shirt with 'That's what she said' written on it (an American Office reference and my favourite phrase). To escape the danger, I sat on some rocks by the beach and read for a couple of hours. It was warm but not hot; in fact as the afternoon drew on it became chilly, so I cycled home.

While I was tucked up under a blanket on the sofa, I began thinking about what I wanted in life. I didn't have the whole picture but I knew I wanted to live near a beach and have a bike. As far as life goals went, I felt they were achievable. I already had the bike so I just needed to fly the nest and get my own place (no matter how small). I decided I'd be happy living in a mobile home, like the cabin. I only needed a bedroom, a bathroom and a kitchen. An outside area would also be nice as I loved having breakfast outdoors. I went to bed visualising what I wanted, hoping it would one day manifest into reality.

On Wednesday, I woke up to see a dark splodge on the ceiling. The splodge moved. Blurry-eyed, my immediate concern was that it was a spider, but upon getting out of bed, I relaxed - it was just a cockroach. It wasn't a welcome guest but at least it wouldn't kill me and with the help of a chair, a broom, a glass and a piece of paper, it was soon evicted. I then made preparations for the day, as I was going on a sea kayaking trip with Maddy to see dolphins and whales. When I'd seen the kayakers the day before, they seemed to have been spoilt for choice of sea creatures to look at so I couldn't wait.

However, it wasn't meant to be. I received an email saying the trip was cancelled due to strong winds. Never mind. I'd seen plenty of whales up close in New Zealand so it wasn't the end of the world. Instead, I read at my favourite spot on the beach, until it was time to meet Maddy for lunch. We strolled up to the lighthouse together and saw a few distant whales, spurting water into the air. Unfortunately, they weren't close enough to take photos but I was content just watching. Before parting, we enjoyed chatting over a couple of drinks at a beach bar and then I cycled back to the cabin and began packing up the Green Turtle.

Australia: Sydney - Falling In Love

20TH - 26TH SEPTEMBER 2018

On Thursday morning, I was ready at reception at 6:40am, as agreed on Monday, but the bus was noticeably absent from the car park. When 7am came and went, I began feeling nervous - had the driver forgotten me? I knew the bus would have to go past me to reach the highway so I walked to the main road and waited, ready to jump into the path of the bus when I saw it. By 7:30am, I was growing increasingly anxious (and more than a little grumpy). A few guys in 'utes' kindly stopped to ask if I needed a lift into town and I wondered if 750km to Sydney counted as 'town'. Finally, at 7:40am, just as I was losing hope, a small white bus stopped at the side of the road. The driver had got the message to pick me up at the park but had come for me *last* instead of first.

The bus wasn't particularly comfortable and it was a tedious ten-hour journey to Sydney. When I arrived, I immediately took the train to Ashfield. My friend Jon (who I'd met in Thailand a couple of years before) had kindly offered me his spare room for a couple of nights and was at the station to pick me up. I was excited to see him again but not as thrilled as I was to finally meet his dogs, Pepper and Niilo. I'd been going gooey over them since he'd first posted adorable puppy photos on Facebook.

Pepper greeted me by coming and sitting on my lap as soon as I sat in the car. Jon warned me that Niilo was a little 'special' mentally; he did come across as a little lacking in common sense but he made up for it in cute fluffiness. We had a relaxed evening catching up over cider and when his fiancée, Amy, returned from work, we all tucked into pizza. We soon got talking about spiders and snakes which freaked me out, especially when Jon said he'd seen dangerous brown snakes in the

Blue Mountains a few times, which was where we were due to go that weekend. The thought of the snakes didn't stop me sleeping well that night though.

On Friday morning, I was woken by the sound of eager paws scratching at my door. Amy and Jon had gone to work and the dogs clearly knew I was there. I was desperate to go back to sleep so I didn't open the door. Their feet pitter-pattered away towards the kitchen so I started dozing again, only to hear Pepper and Niilo outside the glass door (which led out into the garden) to my room a few moments later. I couldn't help smiling as the pair trotted backwards and forwards between the two doors, desperate to rouse me. Laughing, I opened the back door and they came rushing in to see me, tails wagging. From that moment on, they became my shadows. I was supposed to go running but it was hard to leave them. I loved watching them play: they'd jump on each other, play-biting and drooling on one another. I was smitten.

Eventually, I dragged myself away. The sun was shining but it was pleasantly cool - perfect running weather. I ran across the ANZAC bridge and it wasn't long before I caught sight of the Sydney Harbour Bridge. As I ran underneath it, I saw the Sydney Opera House for the first time. It was surreal to see the impressive building in person but I noticed one thing that bothered me - it was *beige*. I'd always thought it was white but it must just look that way in photos.

Stopping for ice cream, I took in the sights and let it sink in that I was running in *Sydney*, somewhere I thought I'd only ever see on TV. Running over the Sydney Harbour Bridge was fun and provided me with spectacular views of the city. The bridge was really high above the water though so whenever I looked down, my legs felt wobbly. After the bridge, I ran along the harbour, past the Sydney Opera House and then through the Botanical Gardens. My ten mile run ended at Central Station, where I took the train back to Ashfield and stopped for a late lunch.

When I got back to the house, I saw I had a message from Tom: he hadn't been very well. Worried about him, I gave him a call. It was lovely to hear his voice again and we agreed we'd stay in touch more. I spent the remainder of the afternoon in the garden with Pepper and Niilo. When Jon came home, we sat chatting, drinking cider and wine, and eating chicken wings. The dogs made me laugh as they weren't satisfied until they'd herded us onto the sofa, living up to their sheepdog nature. We watched television for a short time but as we were both knackered, we soon said goodnight.

Early on Saturday morning, I woke up ready for the Greenway parkrun - it would be my first chance to do some parkrun tourism. I was excited to run with other people as I'd been missing my running group. The first four people I spoke to were English so it was almost like being home. As usual for parkrun, everyone gathered around for a pre-run briefing. We were asked if there were any parkrun tourists and two of us put up our hands. The other woman (Linda, as I later discovered) was from the Gold Coast in Australia. When I said I was from Shepperton in England, I received a huge round of applause.

The run started promptly at 8am. It made a change to push myself as I was used to a slow sightseeing pace. My final time was just over twenty-six minutes. Afterwards, I stood chatting to Linda and lots of Greenway regulars. They invited us to their usual post-run haunt, the Hungry Grasshopper cafe. It was crowded but Linda and I squeezed ourselves in and both ordered delicious bacon and egg rolls.

As it was getting late, I said goodbye and ran back to see Jon and Amy. They suggested we take the ferry to *The Rocks* (a neighbourhood of historic lanes, just under the Sydney Harbour Bridge) for lunch and drinks. Once we were off the ferry, Jon let me take Pepper's lead but she walked *me* rather than the other way around. Unsurprisingly, she and Niilo attracted *a lot* of attention. Most of it was positive but there was one woman who looked terrified and ran away, as if I was strolling about with a hound of hell.

At The Rocks, we met up with friends of Amy and Jon, an Irish couple called Dean and Kelly. They were open, funny people and I enjoyed their company over cider, wine and pizza. The pizzas had unusual toppings: kangaroo and crocodile. I wasn't sure what to expect but I enjoyed both. Kangaroo tasted similar to beef and crocodile tasted like chicken. I felt a bit guilty eating a kangaroo because I'd eaten one before I'd even seen a live one. I hoped I'd get to see one in the wild before I left Australia. If I did, I would apologise for having eaten one of its relatives.

We returned home and Amy made lasagna with salad, which we ate on the sofa. I'm not a salad fan so I was relieved when Pepper and Niilo dived into it when I closed my eyes for a couple of seconds (I was feeling exhausted and hung-over from the day's drinking). I couldn't keep myself awake so I retired to my room for an early night.

After some much-needed sleep, I woke up at 8:30am, eager for our trip to the Blue Mountains. Sadly, dogs aren't allowed in national parks so we had to leave the furry ones at home - I felt sorry for them as they'd looked so excited when they thought they were coming on our adventure with us.

It took a little over an hour to reach our destination. Our first stop was at the Three Sisters, where we walked around the different – and crowded - viewpoints. Legend has it that the Three Sisters were put into stone by their father, to protect them from the fighting after the three sisters fell in love with three brothers from a different tribe. Their father died before he could undo the spell and they remained bound in rock forever. It wasn't a particularly heart-warming story.

Afterwards, we drove to a much quieter area. Jon took us down a track, trying to find a specific rocky ledge that he knew offered good views. We had to navigate our way past some muddy patches but we eventually found it. The view was indeed spectacular. We were high above the green forest and it seemed to stretch on forever. Giant cloud shadows drifted lazily over the treetops in the valley - it was like a tree-covered Grand Canyon. The only issue was the huge drop down the side of the ledge. If I fell, I'd take a five-second tour straight to the bottom. I braved it and walked out to the rocky ledge, where I sat for five minutes. I couldn't properly relax though as my feet were feeling *dizzy* (the only way I can describe it) and were desperate for me to get out of there. Jon took a couple of photos of me and then I quickly returned to safer ground.

It was soon time to head back to Ashfield. The dogs were very excited to see us. It made me sad to be leaving as I'd grown attached to them. It wasn't the first time I'd bonded with a cute creature. I'd once rescued a damselfly, which I'd named Dave, and then bought him home as a weird kind of pet. I released him the next day, but I like to think we shared some special moments in those twenty-four hours (I'd like to be able to say I was five when this happened but tragically, I was thirty-five).

Once I'd packed, Jon took me to the station. I was grateful to him and Amy. They'd been so kind by letting me stay with them and I'd had a really great time. I must admit that I was somewhat envious of them as they were so obviously happy together, and from an outsider's perspective, they seemed to have a perfect life.

It didn't take long to reach The Pod Hostel. It was clean and quiet: nobody spoke. Just like I couldn't settle on whether I preferred travelling alone or with company, I couldn't decide if I liked quiet hostels. I appreciated being able to sleep easily but the reason I stayed in hostels (apart from the cost) was to meet people. Never mind, I'd only be there for three nights and then I'd fly to Adelaide to stay with my friend Katie.

While I ate the leftover lasagna that Amy had given me, Jon sent me a sweet photo of Niilo sleeping and said the dogs kept checking the spare room, wondering where I was. I told him I'd probably launch myself over his garden fence the next day so I could see them one last time.

After a stressful nightmare about school, I woke up early on Monday. Jon had recommended a trip to Manly so at 8:40am, I found myself on a bumpy ferry. When I arrived, I found signs for a scenic walk and followed them. The quiet path led me through the bush and I saw lizards and a kookaburra. I was aware that I should be mindful of snakes but I didn't feel scared. This was probably because I hadn't actually *seen* a snake in Australia so they were almost fictional in my mind and not something to concern myself with (a bit like goblins or fairies).

Eventually, I came across a historic graveyard for people who'd had to be quarantined before they entered Sydney. Most had died of bubonic plague or smallpox and some of the graves were of young British people. The quarantine station itself is now a holiday resort. Some say it's haunted and you can even take ghost tours there. I continued walking, finding a fort, some old gun pits and a dried-up swamp. After about two hours, I arrived at the stunning Manly Beach. I took a few photos of some surfers but then I had to hurry back to take the ferry as I was due to go whale-watching.

"I went whale-watching, and I was really looking forward to it, but when you see it on TV and you see other programs do it, you're seeing close-ups of these massive creatures, and the music that's added gives you a certain feeling. But in reality, you're stuck on a boat that's bobbing up and down; you feel sick; the whale isn't there on demand; it's miles away...well, all right, not miles, but it's at quite a distance. It wasn't right up close. But that's the reality of it. A lot of people might see these things on TV and think, "Oh, that looks amazing, I'd love to go whale-watching," but it's almost better keeping these things a dream." (Karl Pilkington)

The ferry journey had been a little rocky so I knew we'd be in for a rough ride out at sea. The morning boat returned and lots of green-tinted passengers shuffled out, many carrying small white bags. One lady, after asking if I was about to go out, warned me that they'd seen *no* whales, the sea had been *incredibly rough* and the whole boat *stank of vomit* - lovely. I shrugged and smiled at her, secretly hoping the sea-sickness tablets I'd taken would work their magic.

It wasn't long before we were under the Sydney Harbour Bridge. As we left the shelter of the harbour, the size of the waves increased dramatically and we lost a large percentage of passengers from the top deck. People began picking up sick bags. I enjoyed being thrown about by the pitch and toss of the waves but the drizzly, windy weather made the journey quite cold: I refused to go indoors though in case I missed something. Luckily, we were provided with warm jackets so I was able to stay outside.

As we moved further out into the open water, we began our watch. I hadn't felt hopeful after the last group had been so unlucky but that changed when the boat suddenly stopped. There was an air of tense anticipation. As we rocked to and fro, the captain told us to look to '11 o'clock'. Sure enough, the white puff of a whale's blow could be seen in the distance. It was swiftly followed by the flip of a tail. We'd found humpback whales! Every few minutes they would come up for air and we'd see more water blown and more tails. We never knew exactly where they'd reappear so we had to keep our eyes open and not get distracted, which was easier said than done...

Becoming sidetracked by some dolphins for a moment, I turned to my left to watch them. That was when I heard a roar of excitement. Near us, on my right, was a huge patch of white foam. Apparently a whale had breached, jumping out of the sea to do a flip, and I'd bloody missed it. I was less than impressed. The bastard dolphins had cheated me out of the perfect shot of a whale.

After two hours at sea, we began the return journey. Over the tannoy system, the captain informed us that tea, coffee and snacks were available, so I carefully descended the steps to the small indoor seated area. That was where I found a bunch of green-tinted passengers (I'd thought it had been quiet up on deck). Many were laying on the benches or the floor and had family members looking after them as they gripped their sick bags tightly. I felt a little smug that I felt fine but then the booking instructions *had* instructed people to take tablets before boarding: evidently, not everyone had followed the advice.

That evening, I met Kelly, who I'd met on a group tour in Cuba. We went to the pub for a catch up, mostly talking about things that could kill me (a popular thread of conversation in Australia). This time, I learned about a new danger: the blue-ringed octopus. It was able to release enough toxin to kill ten humans. Often, people don't realise anything is wrong until the paralysis sets in (while leaving them fully conscious). They usually die from respiratory issues and there is no anti-venom to save them. I was devastated - the octopus was my favourite animal. Apparently the blue-ringed octopus was tiny and liked hanging about in rock pools. I usually loved knocking about in those too. Thank you Australia for ruining rock pools for me!

We didn't stay out late as we were both tired. I'd been feeling exhausted and wasn't sure why (it may have had something to do with rushing about all the time). As I lay in bed, I felt like I was still rocking on the boat: even though I was shattered, the 'at sea' feeling made it difficult to sleep.

On Tuesday morning, I was at the train station. I was moving towards the escalator when I saw a man struggling to get on with his suitcase. I rushed to help but before I could get there, he fell, getting carried up in a heap. Someone stopped the escalator so some men could help him stand. I ran to the top of the stairs and back down the escalator so I could at least grab his case for him. Then I went to find help as he'd cut his leg and it was bleeding. Once I knew he was ok, I took the train to Cronulla, a surfing reserve. Apart from the surfers, the beach was deserted. As I was walking, I came across some rock pools. Usually I would've gotten right in there, poking away at things and picking up rocks to see what was hiding underneath, but not this time. I fought my urges and kept my hands to myself.

After my walk, I took the ferry to Bundeena, where I enjoyed another deserted beach: it wasn't a bad life. Next, I did the cliff-top walk, which offered amazing views out to sea. As the path moved inland for a while, it became more wild and sandy. There were also a lot of tree roots which I occasionally mistook for snakes, but apart from that I only saw kookaburras and giant red ants. I didn't see a single human until I reached a geological formation known as The Balconies. It was the perfect spot to sit and watch the waves crash against the rocks. However, a large group of noisy Koreans arrived and broke my bubble of peace so I made my way back to the ferry. The rest of the evening was spent relaxing and packing. It was a shame to be leaving Sydney but I wondered what excitement Adelaide would bring.

Australia: Adelaide - Koala Hunting

26TH SEPTEMBER - 5TH OCTOBER 2018

My friend Katie picked me up from Adelaide airport on Wednesday evening. I'd met her on a walking tour of Budapest in 2014 and as we'd both been alone, we'd stuck together. We'd kept in touch and Katie had given me an open invitation to stay if I was ever in Australia.

I was excited to be away from hostels and cities, and experience life in the countryside. Katie lived on an orchard: her family had lived on the land there for over one hundred years. Obviously, my first concern was spiders, as old houses and arachnids are natural companions. It wasn't long before I encountered one. The toilet was outdoors and on my first visit, I looked above the doorway to find the type of spider I hated most: a hairy, black beast with a chunky body. I called Katie, who kindly evicted the intruder but I was on the alert.

Despite being nervous about spiders, I fell asleep quickly. The house was blissfully silent so I didn't wake for nine hours. I'd been on the go for seven weeks and my body was telling me it needed a rest. Thursday morning was therefore spent in bed, reading, and then I pottered around the orchard, taking photos.

Soon, Mr. Canon and I left the borders of the orchard and entered Blackwood Forest. It was a photogenic haven. While I was exploring, an excited dog bound up to me and dropped a saliva-covered ball at my feet. I picked it up, making as little physical contact with it as possible, and chucked it. The dog leapt after it, snapped it up and returned it to me. That's when its human, a chatty octogenarian, joined us. We discussed my travels and he said I was brave going alone, especially as I was only in my twenties. I told him I was actually forty and he looked surprised. Since travelling, a few people had assumed I was younger than I was (they obviously hadn't looked closely). It was flattering, although it didn't change the depressing truth that I *was* actually forty.

That evening, Katie's family came for a dinner. It was nice to meet her parents (Carla and Peter), sisters and partners (Michelle and Luke, and Sarah and Adam) and her nephew, Harvey. To my delight, Sarah also brought her puppy (Albert) with her. He was adorable and I gave him lots of hugs. Katie's relatives were very welcoming and it was pleasant to feel like part of a family as I'd been missing my own.

On Friday morning, I went running. I wasn't enthusiastic about it and neither was my body. My legs felt heavy, my shins felt tight and even the slightest incline caused me to stop and walk. I managed three miles and then I stopped to sit on a tree stump in the forest for an hour, almost meditating, to watch the grass wave in the breeze. The break must've done me good as the mile home felt much easier.

In the evening, Katie and I went to the popular Friday night market in Adelaide. We ate Chinese food and treated ourselves to foot massages. I hoped it would help my legs feel more relaxed, ready for the scenic Brighton seafront parkrun on Saturday morning (which I'd also got Katie to sign up for).

At 8am, we were ready at the start-line. It was sunny but the sea breeze kept me cool, so I ran the five kilometres in a similar time to the week before. Katie had intended to walk it but ended up running it *all*. I was very proud. To reward ourselves, we ate breakfast at the sailing club. The rest of the day was very relaxed. We spent time with Katie's family, had lunch at the Duck Inn and then I wandered around the orchard, taking more photos. On the way back to the house, I came across a flock of gallahs. I chased them but they flew away before I could get a good shot. As usual, I spent a lot of time staring up at gum trees for koalas. I couldn't believe I'd been in Australia for two weeks and hadn't seen a single one. Katie's sister had seen one in the orchard on Friday though so it was surely just a matter of time...

Bright and early on Sunday morning, we were ready for the Bay to Birdwood (a vintage car parade). Katie's family owned two vehicles from the 1920s: a green truck and a fine-looking, white Hupmobile. We left the orchard at 6:30am to drive to the Bay. Peter and Sarah were in the truck while Diligent (a mechanic) drove the Hup. Adam was up front with him and Katie and I were in the back. The car wasn't fully enclosed so it was freezing. We wore lots of layers and used blankets to keep ourselves warm.

Hundreds of vintage vehicles gathered in a field near the bay. They were all so beautiful: I could see how much work and passion had gone into restoring them. At 8:30am, the parade began. One by one, the vehicles left the field to begin their journey to Birdwood, up in the Adelaide Hills. There were lots of people dressed up, matching their clothing to the era of their vehicle. As we drove through the streets of Adelaide, the crowds waved at us and we waved back. I hadn't realised how popular it would be; people of all ages lined the streets and many set up camp in the road's central reservation.

The Hupmobile did well to keep going, even on the tough hills, whereas the truck had a few issues. However, within a couple of hours, both vehicles reached Birdwood. We bought lunch from one of the many food stalls and then Katie, Sarah and I lay on the grass, enjoying the sunshine. Again, I stared hopefully into the trees, looking for koalas. By 1:30pm, it was time to head home. Sarah jumped in the back with Katie and I, and we were on our way. I was busy admiring the scenery when we suddenly stopped. A koala was on the road! I was so excited to finally see one - they *did* really exist. The koala quickly found a convenient tree to climb and we were able to get photos before it disappeared.

We set off once again. It was more relaxing to travel without the constant waving and I began to doze. That's when the car's engine made a strange noise. We pulled over. The men fiddled with the car but it wasn't going anywhere. Diligent and Adam needed to get back so they ordered an Uber and left us girls to wait for assistance. Putting a blanket on the grass verge, we played music and waited for Peter to arrive with the truck. As we sat there, people in cars waved at us, perplexed: they must've thought we were there for the car parade, just late to the party. To prevent further confusion, Sarah opened the car's bonnet so people would understand that we'd broken down. After ninety minutes, Katie's Uncle John arrived. He said the car couldn't be fixed where it was and would need towing. John then told us that the truck had also broken down. What bad luck! We finally made it home just after 6pm, by which point we were knackered - an early night was required.

As it was a public holiday (Labor Day), we had a lazy start on Monday. We ate lunch with Katie's family and then drove to Cleland Wildlife Park. I was very excited as I was going to meet a koala and feed some kangaroos. The park didn't disappoint: we were able to stroke a Koala named Brownie and have our photo taken with him. He was adorable, and like me, obsessed with food.

Next, we visited the kangaroos, which were very entertaining. I loved watching them bounce about. We tried feeding them with pellets we'd bought at the park but most weren't interested, preferring to eat the grass instead. In addition to koalas and kangaroos, we saw Tasmanian devils, wombats, lizards, dingoes, wallabies, bandicoots and a range of poisonous snakes. It was fascinating to see a legendary brown snake up close but I was glad we were separated by a glass window.

As it was Katie's birthday the following day, we next drove to Hahndorf, a small German-style town, for a celebratory evening at Hahn and Hamlin, a small artisan cafe run by one of Katie's friends. We had the place to ourselves and it was full of her friends and family. The food was delicious and I enjoyed meeting some new people. Once most had gone home, four of us sat chatting over leftover dessert and tea. I'd had a wonderful evening and felt like I was part of the family - I was already dreading leaving at the end of the week.

On Tuesday, we went for a walk along the river to the bakery, where we met Michelle, Luke and baby Harvey for lunch. The bakeries in Australia did fantastic cakes: they were usually twice the size of the ones at home and were often a meal in themselves. I'd been working my way through the different types, from peanut butter cronuts to cream-filled berliners. They were all amazing.

Afterwards, we went to the camping shop, as I needed a sleeping bag for my upcoming tour of Australia's west coast. The trip would involve camping in the desert - I wasn't particularly enthusiastic about the prospect, as by staying with Katie, I'd grown used to home comforts and wasn't up for life back on the road.

Next, Katie and I went to Henley Beach, hoping for a pretty sunset. The sky had steadily been growing cloudier and darker over the course of the afternoon so we hadn't held out much hope. However, when we arrived, Mother Nature did not disappoint. We wandered along the beach, past the pier and sat on the sand to watch the beautiful changing colours of the sky. As the sun slipped beneath the horizon and the warm colours became increasingly muted, storm clouds gathered out at sea and the temperature dropped significantly.

To warm up, we went for fish and chips, meeting up with Katie's sisters. We decided we needed dessert and that's when we heard the first rumbles of thunder. Sitting outside a bar with our ice creams, we watched the storm. Lightning zig-zagged angrily across the sky and thunder boomed, seemingly right above our heads. It wasn't long before we had to find shelter, as sheets of heavy rain flooded the pavements. There was a lot of laughter and excitement as the storm progressed but it finally overtook us, racing for the hills. It was a perfect end to the day.

Wednesday was chilled as Katie was working. I ran by the river and then enjoyed a marathon of Macloeod's Daughters, an Australian TV series that Katie had introduced me to.

On Thursday, I went for a walk and bought a hoodie and a long-sleeved top from the charity shop. I hoped they would keep me warm on the cold nights in the desert. However, I was more concerned by what might *bite* me in the desert - I hoped my good luck would last.

In the evening, I had a farewell dinner with Katie, Sarah and Amy (Katie's sisters). We had a giggle talking about our childhoods. Sarah and I found that we had lots in common, like sticking stuff up our noses as kids, liking weird smells (such as petrol) and annoying people on purpose - it must be something to do with being the youngest in the family.

I'd enjoyed a blissfully relaxed few days in Adelaide and had been able to message and talk to Tom a lot, which had been wonderful. I felt we were getting to know each other and were growing closer, despite being separated by thousands of miles. I'd really loved spending time with Katie and her family. They'd all been very welcoming and I'd felt very much at home. Leaving would not be easy.

Australia: West Coast Tour - Brown Snakes & Broccoli

Katie took me to the airport on Friday morning and kindly waited with me until it was time to board. I shed a few tears as I left the gate; however, by the day's end, I'd booked a flight to Melbourne in March and would return to Adelaide from there. I also arranged to meet my niece in Bali over the Easter holidays. When I landed in Perth, I collected the Green Turtle (which was now even heavier with a sleeping bag strapped to it) and took the bus into the city. The large Perth City YHA was easy to find and seemed pleasant enough.

I wasn't sure what to expect with the upcoming tour. I knew I'd be one of nineteen people and that we'd be camping, cooking our own food and seeing lots of sights along the West Coast. The website had stated that the tour was aimed at the 18-35 age group so I wondered if I would be the oldest person. As it turned out, the group was quite mixed in terms of age, with a roughly even split of males and females. With the exception of Joel, who was twenty-five, all the men were older than me. The girls were in their twenties and thirties and were mostly German or Swiss. There was also a Canadian, an Irishman, a South African, a French father and daughter, a fellow Brit and three Australians.

Everyone seemed friendly although I couldn't decide where I fit in. I often felt awkward in large groups of people, which meant I had a tendency to keep myself to myself. I wanted to enjoy myself though, so I knew I'd have to force myself to chat to people, even if I felt paranoid they wouldn't want me to.

We all met at the hostel's reception at 7am. Our dreadlocked guide pulled up in a grubby white bus and introduced himself as Damian. We put our bags in the back and began our journey of over 2,600 miles. First, we stopped at the Pinnacles, a cluster of rocks jutting out of the sand. It was a strange sight and more than one of the rocks looked like penises. Damian told us that if two people curled up by the base of one, we could be the testicles - lovely.

Our next stop was at Jurien Bay, a white sand beach with turquoise water, but before we could dip our toes in the water, we had to make lunch. Damian told us he was keen for us to eat healthily and talked a lot about salad, broccoli in particular. As all meals would be group meals, it didn't bode well for me: I hated vegetables and I certainly did not do salad. Lunch was a massive beetroot, cauliflower and broccoli concoction. Thankfully, there was also bread and cheese available. I would end up having cheese sandwiches almost every day for lunch as there was never any deviation from the offering of salad. Damian joked that his passengers always complained about the lack of variety in the lunches and grew to hate the broccoli that turned up in every meal. I couldn't say I was surprised.

After lunch, we drove to our second unusual sight of the day: a large pink lake (the colour being due to bacteria). It was pretty impressive. Soon after, we visited Eagle Gorge Point. We were able to watch playful whales breaching, leaving masses of white foam behind them as they crashed back into the ocean - they were a joy to watch. As we started driving again, we saw kangaroos. It was exciting to finally see some in the wild.

Lastly, we stopped at Jake's Point, where the waves were particularly feisty. The colours of the sky gradually became warmer, readying for another amazing sunset. While taking photos, I got chatting to an older man who said he'd surfed the beach there every day for twenty-seven years. He was quite a character and told me about a time when a shark bit his foot (I was pleased to see he still had both feet). He let me take his photo and then strode out into the ocean to continue his love affair with the waves.

That evening, it was my group's turn to make dinner. We prepared chicken fajitas with salsa, cheese and beans. My group was also tasked with preparing spiced potatoes for dinner the next evening so we left them in the oven to slowly cook. I checked on them a couple of times but Damian kept telling me to leave them in longer. I was dubious so I turned down the temperature of the oven. We had to get up at 5am so I went to bed early, entrusting the potatoes to the others. I shared a room with some girls from my group, who all talked loudly in German. I felt awkward as I had no idea what they were discussing, so I put my ear plugs in and went to sleep.

I awoke at 5am to a strange smell. I went downstairs for breakfast and the aroma grew stronger. That's when I realised that the potatoes were still cooking. They were small, smoking, black rocks. Oops. My group would never be forgiven for this error and jokes would religiously be made at our expense whenever it was our turn to prepare a meal.

An hour later, we left for Kalbarri National Park. Our first stop was at Nature's Window, a small natural arch. The hike to it, on the rim of the canyon, was amazing. I loved the striking, red-hued geology of the area, where the rocks had been stacked in layers over millions of years. I sat on a ledge, listening to the bird song and admired the view. It was very peaceful. Well, for a short while at least. A loud drone appeared from nowhere, sounding like a giant bee. I hate drones; therefore I gave this one the finger when it came near me and tutted loudly at the woman controlling it.

As if the drone wasn't irritating enough, a million flies awoke with the growing heat of the day. They weren't biting ones but they were annoying and enjoyed sitting on my face or trying to fly into my ears.

My ponytail was useful for flicking them away: I had a sudden respect for horses, which have to put up with that sort of crap all the time.

Our next stop was at the Z Bend of a river. The hike was a little more challenging than the first, with lots of rocks to navigate to reach the river. There were helpful ladders in places; these were easier than clambering over bare rock.

At lunch, another salad was prepared. I popped to the cafe for a cold drink and accidentally came out with a chicken panini and a slice of cake. Damian looked unimpressed and made a sarcastic comment but I didn't pay any attention - I was a grown woman and if I wanted a panini, I would have one!

As you might be able to tell, I never completely warmed to Damian. It was his last trip of the season and I thought it showed in his attitude. He wasn't as approachable as guides I'd had on other group trips and often seemed ill-tempered. When cooking, he'd get grumpy if we did something the wrong way. God forbid that we should put the tomato *in* the salad - that was a big no-no. However, he was good in other ways. For example, he could be funny when he wanted and sometimes told terrible jokes that would have us all groaning. Also, he'd always stop if he saw any wildlife he thought we'd be interested in and he was knowledgeable about all things Australian.

That night, after a long drive, we arrived at the Monkey Mia hostel. We had dinner and then enjoyed an early night. The next morning, we all went to the beach, excited to see the famous dolphins. We weren't disappointed: three dolphins were there, ready and waiting. Everyone formed a long line at the water's edge and we were told to enter the sea up to our ankles. A lot of information was given about the particular dolphins we were seeing - at forty-two, one of them was older than me. The other two were mother and daughter. The dolphins followed the woman as she spoke and they came really close to us.

Dolphins can't see above them so they would turn curiously, with their eye out of the water, to look up at us. They were as interested in us as we were in them. Some people were chosen to feed the dolphins, which were only allowed three fish each. There was a strict limit of how many fish each dolphin could be given as previously, there had been a problem with overfeeding: the dolphins hadn't needed to hunt for themselves and were therefore neglecting to teach their calves how to hunt. This meant few survived into adulthood. Thanks to the new limits, fewer calves were dying.

Once the show was over, we returned to the bus. Our first stop of the day was at the stunning Shell Beach, which was formed of millions of tiny white shells. After a paddle in the sea, it was Group Two's time to make lunch: *another* salad. People groaned when it was announced that it was our turn but apart from someone cutting a finger, it all went smoothly. We finally reached Coral Bay at 6:30pm; it had been a long drive. The hostel provided free burgers so we were given the night off from cooking and relaxed at the hostel's bar. I was tired though so I went to bed early.

For the first time since leaving Perth, we had a 'free' day. It was great knowing I didn't have to do anything in particular for a few hours. After a morning run and a chat with Tom, I did my laundry and read by the pool. Just as I was about to head to lunch, I bumped into Brian, Joel and Scott and we visited the restaurant next door. I had fish and chips, which was *so* much better than salad.

After lunch, I played volleyball in the pool with Joel, Meghan and Roger. I felt sorry for Joel for being paired up with me as I was rubbish. He'd often put his head in his hands and laugh at my pathetic attempts to get the ball over the net and then sarcastically high-five me whenever anything remotely acceptable occurred, like the ball skimming my fingertips (because at least I'd touched it). Nobody kept score thankfully.

At 3:30pm, Damian gave us a ten minute warning: it was time to get back on the bus. We had a short drive to reach the Yardi Creek campsite. We would be sleeping in small permanent tents there for two nights: Annie (a fellow Brit) and I chose one of the tents and put a rock outside it so we would remember which was ours.

After dinner, I sat chatting with Brian, Shane and Russell, discussing our favourite movies and purposely misinterpreting what Russell (an older Australian) was saying to make it sound inappropriate. Russell was an 'interesting' character (or less politely, a racist moron). He liked to share his strong opinions on many topics, including the royal family, Sadiq Khan (London's mayor) and Muslims. As the trip progressed, he upset many with his unwanted opinions and people started avoiding him. We spent the evening around a large campfire, talking and laughing. I wasn't overjoyed when Russell sat next to me. He kept on about me not wanting children and told me, "You're not an ugly woman; you could do well for yourself if you wanted to." I believe it was meant as a compliment...

On Wednesday, we visited the aptly-named Turquoise Bay. Up until then, I'd been too scared to enter the ocean, but I couldn't resist the clear water and happily jumped in. We'd gone to Turquoise Bay to snorkel which wasn't something I generally cared for. I always ended up choking on sea water and were I to see something scary (a shark or a jellyfish), I'd panic; therefore I didn't swim where my feet couldn't touch the sand. I used the snorkel for a few minutes and saw some large fish. I wasn't overly impressed so I swam back to shore to swap my snorkel for my camera.

Our next stop was at Oyster Stacks, another snorkelling area. I didn't bother going in this time, and chose to sit on the beach instead. I was glad I did, as we saw killer whales out at sea. I never tired of watching whales, no matter how often I saw them.

That evening, we drove to the beach to watch sea turtles lay eggs. The turtles clearly hadn't got the memo though, as they stood us up. We did see a crab. Joel tried to catch it and ended up with a bleeding finger when it fought back (which served him right in my opinion). We lay on the beach, staring up at the stars. We could clearly see the Milky Way and I saw more than one shooting star: I made a wish on each. One of those wishes was for a broccoli-free meal.

After a good night's sleep, we were on our way. We were going to Karijini National Park for three nights, which meant a 700km drive. I don't need to go into detail about the journey. Let's just say that if I were to have played a game of Eye Spy, I would only have required the letters R, S, B and D (road, sky, bushes and dirt). The only exciting thing to happen was finding a huntsman spider in a public toilet. It was a little bigger than the size of my palm so it wasn't big, you know, for a huntsman.

Lunch was yet another salad. Even the people who liked salad were bored with salad, mostly because they predominantly consisted of uncooked broccoli. The food situation made me increasingly happy that I would be leaving the tour in Broome (most were carrying on to Darwin for a further twelve days). I couldn't wait to be alone again as I wanted to be able to make my own decisions about when I woke and what I ate.

We finally reached Karijini at 6:30pm. I shared a permanent tent with Annie again. For dinner, my group prepared a tasty chicken curry and then we sat around chatting until bedtime. We were far from civilisation and light pollution so the stars were stunning. I made wishes on more shooting stars before heading to bed.

Friday did not start well. Someone unexpectedly opened the hatch on the bus and I walked straight into it with my head - ouch! Then, as I was about to put a can of drink into the ice box, I dropped it and it exploded. With the luck I was having, I didn't think I should be allowed near any of the dangerous gorges we were about to visit. When we reached Handcock Gorge, the sign indicated the hike was a Class Five (the hardest level, only for *very* experienced bush walkers). It did not fill me with confidence. We descended some steep, rocky steps to the bottom of the gorge and then began walking along the water that ran through it. Before long, we had to climb slippery rocks. I banged my head hard on a pointy protrusion within five minutes. I decided to stop: I'd had enough.

Damian was surprisingly encouraging and talked me into trying the next section. I left my shoes, clothes and bag on the rocks and *swam* through the gorge (the water was deep in this section and swimming was easier than climbing the rocks on the side) and out to a small water hole. It was then time for the 'Spider Walk': a very narrow passage where we had to move sideways (more like crabs than spiders), straddling the water (which was littered with sharp rocks), with our feet on one side and our hands on the other. It finally led out to a large body of water: Kermit's Pool, where we enjoyed a swim.

Next, we visited Weano Gorge. To get there, we had to do the aptly-named 'Handrail Pool Walk'. This was where a metal handrail was available to help us down a practically vertical section of slippery rocks. I took it slowly and managed not to fall. Once we were all down safely, we spent more time swimming. It was the perfect place to relax and appreciate the scenery. However, I soon managed to slice the back of my thigh on a sharp rock - it really wasn't my day.

That evening, I sat with Lauriane. Feeling brave, I spoke a few sentences of poor French. We then spent the night laughing hysterically, mostly at the random crap I was coming out with. Her dad, Louis, joined in too. He didn't speak much English so he was glad to converse in French, even at my low level. I taught them the French song I'd learned at school about birthdays and we listened to it on YouTube. I went to bed with a headache from laughing so much.

On Saturday, we visited Knox Gorge: *another* gorge. Annie and I were fed up with them as they always involved risky hikes. This one was no different. In fact the hike down was the worst yet, as it was like climbing down a land slide: the path was covered in fallen rocks. When we reached the bottom, Damian told us that the next part of the hike would be even *more* challenging. Annie and I looked at each other and shook our heads. We stayed behind and spent the morning swimming instead. When the others returned, a couple of people said the climb had been a bit hairy, so we were glad we'd stayed behind, even if Damian seemed grumpy with us.

In the late afternoon, the others hiked more gorges. Annie and I went to the campsite bar instead with the drinker of our group (another defector) and two other Australian men, Joel and Leith. It was nice to talk to different people for a change. The group dynamics at the camp had been getting weird and there was an undercurrent of bitchiness developing between a few people. We were also getting increasingly fed up with Russell. My revenge was subtle but effective: every time our group was cleaning, I'd give him some washing up to be redone (as he always did such a terrible job). He'd get genuinely annoyed and call me the washing up police. I could tell he wasn't used to lifting a finger at home as he had a clever way of looking busy while doing very little.

After dinner, I heard Damian shouting about a snake so I went over to see what the fuss was about. A deadly brown snake was in our camp. I was mesmerized by it and had to remind myself to keep my distance as its bite could be fatal. Damian was worried that it was so close to our camp so we kept an eye on it. Eventually, it moved backwards, slyly disappearing into the bushes.

Some of the girls were nervous to make the five minute walk to the shower block in case it reappeared, so we went to the bathroom as a small group. Meli was just asking me to protect her when it slithered right in front of us. She and a couple of others ran back to the tents screaming, but Lauriane and I watched until it was out of sight. I've never been scared of snakes. I grew up with a brother who kept them as pets so I became immune to the sight of them at an early age. However, I had a healthy respect for them, especially the venomous ones. I walked slowly to the toilet. Having seen a snake for myself, I could no longer wander about carefree like I was camping at home. I used my head torch to sweep the path ahead of me but I had no further encounters.

Sunday wasn't exciting. We stopped at Port Hedland, an uninteresting iron ore port, and then continued on to the Pardoo Station. My group prepared dinner and I was put in charge of the potatoes. This time, they didn't end up burned to a crisp! There was still a weird atmosphere though, so I chose to spend most of the evening alone.

We had an early start on Monday and made it to Broome by lunchtime. We finished the trip on a high as we visited the amazing Gantheaume Point. The red rocks looked like the surface of Mars and contrasted beautifully with the turquoise sea. We even saw dolphins leaping about in the water.

The trip was over: all 4200km of it. Everybody was staying at a different hostel to me but I didn't say goodbye as we were all in town until Friday - we would still see each other. The trip had been a great experience and I'd seen some beautiful landscapes but I was looking forward to some alone time.

Australia: Broome - Do Not Go Out Alone After Dark!

15TH - 19TH OCTOBER 2018

"Everyone thinks you should be happy; it's all about living the dream. But if you're living the dream, how do you know if you're awake or asleep? That's what I quite like. I quite like having bad dreams. You wake up and go, "Thank God for that." If your dreams are better than your real life, what is the point? Your dreams should never be better than your real life. Unless you're a sloth, because then they're asleep a lot, aren't they? (Karl Pilkington)

I loved my time in Broome - in fact I had one of my happiest moments there. Travelling wasn't always comfortable, but in Broome, I felt like I really *was* living my dream. But to fully appreciate your dreams, you need the occasional nightmare. I had one on my first night...

'DO NOT GO OUTSIDE ALONE AFTER DARK!'

This important advice (I could tell as it was underlined twice) was given in the bathroom of the Kimberley Klub YHA. It wasn't the only helpful poster: I was also advised against having unprotected sex. It wasn't only fornification that was risky, so were the local bacteria. A poster showed a nauseating photo of someone's hand that appeared to be necrotizing after contracting a nasty infection.

Feeling a bit sick, I left the bathroom and let myself into my private room. It wasn't long before I was wondering what the others were up to. I was never satisfied: when I was alone, I wanted company and when I was with people, I wanted to be alone. I wished my brain would make up its mind. I soon arranged to meet the others at their hostel. I checked the map and found it was a five minute walk away. As I opened the door, I recalled the poster: DON'T GO OUT ALONE

AFTER DARK! It was only 7pm - how bad could it be? When it said 'after dark', it meant after 10pm, surely? I decided I'd be fine.

I stepped out of the safety of the hostel and scanned the vicinity - it was dark and utterly deserted. The dull street lamps barely illuminated the streets. It was noticeable how few houses there were: much of the land seemed disused. There weren't even any cars on the roads. I turned round and stepped back into the hostel to give myself a pep talk.

Telling myself not to be a baby, I went outside again, where a gang of rowdy aboriginal teens were pushing each other around in shopping trolleys. I'd been told that the kids were often the worst for breaking into cars and intimidating people, so I waited for them to pass. Once they got up the road a bit, I followed, maintaining a safe distance.

Successfully making it to the next junction, I checked behind me, only to find a drunk staggering about. Where had he come from? I was sandwiched. I couldn't walk too fast as I'd catch up with the teenagers and I couldn't walk too slowly as the drunk zombie would catch up. I crossed the road to put some distance between us and tried to conceal myself behind some bushes. I regretted my decision to go out. My heart was racing. I saw a side street and ran towards it but the new road was even darker and a hefty man was coming towards me. Three other men, who were sitting on the ground, also began shouting and swearing at me. I froze in panic.

That was when I noticed the golden arches of a McDonald's around the next corner. I ran into the middle of the road and sprinted as fast as my flip-flops would allow. Once in the safety of McDonalds, I ordered a box of chicken nuggets and tried to make a decision. I was genuinely scared to go outside and was effectively stuck between the two hostels. *My* hostel was further away but at least I knew where it was. The other hostel was closer but I had no idea where the entrance was, as it was surrounded by a tall fence to protect the guests.

I settled on returning to my hostel and ran there without incident. The receptionist offered to order me a taxi and told me a few scary stories about things that had happened to previous guests. That was when Adam (a friend of Damian's) came in, thinking we were meeting there. I told him he was at the wrong hostel and he kindly offered me a lift.

It was good to catch up with everyone. We sat at the hostel bar, had a few drinks and played drinking games. We also watched an angry aboriginal woman destroy a truck with a hammer on the other side of the fence. She completely smashed in all the windows. I wasn't sure if it was a random attack or some act of revenge but it reiterated that I shouldn't go out alone after dark.

By 11pm, I was tired. Damian told me not to waste my money on a taxi and offered to walk me home. He was a big guy so I felt safe with him (not very feminist, I know). However, he didn't want to go the long way round and said we'd take the short cut through the dried-up stream. This would've been fine except that the gate was locked. "It's all good," said Damian. "We'll scale it."

The gate was taller than both of us but Damian climbed over it easily. I was less confident. With difficulty, I wedged my foot in the gap by the latch. I then lifted my other leg over the top of the gate so I was straddling it. That was when I got stuck: a thread of my rather short shorts was hooked on the metal railing, right by my privates. It was a bit awkward, but Damian managed to unhook me so I could get my other leg over and safely jump down onto the ground. From there, it was an easy walk back to the hostel, where I had a long conversation with Tom before going to bed.

Tuesday morning was spent by the pool. There were many comfortable sofas to lounge on at the hostel and best of all, lots of hammocks. It was an ideal place to chill. As it was low season, it wasn't busy and was quiet at night. The only real noise came from the local airport, which was a ten minute walk from the hostel. The airport was small but roaring planes would occasionally sweep down from the sky to land. They were sometimes so low that it seemed like they were about to crash into the town.

At midday, I received a message from Claudia asking if I wanted to join some of the group for lunch. We went to the Dragonfly Cafe in town, where I had a mango smoothie and poached eggs with bacon. The group was formed German speakers so I had no idea what they were talking about. As I sat there awkwardly, I wondered why they'd bothered inviting me. We'd originally planned to explore the town but there was a large bushfire in the area and as a result, the air was smoky and ashy. It burned the backs of our throats and stung our eyes. We arranged to meet at 5pm to watch the sunset and returned to our hostels instead.

I wasn't sure the sunset would be very impressive with all the smoke but one of the girls told me smoke enhances a sunset. She wasn't wrong - it was stunning. Smoke hung in the air and created hazy layers, which only added to the beauty. The colours were powerful and there was a striking contrast between the turquoise water and the coral sky. Unlike most of the others, I chose *not* to swim in the sea. On Monday, they'd had to close Cable Beach when a four-metre crocodile had been sighted. Imagine swimming in the clear blue water and turning your head to find a dirty great crocodile eyeing you up. Sod that!

We sat on the beach and watched the sun as it ducked below the horizon. As the evening darkened, the colour of the sky became more intense until it was deep crimson. It wasn't long before the brightest stars began shining. Mars and Venus even made an appearance. I couldn't look away. I had all my favourite things in one place: sea, sunset and stars. Life was good.

On Wednesday, I hung around the hostel pool and at 4pm, returned to Cable Beach with the others. This time, not even the thought of crocodiles could stop me from swimming in the crashing waves, which had turned golden in the evening light. It was then that I had one of those rare euphoric moments, where life felt perfect. The sky was still clouded with a fine veil of smoke and the sun was a perfect vermillion orb, sinking through the haze. I watched it set from the warmth of the ocean and in that moment, I knew I'd made the right decision to travel.

We spent the next couple of hours drinking and messing about on the beach. I danced with Joel and chatted with Lauriane about men and relationships. I'd miss her dirty laugh and I'd miss practising my French with her too. After dark, we visited an open air cinema, where deckchair-style chairs were arranged in rows. It was strange watching a movie outside. Bats were flying around and were regularly silhouetted against the screen. The movie, Crazy Rich Asians, was terrible but not as bad as the mosquitoes that were buzzing around us. Somehow, I escaped with no bites; others weren't so lucky.

After the movie, Shane and Brian walked me home and I hugged them both goodbye. I would miss Brian, a gentle, Australian giant. We always had good conversations and it surprised me that we shared a love of Pride and Prejudice. Like me, he could recite the first line by heart. I also liked Shane, a calm Irishman who was skilled in the art of conversation. He would really listen to people and ask lots of questions. This was rare, as many people prefer to talk only about themselves. It was the last time I'd see everyone. I didn't want to make a fuss so I didn't say goodbye to the main group and just said I'd see them the next day. However, I knew I wouldn't.

On Thursday, I woke up early and ran five kilometres. The heat was stifling and there were still traces of smoke in the air. It felt good to get back to it though, as I'd not had the opportunity to run while I was in the bush. In the afternoon, I went into town. The rest of the day was spent by the pool. I felt sad watching the sunset from the hostel and missed Cable Beach. I wondered if the others were there without me.

On Friday lunchtime, I walked to the airport. I only had four more nights left in Australia before I departed Perth for a month on the Indonesian island of Bali. I felt nervous about it. Everything was out to kill me in Australia yet apart from at night in Broome, I'd always felt safe there. I was less certain about Bali and South-East Asia in general. I told myself to be brave. After all, if I'd survived Mongolia, surely I could survive the much more touristic island of Bali?

Australia: Perth - Licked By a Quokka

19TH - 23RD OCTOBER 2018

Late on Friday afternoon, I arrived at my Perth accommodation: The Downtown Backpackers Hostel. There was one problem. I couldn't get in. I was tired and really needed to visit the bathroom so I wasn't best pleased. The hostel was locked up behind a secure fence and there was no doorbell, just a number to call. I rattled the gate in frustration and did the *wee dance* while the minutes ticked by.

Eventually, I smiled sweetly at a passerby, who called the number for me. After twenty minutes of waiting, I was allowed inside. However, I soon wished I'd stayed outside. The kitchen was a mess and could have doubled as a science experiment for people studying types of lethal bacteria. Unwashed woks and rice clogged up the sinks, and the grimy dishcloths and tea towels turned my stomach.

It's ironic that the hostel name included the word 'backpackers' because no-one there (apart from me) was a backpacker. Everyone lived there long-term and took up *all* the shared space *all* the time. In the evenings, they would lay on the sofas with their duvets so there was no room for anyone else. Nobody ever looked up from their phones when I said hello. In fact, I didn't have a single conversation there in four days.

However, its worst crime was the awful bed (I use the term loosely). It was the thinnest of mattresses on a wooden base. I had to steal the mattress on the empty bed above me to give me a little more comfort at night. It was safe to say that I hated the place and couldn't wait to leave. To have my revenge, I vowed to leave a less than positive review when I checked out - that would show them!

After an awful night's sleep, I felt exhausted yet excited because I was off to meet the world's happiest animals: the quokkas of Rottnest Island. First, I had an appointment with the Claisebrook Cove parkrun. The course was a flat, out-and-back course along the river and the weather was pleasantly cool. It was a relatively popular event, with nearly two hundred participants. At 8am, after the usual parkrun briefing, we were off. As I ran, I was out of breath but I didn't feel I was going at full pelt. Overtaking a few people on a killer hill at the end, I crossed the finish line to find I'd done it in less than 25 minutes - result!

I made breakfast (touching as little as possible in the kitchen) and showered. I then met Claudia at the YHA. She'd been on the West Coast tour, and like me, had finished in Broome. We took the train to Fremantle and from there took the ferry to Rottnest Island. The sea was choppy, but despite forgetting my sea sickness tablets, I felt fine.

As soon as we arrived on the island, we were provided with bicycles. The roads around the island were hilly so it was hard work at times. I was disappointed not to immediately see quokkas: I thought there'd be loads. However, we soon found a small crowd of tourists surrounding what looked like a large rat. It didn't take long for us to realise it wasn't a rat - it was a quokka! We jumped off our bikes and grabbed our phones to take photos. It was a cute little thing, like someone had combined a small kangaroo with a rat and a rainbow. Due to the crowd, I was a little conservative with my photography and didn't try for a quokka selfie. After all, I didn't want to look *uncool*.

After a few more miles on the bikes, we saw a young couple bending down by some bushes - there were more quokkas! This was the dream: two adults with young. The couple left, so it was just us and four of the happiest animals I'd ever seen. There was a no touching or feeding rule concerning the little critters. However, I don't think anyone had informed the quokkas, as while I was down on the ground trying to get a selfie, one began licking me. Another nibbled my bag. I tried to explain about the rule but they didn't seem to care. We finally tore ourselves away to continue our journey. We ate our packed lunches at Cape Vlamingh while we enjoyed the sea view, and then finished our cycle of eighteen miles around the island (my bottom really hurt).

Close to where we'd started were a few shops and cafes, and lots of quokkas. We spent ages following them around with our phones, trying to get selfies. One kept trying to sit on my lap and another was clueless about how to have its photo taken - it kept putting its face right up to my phone instead of staying still and smiling. It was very funny! Once we were done, we had pizza, handed the bikes back and returned to the ferry. It had been an amazing day.

I wish I could say Sunday was as good but it rained all day. I missed Broome and was pining for the sun, the pool and the glorious sunsets. Instead of going out, I stayed in my room all day, booking transport and accommodation to fill in some of the gaps in my travel calendar. I also called Tom a couple of times on WhatsApp which really cheered me up. It was nice having him to talk to when I felt down and I think he enjoyed talking to me too. I tried not to think about how long it would be before I could talk to him again in person.

When I woke on Monday, I felt lethargic but I still forced myself out for a run. First, I ran to the Shepperton Road sign for a selfie with my Shepperton Running Group vest on and then I continued along the river, through the quay and up to King's Park. It was huge with gorgeous botanical gardens. While I was there, a French man stopped me, pointing at my running t-shirt. His name was Lionel Rivoire and he'd just finished running from Sydney to Perth, doing roughly seventy kilometres a day for fifty-eight days. He was so inspiring and he wasn't even limping. I felt bad that I couldn't even be bothered to run three miles back to the hostel.

The following day, my nerves about Bali began to get the better of me. I'd been given lots of warnings about drunken Australians, drink-spiking, scooter-death statistics, ATM fraud, Bali belly or bag thefts. When I'd decided to go, I'd been under the impression that it would be paradise on Earth but maybe I was wrong.

"I think it's a problem when something's a dream because it'll never live up to your expectations. It's better to go somewhere thinking it'll be horrible, and then be pleasantly surprised." (Karl Pilkington)

I agreed with Karl completely. I usually expected the worst. I liked to believe I did it in a tongue in cheek kind of way though as I didn't like to think of myself as a 'glass half-empty' type of person. Often I *was* pleasantly surprised. Other times, I'd turn out to be right and things *were* as crap as I'd expected - case in point, my hostel. On the bus back to Perth, I'd thought to myself, I bet I'll wish I'd gone back to the YHA: I'd liked the YHA. I was right. I *had* wished I'd gone back to the YHA, with its comfortable beds and clean kitchen. Oh well.

Indonesia: Bali: Seminyak - From the Back of a Bike

23RD OCTOBER - 1ST NOVEMBER 2018

Apart from an annoying child kicking the back of my seat for three hours straight, the flight from Perth was uneventful. Getting through passport control and customs was also less hassle than I'd expected. After collecting the Green Turtle, I found a man holding a board with my name on and he whizzed me away to the Kosta Hostel. I checked in within ninety minutes of landing; it was lovely and felt more like a hotel than a hostel. I had an early night as I wasn't feeling great: my sinuses were blocked and I couldn't breathe. After the bed of torture in Perth, my new bed felt like heaven so I was out like a light.

Wednesday started with delicious, healthy, wholemeal pancakes from the hostel cafe. I particularly enjoyed the warm, caramelised bananas that topped them. Feeling grotty, I sat at the pool and read. I also befriended a young English woman from Essex, Jody. We arranged to meet for dinner at the hostel that evening. Both the company and the satay chicken were good and I felt more relaxed as we discussed our travels and ongoing plans.

Thursday was spent much in the same way, although I became a little braver and visited the local Circle K shop a few metres down the road. While I was out, I found a spa. It was only five pounds for an hour's whole body massage. The establishment was basic but the massage was fantastic and as it was so cheap, I'd be able to afford to have one daily.

For the first two nights, I'd shared a three-bed dorm with two young Australian girls, who were self-claimed Instagram addicts. They would spend their time researching the hippest places to be seen, take a taxi there, take some selfies and then come straight back to hunt down the next location. It seemed a tiring to me as it wasn't what I thought travelling was about, but to each their own.

The Instagrammers left on Thursday and were replaced by an American woman who always wore headphones. She explained that she'd just split up with her boyfriend and didn't feel sociable. I got the message and from then on, perhaps rather uncharitably, I referred to her as Sad Sack.

After another massage on Thursday, I bumped into Jody, who asked if I wanted to go to the beach to watch the sunset. I thought it was a brilliant idea as it would force me out of the safety of the hostel. Using an app called 'Grab' (like Asian Uber), she called us a taxi. We picked a beach bar and sat under some colourful umbrellas to watch the stunning sunset. We then had dinner at a funky pizzeria. Bali wasn't nearly as bad as I'd thought. I changed some Australian dollars into rupiah without being conned and we even walked back to the hostel in the dark without being robbed or run over. Result.

However, as much beauty as there was in Bali, it wasn't perfect. The streets were often crowded with traffic; scooters were *everywhere* and they didn't stop for pedestrians. The pavements, when there were pavements, were often crumbling or full of holes and the smell of drains was never far away. There were signs warning about bag snatchers and using ATMs was also something to be wary of, as skimming is a huge problem in Bali and many tourists become victims of fraud. To an expert worrier like me, the possible dangers were exhausting. Luckily, I'd brought a lot of Australian dollars with me so I didn't need to worry about finding a safe ATM for a while. When it was time, I'd look for a bank with a guard, as apparently this was the safest option.

On Friday afternoon, I walked to the beach alone. I was there early so I had plenty of time to take photos of the sunset. After the sun had set,

I ate dinner at a restaurant close to the beach and then had another massage at a spa. I'd been worried about walking back on my own in the dark but it was fine.

I woke on Saturday with the intention of running. However, I still felt unwell so I went back to sleep. That was when I noticed that Sad Sack's bed was empty - she hadn't come home. I hoped she hadn't gotten herself into any trouble. After a dip in the pool, I walked into town for my daily massage, meal and ice cream. I then walked along the beach for a few miles.

By the time I got back to the hostel, it was just after 8pm. While I wrote my blog by the pool, some loud American men were playing the drinking game 'Never Have I Ever'. I had to raise an eyebrow when the topic turned to who had done a particular sexual act. Only one of them *hadn't* done it so they asked my opinion on whether or not it was something that women liked. They chose to take my non-committal laugh as confirmation that it was.

I declined an invitation to join them, and returned to my room. I was honoured when Sad Sack took off her headphones to say hello. She was alive! After explaining that she'd been out *partying* and had spent the night at a hotel in Kuta, she told me that she felt unwell and wanted some peace. With that, the headphones went back on and she turned her back to me.

As I lay in bed, I began to wonder if *I* should've been partying. Was I boring? Should I *party*? The more I used the word 'party' as a verb, the older I felt. I liked sleeping. I didn't fancy going out by myself and getting drunk. I couldn't be braced for danger if I was inebriated. Instead, I decided to invest in an ankle bracelet, or an elephant vest. Then I would feel more like a *proper* traveller. I didn't need to go to extreme of *partying*.

On Sunday, I checked out of the hostel. I was actually a little sad as I'd felt at home there and would miss its cute but crazy kittens. I used

Grab to call a taxi. It wasn't a long journey and I was soon checked in at the Balinea Villa and Spa, where I had my own little place for the next four nights. It hadn't been expensive but it was still double my usual accommodation budget. However, it would be my birthday in a couple of days so I'd wanted to treat myself.

The villa was pretty with flowers arranged on the huge bed. The bathroom was a bit unusual though as it was outdoors. It was private but I couldn't help wondering who'd hear me when I was on the toilet or whether anyone could see me showering. The Balinea had stated that it wasn't suitable for children (a key reason for booking) so imagine my dismay when I found the pool was occupied by two boisterous ten-year-olds. From what I could work out, the French owner (Jeff) had his family staying so it was clearly a case of bad timing.

By 5pm, I decided that I ought to venture out into my new locality. If possible, the roads were even busier and more crowded with scooters. They even used the pavements to overtake so it was really tricky to walk safely. I persevered, dodging caved-in drain covers, and reached the beach in thirty minutes - just in time for sunset. I didn't stay long as parts of my journey had been next to deserted areas so I set off while there was still a little light left. I found a cheap but busy restaurant for dinner, bought an ankle bracelet and then returned to the Balinea for an early night.

I woke up at 10am. I wasn't sure what had happened since I got to Bali - all I wanted to do was sleep. My body and brain were also in agreement that running was not on the menu. My body couldn't be bothered and my brain wasn't happy about the road situation. I decided a week off would be ok. Breakfast at the Balinea was delicious: eggs, pancakes, fresh fruit, fresh juice and yoghurt. I ate like a pig to avoid needing to buy lunch, and then rolled myself onto my sun lounger to read.

It wasn't long before I had itchy feet. I'd read about Tanah Lot, an island temple by the sea, and asked Jeff about it. He offered to find a price for me. He came back with a cost of twenty-five pounds for a car and driver. It was too expensive so he suggested going by scooter. I wasn't happy about the prospect. I'd been on the back of a bike in Uganda, and had even driven one myself in Thailand, but the roads in Seminyak were crazy. I was quoted a price of fourteen pounds for a scooter and driver, who would guide me around the temple. Despite my fears, I agreed to it but I couldn't help picturing myself coming off the bike and my skin being torn off on the tarmac.

My brain is a catastrophiser and often plays movies of possible worst-case scenarios, like an over-protective mechanism for self-preservation. My brain's heart is in the right place, even if it's a little over-dramatic. If I'm somewhere high, images of me falling to my death are shown. If I'm at a restaurant, the movie shows me getting food poisoning. If there are lots of mosquitoes, I'll get malaria. If I'm swimming in the sea, there will be sharks. It's exhausting. I tend to ignore the movies otherwise I'd never leave the house but I think my body may have an addiction to cortisol (the stress hormone).

At 4pm, Ketut arrived and I climbed on the back of his bike. I took hold of the rail behind me and tried to act cool, but my thighs betrayed me as they had a death grip on him. Ketut was clearly an experienced driver. He weaved in and out of the traffic easily and undertook on the pavements like a pro. When we finally reached the quieter roads, I was able to relax a little and enjoy the feeling of speeding along with the wind cooling my skin.

After forty-five minutes, we arrived at the temple. Ketut guided me around, stopping to take obligatory photos of me at key points. It was very scenic at sunset: apparently everyone knew that, as tourists descended on the small island like seagulls on a dropped bag of chips. I didn't like the crowds so Ketut pointed out a peaceful area on a rocky outcrop, further up the beach. As we watched the sunset, Ketut joked that it was a romantic moment for us, which made me laugh. By 9pm, we were back on the bike. Somehow, there was even more traffic, so I grabbed his waist like a frightened baby monkey and held on tight.

When I got back, the French people were having a party so I couldn't sleep. At 1am, I went out, a tad sour-faced, to get water from the cooler. Jeff was very apologetic and promised they'd keep the noise down. In the morning, to say sorry, he offered me a complimentary massage. He asked if I'd prefer a male or female masseuse but suggested a male with strong hands would be best. I agreed, and at midday, was led to the spa room by a young Balinese man, Dulle.

The massage was *unconventional* to say the least. For a start, he told me to take off *all* my clothes. He also didn't cover me at all. I wasn't shy about being naked so I wasn't overly worried. Dulle was an able masseuse and he worked wonders on the tight muscles in my lower back and bottom (probably from being on the motorbike the day before). But as he continued, I began to wonder what sort of massage the owner had arranged. Did he think I needed cheering up? Let's just say it was a *unique* experience and leave it at that...

Feeling relaxed, I returned to my lounger to catch up on the news. I discovered that a Lion Air plane had crashed in Indonesia on Monday, killing all 189 passengers and crew. It was truly awful. My catastrophising brain counted how many flights I still had to take and opened the curtains for the premier showing of 'Worst Case Scenario 1,040,889'. I couldn't let it put me off flying though and told myself that I was more likely to die on the dangerous roads in Bali than on an airplane.

I woke up bright and early on Wednesday. Happy birthday me! It was weird to be alone and it didn't feel like my birthday at all. As a birthday treat, I'd booked a luxury package at a hotel spa. I braved another scooter ride and soon arrived, ready to be pampered. Upon arrival, I was welcomed with delicious cinnamon tea. A lovely lady called Dian looked after me for three and a half hours in which time I had a foot massage, a facial, a body scrub, a manicure and a pedicure. It was all wonderful but by the end, I was fed up with being poked and prodded. Once my nails were painted and dry, I escaped and had long WhatsApp calls with my mum and Tom. I really wished I could've seen him but I'd have to settle for just speaking to him.

I was famished, so I ate turmeric chicken and rice, followed by homemade apple pie and ice cream at what was becoming my favourite restaurant. I then watched another incredible sunset. After that, I didn't know what I wanted to do. I felt I should have a birthday cocktail at a bar, but when I asked myself if that was what I wanted, I found it wasn't. Instead, I took a scooter back to the villa and enjoyed a cold coke while reading in bed. Jeff had kindly left a nice 'Happy Birthday' note on my bed with some chocolates, so I munched on those. It had been a good birthday, despite having spent it alone.

Indonesia: Bali: Ubud - Climbing a Volcano in the Dark

I left Seminyak on Thursday and took a taxi to Ubud. My accommodation was on a busy market street so cars couldn't squeeze down there. Scooters could though and there were many. People even did their shopping on them, not bothering to climb off. I loved the market but there were too many beautiful things to buy: statues, jewellery, dresses and sarongs. One thing that immediately struck me was the large number of penises available: wooden ones, painted ones, shiny metal ones - all sorts. Now don't get me wrong, I'm not opposed to penises, they have their place in the world, but I didn't see why they were so popular in the Balinese markets. Most were sold as bottle openers, but some were so big that I couldn't even get my hand around them. Surely this would make bottle opening a tricky task?

It was difficult to find Indy House as the buildings were hidden behind crowded market stalls, but eventually, I found a small sign pointing down a narrow alley. The guest house was homely and my room had intricately carved wooden doors. After a quick shower, I was back at the market. It took me a while to get into the bartering thing as I was too lazy to quibble over what amounted to fifty pence. However, it was important to play the game. When I asked the price of the vest, I was told it was 200,000 rupiah. I offered 40,000. The guy laughed and lowered his offer to 160,000. I returned his laugh and increased my offer to 50,000, to which he said 120,000. I offered 80,000, which he declined, so I shrugged and started walking away. He soon changed his mind and called to me, "Fine, fine, 80,000." I was happy with that.

With my shopping done, I wondered what to do next. A friend had mentioned the Sacred Monkey Forest but I didn't trust monkeys: they were shifty and prone to theft. However, I soon found myself at the entrance. I removed anything on my person that could be easily stolen and secured my bag so that it wouldn't be molested by opportunistic monkeys. It was with trepidation that I entered the forest. I didn't see any monkeys initially, so I breathed a sigh of relief. That's when I heard a scream. A monkey had jumped from a branch onto a woman's head. People were telling her to stay calm but she was in full panic mode. I must admit that I found it funny, as did a few others. The monkey wasn't doing any real harm but it seemed oblivious to her yelling. I was just grateful that it wasn't me.

A few metres into the forest, the number of monkeys increased dramatically. Observing them, I remembered how close they were to us, their behaviour being very human at times. Saying that, I once saw a monkey stick its finger inside another monkey's bottom, lick it and double dip - not many humans do that I hope. While I watched, a huge male monkey entered a group of smaller ones. They all stopped what they were doing and made way for him, like he was important. He lay on his back with his arms and legs spread: another monkey warily approached and began busily grooming him. Others soon joined in, making it a working party. It was a funny sight.

As expected, lots of people were posing with the monkeys. They'd sit next to one while their friend took a photo. Multiple times, monkeys would climb onto them and the person would laugh. However, as the monkeys made themselves at home, it wasn't long before their smiles faded and morphed into nervous grimaces. Not only would the beasts climb all over them, they would tug on their earrings, necklaces and bags. One got away with a woman's sunglasses. I wasn't having any of that so I opted for a selfie where the monkey was a safe distance away.

By the time I left, it was almost sunset, so I went for dinner and then spent the rest of the evening relaxing on my terrace. Somehow it was almost 2am by the time I made it to bed. I set the alarm for 8:30am and went to sleep. A cock began crowing loudly at 6am and wouldn't stop. I tried ignoring it but it was useless. I was wide awake. There was nothing else for it: I put on my trainers and ran. The route took me through pretty green rice fields on a narrow path. It wasn't so narrow that motorbikes couldn't get down there though and I often had to jump out of their way. It kept me alert at least. On the way back, I noticed a sign for yoga classes, so I made a note of the times.

Breakfast at Indy House consisted of tea, fresh fruit and banana pancakes. I'd never had banana pancakes before and was delighted by how delicious they were. The route I was taking through Asia is actually known as the Banana Pancake Trail, named after the banana pancakes aimed at western backpackers on the popular route. After breakfast, I showered and returned to the yoga studio. There were only six of us in the session, which was held in a bamboo hut. The views over the green fields were incredible and as we moved through the session, I enjoyed the sounds of crickets, birds and the breeze.

Afterwards, I stopped for lunch and decided to make a withdrawal from an ATM. Finding a proper bank wasn't easy but I finally found one with a bank of ATMs that were watched by a security guard. Checking the machine for anything dodgy, I put in my card and tried withdrawing 3,000,000 rupiah. My card was returned. I entered 2,000,000 and the same thing happened. I finally tried 1,000,000 and got lucky. The machine started counting my cash and opened a panel to reveal my money. It was like a school photocopier - all the notes were jammed in the mechanism so I had to work hard to dig them all out before the panel closed. I counted it out to make sure I had the right amount and then stealthily shoved it in the secret pocket of my running leggings.

After a much-needed nap, I took a shower to revive myself. It wouldn't be long before my friend Shinta arrived. I'd first met Shinta in an online chat room, twenty years previously. We'd stayed in touch over the years, becoming online friends, penpals and then Facebook friends. Now we were finally going to meet in person. Shinta was from Indonesia but lived in Jakarta and had flown to Bali so we could spend a weekend together. It was lovely to meet her. Shinta was kind enough to give me a birthday present of a beautiful, printed tunic, which I could wear as a dress. Leaving the guest house, we walked to a restaurant, where we talked about our travels and our lives. It didn't feel like we'd only just met as we felt so comfortable with each other. As we were both tired, we had an early night.

After breakfast, we hopped into the car that Shinta had organised. Our driver was very nice and looked after us well throughout the day. Our first stop was at the Goa Gajah Temple, or Elephant Cave. It was very quiet and we practically had the place to ourselves. I had to wear a sarong to cover my legs which was usual practice in a Hindu temple. The temple was pretty and I liked the elephant stonework on the front of the cave.

We were soon on our way to our next stop, the Tegenungan Waterfall. As we left the car, I noticed a pretty black and gold satin dress at one of the market stalls. Shinta did some bargaining for me and as it was the start of the day, the seller was happy to reduce the price. The waterfall itself was wonderful: wet, loud and splashy, as a good waterfall should be. We took a few photos and then climbed back up to the top. I tried not to look at any of the other dresses or the vibrant kimonos.

Our third stop was at the Tirta Empul Temple. It was a soothing place and somewhere I'd been excited to visit. I'm not a religious person, but I believe there is *something* out there. I wanted to bathe in the sacred waters of the temple and to do that, I needed to hire a green sarong. Shinta helped me to tie it securely so I could wear it as a dress without flashing anyone. An offering needed to be provided, so I paid for a small green bowl fashioned from a leaf, filled with petals, incense and sweets. I said a prayer and then placed my offering on the altar. It was then time to enter the cool, holy waters for purification.

As it was a Saturday, it was busy so I had to queue to access the first fountain. I put my hands in a prayer position while I thought about something I hoped for, and then I splashed my face before putting my head under the spout of cold mountain water. I then moved into the queue for fountain number two (in total, there were fifteen to visit). As I stepped out of the water, a young Indonesian woman asked if she could have her photo taken with me. I was confused but agreed. Then her friends wanted photos too. Shinta smiled and explained that some Indonesians feel it's special to have their photo taken with a westerner. I didn't mind and was happy to oblige.

Once I'd changed, we drove to the Tegallalang Rice Terraces. As it was lunchtime, we visited a restaurant overlooking the vibrant green terraces. I'd not been feeling great for a couple of days so I stuck to simple food. Soya played havoc with my endometriosis: I'd been in a lot of pain so I had to try to cut it out of my diet.

After lunch, we explored the beautiful terraces. I enjoyed it but became annoyed with having to keep paying to cross different pathways, especially as we'd already paid to enter the terraces. Our final stop was at a restaurant with an outside terrace overlooking the active volcano, Mount Batur. We enjoyed a cold drink while admiring the view. It wouldn't be my last encounter with the volcano as I'd booked a tour to hike up it a couple of days later.

On Sunday, we visited the Pura Taman Kemura Saraswati temple where we saw pretty pink lotus flowers. Next, we hiked the Campuhan Ridge Walk which overlooked the jungle. The path was somewhat undulating and a little too hot due to the lack of shade so we didn't walk too far. By the time we'd had lunch and Shinta had bought some presents, it was time for her to leave. I'd had such a fun time with her and I was grateful we'd finally had the chance to meet.

As I waved farewell to one friend, it was time to welcome another. Mel arrived at Indy House in the late afternoon and we sat chatting on the terrace. I knew Mel from the Shepperton Running Group. We'd discovered that we'd be in Bali at the same time so had arranged to travel together. Once Mel had settled in and given me a birthday card and present from Tom (a very handy phone tripod with remote control for selfies), we went to dinner. A local restaurant specialising in suckling pig had been recommended to me so we gave it a try: the pork (complete with crackling) was succulent and delicious.

Afterwards, we went for a short walk. We weren't concerned when it started drizzling but it wasn't long before the drizzle turned to heavy rain. We sheltered under a shop awning before deciding that the rain wasn't going to stop. We couldn't hide all night so we ran. The market street quickly turned into a shallow but fast-moving river so running was a challenge. By the time we arrived home, we were soaked. We hung our clothes out to dry and sat enjoying the storm. We both slept well that night.

At 6am the next morning, we went for a short run. It was great to have a running buddy again. As a birthday treat from Mel, we spent the day at a resort called Jungle Fish which we reached by motorbike. Jungle Fish had a large infinity pool overlooking the jungle and we had a wonderful day relaxing, swimming and trying the different drinks - I particularly loved the strawberry cookie milkshakes.

By 9:30pm, we were ready for bed. We set our alarms for 1:30am as we were going on the sunrise trek at Mount Batur (an active volcano which last erupted in the year 2000). I don't think either of us was pleased to be woken at such an ungodly hour but we forced ourselves out of bed and dressed.

As we walked out into the street, it began raining. We put on our cheap, plastic ponchos and stood in the rain, waiting for our driver, who was late. Two young English girls were in the back of the yellow car and when we arrived at the start of the walk, we were joined by four Americans (a group of three men and a single lady who the guide referred to as 'California'). We were given torches and then we set off. Fortunately the rain stopped. The hike started out easily enough on a tarmac road but after ten minutes, the *real* climb began. The path was dusty and littered with small volcanic rocks, but it was manageable.

The American men were annoyingly loud while we walked and constantly bitched about their friends and droned on about investments and mortgages. I really wasn't in the mood for them. 'California' had clearly not considered what she was about to do before dressing as she was wearing white, leather slip-on shoes and carrying a canvas tote bag, like she was popping to the shops. Our guides weren't impressed as she kept holding us up so they made her go first to set the speed of the group.

The journey became more treacherous as the trail became steeper and more slippery. There was a thick layer of volcanic sand and gravel, and few large rocks to get a firm foothold on. This meant it was easy to fall. Every time we rested, we would look below us at the long but broken line of torches snaking up the volcano to witness the sunrise. The trail of torches could also be seen above us, creeping towards the summit. The lights seemed so high and the remaining footpath appeared noticeably steeper. I was glad it was dark because if the true nature of the trail had been revealed in the daylight, I'm not sure I would've wanted to carry on. My fear of falling gnawed away at me. I was anxious about what was to come and even more concerned about getting down again. We had to stop a lot for California so eventually the guides decided that one of them would hang back and do the journey slowly with her and let the rest of us go on ahead. As the hike increased in difficulty, our speed decreased. Mel and I were sent to the front to 'set the pace' which was a little mortifying.

Thankfully, a Balinese angel in green tracksuit bottoms came from nowhere. He saw I was nervous and started giving me a hand whenever I needed it. I really appreciated his help and decided to give him a tip at the summit. After ninety minutes of walking, we reached a rest station. Green-trouser man gave Mel and me a drink as he said we needed sugar. We thought he was a friend of the guide but it turned out that he was just looking for an opportunity to make money. Once we'd finished our drinks, he charged us 30,000 rupiah each for them (they were usually only 10,000). He'd helped us out a lot so I didn't mind but any thought of a tip was abandoned. He then buggered off, leaving us to do the final (and hardest) bit without his help. How rude.

The final part of the hike was horrible: more vertical, more slippery and much scarier. This time, the guide took my hand and half dragged me up. I asked if we'd be returning the same way and he said no, as it was too dangerous - we'd take a longer but gentler path back to the cars. I was so relieved! We were nearing the summit by 5:15am and there was some grumbling within the group about how the vast clouds would likely block any chance of us seeing the sunrise. This would've rendered our tough trek a little futile so we all kept our fingers crossed that Mother Nature would have mercy on us.

After lots of fear, sweat and doubt, we reached the top, where the path levelled out. We were delighted when the clouds drifted away and revealed the first tangerine glimmers of dawn. Looking around, peaks of nearby mountains and the imposing silhouette of the bigger, feistier volcano, Mount Agung, could be seen through the clouds. It was breathtaking. Well, until the veil of cloud returned, hiding the beauty from us once again. But as it became lighter on the volcano, the clouds once again drifted away, just in time for the sunrise. The growing daylight also revealed the caldera of Mount Batur. At 5:50am, the sun slinked over the horizon. I was happy we'd completed the journey to see it, even if it had been *much* more challenging than we'd anticipated (I'm not sure Mel's ever forgiven me).

The top of the volcano was busy but people were spread out so it didn't feel overcrowded. Everyone was busily taking photographs. Seeing a suitable viewpoint, I moved there to take a few more snaps.

Someone tapped me hard on the shoulder and asked me to move. Bristling with irritation, I didn't turn around but took a couple of big steps to the left and carried on. This apparently wasn't enough as I was asked to move again. This time, I turned around. A plump, curly-haired redhead in a tight vest was stood before me with a couple of his grinning cronies. I told him that there was plenty of space, to which he stated firmly, "I was here first and you're in the way." What a twat! I looked him in the eye and called him an arse. His friends must have found it funny as they laughed like hyenas when I walked away.

Luckily, it was time for breakfast which eased my anger. We were given boiled eggs, sweet bread rolls and bananas. Whilst eating, the view continued to improve as the sun lit up the valley below. Eventually, our guide took us to visit the summit. This meant hiking a narrow ridge path with a precipitous drop on our left (into the volcano) and a slightly less dangerous drop to the right. I kept my eyes on my feet and walked with as much confidence as I could muster to the summit sign. Mel, considering she was afraid of heights, bravely made it too. At 1717 metres, we were at the top of an active volcano. It was photo time, so I turned my back to the caldera and stood next to the sign. My legs felt wobbly, as if they knew that only two steps behind me, was a practically vertical drop. I tried holding onto the signpost but it was as wobbly as my legs which made them even shakier.

Finally, it was time to start our descent, but not before we made a quick stop to see where steam was flowing from cracks in the rocks. Before that, it had been easy to forget that the volcano was still active. The footpath down was much more tolerable than the one we'd taken on our ascent. It was still ashy and slippery but not nearly as dangerous. It was nice to get back to the guest house and take a shower, as we were covered with grey volcanic ash. We then packed, ready for our next stop – Candidasa.

Indonesia: Bali: Candidasa - Red Bottoms

6TH - 10TH NOVEMBER 2018

After leaving lush Ubud, we went to the D'Tunjung Resort in Candidasa, where we stayed in a cute little bungalow. Almost as soon as we arrived, we visited the pool, which was right next to the ocean. The view was pretty, with small islands visible in the distance. In the evening, we ventured out into 'town'. There wasn't much around, just a few small shops and restaurants, and the odd spa.

On Wednesday, we had a pool day. This would've been fine except I forgot to put sun cream on my bottom, and by lunchtime, it was very red and very sore. That evening, we went for a walk and I bought some aloe vera gel for my burning cheeks. We then visited a spa for reflexology.

While we were there, Mel laughed and pointed at something on the spa's menu. For only 100,000 rupiah, we could have a *vagina ratus*. According to the internet, a ratus is a traditional spa treatment, sometimes referred to as vaginal fogging. A ratus is supposed to decrease vaginal 'stress' (I didn't even know how to tell if my vagina was stressed: it had never asked me for any time off). Apparently, other benefits included regulating your menstrual cycle, eliminating unpleasant odours and er...tightening!

Thursday wasn't much different to Wednesday, except I stayed in the shade and kept my bottom covered. I also went for an early morning run. The five kilometre route along the main road wasn't particularly interesting but it was relatively easy as long as I avoided the potholes, dogs, cars and scooters.

That evening, we went for another walk. We popped to the shop and couldn't help but notice that the floor was covered in what looked like maggots and ants. Upon closer inspection, I saw that the 'maggots' were actually dropped wings. It was Bali's flying ant day. The *special occasion* was bad enough at home but the Indonesian version was even less fun, as the ants were *much* bigger. They were fluttering around everywhere and crawling all over the floor. The shop was completely open at the front so there was nothing to prevent their mass entry.

I was treading carefully, trying to locate my favourite electrolytes drink (Pocari Sweat) when Mel asked me to come over to the fridges. "Be quiet and walk slowly," she said. What had she found? I felt a little nervous as I peered around the corner. I needn't have worried though, as it was just a big, beautiful lizard with blue spots. It was having a field day with all the ants. I went to take a photo when one of the large flying ants flew straight into my cleavage. I yelped and fished it out but I spooked the lizard, which ran for cover under the fridge.

On Friday, we fancied a change of scenery so we visited Padangbai. There wasn't much there apart from the ferry terminal so we continued on to White Sand Beach on foot. We used my map app to find the path, which took us through a dodgy gravelled area that was hard to walk on in flip-flops. We decided to brave it and after a short walk and quite a few stairs, we found ourselves at the beach. Huge waves crashed loudly on the white sand beach so it wasn't a safe area for swimming.

We noticed two girls picking up plastic litter so we joined in. Each wave brought more plastic: flip flops, lighters, straws and plastic bottles. Between the four of us, we collected a box-full in ten minutes. It made me a little depressed. At least we'd done something to help, even if it was a tiny contribution.

Once we got back to the bungalow, we sat by the pool and then returned to our favourite restaurant for barbecued pork and fried pineapple - it was delicious.

We had an early breakfast on Saturday morning as we were leaving for Uluwatu. However, we'd booked a driver for the day as we wanted to explore. Our first stop was at Pura Lempuyang (sometimes known as the Gates of Heaven as it's so high up).

Dewa picked us up at 8am and drove us towards the temple. We were only a couple of miles away when he quickly put on his seat belt: we'd come to a police checkpoint. Mel and I had no idea what they were checking for but thankfully they had little interest in us. Dewa showed some papers to the police and then parked up and went over to a table to be processed while some scary-looking officers waited by our car. Eventually, Dewa returned, looking a bit pissed off. He was holding what we assumed to be a fine. We asked him about it but he avoided our questions and pretended he couldn't understand us.

Drama over, we continued on to our destination through heavy rain. After parking, we were taken by shuttle bus up a steep hill to where the temple stood. Once inside, we joined the queue so we could stand at the Gates of Heaven for a photo. A young Indonesian man sat on the ground taking photos for tourists (for a fee of course). It was entertaining watching people being photographed as some took themselves very seriously. A German man attempted to do a sort of break-dancing back-flip and looked genuinely annoyed whenever he got it wrong. When he got onto his Superman pose, Mel and I could no longer contain ourselves and broke out into hysterics, along with many others.

By the time it was our turn, the weather had improved: the clouds parted and we could see the imposing Mount Agung centered between the two gates. We did a *normal* pose, a jump and then a cheesy one, as if we were shielding our eyes from the sun while we gazed majestically into the distance. They came out well so we were pleased. We then climbed up some stairs to admire the stunning views over the valley.

Our next stop was at Taman Tirtagangga, a tranquil water garden. In the ponds were several ornamental statues and stepping stones that could be used to pass from one side of the pond to the other. There were also many koi carp. We took some photos and then jumped back in the car and continued on to Virgin Beach. It was nice to lie on a shaded lounger and enjoy a cold watermelon juice.

As usual, it wasn't long before someone annoyed me: some Russians in bright green shorts were playing frisbee and it kept getting far too close for comfort. I used my best evil glare to warn them away but they seemed impervious. Eventually, their toy ended up in the waves. They searched for ages but couldn't locate it - the sea had stolen it. Mel and I felt a bit smug: it served them right.

After leaving the beach, we had a dull three hour drive to Uluwatu. We checked in at the Padang Padang Inn and then the driver took us to the Uluwatu Temple. I wasn't impressed when I saw signs about monkeys. I'd survived my experience in Ubud but would I be so lucky again?

As we walked around, we didn't see many; in fact, we'd almost forgotten about them while we watched the sun setting over the sea. That's when we heard a commotion. A large male monkey, and a smaller female one, had jumped onto the wall, forcing a man to abandon his expensive camera. A small group of us watched uncomfortably as the monkey sat mere inches away from the device. Would it get knocked over the cliff? Would the monkey snatch it and run off with it? The camera wasn't even mine and I felt tense. Monkeys can be aggressive and this one was huge, so nobody attempted a rescue. A couple of people tried enticing the monkey away with food but to no avail.

The day was eventually saved by the female monkey when she waved her bright red undercarriage (even redder than my own burnt behind) at the male. This grabbed his attention straight away and he sped off towards her. The relieved man grabbed his camera quickly, while the male monkey broke the tension by jumping on the female and enthusiastically mating with her from behind - his feet didn't even touch the ground! What happened next had us in hysterics: the female changed her mind and turned round to slap the male in the face. Humiliated, he ran off to sit on a wall, looking dejected. I was glad we'd chosen not to go to the fire show we'd seen advertised, as the unexpected monkey porn had been much more amusing - we giggled about it all the way to the hotel.

Indonesia: Bali: Uluwatu & Seminyak
- Shaken Awake by an Earthquake

Uluwatu was a quiet place so we spent most of Sunday by the pool. I called Tom for an hour (as soon as I knew he was awake) while I walked around the gardens to get a little exercise – this became a daily ritual. In the late afternoon, Mel and I walked towards Bingin Beach. A walled path led us to a steep set of uneven steps: we descended these through a maze of small cafes and restaurants to a small and shadeless beach, but as it was so hot, we didn't stick around.

On Monday, I busied myself at the pool with travel arrangements. Making plans soon soured my mood however, as I became frustrated when I realised I couldn't afford to do everything I wanted to do or visit all the places I wanted to visit. Goodbye Whitsundays! Goodbye Komodo Island! Goodbye Maldives! My tight budget was the bane of my existence. Before I'd left, I'd naively assumed that fifteen grand would provide me with relative freedom for a year. It hadn't. I could've done things more cheaply, like booking ten-bed dorms instead of four-bed dorms, or choosing hostels over guest houses, but I didn't want to. I wasn't in my twenties anymore and needed privacy and peace.

Leaving my planning behind, we went for a walk and came across a yoga centre offering Sound Healing. Intrigued, we decided to try it that evening. We continued on to Uluwatu Beach but were too lazy to follow the steps all the way down and instead ate at a restaurant overlooking the beach. Apart from the odd monkey, it was a perfect place to enjoy the sunset and watch the surfers play in the golden waves. Once the sun dipped below the horizon, we left for our class.

The open yoga studio was outdoors, on a raised wooden platform. To set the mood, the lighting was dim and calming music played while aromatic incense burned. Yoga mats and pillows were placed in a neat semi-circle so we lay down. The teacher didn't speak much but she was always active. At different points, she would place large singing bowls on our bodies and tap them. With each tap, the bowls would vibrate. Sometimes she'd tap the bowls and wave them over us while they vibrated. I wasn't sure I felt *healed* but I felt very calm by the end.

Over the next few days, our routine followed the same pattern of eating, walking and sitting by the pool. Each day, I would call Tom and we'd talk for ages. It was so nice to be able to catch up on a daily basis, especially as the time difference had made it so difficult when I'd been in Australia. However, I was beginning to feel Bali-ed out. As I told Mel, it was a great place to hang out for a couple of weeks but a month was pushing it. Bali must've taken offence to my comment, as it would soon rumble in reply...

When I first woke up, I was confused. I didn't need a wee. It was still dark. There weren't any loud noises, so why was I suddenly wide awake? It took a couple of seconds to realise that my bed was shaking. It wasn't just the bed: the whole room was trembling. I didn't hear much, just a low rumble and some rattling. The intensity increased as I was gently rocked from side to side. It was an earthquake! Vague advice such as 'hide under a table' or 'shelter under a door frame' went through my head. With my heart racing, I stood up and said to Mel, "I think it's an earthquake." She calmly replied, "Yep."

Only thirty seconds could've passed between me waking and Mel's reply but it felt longer. The strange shuddering subsided so I sat back down, feeling weirdly calm. I had a lot of questions. Where had the earthquake occurred? Had anyone been hurt? Would it happen again? Would there be a tsunami? I was snapped out of my thoughts when I heard movement in the corridor.

Sticking my head out of the door, I saw people making their way downstairs, towards reception. Nobody seemed overly concerned so we stayed in our room. We checked the internet and found a website which told us the earthquake had occurred out at sea, only eighty-six kilometres south of Bali. Depending on which website we looked at, it was classified as between 4.9 or 5.3 on the Richter Scale.

We were both a little shaken up and felt lucky that the quake had not been any bigger, especially when the epicenter had been so close. I messaged Tom, to tell him what happened. He was worried but glad we were ok. Once we felt sure it was over, we turned out the light. That night, I had a lot of dreams where I was walking in houses that fell apart. A thunderstorm also raged outside. Bali was really unleashing its wrath. We were relieved when we woke up that there had been no aftershocks. The website also said there was no imminent danger of tsunamis. Mel and I were both excited that we'd felt an earthquake: it had been a new experience for us both.

Friday was our last full day together so we went shopping in Jimbaran. We both got everything we wanted. I found some black bikini bottoms (my old ones were getting a bit weathered), some banana body lotion, and a Christmas card and present (a little metal statue of a monkey covering its eyes – a private joke) for Mel to give to Tom. Unsurprisingly, locating a Christmas card proved very difficult so I was ecstatic when I finally found one, even if it wasn't *quite* what I'd wanted.

On Saturday morning, after a quick haircut at a local salon, I had lunch with Mel. I felt a little depressed: I wasn't happy about the prospect of being alone again. Our driver picked us up after lunch and for once there was no traffic, so we arrived at the airport early. I sadly hugged Mel goodbye, jealous that she was returning home to her friends and family. I wished I could go home and see Tom.

Once Mel had disappeared inside the terminal building, the driver took me on to the JS Guest House in Seminyak. By late afternoon, I was at the beach. I'd missed my sunset strolls and loved how the sea turned gun-metal grey as dusk closed in. Around me, most people seemed to be in couples or with friends. As I walked, I felt sure I could recognise other solo people: we would make prolonged eye contact and almost smile as we passed each other by. It was as if we both wanted to say hello but felt too shy.

It was hard to know how to spend the next two days. I didn't want to spend much money so the beach would have to suffice. I started the next day with a five kilometre run but was dismayed by how much plastic had been washed up on the beach. I spoke to a local about it and he explained it was to do with the winds at that particular time of year. I saw a group of people picking up beach rubbish: hotel employees and some tourists. I grabbed a pair of gloves and got stuck in. Each wave brought more plastic, leaving it at our feet as unwanted offerings. It didn't seem like we were making even a small dent in it, but by the time I left we'd filled thirty large sacks so I guess we made a difference.

As I went to bed that night, I felt relieved to be flying to Singapore the next day. I needed a change of scenery and hoped that I'd get to meet some new people so I didn't feel so alone.

Indonesia: Singapore - Singapore Fling

Yes, you read right. NOT a Singapore *Sling*, the famous cocktail, but a *fling*. Singapore was like a short but passionate affair. I was seduced on the first date and thought we were going to be very happy together. However, a couple of days in, we had some disagreements - it wouldn't be a happy-ever-after love story after all...

I arrived in Singapore at 1:30pm. Considering it was one of the most expensive places on Earth, I was surprised at the price of a metro ticket: a journey into the city cost just one pound. From the station, it was a short walk to the Dream Lodge hostel. I had a list of free things to see and do in Singapore so I quickly freshened up and made my way to Little India. It was so vibrant and photogenic. There were rows of colourful shops and the roads were decorated with banners. Also, the street art was stunning. However, one thing struck me as I wandered: there were few females. In fact, I could count them on one hand and those I could see, like me, were tourists. Large groups of men stood chatting to each other but there was not one woman amongst them. Some of the men stared a lot, which made me uncomfortable so I stuck to the busier rows of shops. It wasn't long before I was persuaded into eating at one of the many Indian restaurants by a rotund, cheery waiter. Even though it was quite expensive, I couldn't resist the delicious smell of curry. I ordered my favourite: chicken tikka masala with naan bread and rice.

With a full tummy, I wandered in the direction of the Rochor Canal. The sun was setting but everyone I met by the water's edge was friendly and loads of runners sped past me. I felt very safe, even walking alone in the dark. I loved the feeling that I was back in civilisation (no offence to Bali), and enjoyed the proper road crossings that vehicles actually obeyed, and the wide, level pavements. Singapore was behaving like a real gentleman and the bright, colourful lights seduced me. There was always something to see around the next corner: The Flyer (the Singapore version of the London Eye), the Marina Bay Sands Hotel, the malls, the sky scrapers, the palm trees and the famous merlions.

Crossing a bridge, I noticed some towering flower structures, which were part of the Gardens by the Bay complex. If I hurried, I'd make the 8:45pm light show. It was very popular and I groaned when I saw the queue. But then I realised people were queuing for the elevator, not the stairs. Despite the heat, I hurried to the top. I passed through the glitzy shopping centre, went into the gardens, and found a comfortable spot to sit and watch the show. Mesmerising lights danced to vintage music and the giant flower structures, which were covered in green vines and plants, lit up like rainbows. It was lovely to watch dads dance with their kids and couples dance with each other. After the show ended, I walked back to the hostel. The city was still busy and shops were still open, even at 10pm. Singapore certainly wasn't dull - we'd *definitely* be having a second date.

At breakfast the next morning, I met a couple, James (who was English) and Joanna (who was Polish), from Cardiff. We chatted for ages: it was so refreshing to talk to other travellers. My first stop of the day was the Arab Quarter, which was even more interesting than Little India. There were beautiful shops, cosy cafes and even more intricate street art. I spent a couple of hours there, photographing alleys, bicycles and the mosque.

Seeing as I'd loved Little India and Arab Street so much, I was excited to visit Chinatown next. However, it didn't live up to my expectations as it seemed to lack atmosphere (maybe it was just the time of day I was there). I visited a hawker centre for a cheap meal of rice and roasted pork - I must admit I played it safe with my food choice but I really didn't fancy a *pork innards* sandwich...

As I walked towards *home*, it began pouring with rain. My idea for an evening run was out of the window - I didn't fancy running through huge puddles. I looked like a drowned rat by the time I reached the hostel, so I showered and changed into some dry clothes.

In the bathroom, I found something that gave me great joy - a sharing box, containing items people had left behind. I had quite the haul: a half-full bottle of after sun; an almost full bottle of sun cream; a 50% DEET spray (for those pesky mossies); and an unopened bottle of detergent for hand-washing clothes. It was better than Christmas (which wasn't difficult as I hated Christmas).

Feeling fresher, I went downstairs to meet James and Joanna. James was clearly an over-thinker like me as he worried about everything. He hadn't been feeling well so he went to bed, but Joanna and I chatted all night. As we talked, we drank rum (quite a lot of it) and I was quite drunk by the time I got to bed.

I didn't feel great the next morning. I had a little breakfast but my stomach couldn't handle more than a bowl of cereal. As the day progressed, I felt increasingly sick. While I was out, I had to have several breaks to sit down and take deep breaths. It didn't feel like a hangover though. Maybe I had the same thing as James, as he'd been feeling queasy and tired too. I didn't know it then, but it was start of the end of my romance with Singapore.

I took the metro and arrived at the start of my walk at 10am. At 10:02am, it started raining. I hid under a bus shelter and waited for it to stop but it only grew heavier. Eventually, I embraced the weather and strode out into the downpour to climb the steps that led to the top of the Southern Ridges hike. Parts of the walk were covered but most of it was out in the open so I was soon sopping wet. Soon enough, lightning lit up the gloomy sky. The storm must've been directly above as deafening thunder and streaks of lightning occurred simultaneously. I loved it - storms excite me. However, something told me I was being a bit silly. I was standing on a ridge, high above the city, holding an umbrella in an overhead thunderstorm. I then noticed a sign that confirmed said silliness: *For your safety, do not enter the park during, or just after a storm.* Why didn't they put these signs at the *start* of the walk?

To further test my silliness, I crossed a wide, metal bridge that took me above the treetops: the Hendersen Waves, the highest pedestrian bridge in Singapore. The bridge seemed to go on forever as the storm raged above me. I was grateful when I reached the other side without being struck down and felt I'd passed some sort of test. By the time I reached the end of the six mile trail, the rain stopped - typical.

I still felt icky, so I took the metro to a mall and enjoyed the benefits of the air conditioning. It probably wasn't the best idea, as I found myself in an H&M store. I tried a bikini and a playsuit on and annoyingly, they fit perfectly. I couldn't choose between them so as they were in the sale, I bought both. I had no will-power but it was nice to have new things!

I discovered the mall was close to Sentosa Island, so I walked along the boardwalk to get there. I was amused (and dumbfounded) that the boardwalk also featured a travelator. It wasn't a long walk so was it really necessary? Amazingly (to me anyway), I was the only person *not* using it. It conjured up images of the movie Wall-E, where humans grew obese because they travelled everywhere on floating chairs. I worried for the future of humanity.

I got as far as the entrance to Sentosa and decided it looked a bit like a theme park. I lost interest and returned in the direction of the metro station. I went straight to bed when I returned to the hostel, hoping I'd feel better in the morning.

I didn't. I felt worse. I didn't eat much for breakfast but I felt up to visiting Little India with Joanna. As it was still morning, it was quiet and lacked the atmosphere I'd enjoyed on my first day. The Arab

Quarter was a little busier though and I enjoyed showing Joanna around my favourite streets. As the sun was out, the heat was stifling. I was glad when we reached the hostel. Not just because of the weather but because my stomach was cramping. I rushed upstairs and sat on the toilet for a long time. It was the first of many visits that afternoon. My romance with Singapore had definitely turned sour.

On Saturday morning, I woke up bright and early. I checked my phone and was delighted to find I'd been awarded Third Female Runner of the Year in the Shepperton Running Group. I was sad I couldn't have been there to collect my trophy in person but it had been put in Mel's safe hands until I returned home. As I began moving about, I mentally checked my health. I didn't feel sick and my tummy was no longer gurgling - I could go to parkrun!

I was on the metro by 6:30am. Not that the parkrun was near the metro - it was a two mile walk from the station. I arrived five minutes before the briefing and was *glowing* thanks to the humidity. As always, the parkrun team was mostly English so it was almost like being home. Despite the heat, I really enjoyed the run and it was so good to run with other people for a change.

My flight was at 1pm, so I didn't hang around afterwards. I half-jogged to the station, hopped on the metro and was back at the hostel just after 9am. Joanna and James were in the kitchen so we had a final breakfast together and said our goodbyes. I then went to the airport – it was time to visit Thailand.

Southern Thailand:
Karon Beach - Island Hopping

The flight was thankfully short and I soon landed at Phuket Airport. Before I knew it, the Green Turtle and I were queuing for the ATM. I was tired and couldn't have read the screen properly, as I was surprised (and annoyed) to find that I'd been charged six pounds to take out less than one hundred pounds. After doing some research, I learned this was the standard charge at all Thai ATMs. If I'd known, I would've withdrawn more.

I bought a bus ticket to Karon Beach and waited for the bus. Fifteen minutes later, a Thai man barked at me to come over. 'One?' he questioned. I nodded and he rolled his eyes at me, throwing my bag on top of another. He did the same to another woman. We shrugged at each other, unsure of why solo travellers offended him so much. He then yelled at both of us, 'Get on! Now! Go!' Smiling nervously, we hurried into the last two seats. I was squashed in the back with the luggage, practically sat on the lap of a young German man who said he'd also been shouted at.

One by one, people were taken to their accommodations. I knew I'd be last as I was the only person going as far south as Karon Beach. The bus was cramped and bumpy but luckily my seat-mate was dropped off first, so I had room to make myself more comfortable. The driver had been so unfriendly that I was wary when he ordered me to sit up front with him, but as the bus emptied, he became more cheery. By the time it was just the two of us, he knew all about me and had given me tips on where to go and what to do. He wasn't so bad after all.

Eventually, I was dropped off at the JJ Guesthouse. My room was simple but spacious with a queen-sized bed and a fridge. As I passed through reception, I noticed that the guesthouse offered discounted day trips. I worked out that I could do a couple as long as I was thrifty the rest of the time. With that in mind, I went to the market for dinner. Watching where the locals went, I queued for some delicious barbecued chicken and pineapple on a stick. I also treated myself to a banana pancake before heading to bed.

I woke on Sunday feeling refreshed. I'd been worried I might get bored in Thailand so I decided to create a daily routine: I liked routines. I decided to run most mornings and go walking in the afternoons. I'd also visit somewhere new each day.

After breakfast, I went to the beach. It was beautiful (well, apart from the crowds and the large man-bellies hanging over too-tight Speedos). By lunchtime, I was hot, sandy and restless. I'd seen a viewpoint on a map so I thought I'd try and find it. The walk started off easily but the last mile was tricky as I had to walk up a practically vertical dirt road and then along an equally steep main road with no pavement. By the time I reached the viewpoint, I was drenched with sweat. It was worth it though, as the views over Karon Beach were gorgeous.

My alarm went off at 5:50am on Monday and I went for a quick two mile run before going on a tour to 'James Bond Island'. Twenty minutes after I was picked up, I remembered why I rarely enjoyed group trips: I'd be accompanied by *other people* and we'd have to do the tedious pick-ups and drop-offs (I was somehow always first to be picked up or last to be dropped off). It took ninety minutes to pick up just four groups of people as the driver kept getting lost.

Firstly, a polite French couple boarded and then an older Indian couple. The woman's daughter was going on a different trip and hadn't yet been picked up so she was yelling down the phone to the company at regular intervals. The French people and I rolled our eyes at each other. We were then joined by a Thai family with two screaming children who kept kicking my seat. I quickly moved and used my headphones to drown them out.

Finally, we picked up a young Indian couple. I was buckled into my seat while we were driving at speed and the woman decided she wanted to speak to the driver. She tried to climb over me until I raised my eyebrows at her - there was nowhere for me to go unless we stopped the minibus and I got out. Huffing, she sat down. Her husband then tried. He trod on my foot, trying to get past me by almost climbing onto my lap and then shouted at me to 'Just move!' I replied with two choice words which shut him up.

By the time we got to the harbour (two and a half hours after I'd been picked up), I was pissed off. We were ushered onto the pier and then onto our boat, where things settled down. I sat at the front so I could turn my back to everyone and pretend they didn't exist. The views were incredible as we moved through the water and I could see the distant outlines of rocky islands jutting out from the ocean.

Our first stop was at an island named Ko Phanak, where we were put into canoes. I was disappointed not to be able to paddle myself as each canoe had a dedicated 'crew' so all I only had to sit there. We were taken through a large cave that smelt like fruity old socks. I soon realised it was the smell of bats - hundreds of them hung from the ceiling. The cave was quite low in places: some people seemed a little claustrophobic but I enjoyed it.

Once we were back on board, we were taken to the nearby Ko Hong Island, where we had a similar experience. We also had lunch, a tasty buffet of chicken curry, chicken drumsticks, pineapple fried rice with vegetables and noodles. I had two large helpings to make the most of a free meal.

In the afternoon, we went to James Bond Island (which features in *The Man with the Golden Gun*). It was gorgeous but crammed with tourists. People were vying for selfie spots and some were quite rude about it. While I was taking a photo of the island, I heard a woman say to her friend, 'Wait until *she* (pointing at me) goes so she won't be in the way.' I wanted to push her in the water but instead, I took photos for a very long time, until she eventually stormed off.

Once we were back on the boat, it was time to return to Phuket. On the way home, loud music started playing and three Thai men came up the stairs dressed up as women. They proceeded to give the men lap dances. A few loved it while a handful ran away in fear. Others were resigned to their fate and just accepted it miserably. It was very bizarre.

On Tuesday, I went for a four mile beach walk. As always, it was good for people-watching. I noticed lots of Russians seemed to favour the stand-up style of sunbathing. They would stand silently, like sunflowers, facing the sun. It looked strange but as standing burns more calories than lying down, it wasn't a terrible idea.

My afternoon jaunt was to the Karon Temple. I'd hoped for some peace but it was set inside a market so it wasn't quiet at all. It was beautifully decorated though so I was glad I'd made the effort to go. Afterwards, I returned to the beach to watch the sunset.

On Wednesday morning, I woke up early for a run. I was then picked up at 8:30am for a tour to Racha Island, which was thirty minutes away by speedboat. I was picked up promptly (first as always) but this time the pick-ups were quick and we were at the harbour within thirty minutes. The speedboat was great fun and we soon arrived at a small, beautiful beach. I sat on the sand, reading and people-watching. I giggled at the *sexy* poses that the Russian women loved so much: one hand on the hip and the other arm bent behind the head. They even did it on top of spiky rocks – ouch! I had to laugh when one woman was posing on the sand and a rogue wave hit her full in the face.

By 3:30pm, I was back on the boat. However, on the bus to the guesthouse, it hit me that I hadn't spoken all day except to say 'thank you' or 'yes'. It was a good job I was dropped off first, as by the time I got back to my room, I was an emotional wreck. I hadn't had a two-way conversation in four days and I suddenly felt incredibly lonely. I might not have been a people person but I did need *some* people. I spent the next two hours crying, longing for home. I never expected to feel so lonely when travelling and I felt ungrateful for wasting my time feeling sad, but I couldn't help my feelings. I found myself calling Tom. We spoke for a very long time; in fact I didn't go to bed until 5am.

The alarm woke me at 7:45am. I felt drained and didn't want to go on yet another trip to be surrounded by people I didn't know. Regardless, I ate breakfast and readied myself. I was picked up second (for a change) and then two young German girls joined us. As we walked to the speedboat, we began talking. Their names were Lea and Neele and they were travelling for six months. They'd been to some of the places I was going to go to and I'd been to some of the places they were going to go to, so we swapped stories.

The journey to Coral Island only took fifteen minutes so we were there by 10am. I sat with the girls and we looked after each other's bags while we took turns to swim in the sea. At midday, we went for our free lunch together and then enjoyed a walk along the beach, taking photos for each other. The time passed quickly and it was soon time to board the boat. Talking to the girls eased my sense of loneliness so I felt much happier by the time I got back to the guesthouse.

Southern Thailand:
Rawai - Boxing Lessons

I had a lazy Friday morning and booked a flight, one that would take me away from Asia, from Sri Lanka to Paris, on 23rd May. The flight wasn't for six months but I still felt excited about the prospect of being closer to home. Not that my trip would end there as I intended to travel around Eastern Europe until the end of July. When it was time, I walked down the road with the Green Turtle to find an over-priced tuk tuk to take me to Rawai. As the journey was so short, I soon arrived at the Rawai Studio Apartments. I was quickly checked in and shown to my spacious room, which had a huge bed and a kitchen.

My first stop was to buy food: yoghurts, milk, cereal, bread, butter and eggs. On my brief walk to the shop, I noticed that there wasn't much around and wondered how I'd spend my week. That's when I noticed posters along the roadside. There were adverts for boxing, yoga, villas and even floatation therapy. I was intrigued by a few and took photos so I could look up the websites when I got back. I thought it might be fun to try a few new experiences, especially floatation therapy, where you lay in an isolation tank filled with salt water and float. I booked it for Sunday afternoon. Next, I looked up the boxing. Ali's Boxing Gym offered Muay Thai lessons for beginners for 250 baht. I emailed them and booked a lesson for Saturday. It seemed I would be pretty busy after all...

I woke early on Saturday for a short run. The first route I tried was guarded by scary dogs that growled as I drew near. I didn't fancy a fight with them so I turned around and went a different way. By the time I got back, I was shattered and desperate for a cold drink and a shower.

While I ate breakfast, I started feeling nervous about boxing. Would I feel out of place? However, I had no reason to worry. At 11am, I turned up at Ali's Boxing Gym. There were a few people there but most were just finishing their morning training. While I waited, I met a British woman named Nicola, who was travelling long-term. She'd got hooked on Muay Thai Boxing and had ended up living on Phuket for almost a year. It was nice to chat to a friendly face and I felt at ease straight away.

Ali, the gym's manager, handed me a skipping rope and told me to skip for fifteen minutes. I hadn't skipped in years: it was knackering. Ali told me I had athletic legs and asked if I was a runner. I replied that I was and he told me that boxing was a good way for runners to improve their upper body strength. It was definitely what I needed as my arms were pathetically weak.

Once the skipping was completed, Ali showed me some punches. I was crap. There was so much to think about: how to make a fist, how to move my hips, how to move my feet, etc. I was all over the place and Ali didn't know what to do with me. That's when Nick came over. Nick was an amazing, patient teacher who started from the beginning. He taught Muay Thai classes to kids so he was fully able to handle my ineptitude. We started with posture and foot work. He told me I had fantastic posture but it wasn't a compliment. I needed to be more slouchy so I could protect myself.

Once I'd done a good enough job with the footwork, we moved onto punches. He made me use a rubber band to help me with the technique. It took quite a while but I was finally able to punch with my left hand correctly. That's when I suddenly had the urge to throw up and the room went spotty. I made it to the bathroom and put my head between my knees. Nick was kind enough to run out and get me an energy drink as he thought I needed electrolytes. The drink helped but we took a break and chatted to Nicola. I learned that Nick was part Canadian and part Iranian. He'd also become hooked on Thailand and like Nicola, had been there a long time. I didn't feel great but I decided to carry on as I'd really been enjoying myself. To finish the lesson, we practised the punches and then worked on defensive techniques. Nick said he was proud of how far I'd come and offered to meet me again on Monday.

On the way back, I bought a big bottle of water and chugged it down. I still had butterflies in my tummy. I knew why though - I was about to rent a scooter. The thought of it scared me. What if I was knocked off or did something stupid and ended up hurting myself? The guesthouse rented out bikes for only 150 baht a day. I chose a blue one that looked slow. I thought I'd try going to Rawai beach which was only a couple of miles away. I kept to the left and tried to feel confident. It didn't work: I had a death grip on the handles and my whole body was tense.

After fifteen minutes on the dual carriageway, I saw a sign for Chalong Temple. Oops - I'd gone in the wrong direction. I was scared to turn so I drove the wrong way for another ten minutes. Finally, when the road was unusually quiet, I crossed both lanes, made a u-turn and drove in the correct direction.

I must've missed the sign for Rawai Beach as I found myself down in the very south of Phuket. I visited Phrom Thep Cape and Nai Harn Beach instead. Both were very beautiful but I couldn't settle as I felt the need to get back on the scooter. Part of me wanted to return to the guesthouse but I made myself drive to my favourite restaurant in Karon Beach.

As I ate dinner, the sky turned stormy. I didn't fancy driving in bad weather so I clambered onto the scooter. This time I felt more relaxed. The journey between Karon Beach and Rawai was very quiet and I found myself enjoying the journey along the winding road. I made it back in time for sunset and breathed a sigh of relief as I parked up: I had survived.

Early on Sunday morning, I was back on the scooter to visit Big Buddha, up on a huge hill in Phuket. It was the highest point on the island and the views were supposed to be wonderful. The roads were quiet and I reached the turning for the Big Buddha without any issues. I'd been concerned about the steep climb up but I needn't have worried as my bike was up to the job. The Big Buddha appeared to be looking down over Phuket. I wandered around and took in the views - it was hazy but beautiful. The descent was uneventful and before long, I was at my next stop, the amazing Chalong Temple. There were a few couples having their wedding photos taken and they looked regal in their traditional outfits.

By 1pm, I was back at the guesthouse so I showered and napped until it was time for my floating session. When I arrived, I was shown to my room. There was a shower, toiletries, towels and a large door that led to the floatation chamber. I was told to shower before I entered the water. Once I'd showered, I stepped into the chamber and closed the door. The space was lit by a blue light and gentle music played. It was very relaxing to be buoyed by the magnesium-salt-filled water. The music stopped after fifteen minutes so I floated in the silent darkness.

I'd like to say I had a blissful, meditative moment, where I felt at peace with myself and the world, but I didn't. Apparently lots of people sleep while they float but I couldn't nap in such a strange environment. I thought about what shopping I needed to buy on the way home and my plans for the rest of the week instead.

After what felt like forever, the water started bubbling. This was my signal to get out. I showered and exited the room. It had been an interesting experience but it wasn't something I'd do again. As I paid, I chatted to the receptionist about travelling. We got onto the subject of running and she pointed out a poster on the door. A man called Jay was offering himself up as a running buddy on Wednesday mornings. I felt excited to have someone to run with. Using Instagram to contact him, we arranged to meet that week (something I would later regret).

On Monday morning, I was back at the gym for another session with Nick. Nicola was there too. We did a lot of practice of the basic punches and blocks, and then once I was ready, he put some gloves on me. We did some pad work and he moved around so I had to shadow him whilst getting some jabs in and defend myself from his fake 'hits'. He laughed out loud at one point as I left myself wide open and he asked what would happen in a fight if I did that. I told him I'd get slapped. He quite rightly pointed out that boxers do not 'slap'.

As we went through the lesson, I found that I could distract him by getting him to talk about diets and nutrition (his favourite subject). This allowed me to get in some sneaky rest breaks. I'd learned this technique from the children I'd taught. They would sometimes distract me from my teaching by talking about something they knew interested me (like octopuses). I often fell for it and before I knew it, we'd be watching a YouTube video of an octopus opening a jar. Towards the end of the lesson, we moved onto the punch bag. It was hard work trying to hit it with a respectable level of force and my knuckles really hurt, even with the gloves on. I'd definitely improved though and I was proud of myself.

Tuesday's boxing lesson was more intense and sweaty. We practised punching for a while and then moved on to different techniques for using elbows and knees. I was actually good with those and got the hang of the spinning elbow quite quickly. This was where you face your opponent, turn away but then spin to hit them in the face with your elbow. It was great fun!

After doing it twenty times, I got a bit dizzy so we moved onto knee work. I liked using my knees. He practised with me kneeing into the pad multiple times and then he had me grab his head while repeatedly thrusting my knee up into his face (well into the pad anyway). I was a bit gentle at first but he told me to really go for it. I loved it as it made me feel confident. He said it was a good self-defence technique if I ever needed it and suggested I do it if someone insulted me.

Considering how rubbish I'd felt the week before, I couldn't believe how different I felt a week on. The boxing gym felt like home. I could go there and chat to people and feel part of something. The bike helped too: it made me feel more independent and free.

Being a creature of habit, I found myself at Karon Beach again on Tuesday afternoon. I had a dip in the sea and then sat on the beach, watching the parasailing. When the boats moved off, lifting the tourists into the air, the Thai guys would jump on the parachutes behind them. They had nothing to secure them and would just stand on the ropes. I couldn't decide if they were brave or stupid.

As I watched the boats, I noticed how dark the sky had become. Lightning struck out at sea and was immediately followed by a loud clap of thunder. I was glad I wasn't one of the paragliders! The storm came quickly inland and I was soon drenched. I didn't bother hiding though as it was warm and I had beachwear on. However, lots of people crowded under shelters, standing in their bikinis and swimming shorts. I thought it was odd. Were they worried their swimsuits would get wet? After dinner at my usual place, I hopped back on the bike, taking a different route. I soon regretted it though as the road was fast and busy. Staying on the left, I kept my speed up enough to not cause a traffic jam.

Sandy, wet and a little tense, I arrived at my destination: a building where massages were given by the blind. It was dark and very basic inside but the atmosphere was friendly. A few people were sat about chatting but I was the only actual customer. I was given a dry robe to wear and told to lay down on one of the beds. A blind Thai man came over and started massaging me while another man sat belching repeatedly (I couldn't help laughing). My masseur cackled whenever he found a tight spot and I'd hold my breath while he stuck his elbow/fist/knee/fingers into it. It was like his blindness enabled him to more easily locate areas of tension. I felt the massage was doing me good though, more so than the foot massages I usually favoured. The session ended with a weird stomach massage and then a face massage. It only cost 150 baht so I left a large tip.

The next morning, I was up at 6:30am, ready to run with Jay. I met him at the gym and we were joined by two other women, both named Julia. We set off towards Nai Harn Lake. The two Julias hadn't run in a while so I was soon out in front. Many people were taking advantage of the pretty lake: runners, walkers, tai-chi-ists and cyclists. I ran on the road as opposed to the pavement as several tiles were sticking out and I didn't want to fall over (a *bad* decision in retrospect). The route around the lake was two kilometres. I was almost around when Jay caught up with me. We were discussing marathons when suddenly I was falling: I'd tripped on one of the protruding reflectors in the road. The first thing that made contact with the ground was my elbow. Then I skidded towards the kerb, face-first – smash!

Initially, I lay there in shock. I then did a mental check for damage. My face felt sore and my hand instinctively reached for my nose which was bleeding heavily. Jay kept asking if I was ok but I could only groan. Once I felt able to, Jay helped me to sit on the kerb. Three cyclists came over to help and one kindly poured bottled water on my grazed elbow and hand. My other hand was still under my nose and was filling with blood again. Jay took off his t-shirt and gave it to me to help soak it up. Somehow, apart from one large spot of blood, my white Shepperton Running Group t-shirt remained clean. I could feel my lip swelling and my nose hurt - had I broken it?

Jay and I moved to a bench and sat there until I felt up to walking. Once we got to the gym, he fetched some ice to put on my face, and we sat chatting until I felt able to return to the apartment. Jay waved me goodbye as I got on my scooter and drove off. I felt bad for him as he clearly felt guilty about the situation (not that it was his fault in any way).

When I returned to the guesthouse, the receptionist looked at me in shock and insisted on taking me to the clinic, as she was concerned about my nose. We got on her scooter and were there in five minutes. Nurses took photos of my nose and sent them to a doctor. The reply came quickly - I needed stitches to fix a deep gash at the top of my nostril and an x-ray. I'd never broken anything in my life and had never had stitches. I felt very alone and quite scared, so I called Tom and my mum to tell them what had happened. They were obviously worried but glad it hadn't been worse (at least I had all my teeth).

I took a taxi to a recommended private hospital near Phuket Town. I was put on a gurney and seen immediately. Within fifteen minutes, I'd had an x-ray and was wheeled into a treatment room. After that, a doctor patched me up. He injected anesthetic into my nose (which was unpleasant) and put three stitches in it. I didn't feel any pain, just the pull of the thread. The doctor then informed me that my nose was indeed broken. It was only a small break thankfully so no surgery was needed, just painkillers and time. The lovely staff diligently cleaned my wounds. Although I knew it was necessary, it really hurt when they scrubbed my grazes. Once the grazes were clean, they were covered with squishy, flesh-coloured material, a bit like that of a blister plaster.

Only an hour after I'd arrived, I was back in the taxi with an ice pack, painkillers, muscle relaxants and a course of antibiotics. I was also over two hundred pounds poorer. My travel insurance would cover anything after the first one hundred pounds but it was still a lot of money to lose from my budget. I spent the rest of the day curled up in bed, feeling sorry for myself. By the evening, the grazes were weeping. I pulled a couple of the plasters off and dabbed the ooziness away: the wounds dried up quickly. Before long, I'd peeled off all but one of the plasters. The grazes stung when the air reached them but they looked much better once they dried out - I preferred scabs to oozing.

On Thursday morning, I was feeling bruised and battered. My face was scabby: not big black scabs, but light brown ones that cracked easily and looked more like burns. I'd been due to have a lesson with Nick, so at 11am, I walked to the gym. A few people did double-takes when they saw me but I held my head up high. I saw Ali first, who kindly gave me a banana and a sports drink.

When Nick arrived, he was disappointed we couldn't do our lesson. I was too, so we sat and chatted for a couple of hours instead. He asked if I'd gotten into a fight: when I told him how I actually broke my nose, he suggested I tell a different story, one where I'd upset a lady-boy and we'd fought. He really made me laugh, even though it hurt my face to do so. Nicola came over for a chat and told me she would soon be having her first real fight. I would have loved to have watched. She looked so frightening when she was training. I certainly wouldn't have wanted to go up against her! I hugged everyone goodbye and thanked them for making me feel so welcome. I was so pleased I'd seen the boxing sign and was grateful I had some valuable new skills (should I ever need them).

Southern Thailand: Phuket Town - Recuperating

I woke up on Friday in less pain - progress! I wasn't looking forward to changing accommodation though as I really didn't have the energy. Reluctantly, the Green Turtle and I began the hot, long walk to the bus stop. I made it a third of the way easily enough but it was tricky when my hand and elbow were still so sore. Just as I was getting tired, a kind Thai woman pulled over and insisted on taking me to the bus stop. She balanced the Green Turtle on her scooter and I hopped on the back. I was so grateful.

My next job was to find a blue 'bus' (an open van with two rows of benches in the back). I waited at what I thought was a bus shelter but I missed the first one as I was distracted by a dog. A man on a scooter approached, asking if I wanted a taxi. He distracted me just as the next bus came so I missed it. We negotiated and he agreed to take me to Phuket Town for 100 baht. The bus would've cost 50 baht but the taxi would take me right to the door of my accommodation, which would save me a long walk.

He squeezed the Green Turtle in by his feet and off we went. I dropped my bag off at the Vitamin Sea Hostel and then he took me to Dibuk Hospital for my appointment. I was shown into the ward and immediately seen by the same doctor and nurses I'd seen on Wednesday. I was told my nose was healing well and that there was no infection. They cleaned me up, changed my dressing and told me to come back on Wednesday to have my stitches out.

Leaving the hospital, I stood on the side of the busy main road, waiting for a blue bus. Four taxis pulled over but they were charging three times what the bus would so I waited. It wasn't long before I saw one. Relieved, I waved it down, but it cruised right past – how rude! When I saw how full it was, I let him off: there'd be another. Within two minutes, an emptier bus came and took me to the fruit market in Phuket Town. From there, it was a ten minute walk to the hostel.

I checked in and then rested on my bed, chatting to the three British girls in my room. By 3pm, I was hungry so I ate at a nearby cafe and then walked towards Monkey Hill. The road up the hill was very steep. A lot of people were walking up and some were even running (albeit very slowly). People kept doing double-takes when they saw my face. I just smiled and they nervously smiled back. With my bruised knuckles, maybe they thought I'd been in a fight and didn't want to upset me.

As I continued up the hill, I began worrying about the monkeys of Monkey Hill: after all, it wouldn't be called that for nothing would it? They were waiting one and half kilometres up and there were loads of them - I felt like Pacman avoiding them all. Despite the signs saying not to feed them, people were doing just that. As usual, I kept my distance.

At the top, the views over Phuket were very pretty, although partially blocked by some bushy trees. I couldn't relax though, as a monkey took a fancy to me on the rectangular viewing platform and was eyeing up my camera. Every time I went to take a photo, it approached. I walked to the next corner and it followed a few seconds later. We lazily circled each other for two minutes (the slowest chase ever seen in Thailand). Thankfully, someone showed up with bananas. The pesky thing stopped harassing me in favour of free food and I was able to quickly take some photos and hurry back down the hill.

On Saturday, I had a lazy morning before venturing out at midday. My nose felt and looked much better as the scabs had miraculously fallen off (cough...). I went on a tour of Old Phuket Town with Mr. Canon. It was full of colourful old buildings and street art and I loved wandering around the different streets, exploring little alleys and taking photos. Phuket Town became the highlight of my time in Thailand. I explored for a good few hours and managed not to spend much money, despite wandering into many shops. At the fruit market, I stopped to buy some passion fruits. I'd never actually eaten one before. They were delicious – a new favourite!

By 5pm, I was back at the hostel. When I returned to my dorm, the two younger British girls had left and a German girl, Neela, had arrived. She'd been on an eight-day diving trip where she'd burst her ear drum on day two. I'd burst mine a couple of years before so I could sympathise. I named our dorm the Room of Mishaps: a broken nose and now a burst ear drum. She wanted to go out for dinner so we went to a restaurant near the market and sat chatting for hours. We also arranged to go walking the next day.

When I went to bed, I set the alarm for 7am so I could run the next morning. I felt quite apprehensive as breaking my nose had dented my confidence. However, the only way to get over it was to get back out there. On Sunday morning, I was out of the door by 7:15am. I walked for a while before starting to jog slowly towards a large park I'd noticed on the journey to Phuket Town. Suan Luang King Rama Park was about a mile and a half from the hostel. There was a four kilometre track around the perimeter and there was not a reflector in sight. It was busy but there was plenty of space. Falling was still a concern though. I felt I couldn't trust my own feet anymore and kept picturing my face slamming into the kerb.

I was glad to get back to the hostel without injuring myself. I'd run five miles which was the furthest I'd managed in a while. Once I'd showered and had breakfast, Leela and I set off on our walk. We decided to visit the Khao Rang Viewpoint, up another hill. Luckily it wasn't as high as Monkey Hill and there were fewer monkeys. The views were also nicer as they weren't obstructed by trees. After we'd descended, we looked in some shops as Leela wanted to buy gifts. We then had lunch and I took her to the fruit market where we bought more passion fruits. The lady recognised me and smiled.

When we returned to the hostel, we met a British guy called Akshay, who was travelling for six months. He wasn't feeling well as he was suffering with a cold (another one for our sick and injured club). Neela and I had made plans to visit the night market so we invited him along.

The three of us set off at 5pm. The large market sold all sorts, including fake designer knock-offs, tourist tat, clothes, toys and local crafts. We were all hungry so we weaved our way to the food section, where we had crispy pork and rice. Neela left to go clothes shopping so Akshay and I carried on eating, sharing satay chicken, blueberry doughnuts, chocolate waffles, coconut pancakes and fruit smoothies. Once our bellies were full, we returned to the main market, where I bought some purses and an adorable, crocheted octopus. I was skint, so we returned to the food market to wait for Neela. Once we were reunited, we walked home.

Leela checked out on Monday morning as she was leaving to meet a friend in Krabi. I didn't feel like doing much so I had a day of travel planning while sitting on the hammock-style ceiling of the hostel. I'd been planning on *not* planning Vietnam but I'd recently discovered I'd be there during their new year in February; therefore booking ahead would be wise. I did lots of research into visas, buses, trains and accommodation and after four hours, Vietnam was sorted. I was going to start in Hanoi and work my way south over three weeks.

On a roll, I began making plans for my Eastern Europe trip and booked some accommodation. By the end of the day, I was overwhelmed as I felt I had so many bookings and so many places yet to see. I had to remind myself to keep taking my journey in small steps. I'd made my bookings and could now forget about them and concentrate on my more immediate travels in Thailand.

In the evening, Akshay and I found a restaurant which was cheap and full of locals. The food there was great and we could see why it was so popular. We were both tired so we didn't stay out for long. Nobody else had checked into my dorm so I was alone. It felt strange after being used to company but at least I slept well.

On Tuesday, I started the day with another run. The park was quieter as it was a weekday, although the roads leading it to it were busier. I didn't know what to do with myself for the rest of the day but ended up doing Christmas shopping for when I met up with my niece in Malaysia. In the evening, I had a farewell dinner with Akshay.

Wednesday morning began with a three mile walk to the hospital. I had to cross a couple of busy dual carriageways but at least if I'd been hit by something I would've been close to medical help. I was nervous about having the stitches out. Would it hurt? It did actually, but only a little. The doctor, a different one this time, told me my wound had healed well and had closed up completely. The fracture would also heal in time. The nurse, who had been present on all three visits, wished me well and said she was impressed with my quick recovery.

I took a blue bus back to the hostel, picked up the Green Turtle, and said goodbye to Akshay. It was a sweaty fifteen minute walk to the bus station, where I took the 12pm airport bus. Leaving Phuket Town made me sad. I'd enjoyed spending time with my friends from the hostel and it had been a good place to quietly recover from my injuries. There were also a couple of random people I'd miss. I loved the lady at the restaurant near the hostel - she would always tell me off for not eating my salad and would always ask how my nose was. I'd walk past her a couple of times a day and she'd smile and wave every time.

I'd also miss the old man down a side street I used to cut through. He must've been about seventy and had no teeth but his wrinkled face had so much character. The first time I'd seen him was on my first run, when he'd pointed at my nose and given me a gummy cackle. In broken English, he'd asked what had happened so I'd mimed running and falling down. I think he understood as he rolled his eyes and laughed again. I saw him a dozen times on various outings. He was always in the same place, night or day, and he'd always point to his nose and laugh when he saw me. I'd miss my interactions with him.

Southern Thailand: Ko Lanta Island - Mishaps & Adventures

12TH – 21ST DECEMBER 2018

The bus dropped me off on the main road, half a mile from the Hero Phuket Guesthouse. Sweaty and tired, I finally reached my destination, having navigated a labyrinth of small roads. I tried to check in but was told they'd overbooked and needed to move me to a different guesthouse. A man grabbed my bag and walked me to The Soodsoi Resort. I was put in a little bungalow which actually looked much better than the Hero Phuket. My friend Katie was on a plane to meet me so I messaged her to inform her of the change of accommodation and then walked to a nearby beach for an hour. Katie called at 8:45pm to say she'd landed and then took a taxi to meet me. It was lovely to see her again. We had a good catch up and then went to sleep.

On Thursday morning, we were at the Hero Phuket for 8:30am, where we were given a cold fried egg and frankfurter for breakfast (at least the toast was warm). A woman was sleeping on a sofa: apparently she'd been double-booked too. It didn't fill me with confidence for our booking there the following week. Our pre-booked taxi to the Rasada Pier arrived early and drove us away. We'd take a ferry from Phuket to Phi Phi Island and from there go to Ko Lanta Island. The two-hour ferry journey was very pleasant; I sat outside in the sun and Katie stayed inside to snooze. I took a selfie and was pleased with how normal I looked. I'd taken the plaster off my nose that morning and you could barely see where the stitches had been.

Phi Phi Island was very pretty but sadly we didn't have time to explore properly. By 3pm, we were on a different boat and on our way to Ko Lanta. We arrived at 4:30pm and were picked up by the couple who ran our accommodation: The Cat Bungalow. We checked in and our cheerful host, Oi, told us where to go and what to do on the island. A lot of it involved renting scooters. I was apprehensive as I was scared of further injury.

Once we'd settled in, we walked to a market. The main road ran down the edge of the western coastline of Ko Lanta and was full of massage spas, restaurants and small shops. It was being dug up and resurfaced while we were there, which made walking on it tricky. The market was two miles north of our accommodation. There was fish on offer and a lot of fruit, but otherwise we found nothing tempting. Instead, we ate at a restaurant Oi had recommended, a cute place with Thai/English translations written on the walls.

On Friday, we ate breakfast at the guesthouse. We then went to a local beach. Straight away, we were lured by a massage hut: it was so relaxing to listen to the sound of the ocean while someone rubbed our feet. After, we continued along the beach until we found a bar offering free sun-beds. We spent a couple of hours there, reading, before stopping for lunch and continuing on to the quiet Long Beach, which was lined with palm trees. We stayed until 6pm. It was too cloudy to expect a decent sunset so we began the long walk home. Making our way along the dusty road, I noticed a glimmer of red above us. As the colour grew in intensity and spread across the sky, we began to regret leaving Long Beach. We made it to Relax Beach but only caught the end of an amazing display.

After a sleepless night in our hot room (which lacked air conditioning), I was up early on Saturday for a five kilometre run along the bumpy main road. Later on, Katie and I hired scooters from Oi. It would be Katie's first time. Things started out well: we drove slowly, with me in the lead, and went south, towards Mu Ko Lanta National Park. We were a couple of miles down the road when I noticed that Katie was no longer behind me. As I waited, I started feeling anxious - had something happened? A truck going in the opposite direction went past me, stopped on the side of the road and someone got out. That's when I knew something had gone wrong. Turning my bike round, I kept my fingers crossed that it wasn't anything serious. When I got there, the kind stranger had picked up Katie's bike for her and to my relief, she was standing. Her legs looked fine but her elbow was badly grazed.

I knew she needed to get it cleaned properly so I looked up medical centres on my map app and we set off to a nearby town. We found a clinic and the nurses cleaned Katie up and gave her an abundance of medical supplies so she could clean and dress her wound daily. I expected her to want to return to the guesthouse but she insisted on carrying on. The journey to the national park was only another seven miles away but it felt longer. I was anxious that something else would happen and kept an even closer eye on Katie, checking my mirrors every couple of seconds. As we approached the park, the road became more winding and hilly. Luckily the surfaces were good so that made it easier.

At the entrance to the national park, we paid and parked up. We walked to the quiet beach and took photos of us on a picturesque wooden swing hanging from a tree. After, we began the nature trail. It started with a long set of steps - some came up the top of my knee so they took a fair bit of energy to climb. We passed through thick forest and green foliage. Thankfully we didn't meet any monkeys or mosquitoes. Thick vines and fallen trees blocked our way numerous times so we had to maneuver ourselves around them. One of the concrete bridges had also collapsed so we had to climb under it. It certainly kept things interesting! The trail finished abruptly and we were suddenly back at the car park. There wasn't much else to do so we got on the bikes and drove north towards the Khlong Chak Waterfall. A mile up the road, it started raining. Within two minutes it turned into a downpour. We parked the bikes under a tree and waited for it to stop.

It didn't seem like the rain was going anywhere so we continued on slowly, stopping for lunch at a scenic cliff-top restaurant. We could see a secluded bay below, while above us, clouds clung to the tree-covered hills. As the rain eased off, we left. The falls weren't far away and we were soon taking a right turn, which led to the parking area. All was going well until the road surface changed. I made it halfway up a gravel-covered hill before losing my nerve. We decided to turn back. Returning to the main road, we left our bikes next to a travel agency and continued on foot.

There was no entrance fee for the waterfall but someone soon approached us to inform us that a hiring guide would be best. We didn't want to pay 200 baht each so we decided to go by ourselves. To find the falls, we had to follow the stream. This was easier said than done as the path frequently went *through* the stream. Sometimes there was a path to the right of the stream and this would take us higher above it, into the trees.

The further we went the more challenging the trail became and we soon had to clamber over slippery rocks. I wasn't sure it was worth continuing on. Katie seemed quite up for it though, despite her injury, so we ploughed on. Two kilometres in, we reached a Y junction. We took the left branch and found ourselves in Bat Cave, which was impressive and *very* dark. We didn't venture too far in though as we didn't have torches. After, we continued on to the waterfall.

The waterfall itself was a disappointment. The morning's rain had clearly not been enough to spur it into action. It was a case of the journey being more exciting than the destination. Time was getting on so we turned back. We followed a small group of Germans who seemed to know where they were going. They did up to a point but they must've missed a turning as we were suddenly lost. Hoping for the best, we continued by the stream, climbing over rocks and fallen trees until we reached the path we'd come in on.

As we left the parking area to walk to our bikes, we discussed the high-pitched sound that had been our constant companion. It was *so* loud, it was almost unpleasant. When I researched it, I discovered it was a cicada, a type of insect. I was awed that something so small could make such a racket.

The journey home seemed longer because I was worried about one of us having an accident. As we went through a gravelly section of road, Katie called out to me as I'd almost missed the turning for the guesthouse. I pulled into the centre of the road with Katie just behind to my right. All of a sudden, she shot forwards, knocking my left foot and coming to a sudden stop just in front of me. It scared the life out of me and I almost accelerated by accident. I told her to go ahead (my heart couldn't take any more surprises) and followed her up the hill.

That evening, we walked to the beach for dinner. It was so pretty with all the coloured lanterns hanging in the bars and restaurants. After dinner, Katie lay on a sun-bed with a pineapple juice and I relaxed on a hammock with a much-needed Amaretto Sour. A storm was going on out at sea and we enjoyed watching the lightning illuminate the night sky. It was a perfect end to an adventure-filled day.

Apart from doing a five mile run on Monday, the next two days were beach days. The weather was overcast but it was nice to read by the sea. We visited a beach bar both evenings and on Monday, discovered the New Ozone Resort. The bar served good food and wonderful Pina Coladas. It was relaxing sitting on our little cushioned platform, watching the sunset.

On Tuesday, we were up early for our Four Island Tour with Tin Adventures. It didn't take long to reach the pier and from there we were separated by our destinations. We waded to our speedboat, which then tore off through the waves. I sat at the back, looking out at the foamy sea behind us. Our first stop was at Emerald Cave. We all jumped into the sea and Katie was given a life ring so she could keep her injured elbow raised out of the water.

Swimming, we entered a darkened cave in the cliff wall. One of the couples couldn't swim well and they were flapping about all over the place. I stayed well behind them as I was worried one of them would kick me in the face with a flipper (I was still protective of my broken nose). Before long, we could see daylight. We swam out onto a small beach which was backed by a stunning jungle-like forest - *this* was where the name Emerald Cave had come from. The only way to get there was via the cave so I felt like I was in a secret place.

Our next stop was at Ko Kradan Island, where we spent a couple of hours on the beach and had a buffet lunch. We'd been provided with snorkels so I did it for a few minutes. The fish were very colourful and there were many. Snorkelling wasn't really my thing so I found a dead tree to lie on and enjoyed the sunshine instead.

Our third stop was for more snorkelling by Koh Chueak Island. This would've been fine except it started raining heavily. It was tricky snorkelling in the choppy sea and feeling sick, I returned to the boat. This was a mistake as the boat was rocking and within minutes, I was ready to puke. Forty minutes we had to stay there, but finally, we were on our way to the fourth stop: Ko Nga Island. I was desperate to get onto dry land and calm my poor stomach. It seemed to work - I spent thirty minutes walking on the beach and eating brioche.

By 4pm, we were back on Ko Lanta. Minus the nausea, the trip had been great fun. The Tin Adventure guides had been so cheerful and had really looked after us.

On Wednesday, Katie and I went our separate ways. I'd been up late chatting to Tom on WhatsApp (trying to resolve an argument) and had run early, so I wanted to sleep. Katie took a scooter and visited some shops. Once I'd finished my three hour *nap*, I sat in the garden talking to Oi. I discovered she had a baby who lived with her mum in Bangkok.

She worked too hard during the high season to look after a young baby but she missed him terribly. I felt sorry for her for being in such a tough situation.

On Friday, I hugged Oi goodbye and Katie and I hopped in the back of a van to go to the pier. The ferry trip was fun - I sat at the very front of the boat with my legs hanging over the side, enjoying the sun and cool breeze. I was staring out to sea when something caught my eye: a silver fish, about thirty centimetres long, jumped out of the water. It didn't just jump once - it kept on jumping, like it was flying. I pointed it out to the French guy I'd been talking to, who said it was a flying fish. It was very cool and as the journey continued, we saw more.

Our ferry stopped at Krabi which looked amazing with all the rocky islands, perfect beaches and clear seas. I was glad we'd got to see it even if we couldn't stay. We were then transferred to a different ferry which took us to Phuket and from there we were driven to the Hero Phuket Guesthouse. This time they had a room for us, though it was small, cramped and smelt slightly of sewage.

On Friday morning, Katie and I were once again served cold fried eggs and frankfurters (breakfast at the Hero Phuket was not its strong point). However, the owner, Hero, was sweet, which it made it hard for me to leave a bad review. After breakfast, he dropped Katie off at a fancy spa hotel (she had a later flight), where I hugged her goodbye, and then he took me to the airport so I could fly to Malaysia to meet my niece, Kerry.

Malaysia: Kuala Lumpur & Penang - A Very Kerry Christmas

21ST DECEMBER 2018 - 2ND JANUARY 2019

We'd both been due to land at 4pm but Kerry's flight had been delayed by over three hours. It could've made meeting at the airport tricky, but as it happened, my flight was delayed too. By the time I'd taken the train from KLIA2 to KLIA (different terminals), it was almost time for her plane to land. I impatiently waited at arrivals, feeling excited to see her. Finally, at 7:30pm, she walked through: she saw me before I saw her. It was lovely to be with her again. Dithering about how to get to the hotel, we settled on taking a metered taxi. Due to the Friday night traffic, it took over an hour. We checked in at the Big M Hotel and were pleased with our room. As it was late, we popped to an ATM and then went straight to bed. I set the alarm for 6:30am so I could go to parkrun the next morning.

I almost ignored my phone when it woke me - running was the last thing I wanted to do. However, I forced myself out of bed, got dressed and ordered a Grab taxi to take me to Taman Pudu Ulu Park. The parkrun wasn't very busy: there were only sixty-nine people. There were quite a few tourists though and I got chatting to a friendly couple from Liverpool, Sean and Alex. Sean wasn't running but Alex did. Apart from the heat and humidity, it was fun. I even borrowed a Santa hat to enter into the Christmas spirit.

It was a sunny day so Kerry and I decided to visit the famous Petronas Twin Towers. By the time we got there, tickets were almost sold out but we managed to book some for 4:30pm. Just as we were about to return outside, we noticed a shopping mall through a walkway. We followed the bright lights into a winter wonderland. I was surprised how popular Christmas was in Malaysia - there were towering

Christmas trees, toy soldiers, lights and decorations wherever we looked. Festive music poured out of all the shops: the mall was vomiting Christmas. Kerry and I weren't Christmas people but we enjoyed the novelty of Christmas in a different country and took numerous selfies with the festive displays. We found a reasonably-priced restaurant for lunch called Secret Recipe, where we both ordered satay chicken. Throughout the meal, I couldn't take my eyes off the cakes by the counter. I was too full to enjoy dessert properly so I insisted we return there for afternoon tea.

Next, we stopped at the pretty Kuala Lumpur Eco Park, where we climbed towers and walked over suspended canopy bridges. The sky looked black in the distance though - a storm was coming. Soon enough, it was time to return to the Petronus Towers. We made it inside just as it started to rain. We spent more time in the shopping centre (unsuccessfully looking for a Santa hat) and then queued for our tour. We were given passes on lanyards and then our group was squeezed into the tiny elevator, where we were taken to the Skybridge. The bridge, connecting the two identical towers, was located on the 41st floor and we were given time to look out of the many windows.

In the distance, the thunderstorm lit up the gloomy sky. Once we'd taken photos, we were ready to return to the elevator and leave. I was disappointed that we wouldn't get to go to the top. However, when we entered the lift, the woman pressed the button for the 86th floor - hurrah! From the top, the views over the city were even more fantastic: cars looked like tiny toys. We took a few more photos and then descended to the ground floor. On the way back to the hotel, we returned to Secret Recipe for delicious cake. I had tiramisu gateaux and Kerry had chocolate sponge.

The next morning, we took a taxi to the airport and flew to Penang. We collected our luggage from the carousel and then waited outside for our taxi. We started putting our bags into what we thought was our taxi but the driver looked panicked, probably because he was there to pick up his wife! Another driver waved and pulled over. He put our bags in the boot and we opened the car door, but just as we were about to step in, a middle-aged man hurried over, asking if we were sure the taxi was ours. We weren't and it wasn't. I ran inside the airport to use the free WiFi and check where *our* driver was. By the time I got back outside, he was there and Kerry was loading the bags into the boot.

When we arrived at our accommodation, The Studio at Mansion One, we were met by the Indian owner, a rotund, exuberant man, who showed us around the flat and explained where to find shops, restaurants and things to do. He pointed out the washing machine and told me that I would know more about that than he did (presumably because I was a woman). I narrowed my eyes at his sexist comment and he swiftly changed the subject. I was surprised that the flat was in a towering apartment block as I'd been expecting a more modest building. We were on the 15th floor and had great views of the island from our balcony - we could even see the sea. Over the next few days, I spent several enjoyable hours there, watching the world go by below or evening storms rage above.

Once we'd settled in, we went for a walk in the local area, where we found a huge shopping centre. Kerry treated me to a Nando's as a belated birthday present. On the way home, we stopped at a supermarket to buy food. I was looking forward to poached eggs on toast again and was even able to buy proper Lurpak butter (but sadly no Cathedral City cheese).

On Monday (Christmas Eve), we walked to the Penang Botanic Gardens. It was free to get in and the undulating paths took us all around the different sections of the gardens. We stopped to take photos on a pretty bridge and did our best to avoid the perpetual irritation of the monkeys. It was very humid so we stopped for cold drinks and ice creams. We were peacefully sitting on a bench when a monkey approached. It had its eye on our drinks. Thankfully, we stood at the same time the monkey lunged. Kerry and I ran around some Chinese tourists and safely escaped to a different bench. After a wander around the shopping centre, we were back at the apartment just before sunset, which I watched from the balcony. Towering storm clouds had gathered and lightning started shortly after the sun ducked below the horizon. At one point, forked lightning struck the same area three times - it was fun to watch.

On Christmas morning, I went for a run. The route was flat and on good pavements, so apart from the heat, it was relatively easy. Lots of people wished me Merry Christmas as I ran past and I wished them well in return. Kerry was awake by the time I returned so we exchanged gifts and put on our Christmas accessories (I wore my hat and Kerry wore a Christmas t-shirt). We wanted to spend Christmas Day on the beach so I ordered a taxi to take us to Batu Ferringhi. The sandy beach there was a couple of miles long and wasn't too busy. It was weird being on a sunny beach on Christmas Day - it didn't feel like Christmas at all. Christmas dinner was a spicy curry at a beach café.

By 5pm, it had clouded over, so we decided to go home. Unfortunately, we couldn't find any free WiFi so we couldn't call a taxi and had to take the bus instead. Even though buses were supposed to come every ten minutes, we waited over half an hour for one to turn up. We squeezed onto the busy bus and had a cramped, bumpy journey home on the winding roads. It took an hour to get back as there was so much traffic. We spent our Christmas evening in the traditional way: watching movies and eating.

On Wednesday, we took a taxi to Penang Hill. To reach the summit, we could either take the funicular train or walk. Kerry would've killed me if I made her walk up so we each paid for a one-way ticket. There was a lot of queuing and it took over an hour before we were squeezed into the tiny carriage. The steep journey up (supposedly the steepest in the world) was two kilometres long: we stood at the front of the car so we had a good view. At the top, it was rather cloudy so we couldn't see much. We wandered around and then ate at the small food court. As we'd only bought one way tickets, we had to walk down on foot, which meant descending over two thousand stairs. However, first we had to find them.

I used my map app to choose a trail and we took the Viaduct Road. There must've been some large landslides in the area because the road was almost impassable. On one bend, half of the road had been washed away and further along, the road was almost completely caved in, so we gingerly side-stepped our way around gaping holes in the tarmac, piles of mud and fallen trees.

Soon enough, we found the stairs that would take us through the ancient jungle. We hardly saw any people but we were joined by huge ants, a monkey and several mosquitoes (which ate Kerry alive). In places, there were no steps at all and we had to navigate our way down steep, muddy 'paths' with only a rope for support. Kerry fell into a particularly muddy patch. It was around this time I detected that she wanted to throttle me. We eventually reached the bottom and took the bus back to town, sitting in silence. The atmosphere was tense between us that evening.

On Thursday morning, I did a quick run in the rain and then jumped on Kerry to check we were still friends. Once I'd showered and we'd had breakfast, we walked into George Town. Our first stop was at the Upside Down Museum. There were people in each room who took photos for us and told us how to pose. The pictures came out well, and when we turned them upside down, it looked like we were defying gravity.

That afternoon, we visited the old wooden jetties which were part of the George Town heritage. The buildings were all on stilts in the water. Some of the jetties were narrow with no barriers, so they were a little scary, especially when we had to cross paths with people coming the other way. The water was stinky so we did *not* want to fall in.

Once we left the jetties, we strolled around Little India. It was bustling and colourful with lots of street art - I loved it. It wasn't an easy place to explore however as traffic on Penang was terrible and it was difficult to find road crossings. We had to walk out in front of cars and hope they stopped. I was always in charge of this; if Kerry had been in charge we would've stood there all day. We passed a hawker market so we popped in to see if we could find any pancakes. Instead, I saw roast pork. It was hard to find pork in Malaysia due to the large Muslim community so I couldn't resist. After, we continued to Fort Cornwallis (apparently the best preserved Fort in Malaysia). It was a bit run down, and as they were doing preservation work, there wasn't much to see.

As we started walking towards home, we passed an old Protestant Cemetery. I loved exploring cemeteries so we entered via an old metal gate in the corner. We were the only people there but it didn't feel creepy. The cemetery had been partly destroyed during World War Two so only the graves in the centre still stood. The others were sadly unmarked. I took some photos and then we went home.

I woke on Friday feeling exhausted so when the alarm went off for a morning run, I ignored it. It was our last full day in Penang so we returned to Batu Ferringhi for a well-earned beach day. That evening, I had a discussion with Tom that didn't end well. It didn't seem like there was a way for us to be together and I spent a couple of hours crying on the balcony. For the hundredth time, I wished I hadn't met him so I could've enjoyed my trip without the constant emotional rollercoaster.

On Saturday, we hung out at the apartment until 1pm. We then spent the rest of the afternoon at a spa until it was time to go to the airport. Our flight back to Kuala Lumpur was a little delayed but I was delighted when my bag was the first to arrive on the carousel – it had never happened before! We checked in to the Big M Hotel. It was around this time that I started worrying about bed bugs. I'd read about them in the Solo Female Traveller Facebook group I'd joined, and started to get paranoid. After pulling up all the sheets and checking the mattresses (much to Kerry's amusement), I decided we were safe. Over the next few days, I checked my upcoming accommodations for online reviews relating to bed bugs. I found that my next hostel had received many recent complaints about them so I quickly found an alternative. I had to change a couple of future bookings, but it was better to be safe than sorry (bed bugs are really difficult to get rid of and people often have to throw out all of their belongings).

On Sunday, we visited a large mosque and then walked along the 'River of Life' to the large Central Market. I found Kuala Lumpur to be a strange city. Some of it was lovely but other parts were really run down. Usually, the river is the most beautiful part of a city but this wasn't the case there. The riverbank was falling apart and the path that ran along it was cracked and often impassable. People appeared to live under one of the bridges and I even saw a young couple washing in the dirty water pouring from one of the drain outlets. It made me grateful for what I had in life. That night, we found a quiet Indian restaurant for dinner. We tried to place our orders but the surly waiter informed us that there was no naan bread and no chicken tikka (which were *two* of the three things I wanted). He had a really bad attitude so we walked out. Luckily, we found a better restaurant next door, the Betel Leaf. It was busy (a good sign), with friendly waiters and delicious curry. Things definitely worked out for the best.

On Monday, we walked to the Butterfly Park in the Botanic Gardens. The butterflies were spectacular but it was hard to get photos of them. As it was New Year's Eve, we returned to the hotel to shower and then went out again. We didn't know what to do with ourselves but we knew there'd be a firework display at the Petronas Towers. It started raining just as we arrived so we quickly went into the crowded shopping centre. Seeking refuge, we ducked into a bookshop. I was disappointed that most of the books were wrapped in plastic but there were a few to look through to pass the time.

At 10pm, the shopping centre closed. We joined the throng of people being ejected into the crazy horrors of NYE. There was a constant stream of horns blaring and people selling tat, like light-up Petronas Towers headbands. We lasted ten minutes before Kerry suggested we watch the fireworks from the hotel's terrace. It was a relief to leave the crowds and noise behind. We bought cider and sat outside at a small table, waiting for midnight. I'd like to say our plan worked perfectly but a nearby skyscraper blocked the fireworks almost completely from view. Never mind.

New Year's Day was Kerry's last day in Malaysia. We slept in and then returned to the shopping centre, where we had a Nando's and some cake. After a walk around KLCC Park, we returned to the hotel. I ordered a taxi for Kerry and she left at 7pm. It was strange returning to the room alone and I missed her already. However, I received some unexpected news from Tom that made me feel more positive about the future. His situation had changed, and when I finally returned to England, we could be together. The realistic part of me doubted if things would work between us as I was notoriously crap at relationships, but the positive part looked forward to giving it my best shot.

'I never believed my mum when she finished the story with, "And they all lived happily ever after."

"No they didn't. I don't believe it," I'd say. I preferred Humpty Dumpty - nice and short, and a realistic ending. He never hurt anyone, but he had a little accident and died. Shit happens. That's life isn't it?'

(Karl Pilkington)

Malaysia: Ipoh -
A Love/Hate Relationship

The train arrived in Ipoh at 3pm and I lugged the Green Turtle towards the De Cafe and Rest House (a hostel). I overtook a man holding a small child, who asked if I needed a lift. I explained that my hostel was nearby so it wasn't necessary. Laughing, he told me I must be strong as my bag looked very heavy: weighing in at fifteen kilos, he wasn't wrong.

I had trouble locating the hostel as the signage hadn't been obvious, but a local shop owner pointed me in the right direction. My dorm had ten beds, in the style of a capsule hostel. There were only two other girls in the room and we had the whole place to ourselves (probably because it was the holidays).

After a shower, I left the hostel. I fell in love with Ipoh as soon as I saw the amazing street art. Some was old and faded but it was all beautiful. Ipoh was my favourite kind of city: grimy but charming, and very photogenic. However, first impressions could be deceiving...

Ipoh had many alleys to explore and I enjoyed getting lost in them. I didn't come across many people but there were some tourists and a few elderly men about. I tried smiling at them but they mostly narrowed their eyes at me suspiciously. A couple smiled though and one man even waved. I passed many stray dogs. They were chilled thankfully, not like the scarier strays in Thailand. I got upset when I noticed that one had a large growth, maybe a tumour. However, upon closer inspection, it turned out to be his balls.

As I'd left it so late to go out, it wasn't long before the daylight waned. I hadn't eaten all day so I stopped at the BBQ Lamb Café: the meat was cooked to perfection and served with chips and rice. Halfway through my meal, I was joined by an unexpected dinner guest - a ginger cat. It jumped up onto the chair opposite and hungrily stared at the lamb. Being a soft touch, I shared. Once we'd finished, we sat in companionable silence. However, when I suggested splitting the bill, it crept away.

After paying, I returned to the hostel and snuggled up in bed. There was no sound-proofing in the building so I could hear *everything* from outside: a constant stream of cars, motorbikes screeching along the alleys and the call to prayer, which sounded regularly for long stretches of time (my ear plugs therefore came in very handy).

On Thursday morning, I checked the forecast and saw that the weather was *cool* and cloudy - *only* 33°. It was running weather, you know, for Malaysia. I only managed three miles as despite the forecast, it was sunny. I followed a path along the river which was prettier and better maintained than the one in Kuala Lumpur. It wasn't all easy though as the path crossed a couple of five-lane roads and there was no crossing. I had to carefully cross each lane, one at a time, and hope for the best.

Once I'd returned to the hostel and showered, I walked to the shopping centre to enjoy the food court and the air conditioning. Malls were my saviour when I craved normality as I could almost pretend I was at home. I couldn't resist buying a t-shirt saying: *Are we having fun yet?* It's what I regularly asked myself about my travels.

The next morning, I took a taxi to the Kek Look Tong cave temple. The driver belched throughout the journey, about once every three seconds, and I had to try hard to stifle my laughter. Once I was out of the car and had released my pent-up giggles, I walked to a small pond and was surprised to see it was full of turtles of all shapes and sizes. It looked very crowded and I hoped they were ok.

The cave itself was amazing. Different shaped stalactites hung from the roof, some resembling frozen waterfalls. Throughout the cave complex were beautiful statues, including a golden Buddha. I was relieved it was quiet as it allowed me to fully enjoy the experience.

At the rear of the cave was a large exit into the gardens. The views of the tree-covered hills and the large lily pond were phenomenal. I followed a footpath around the pond and happened upon a strange pebbled path where every pebble had been individually cemented in place. Watching the locals, I discovered I was supposed to remove my shoes and walk along it, like a walk of pain. It was like trying to walk barefoot on Brighton beach. I learned to look for the larger, flatter pebbles as these hurt my feet less. It was a great way to practise mindfulness as the only thing I could think about was the path before me and where to tread next.

It was hard to drag myself away from the gardens. It was so calming listening to the birds sing prettily and the distant high-pitched cicadas. But eventually, I was chased away by the rain. I exited through the cave and began the two mile walk to a cultural centre. Along the way, several locals waved and smiled at me. I wasn't sure why. Maybe they didn't see too many tourists walking about the quiet streets. I loved the quirky Qing Xin Ling centre. There was a lot to see: fish, caves, temples, street art, historic vehicles, memorabilia and electronics. I had a feeling I would've enjoyed it more had I been with a friend though.

After, I walked to the Sam Poh Tong cave temple. The last part of the journey was not enjoyable as I had to walk along a busy dual carriageway with no footpath. Then I had to turn onto what I could only liken to a motorway, also without a footpath. I made it there safely, only to find that the temple was closed. However, I happened upon the spectacular Lin Seng Tong temple next door. It was so colourful and full of statues, including a large, golden, sleeping Buddha.

As I wandered, I came across a place where wishes could be hung on a 'love tree'. I wrote my own love wish about Tom on a pink ribbon and used the red string to hang it with the thousands of others. I ate at a nearby restaurant and then ordered a taxi to another temple. The driver sped off before I noticed it was closed. The temple wasn't in a great part of town so I quickly left.

My route home led me through what looked like a go-cart course but upon closer inspection, I realised it was a test centre for motorbikes and motorists. Bemused, I watched the learner drivers do things I'd never seen motorists do in Asia: show patience, signal, check their mirrors and wait for pedestrians to pass. Worried I might get told off for trespassing, I hurried to the exit.

By the time I was back in town, I needed a drink. This was easier said than done as I could not find my usual newsagents. I looked high and low, and went round in circles for an hour. Finally, just as I was about to give up, I found it. I'd forgotten it was set back from the road and hidden by greenery. I must have passed it at least five times. As this was my third visit, the cheery, toothless owner started chatting, telling me how he'd worked in London when he was younger but hadn't liked it as it was too busy. He'd loved climbing Ben Nevis though. It was nice to chat to someone, even briefly and I left feeling happier.

On Saturday, I went running and then tried to decide what to do next. I wanted to visit a different cave temple but the only way to it was via a busy main road with no footpath. I could take a taxi but there probably wouldn't be anywhere with WiFi nearby to order a taxi home. I then decided to hike up a hill but when I did further research, it was not recommended not go alone due to muggings. Desperate, I found a supermarket on the map - maybe I could go there and buy some yoghurt to cheer me up? Alas, halfway up the road it turned into a triple carriageway and I had to turn back.

Feeling fed up, I traipsed back to the shopping centre and bought some cake. After, I found myself looking for an egg poacher. Admittedly, carrying an egg poacher around would've been a bit *Waitrose* of me. I'd certainly never seen one mentioned on any of the 'what to pack' lists I'd looked at before I left home.

On Sunday morning, I went to the flea market. As usual, the ratio of men to women was roughly 4:1. It was *very* crowded and I soon felt uncomfortable, even though I was covered up. Lots of men stared at me, raising their eyebrows suggestively and making comments. One stood right in front of me, glaring with serial killer eyes. I glared right back at him until he turned away. Feeling uneasy, I ducked down a side street and quickly left the market. It was the most vulnerable I'd felt since leaving home. Luckily the river was only a short walk away. Finding a bench to sit on, I took some deep breaths to calm down. Once I felt ok, I popped into my favourite newsagents to buy a drink and have another chat with the owner, who told me to call him Uncle Ram. I took a photo so I could always remember his smiling face.

Upon leaving the shop, I heard yapping coming from some nearby cages. Inside were rescue dogs and adorable puppies. Most of the cages had no tops so the animals could be petted. I could've stayed there all day stroking them as the dogs were all so lovely and friendly.

Slipping some money into the collection box, I reluctantly left and went into a quirky cafe called De Classroom for lunch. I wrote my order on a little shopping list and rang the bell for the waitress to collect it. I ordered some delicious eggy bread and then later had an ice cream sundae. It was a cool place to hang out and I stayed for a couple of hours, writing my blog, despite the happy hard-core music. After leaving the cafe, I called Tom for a chat and then enjoyed a nap in my air-conditioned dorm.

I was abruptly woken by what sounded like the roof caving in, but it was just heavy rain. My dorm was on the top floor and the roof of the building was made of metal so it sounded terrible. Then explosive thunder began. A few drops of water splatted onto my face from a leak in the ceiling - perfect. As I waited for it to stop, I got chatting to two Dutch girls who'd just checked in (the first people I'd spoken to at the hostel). I gave them some recommendations and we discussed Ipoh (they'd already been there for a couple of days). They were also fed up with the creepy men. I was relieved it wasn't just me.

By 5pm, the rain stopped so I ventured out for dinner. The city was dead and most shops had shut early. As I walked down a narrow alley I'd used a dozen times before, I noticed three dogs. I wasn't concerned as the dogs in Ipoh had never bothered me before. Maybe they'd been riled up by the storm but all three rushed at me, growling and snarling. Trying not to panic, I avoided making eye contact with them and inched backwards. They got closer and closer, snapping their drooling jaws at me. I was petrified. Nobody was around to help me so I kept slowly backing away until I made it onto the main street. The dogs didn't follow so I quickened my pace. I walked away without looking back and once around the corner, I leant against a wall, shaking. I had dinner at an expensive café and then returned to the hostel. Climbing into bed, I vowed to stay there until I left for Kuala Lumpur the next day.

Once I was safely back in Kuala Lumpur, I took a taxi to a capsule hotel: The Bed KLCC, which was spacious, modern and clean, with good facilities. My dorm had eighteen beds and each capsule had its own light, blind, power point and locker. After resting, I ventured back to my old haunt, the Suria shopping centre, nestled at the base of the Petronas Towers. I did a little shopping in the sales and then stopped at the supermarket for a huge tub of peach yoghurt which I ate by the fountains in the KLCC gardens. The following day, I stayed in bed, only leaving for food. I was learning that long-term travel didn't mean being a tourist every day: it was sometimes necessary to rest and take it easy.

Northern Thailand:
Bangkok - My New Favourite City

The plane from Kuala Lumpur arrived in Bangkok at 5pm. I took the bus into the city: luckily, I'd been first in the queue as the bus was soon jammed. It was a long journey in the heavy Bangkok traffic so I was grateful to have a seat. Eventually we reached the city, where I transferred to the Skytrain. After that, it was a sweaty ten minute walk to the Kinnon Deluxe Hostel.

After settling into my tiny single room, I went downstairs. This was when I met Sylvia, from Austria, who asked if I wanted to join her and some others for drinks that evening. Feeling knackered, I declined. As we sat chatting in the kitchen, we were joined by Ritchie, from the US, and Fabrizio, from Peru. Fabrizio was a Latino whirlwind: if you weren't careful, you could find yourself swept away by his energy and exuberance.

The little group referred to themselves as the Chang Gang (due to their love of Chang Beer). Fabrizio shared a couple of his beers with me, joking that if I was drunk, I'd join them. However, despite his best efforts, I insisted on them having fun without me. They met up at 9pm to go out but by midnight we were still sat talking in the kitchen. It was great - I hadn't laughed so much in ages.

The next day, I slept in and had a relaxed breakfast with Ritchie, who was perky considering how late they'd all stayed out (and how much they'd drunk). He showed me some photos of the night before: it was clear that Fabrizio enjoyed stripping off a lot. I had a peaceful day and only left the hostel for food and a massage. At 6pm, Christian, Ritchie, Fabrizio, Sylvia and I walked to Lumphini Park. There was a huge crowd of people doing group aerobics which was quite entertaining. Our group split: Fabrizio and Ritchie used the weights while the rest of us ran around the track with hundreds of others. Once we regrouped, we walked back to the hostel and got ready for a night out.

We started off in a civilised manner and ate at a Japanese restaurant, but then Fabrizio bought wine and it all went downhill. We met more people from the hostel and took a big taxi van to the Havana Social, a cosy nightclub in the style of a Cuban bar. Predictably, Fabrizio soon lost his clothes. The night was full of dancing, laughter and lots of alcohol: Prosecco, gin and rum. We'd all chipped in at the start but Fabrizio kept it coming, buying more bottles whenever we ran out.

The evening became a blur. We got back to the hostel at 3am and sat on the rooftop terrace, where I have faint recollections of being kissed by a young Bulgarian man. By the time I reached my bed the room was spinning unpleasantly, so I sat up for a while chatting to Tom on WhatsApp. As I sobered up, I felt a bit guilty about the kiss but it was only a silly drunken thing – it hadn't meant anything. I finally went to sleep at 7am, just as the sun was rising. Needless to say, I didn't make it to breakfast.

Apart from visiting the market for food with the others, I stayed in bed. Then, at 5pm, the Chang Gang left for Chiang Mai. I'd really enjoyed their company and was so pleased I'd met them. I was sad to see them go but my liver breathed a quiet sigh of relief. The hostel was never quite as vibrant after they left.

Once I'd waved the Chang Gang goodbye, I started chatting with Edwin. He was from Taiwan but lived with his husband in Ireland. I'd met him the previous evening, when he'd tried to persuade me to visit some inappropriate 'entertainment' shows. As we both had a very dirty sense of humour, we hit it off immediately and he became my new hostel buddy.

"There's a woman over there just tucking in on a bunch of scorpions. Where's the line between food and insect? She gets up in the morning, there's a spider in the bath. What does she do? 'Oh good, I'll leave the croissant for tomorrow'?" (Karl Pilkington)

That night, Amy, who worked at the hostel, took us to the Chatuchak Market on the subway. It was a long journey and the train was packed (which didn't help my ongoing hangover). The market was varied and thankfully, not too crowded. We saw a stall selling insects. I felt sick looking at the poor, crispy critters. I definitely couldn't have eaten any but we ate other stuff: meat on sticks, banana pancakes and spring rolls. It didn't make me feel any better though and I was glad when it was time to leave.

On Saturday, I was determined to see something of Bangkok. I'd been chatting to a Norwegian woman from the group on Facebook, and we'd decided to meet at the Wat Pho Temple. I was too lazy to work out the subway system so I walked. As I weaved my way through the different streets, I felt content. Bangkok had reignited my passion for travel. I was enjoying the company of others and was going with the flow instead of planning my days rigidly. My walk led me to Sathorn Pier. I took the express ferry down the river to Wat Arun and then another ferry across the river to Wat Pho.

As arranged, I met Christine at the entrance. It was a bit awkward at first as we didn't know each other, but as we walked around the temple, it was clear we had plenty in common. Wat Pho was beautiful, with amazing (not to mention huge) golden statues of Buddha. It was very colourful and thankfully not too crowded.

After, we looked at other temples in the local area, including Wat Ratchapradit, Wat Ratchabopit, Wat Suthat Thepphaararam and Wat Saket. They were each beautiful in their own way so it was impossible to pick a favourite. Our route took us through a few unexpected places, along canals and down narrow alleyways. Some streets seemed to have a single purpose; for instance, there was a whole street devoted to selling golden Buddha statues, another for car parts, another for flowers etc. Knackered, we stopped for an early dinner at a small market and then walked through Chinatown. It was great to see all the stalls selling festive goods in preparation for the Chinese New Year. We parted when we reached my hostel. It had been a fun day and I'd enjoyed Christine's company.

At breakfast on Sunday, Edwin asked if I wanted to join him and a female Chinese couple (Chang and Zhou) on a trip to the floating market. I agreed, my original plans going out of the window. I'd been expecting a market on a floating island, like I'd seen on Lake Titicaca in Peru, but this market wasn't floating. It was surrounded by canals, with people selling boat trips to tourists. We didn't take a boat trip but we spent quite a long time at the market, eating. Once we were full, we found a little footpath along the canal. It was nice to get away from the crowds.

Before hopping in a taxi, we sat in a charming cafe which sold beautiful cacti. The Chinese women (also teachers) had some questions about education in England so Edwin translated for us. Through our conversation, I was told many things about education in China. The women informed me that six-year-olds received four hours of homework per night and this increased as they grew up. School was incredibly competitive and one mistake on a test could cost them their future. High school students often didn't get home until 11pm and would leave for school again at 6am. They had no time for themselves.

Apparently, they had to decide their path when they were eighteen and weren't allowed to deviate from this - a career change was virtually impossible. She told me how she'd wished she'd worked even harder at school so she could have a better job now as an adult. Chang and Zhou were in a relationship but could not be together. One was married to someone she'd only met three times, just to stop her family asking questions.

The conversation was shocking to both me and Edwin, who said things were tough in Taiwan but nowhere near as bad as in China. It made me appreciate my life in England. I was grateful to have grown up able to have free time and to make my own decisions.

The next day, I visited Wat Arun (aptly named the Temple of Dawn). Along the way, I found some interesting places. I loved walking in Bangkok as there was always so much to see and I never knew what was around the corner. I visited Warehouse 30, an old WW2-era building. Inside were cafes, designer goods and a nude (but tasteful) photography exhibition. Just outside was an alley full of colourful street art.

As I continued on, I discovered the authentic Bangkok: small alleys and roads, packed with labouring locals. There were sacks full of fragrant flowers and spices outside of worn, wooden doors. Metal carts were being pushed around, overly full of large boxes and scrap metal. It was wonderful. Eventually, I found a bridge and crossed to the other side of the river, where I entered the stunning, and incredibly ornate Wat Arun. I took photos and then sat on the ground, people-watching. I wasn't in any hurry to leave. I waited for the sun to set but it was very overcast so I left for home.

On Tuesday, I checked out of the hostel and said goodbye to Amy and Edwin. Hopping in a taxi, I went to the Annex Lumphini Hotel to meet my friend Rina. It was lovely to catch up with her. She'd come with her friend Jo, so we made our introductions and then set off. As we walked through Lumphini Park, we looked for the monitor lizards that dwelt there. I asked myself, 'Where would I hide if I were a lizard?' I looked over at the bank of the stream and said, 'There!' I was right, a few metres in front of us, a giant lizard was sat on the bank. Excited, I ran over and took a photo.

Next we visited the Bangkok Art and Culture Centre. It was fantastic and I loved the modern building with its winding staircase. A huge display of colourful plastic baskets was hanging from the ceiling but we had no idea what it was about. Our cluelessness would become a theme. The descriptions that went with the art were written in such a convoluted way that they made no sense. We'd read them numerous times and still walk away scratching our heads.

There seemed to be an over-riding theme of sexuality in the gallery. At first, Rina thought I was just being dirty-minded, but as I stepped through what looked like a vagina to read the information panel, it turned out I was right. It *was* a vagina and it had been made from women's skirts, symbolizing feminism. There was naked surreal art, a weird structure made entirely from cling-film, a sexy slogan made out of moth wings, and testicles and breasts fashioned from wire. As we entered a room with post-it notes all over the wall, it seemed only fitting that my artistic contribution should be a drawing of a penis with 'I love BKK' (Bangkok) written on it.

In the evening, Rina and I ran at Lumphini Park. It was good to have my running buddy back. We only did three miles but it was enough. For dinner, we all walked to a local restaurant. That was when I suddenly felt so tired that I nearly fell asleep at the table - I needed to sleep. I returned to the hotel while they went out for drinks. Despite my tiredness, I felt a little jealous. I didn't have the money to go to nice places and it upset me a little.

By the time I woke up the next day, Rina and Jo had gone out for the day so I met Edwin at a shopping centre called Terminal 21. Over lunch, we had a long, frank talk about our lives. I really liked Edwin and felt like I'd known him ages. We wandered around the shops until 4pm, when we went our separate ways, promising to keep in touch. The mall was a two-mile walk from the hotel and both journeys were an adventure in their own way.

On the way there, my map had led me down some narrow streets where locals resided in rickety shacks. I'd seen no other tourists and had felt rather obtrusive. I'd taken a wrong turn at one point and a man had angrily waved his arms at me to tell me to turn around. I'd finally come to a set of metal stairs, which led to a raised walkway on an enclosed metal platform, next to a polluted stream. It extended for half a mile before finishing at the main road.

On the way back, I purposely took the main road, cutting through the wonderful Benchakitti Park. The park was largely formed of a lake with pretty pink flowers surrounding it. At its edge was a paved track for running, and outside of that, a track for cycling. As I left the park, I cut through an industrial estate. I was surprised to see lots of security guards with whistles. Nobody stopped me passing through but a couple of guards asked where I was going. I said I needed to get to the main road and they pointed me in the right direction. I passed a large building with many flags outside it but I couldn't read the writing to work out what it was. Looking at a map later, I saw it had been a large tobacco plant.

Once I returned to the hotel, I didn't leave, even for dinner. My feet were hurting from wearing flip-flops to do over thirty miles of walking in three days and I was exhausted. Instead, I packed, ready for our flight to Chiang Mai, and had an early night.

Northern Thailand: Chiang Mai - Mud Bathing With Elephants

Once we landed in Chiang Mai, we took a taxi to the We Briza Hotel. After a quick rest, we went exploring. The old part of town took the form of a large square, bordered by a moat, which had several gates to allow people and vehicles through. After eating at a Japanese restaurant, we wandered through the narrow streets, exploring the shops, markets and temples. Sometime after dark, we found ourselves in the night bazaar, which was crowded with hundreds of stalls.

Feeling tired, I returned to the hotel while Rina and Jo continued on. When I got back to the room, I booked a trip to an elephant sanctuary. I was nervous about it because I didn't want to go anywhere where animals were mistreated. I'd done some research earlier in the day and had narrowed the search down to two reputable companies. The most popular option was fully booked so I went with the Elephant Jungle Sanctuary. They had excellent reviews and did not allow visitors to ride the elephants so I hoped we wouldn't regret our decision to go.

On Friday, the girls and I went our separate ways. I took photos in the old town before heading to a meditation session at a yoga studio called Body and Mind. Since Tuesday, I'd been feeling anxious and tearful and I hoped the session would give me some relief.

I was welcomed by a tall American man, David, who was dressed all in white and had a calming presence. David put me at ease straight away and talked to me about Buddhism. I was very interested in what he had to say. We were soon joined by two others: a French woman in her fifties and a young man from Belgium, Gilles.

David led us into the meditation with some soothing chanting. We then sat in silence for ten minutes. I was surprised by how easily my mind switched off. A few thoughts came up but the only thing that disturbed me was some tightness in my hips. David chanted once again to finish the meditation and we discussed in detail what feelings and thoughts had arisen. We were told about the basic beliefs of Buddhists and it made a lot of sense to me: nothing is permanent; people create their own discontentment and we do so by clinging on to things out of fear, becoming too attached. I realised I was guilty of creating my current discontentment. I was always worrying about the future or caught up in the past. Instead, I needed to focus on the present.

Knowing he was married, I asked David how someone could be in a relationship while not attaching. He replied that people should avoid 'clinging' to another person as this is a sign of fear, which creates more discontent. For example, if your partner wants to change career, you shouldn't hold them back because you're scared of the changes it will bring to your *own* life; you should support them. Stepping out of the door, I felt better. The world made sense again and the dark cloud that had been hovering above me disappeared. I was amazed but not surprised. I knew meditation had the power to reign in my constantly chattering mind. I just needed to keep it up.

With a new sense of inner peace, I met my friend Sylvia. It was great to see her again and we had a relaxing afternoon walking around town, visiting temples and markets. We stopped at a Japanese restaurant for lunch and talked about meditation, our careers and our travels. We then explored the south-west corner of the old town where it was quieter. Just after 6pm, we went our separate ways. We hugged goodbye and I returned to the hotel to call Tom. I explained what I'd learned from David and told him that I was feeling much happier - he seemed relieved.

On Saturday morning, we woke up excited to see elephants. We were picked up at 8am, in a 4x4 truck with two benches in the back (it wasn't the most comfortable of rides). Joining us were John and Lauren, and three loud women: a mother (Lorraine), her daughter (Tina) and her niece (Alyssia). The three women did not stop talking.

As the journey progressed and we left the main highway, the road began twisting and turning. The driver didn't allow this to slow his speed though. An uneasy silence took over as Lorraine said she felt sick. I looked over at Rina and she didn't look well either. Thankfully, Jo and I had taken motion sickness tablets so we were unaffected. We could only watch with sympathy as the roads went from bad to worse. The final section of the journey was on a bumpy dirt track which led into the sanctuary. I half expected this to finish them off but they fought their regurgitation instincts well.

We were all relieved when after two long hours, the truck rolled to a stop and we could get out. Within minutes, the horrible journey was forgotten as we became distracted by the elephants in the valley below. After sitting in the hut, we were told about the elephants, which had been rescued from places where they'd been ridden or mistreated. We were told that at this particular camp, humans worked for elephants; elephants didn't work for humans. As far we could tell it was true: the animals seemed content and happily roamed around the extensive property.

After our talk, we were instructed to put on traditional karen tops (to protect our clothing), wash our hands and collect a bunch of bananas to feed to the elephants. We could feed them via their trunks or could say 'bonbon' if we wanted them to open their mouths. We were told not to tease them with the food, just give it to them.

We walked down the hill and the elephants quickly came towards us. They clearly knew the drill and understood that we had food. I always thought I was a fast eater but I was nothing compared to an elephant.

Bananas were swallowed whole and as soon as they were passed one banana, their trunks would eagerly search for the next. As well as bananas, we fed them sugar cane. This needed to be crunched a little first but was soon dispatched. Once all the bananas and sugar cane had been demolished, we collected some thick, tall stalks of grass. The elephants quickly munched their way through those too.

We also fed some baby elephants called Beyonce and Rhianna (a terrible choice of names). They were two and one years old. We were told to be careful as they could get excitable and kick. Next, we walked to another camp and saw some different elephants near a small waterfall. They were playing and roaming free, although always watched closely by the mahouts, who made sure that people followed the rules (a child was quite rightly told off for trying to poke an elephant with a stick).

At midday, we had a tasty buffet lunch. We then got into our swimsuits for the afternoon session. Before we left the hut, we were shown how to make medicine balls (which help keep the elephants healthy) out of rice, salt, bananas, rye and tamarind. We mixed the ingredients together using a large pestle and mortar, taking it in turns to grind it up. Then we used our hands to make the mixture into balls. The banana made the mixture very slimy and I didn't care for it. Taking two balls each, we returned to the elephants. We were told to put the medicine straight into their mouths to prevent contamination with the ground (in case the elephants dropped them).

My messy hands were soon forgotten, as it was time to get in a mud pool and give the elephants a spa treatment. An elephant near me lay down and I gently rubbed mud onto its face and head. This apparently helped to remove parasites. The elephant seemed to enjoy it and I did too. Once the elephants were covered in mud, we all walked to the waterfall and used plastic buckets to rinse them off. By the time we finished, the elephants were nice and clean. We then walked back to the camp and said goodbye to the beautiful creatures. It had been a really special day and as we got back into the truck, we felt happy with our experience. Our happiness wasn't long-lasting though because the return journey was just as unpleasant as the morning one had been. Most people had taken travel sickness tablets this time, but Lauren, who was in the early stages of pregnancy, began feeling sick. Before long, she was throwing up into a carrier bag. Thankfully, once we were back on the highway, she felt better.

Early the next morning, Rina and I went for a three mile run. There were no scenic routes near our hotel so we had to settle for running along a busy main road. After a shower and breakfast, we walked into town to pick up some bikes as we wanted to visit the Umbrella Festival at Bo Sang. On the way back from dinner the night before, I'd made enquiries about bike hire and had found a guesthouse where we could rent them for only a pound each. The man had enough bikes but they were rusty, rickety and uncomfortable, with no gears and ineffective brakes. The only good thing about them was that they were so rubbish that nobody would steal them.

After paying a deposit, we walked the death-traps through the main town. Passing a busy hair salon, where haircuts were only five pounds, I asked Rina and Jo if they'd mind if I made enquiries. We weren't in any hurry and Rina wanted hers cut too, so we locked up the bikes and went in. Joy (the hairdresser) cut my hair shorter than I'd planned but I was really pleased with it. Rina, made a little nervous by the shortness of my hair, ended up having less off than she really wanted, just to be on the safe side.

We stopped for a hot drink and then pushed our bikes to the main road. We were ready to go, when my chain came off. Normally, this would have been fixable but the gears and chain were enclosed in a plastic case; therefore I had to wheel the bike back to the guest house and swap it. I then cycled back to the Rina and Jo, and led the way to the umbrella festival. The ride was a little scary as we were on a busy dual carriageway for seven miles but we survived.

When we arrived in Bo Sang, we parked our bicycles and explored. The festival was held along the main street and the town was vibrant and colourful - there were umbrellas of all shapes, styles and sizes. We watched a traditional parade of Thai women cycle past, all holding umbrellas and smiling prettily. Feeling hot, we took shelter in the gardens of a café and enjoyed cool drinks. We then stopped for some banana pancakes before picking up the bikes and setting off for Chiang Mai. When I went to stop at a busy junction, the brake cable snapped off entirely. It wasn't ideal as I had to cycle back to town without any brakes - it was a good job the road was flat! We arrived back in one piece and gladly returned the bikes to the guesthouse.

On Monday, we took a red songthaew to Doi Suthep, a golden temple on a mountain. Despite having taken tablets, both Rina and Jo felt sick on the winding road. Once we were off the truck, we climbed three hundred steps up to the temple, which was incredibly crowded. While we were there, I was blessed by a happy monk, who shook water over my head and hit me gently on the head with sticks.

After an hour, we began working our way down the mountain on foot. Using my map app, I found a shortcut: a steep, slippery dirt track called the Pilgrim's Path. We soon joined up with the friendlier main road, which we followed downhill. Not long after, we came to another temple, Wat Pha, which was quiet and beautifully set amongst the trees. What I really loved was the small waterfall where I sat listening to the peaceful sound of running water.

Returning to the main road, we walked for a mile and a half until we came to a set of stairs. The steps descended to an overgrown footpath, which took us to a small waterfall. At first the path was quiet but then we bumped into dozens of monks, who were all out for a walk. The track became wider and easier and eventually led down to some rocks and then out to the main road. We walked three miles back to the old town and rewarded ourselves with foot massages. Rina and Jo then went for dinner while I returned to the hotel.

On Tuesday morning, we relaxed at the hotel until it was time for me to leave for Chiang Rai. It had been so lovely seeing Rina again, and meeting Jo, but I'd sometimes felt awkward as I was always conscious that they were on holiday and wanted to make the most of their time. As I didn't have much money, we'd had many meals apart and had gone our separate ways quite often. It wasn't anyone's fault; it was just the way things were. We said our goodbyes and then I took a taxi to the station.

Northern Thailand: Chiang Rai - The Blue, The White & The Black

22ND - 26TH JANUARY 2019

I arrived in Chiang Rai at 4pm. From the station, it was a short walk to the Ti Amo Chiang Rai Central Guesthouse. I checked in and was shown to my single room on the second floor. However, I wasn't alone - a mosquito was lurking. Every time I went to kill it, it flew off. I couldn't relax knowing it was there, waiting to suck my blood and possibly give me a horrible disease, so I took a flip-flop and waited. After a couple of minutes, it landed on the table. Quietly, I approached but it flew off before I could squash it. This continued for an hour until eventually, it landed on the wall and like a ninja, I splatted it!

Feeling victorious, I left the room. Apart from being smaller, Chiang Rai wasn't much different to Chiang Mai ('same, same but different' as the famous Thai saying goes). It was soon dark, and as I was hungry, I bought some chicken satay sticks and a banana pancake from the busy street market and sat on the kerb to eat them. Before I'd even taken a mouthful, a stray black dog approached and looked at me sadly. It was obviously hungry so I shared my chicken.

Next, I found the night bazaar, where I bought some bracelets and small silk bags. I walked past the massage booth the first time I saw it but then I realised how tired my legs were and went back. Attached to the booth was a stall selling linen tops so it was a perfect people-watching spot. Every time someone approached, the young girl serving would stand and greet them, eager to make a sale. I enjoyed watching people try on the tops and could usually tell by their facial expression whether or not they'd make a purchase. One cuddly man was given the extra large size to try on. I felt sorry for him as he struggled to pull it over himself before giving up. He pulled a sad face and wandered off, dejected.

Over breakfast the next morning, I researched what to do in Chiang Rai. The main attractions seemed to be three temples, simply named the Blue Temple, the White Temple and the Black Temple. There were numerous tours offering to take me to all three in one day, but my research showed me I could visit them by myself for a fraction of the price.

I spent the day relaxing, and then at 5pm, I ran towards the Blue Temple, which was supposed to be prettiest at sunset. Even though Chiang Rai was cooler than Chiang Mai, it was still hot. The fumes from the traffic weren't a pleasant addition either and after a mile and half, I felt sick. Not wanting to puke on the side of the road, I bought a cold drink and walked the rest of the way.

The official name of the Blue Temple is Wat Rong Suea Ten (temple of the dancing tigers), named after the tigers that once roamed the area. It was stunning and I loved the intricately painted walls and ceiling. When I'd first arrived, the temple had been swarming with tourists, but as the sun began to set, the tour buses drove away and I could enjoy a little more peace. However, not wanting to run home in the dark, I soon had to make a move. As I ran over a quiet bridge, I was distracted by the sky, which was a gorgeous deep red.

Once I got home and showered, I repeated the previous evening's activities: chicken satay, a banana pancake and a massage. I really was a creature of habit, mostly because I craved the little interactions I'd get when I returned to the same place. During the massage, my masseuse pointed out some women in extravagant costumes. Laughingly, she informed me that they were lady-boys (it was quite hard to tell).

As before, I watched people make their way through the market. I was pleased to see the clothes stall was doing well. A Chinese woman came to browse and when she saw the girl's tiny dog, she grabbed it. The poor thing looked terrified and could only blink in fear while it was man-handled by a stranger. The woman said she didn't want the top but she'd take the dog. The girl wisely took the dog back into her possession before the crazy lady could run away with it. I'd never seen an animal look so relieved.

The next day, my alarm went off at 7am so I could visit the popular White Temple before the crowds flooded it. At the bus station, I looked for the small blue bus I needed. I spotted it easily and a smiling woman, who was sitting by it, told me to take a seat inside. At 8am, I heard a whistle blow, followed by the familiar tune of Thailand's national anthem. Everyone in the bus station stood still while it played. When it was over, another whistle was blown and everyone carried on with their business. The same thing had happened when I'd been in Lumphini Park in Bangkok. The anthem had started at 6pm and everyone had stopped running and stood silently like statues. It had been a strange thing to witness.

The bus left promptly at 8:10am and chugged along slowly for ten miles, spluttering more than a chain-smoker. Eventually, the woman told me it was my stop and the bus pulled over to let me off. The White Temple wasn't hard to locate - even from a distance, its whiteness was blinding. I paid fifty baht to enter and joined the crowds (my cunning plan hadn't worked - it was already busy).

Near the entrance, I stopped to take photos of the temple. I was soon irritated by some obnoxious Chinese tourists, who rudely spoke about me in English, like I wasn't there. They apparently wanted me *completely* out of the way. To annoy them, I purposely took my time taking photos while they tutted loudly.

The White Temple itself, or Wat Rong Khun, was magnificent. According to Google, it isn't a real temple but a privately-owned art exhibit. The owner is an artist called Chalermchai Kositpipat, who designed, constructed, and opened it up to visitors in 1997. The building is painted white to symbolise the purity of Buddha. The interior, juxtaposed against the white exterior, showed images of popular icons such as Superman and Harry Potter amongst hellish flames and demons: a clear message that people shouldn't worship false gods. Images of historic tragedies and nuclear war were also depicted, showing how humans were destroying the planet. To me, the most striking part was the grasping hands reaching out of the ground, reminiscent of Dante's Inferno. They symbolise unrestrained desire: to achieve happiness, you need to forego temptation, greed and desire (easy - *right*?).

In less than an hour, I was back at the bus stop. A blue songthaew soon arrived and I hopped on. The truck was much faster than the bus had been so I was back at the station quickly. I didn't know what to do for the rest of the day, so I relaxed until 5:30pm, when I went running. I'd chosen a circular route, which led me partly along the river, where I enjoying watching the sun setting through the trees.

On Friday morning, I went to the Black Temple, which was actually the Baandam Museum, sometimes referred to as the Black House. To get there, I took the small green local bus, which went north, towards Mae Sai. It was full when I got on, so I stood in the aisle, waiting for our departure. However, when the feisty female conductor stepped aboard, she gruffly shouted at the men on the back row to move. They obediently shuffled along, making room for me. It was a bit of a squeeze and a little awkward for all concerned, but it was better than standing.

We soon covered the seven miles. From the side of the road, it was a ten minute walk to the museum. I paid eight baht to enter and then looked around, trying to get a feel for the place. There were fewer tourists than at the other temples but there were more rowdy school children tearing about.

I couldn't miss the main building as it was very imposing. I noted that it wasn't actually black but dark brown. It was rather macabre so I nicknamed it the S&M Temple. There were several buildings in the complex to explore and their decors all shared common themes: black chairs fashioned from painted cow horns (reminiscent of scorpions), penises, animal skins and lots of dark wood. I had a giggle taking some selfies with a wooden statue with a giant willy, and then I returned to the main road, where a songthaew returned me to Chiang Rai.

Chiang Rai (Thailand) to Luang Prabang (Laos): Mekong Smile River Cruise - Crossing the Border

Bright and early on Saturday morning, I was picked up from the guesthouse by a private taxi (included in the price of the cruise) and we drove 135km, from Chiang Rai to the Chiang Khong border. The sun rose as we sped past lush paddy fields, the warm colours of the sunrise reflecting in the water. When we reached Thai immigration at Chiang Khong, my driver gave me fifty baht to pay for the bus and sent me on my way. I felt like I'd been given pocket money for good behaviour.

Exiting Thailand was simple: my passport was stamped by an immigration officer and shortly after, I joined a small queue for the bus into Laos. The ticket cost only twenty-five baht and while I was paying, a woman offered to exchange my remaining baht into US dollars. I'd been planning on paying with baht, but she gave me US$35 (the cost of my Laos visa) for 1300 baht. The exchange rate wasn't great but it was still a saving of five pounds.

The bus journey was very short. We travelled over the Friendship Bridge, which crossed the Mekong River, and entered Huay Xai, at the border of Laos. Once I'd exited the bus, I completed my visa on arrival form and joined the queue. Luckily, it was quiet so it was soon my turn to be seen. The woman behind the counter was *very* grumpy and snatching my documents, gruffly sent me to the next window. After a short wait, a happier man waved my passport at me and asked for payment. With my visa in my passport, I passed through immigration and waited for my guide. He was supposed to have been waiting to help me with my visa, but I hadn't noticed anyone. I stood around for ten minutes before beginning to wonder whether I should've met him on the *other* side of immigration. Unable to go back, I waited nervously, hoping he'd find me. A young man came over to offer help. I explained my situation and he left to find my guide. Within minutes, Kae was with me - I *was* supposed to have met him the other side! We waited for two older French women to join us and were then driven into town, where we picked up two young American girls (Cara and Jamie) and a British couple (the lovely Janine and Jim).

We were soon dropped off at the slow boat pier. The boat was comfortable and was very spacious for only seven of us. Our guide said we were VIPs, as the cheap public boats crammed over a hundred people in them. Since arriving at the border, I'd been cold for the first time since Perth. It was even chillier when the boat started moving. I had to put a shirt on and cover my goose-bumped legs with a blanket.

After ninety minutes on the river, with Thailand on one side and Laos on the other, we reached Padhai Mountain. From there, we left Thailand behind: we were properly in Laos. Apart from a couple of small villages, the Mekong riverside was completely undeveloped. It was all beautiful green jungle, trees and rock. The boat stopped at a small village. As it was Saturday, the men were taking care of the children (a local tradition). There were many cats and dogs milling around. I was dismayed to learn that some would be eaten by the village's residents (I was therefore glad we weren't staying for lunch). The village had many huts and the people were all friendly. I felt intrusive walking around but the people seemed accustomed to it and visitors brought in money to build a bigger school.

Back onboard, we were served an excellent lunch of fish and chicken with rice. The sweet, delicious fresh mango was the best part though. The rest of the afternoon was spent napping in the sunshine while the boat journeyed down the river. The river itself was fast-moving, with a strong current. Speedboats often zoomed past but I'd read that they were a dangerous way to travel on the Mekong due to the shallowness of the water.

At 5pm, we reached the small town of Pakbeng. Leaving the Green Turtle on the boat, I was driven to my accommodation, the Thip Phavan Guesthouse. It was clean and comfortable and had surprisingly good WiFi. I went for a walk while there was still some daylight. The town was small and consisted of a single main road, flanked on either side with small buildings: homes, guesthouses, shops and restaurants. The view of the sun setting on the river was lovely. I watched from the pier, feeling grateful I'd booked the cruise - so far, it had exceeded my expectations.

In the evening, I had dinner at a restaurant next door to the guesthouse but the pork dish I ordered was bland and overpriced. Free local whiskey was provided with the meal although it was a little potent. I didn't stay at the restaurant long as an obnoxious American was there with a group of friends. She kept shouting her mouth off at the staff and demanding more free whiskey. I was glad to escape to the peace and quiet of my room and have a nice long chat with Tom. I told him all about my journey to Laos and he told me about things at home.

After a good night's sleep, we were back on the boat. Low clouds clung to the valley and it was cold. As I warmed myself with some hot tea, an unexpected visitor came aboard, a Scot named Sarah. She'd been on the public boat the previous day and had *not* enjoyed her experience as it had been so cramped. She'd met Cara and Jamie the previous evening, and liking the sound of our 'luxury' cruise, had decided to join us. Sometime in the late morning, we stopped at another village. There wasn't much to see, just a lot of stalls selling scarves.

When we returned to the boat, we all assumed our usual positions on the benches. However one of the French women decided she wanted to sit *right* where I was. Instead of politely asking if I could budge up, she pushed me and squeezed her bum onto the tiny bit of space she'd created. I didn't say anything, even though I thought it was rude. We ate lunch and then went back to the benches. I was just about to fall asleep when the French woman returned, gave my pillow a big push and squeezed herself onto the end of the bench again. I don't know why she chose *my* space to invade as people were laying on the pillows in all four corners of the two benches and she didn't try to sit on *them*. She could have sat in the middle of either of the benches or on one of the many other available seats.

It wasn't the first time the French woman had been rude: she'd shoved one of the Americans the day before. I made my displeasure clear and a few heated words were exchanged. We then proceeded to begin a petty battle of wills. I, being pig-headed, wouldn't move and she refused to move to an empty seat, so we ended up leaning against the same pillow but facing in opposite directions. Every now and then she'd push back, trying to shove me further away. The others found it hilarious and couldn't believe how badly she was behaving. I just joked (out loud) that she obviously really liked me and needed to be close to me. Eventually, she stormed off and I had no further dealings with her.

Our penultimate stop was at some caves. This involved walking up lots of steep steps and passing many women and children, who were all trying to sell things. The most common items on offer were tiny cages with birds inside. The idea was that we were supposed to set the birds free. However, they would only get recaptured because the birds were trained to return to the sellers - poor things. The caves were dull so I quickly grew bored and returned to the boat. Once we got going again, it took just over an hour to reach our final destination: Luang Prabang. We said goodbye to Kae and the captain, and then a minibus dropped us off at our various accommodations. It had been a really great trip - one of the highlights of my travels.

Laos: Luang Prabang & Vang Vieng - Adventures on the VIP Bus

At 5pm, I arrived at the Sok Dee Residence, where I met up with my friend Natasha. It was so good to see her. Over dinner we had a much-needed catch-up. While we ate, a blind cat joined us. It kept jerking its head up, as if trying to see from its missing eyes. There was clearly nothing wrong with its sense of smell though as it knew when meat was nearby. I tried to feed it some pork but even when I held the meat up to its mouth, it would drop it, and one of the greedy, more visually-able, cats would snatch it up. Natasha suggested its disability made people more likely to feed it and told me not to worry about it. It wasn't skinny so she was probably right.

After dinner, we walked around town. The streets were lit up with lanterns and fairy lights but there were no street lights so we could easily see the stars sparkling in the sky. We soon found ourselves at a night market. One particular stall, run by two children, immediately caught our attention. The girls were selling small, colourful bags, hand-stitched with pictures and text. All were written with poor grammar ('we are happy banana') but this only added to their charm. Tired from her long journey, Natasha wanted an early night so we returned to the guesthouse.

We had a late start the next morning. The cafe we chose for breakfast was fantastic: for only three pounds, I had a delicious breakfast of fresh orange juice, peppermint tea, apple pancakes, coconut ice cream *and* a large bowl of fresh fruit. After, we made our way to Phou Si 'Mountain'. We'd expected it to be bigger but there were only three hundred steps before we were at the top. The views over Luang

Prabang were pretty though. Although it was a little hazy, we could see the river and the streets below, and mountains in the distance.

Back at ground level, we walked over the rickety Bamboo Bridge. The bridge is remade every year so we had to pay a small fee to cross it, which contributed to the cost of the next one. On the other side of the river, we climbed a set of steps, where we found a shop selling handmade jewellery. I bought a beautiful mint and gold necklace, with beads made from recycled paper. We carried on walking until we found ourselves at a different bridge. This one was larger, so motorbikes could cross in both directions. There was a narrow footpath for pedestrians. I didn't think much of it at first but when we were halfway across, I began feeling uncomfortable as we were so high up. The path was made up of three strips of wooden planks, sometimes with large gaps between them. The wood was bendy and cracked, and didn't seem very strong. I was relieved to reach the other side safely.

That evening, I went running. As usual, there weren't many suitable routes so I picked the longest, straightest road on the map. The sunset was a welcome distraction and I stopped to take photos as the sun dipped behind the mountains. Then it was back to running on the busy road, weaving around tuk tuks and breathing in fumes - lovely.

The next day, we were taken by private minibus to Kuang Si Falls. I hadn't expected much, as every other waterfall I'd visited had been a disappointment but this one was incredibly beautiful, consisting of a series of shallow falls and turquoise pools. It looked just like it had in the photos I'd seen online and as we were there so early, there weren't any people to ruin the view. We followed a winding path until it ended at a wooden bridge. As I'd only seen pictures of the shallow falls, I was surprised to see some larger ones. Minty-blue water cascaded down from high in the rocks and again, I was astounded by the beauty. After taking photos, I looked for Natasha but she was nowhere to be found. Noticing a set of steps, I wondered if she'd gone to the top of the falls, so I followed the path, which was unpleasantly muddy and steep. At the top, there was no sign of Natasha so I descended and then walked towards the bear sanctuary, which we'd passed earlier.

I reached the sanctuary but my friend wasn't there so I waited and watched the bears in their enclosure. One was lounging at the top of a large wooden construction when a smaller bear approached. It obviously didn't want company as it leaned down and growled at the visitor, gnashing its teeth. The other bear retreated apologetically. It didn't stay away for long though and soon approached again. This time the bigger bear came down - it was *not* happy. From the middle level of the tower, the bear had a few words with the intruder, which standing up on two wobbling legs, began backing away. I imagined the following conversation taking place:

Little Bear: Do you mind if I join you?
Big Bear: No. Get lost. I've already told you once.
Little Bear: No worries mate - it just looks fun up there. I promise I won't bother you.
Big Bear: This is the last time I'm saying it - SOD OFF!

With a final roar, the bigger bear scampered to the ground and ran at the smaller bear, forcing it to quickly retreat into a hollow. Point made, it returned to the top of its tower while the other bear hastily crept away. The whole thing had been hilarious to witness and I walked away laughing. Finding myself at the entrance, I wondered if Natasha was waiting for me at the minibus. She was.

That afternoon, Natasha visited the palace while I went for a walk. I was by the river when I noticed a familiar head of copper hair - it was Sarah from the slow boat. We wandered together and laughed about the crazy French women. Apparently they'd been at it again on the way into Luang Prabang and had tried to get the minibus driver to drop them off before Sarah, even though he'd had a set itinerary. As she'd exited, she'd smugly told them that *they* would have to wait until last. She said she'd bumped into them a couple of times at the market. I was pleased that I hadn't had *that* pleasure.

At 7am the next morning, we were collected from our accommodation by a songthaew. The next people to be picked up were very familiar: yes, it was my friends, the French women. You can imagine my excitement. When we left the songthaew, we took our bags onto the double-decker 'VIP' bus, which I renamed the 'RIP' bus due to the huge spidery crack in the windscreen, which had been repaired with black tape. The French women, unhappy with their assigned seats, moved to the front of the bus. Soon enough, they had to move again, as the people whose seats they'd stolen turned up. This happened a few times until they finally learned to sit in their own seats.

As the bus moved off, I wondered what the journey would be like. I'd taken travel sickness tablets so I hoped it wouldn't be too traumatic. Once we left the outskirts of Luang Prabang, we were all handed sick bags. It was clear why people might need them: the mountain roads were narrow, winding and poorly-surfaced. Every time the bus went round one of the many blind corners, the driver would sound the horn to let oncoming drivers know he was there. It was terrifying at times. Not long after leaving, we heard a loud wrenching sound. It was never clear what exactly happened, but when we stopped for a toilet break, some men were trying to fix the bus door which looked like it had been partially torn off. It wasn't a great start.

As we crept along the mountain roads, the scenery became increasingly spectacular. Despite a lot of litter along the roadside, Laos was mesmerising. The jagged, majestic mountains, covered in deep green blankets of forest, jutted up into the air, stretching towards the clouds. It was interesting to observe the locals going about their daily routines as we passed through small villages: kids were taking outside showers under taps; women were taking care of their children; and families were happily gutting animals together in the street and.

As we drew closer to Vang Vieng, we descended into the valley, where there were many farms and paddy fields. It was here, at a roadside 'restaurant', that we stopped for lunch. This was included in the ticket price but Natasha and I took one look at what was on offer and decided against it - we didn't fancy food poisoning.

We finally arrived in dusty Vang Vieng at 4:30pm. Thankfully the French women had stayed on the bus, presumably continuing on to Vientiane, so at least we wouldn't bump into them. From the bus stop, it was a two minute walk to the Sansan Resort and Spa. We were supposed to have stayed at a different hotel, but as there'd been a problem with our room, we'd been moved - it was *definitely* an upgrade. Once we'd settled in, Natasha sat by the pool and I went off in search of food. Thankfully I soon found a roti stall, where I stuffed my face with banana pancakes (I was maybe taking the banana pancake trail idea a little *too* literally). On the way back to the hotel, I came across the smell of freshly made pizza. I couldn't resist treating myself to a large slice of the salami pizza, handmade by an Italian chef. It was delicious - the best I'd had in months.

That evening, we met Jim and Janine at our hotel. We had a walk around the busy market and then stopped for dinner at a small German restaurant, where I had an amazing schnitzel with fried potatoes. It was fun to catch up and reminisce about our time on the slow boat. We also had a giggle telling Natasha all about the crazy French ladies. It was a wonderful evening with good friends, old and new.

On Thursday, Natasha and I stopped for breakfast at Victor's Place. I ordered tea with milk, mango juice, fresh fruit and pancakes, carefully pointing at each item on the menu. My tea turned up *without* milk so I asked if I could have some. Victor seemed confused and told me to point at the menu again. He then became angry and grabbing my tea, poured it onto the street. Another did not arrive. When my juice turned up, it was melon and not mango. I gingerly asked for mango and he started arguing that I'd ordered melon. This too was taken away and not replaced. Natasha's order turned up without a problem, but half an hour later, I still had nothing. I went to the counter to ask if I could have one of my drinks and Victor was very rude. Seeing red and feeling *hangry*, I walked out, telling Natasha I'd see her back at the hotel. I ate at the banana pancake stall and then had a slice of delicious salami pizza.

Later on, we went hiking. We crossed a bamboo bridge and followed signs (indicated by white carrier bags on tall wooden poles) to a viewpoint. We'd been expecting a bit of a climb and lots of steps but we hadn't expected the wooden ladders. They weren't very sturdy and the bamboo handrails uselessly wobbled about. When there were no ladders to deal with, we had to scramble up jagged rocks. We made it just over halfway when Natasha said she wanted to stop. I climbed a little higher to see if things improved but the path only got worse so we carefully descended. Instead, we followed signs to a cave. The winding route through fields and forest was beautiful and peaceful, but when we finally reached the cave, a sign pointed up. Laughingly, we agreed we did not want any more 'up' and turned back.

On the way to the hotel, we couldn't resist stopping at a riverside bar, where we rested our hot, tired feet in the water and each enjoyed a cold bottle of cider. We watched people float past on giant rubber rings. A few years ago, this was why tourists had come to Vang Vieng: to tube down the river and drink copious amounts of alcohol. However, there had been too many deaths so it had been stopped. The tubing still happened but there were fewer bars along the way.

On our final morning in Vang Vieng, I went running. As usual, I had limited options. I ran along the main road but it was incredibly dusty and I didn't enjoy choking on fumes. Instead, I ran over the bamboo bridge and over the fields. It was uneven but more pleasant than the road. I hoped that Vientiane, our next stop, would have better running routes.

Laos: Vientiane -
Rage Against the Mosquitoes

1ST - 5TH FEBRUARY 2019

Natasha and I thought we'd try the minivan for our onward journey to Vientaine (pronounced vee-en-tea-en). We paid 50,000 LAK each (about five pounds) and booked the three-hour journey for 1pm. A songthaew promptly arrived and took us to a small bus station, where we were told to wait. Finally, at 2:40pm, two vans arrived. There were twenty-seven of us waiting and we were split into two groups. Our bags were thrown onto the roof of each vehicle and secured with netting and rope. The vans were very uncomfortable as there was no leg room and little suspension. The situation wasn't helped by the poor roads: there were several sections without tarmac and we bumped over the uneven surfaces madly. Sometimes the vans would crash through potholes, launching us from our seats.

At 6pm, we were unceremoniously dumped at a bus station in the middle of nowhere. Most people had other buses to catch, so they ran off quickly, leaving Natasha and me with a young British couple. We all jumped in a songthaew and waited...and waited. Three locals jumped in but as it wasn't full, we had to wait some more. I became grumpy and impatient, especially as hungry mosquitoes were circling.

Realising that no others passengers were coming, the driver transferred us to a smaller songthaew and we were finally on our way. Just after 7pm, three hours later than advertised, we arrived at the VKS Hotel. I'd arranged to meet Jim and Janine, so the first thing I did was to message them. Natasha wasn't feeling very sociable as her poor bunny at home had died that day, so just the three of us went for curry. It was great to see them again and we had a fun evening discussing our travels, past, present and future.

The next day, Natasha and I walked to a temple. On the way, we stopped at Laos' answer to the Parisian Arc De Triomphe: the Patuxai Monument. The monument had a beautifully painted ceiling and was surrounded by pretty fountains. In the small park, there was also a large structure featuring four elephants made entirely from blue and white china cups. I didn't understand its significance but I liked it. Leaving the monument behind, we carried on to explore the impressive Wat That Luang, a golden Buddhist stupa. It is Laos' national symbol and therefore the most sacred monument in the country.

The return journey was a little uncomfortable, partly because of the unbearable heat and partly because I didn't know what to say to Natasha, who was very upset. When we got back, she went for a coffee to spend some time talking to her husband, and I retreated to the coolness of our air-conditioned room, where I promptly fell asleep.

I woke up a little later with five bites so I became suspicious that horrid mosquitoes were lurking. Despite a close inspection, I couldn't find any (though it was difficult to see *anything* against the room's gloomy, grey walls). In the late afternoon, Natasha and I went for dinner at an Italian restaurant. I was pleasantly surprised - Laos really could do pizza! It seemed to be the only Asian country that did it well, as all the other pizzas I'd tried while I'd been away had been terrible.

On Sunday, I did a four mile run on the paved 'boardwalk', which hugged the river. Over breakfast, I got talking to a Welshman, Alun. He'd been to Buddha Park on the local bus the previous day and said it was worth a visit. We therefore added it to our agenda.

Our first stop was at Wat Sisaket. It was older than the other temples we'd seen, with a colourful, painted interior. After, we went to the station and searched for the number 14 bus. A local pointed us in the right direction and we hopped on, sitting at the front.

Buddha Park was unusual. It was designed and constructed in 1958, by Luang Pu Bunleua Sulilat, a sculptor, shaman, priest and 'fuser of faiths'. For this reason, there was a peculiar mix of sculptures: part-Buddhist and part-Hindu. At the back of the site were some gardens, where wilting sunflowers were somehow growing out of the desiccated soil. Amongst them were large plastic reindeer; their presence didn't surprise me, it was just more weirdness in an already weird place.

Once we'd seen enough, we returned to the road and took the next available bus. Mosquitoes danced around me. I managed to successfully squash a couple but Natasha looked at me disapprovingly every time: she seemed to have a strange empathy for them. I was happy for her to be friends with them but *I* certainly wasn't going to be, not when they were possibly spreading malaria or dengue fever about (and not while I was still itching profusely from the previous day's bites). Once we got back, Natasha went for coffee while I called Tom. We didn't do much for the rest of the day, apart from going out to dinner.

We got up late on Monday as there wasn't much left to see. As I was in the bathroom, something zipped past me: a mosquito. Deftly, I splatted it on the floor, hoping it was the one that had attacked me in my sleep. But just as I was dressing, another flew past. I gave chase. While trying to hide from me and my flip flop, it made the mistake of seeking shelter in the safe. I slammed the door, locking it inside! Feeling victorious, we left the room.

We had breakfast at one of the many French cafes. I had an amazing crepe, topped with cream, apple pieces and salted caramel: it was much better than the bland hotel breakfasts. After, we visited the COPE centre (Cooperative Orthotic & Prosthetic Enterprise), which is the main source of artificial limbs, walking aids and wheelchairs in Laos. The centre was very informative and explained that Laos is one of the most heavily bombed countries in the world. It was bombed repeatedly by the US in the Secret War (1964-1973), particularly by cluster bombs (formed of hundreds of smaller grenade-like 'bombies'). Around thirty percent of the bombies (estimated at around 80 million) failed to detonate and it is these that kill and maim people to this day. COPE helps people to rehabilitate and recover from encounters with these devices, providing them with artificial limbs. Thankfully, a lot of work has been going on to safely remove the unexploded devices and the numbers of casualties has dropped dramatically.

At 6pm that evening, a taxi arrived to take Natasha to the airport. It had been wonderful to see her but due to the death of her beloved bunny, I didn't think she'd really enjoyed her time away.

After a pizza, I returned to the hotel room and that is when the real battle began. One mosquito after another appeared from nowhere. No sooner had I killed one, when another would materialise. My trusty flip flop proved a valuable weapon and finally, after a ninety-minute killing spree, the room was mosquito free. Just to be safe, I covered myself in DEET before climbing into bed and calling Tom from under the covers. He thought I was a bit mad for my attack on the mosquitoes and we had a good laugh about it. Once we ended the call, I stayed hidden under the sheet and hoped I'd wake up in the morning well-rested, ready for my flight to Hanoi.

Vietnam: Hanoi - Happy Chinese New Year! (Part 1)

5TH - 8TH FEBRUARY 2019

I hadn't been looking forward to Hanoi because I was aware it would be crammed with motorbikes. Also, Hanoi and Ho Chi Minh City were apparently well-known for motorcyclists snatching bags or phones: I'd read horrible stories about tourists being dragged along the road when they'd refused to let go of their bags or *couldn't* let go quickly enough. In reality, this could happen anywhere, and in my time there, I never once witnessed it. I was always on my guard though, and wore my rucksack on my front whenever I was outside. It made me look like an idiot but I was ok with that.

I'd booked my flight with Lao Airlines so I was pleasantly surprised when I boarded a plusher Vietnam Airlines plane. Not only did the flight depart early but it was almost empty, due to the fact that it was Chinese New Year. Once we landed, I made my way to border control. I'd been expecting some hassle going through immigration, but thanks to my e-visa, it was simple. The officer didn't say a word; he just stamped my passport and waved me through to collect the Green Turtle.

At first, I wasn't worried when I couldn't find my taxi, but as I wandered back and forth, looking for a board with my name on, I became a bit concerned. Eventually, I asked for help from a woman at a SIM card stand. She didn't look impressed but she kindly lent me her phone so I could call the hostel. Initially, the receptionist who answered wasn't very helpful but after a couple of minutes, she understood my issue.

Shortly after, a young man with my name on a board appeared. He picked up the Green Turtle and grunted. He could barely lift it, even though it was less than fifteen kilos. If I could carry it a mile, surely he could carry it a hundred feet? Apparently not - instead, he left it on the ground of the car park, choosing to bring the car to the bag rather than the other way round.

I arrived at the Little Charm Hanoi Hostel just after 10:30pm. It turned out to be a perfect choice of name as most of the staff there really did have *little* charm. There were one or two more helpful people though so I always aimed for them when I needed something. Once I'd checked in, I went straight to sleep.

The next day, I felt really tired so I slept in. In the afternoon, I left to find an ATM. I tried a few but my card kept getting rejected. Having no cash at all on me, I started to worry that it might become a problem. However, when I returned to the WiFi, my Starling Bank app told me I hadn't unlocked my card to allow ATM withdrawals - oops. Unlocking my card, I tried again. This time I was successful. I withdrew the maximum, two million dong. As this wasn't enough, I took another two million out, making me a multi-millionaire! I hid my dong in my bag (snigger) and quickly returned to the hostel to squirrel it away in my locked bag, inside my locked locker.

In the evening, I went for a walk. The traffic was crazy and motorbikes came at me from all directions - everyone seemed to be on the wrong side of the road. Looking for a reprieve, I went to Hoan Kien Lake. It was busy, as people were celebrating Chinese New Year: this was the reason why almost everything was closed. Hardly any shops were open the whole time I was there, which made my time in Hanoi a little dull.

Early on Thursday morning, I ran five kilometres around Hoan Kiem Lake. Luckily the roads were *much* quieter than they'd been the previous evening. The path around the lake was also emptier; just a few people were exercising: mostly runners, walkers and cyclists, but a few were doing tai chi.

That afternoon, I wandered aimlessly, until I noticed some train tracks disappearing down a narrow road lined with homes and cafes. There was some graffiti so I enjoyed exploring and taking photos, walking down the centre of the tracks. I assumed that the tracks were disused but when I later researched it, I discovered they were active. I couldn't imagine living somewhere where trains zipped past less than a metre from your front door. It was something I wanted to see though, so I made a note of the train times.

Moving on, I walked towards the citadel. However, when I reached the gate, I noticed a sign saying that I could only enter if I was dressed 'neatly and politely'. I didn't know what that meant. I wasn't sure my shorts and vest were *polite*, so I kept walking. Eventually, I reached the West Lake. Nearby were some pretty gardens, so I sat in them for quite a while and caught up with writing my blog.

That night, I packed, ready for the two-day Halong Bay cruise the following morning. The hostel had booked it for me with Swan Cruises and I was very excited! I'd paid for my hostel bed up until Sunday so I was able to leave the Green Turtle in my locker and just take a small rucksack. Knowing I had a busy couple of days ahead, I went to bed early.

Vietnam: Halong Bay Tour - 11 Angry Swedes

8TH - 9TH FEBRUARY 2019

I was collected from the hostel some time after 8am, along with another solo girl, Luca (from Germany). As the bus was almost full, we took the only available seats at the back of the bus. Luca and I hit it off immediately. Quietly, we joked that we appeared to be on a bus full of retirees. We were chatting away, when a mature Swedish couple turned and told us to be quiet: our talking was making it hard for them to read. Feeling awkward, we lowered our voices and carried on. A couple of minutes later, the couple turned around *again*. Rather than communicate with us directly, they loudly asked another Swedish couple (who were sat next to us) to request that we lower our voices. With the four of them glaring at us, I told them that we were *not* at a funeral so we would not sit in silence. They did not look happy. As it turned out, it wasn't just *four* of them. Our guide, Vinh, asked us to introduce ourselves and we soon discovered that there were *eleven* in their group - over half of the people on the trip! How delightful.

During his briefing, Vinh warned us to keep our expectations of the trip low. He explained that even though we'd paid a lot of money (a single room had cost US$185), the boat wasn't 'good'. It was also only half-staffed due to the New Year celebrations. He told us that the photos on the website had been taken when the boat was new, but now it was three years old and looked 'not good' from the outside. He went on to say that we could also expect to see cockroaches and mice onboard - better and better! His sales pitch wasn't quite what I'd expected to hear but it made me laugh.

We arrived at the port just after midday and were transferred to the main boat. I was disappointed when I heard Luca was going on a different boat as I'd been looking forward to hanging out with her. The people who weren't in the Swedish group were all in couples or trios, so that left me on my own.

Onboard, we were provided with lemon tea and given the keys to our cabins. I was pleasantly surprised - my cabin was very cosy: it had a small bathroom and a lovely view out to sea. We were *very* lucky with the weather. People had warned me to expect grey skies but we enjoyed sunshine, at least for the first couple of hours. Halong Bay was stunning. We were surrounded by dramatic limestone karsts (big rocks jutting out of the ocean) and the calm water was a tranquil shade of jade.

Lunch was a delicious multi-course meal: I enjoyed steamed fish, chicken curry and grilled pork. We then had melon for 'dessert'. I was a little disappointed because fruit does *not* count as dessert. After we'd eaten, I sat in a solitary spot at the front of the boat. Since everyone was in ready-made groups, I felt more comfortable withdrawing. From where I sat, I could see the captain. I had to laugh, as he was steering the boat with his feet.

Later on, we went kayaking. Most people went off in the double kayaks, which left me with one of the grumpy Swedes. Grimacing, she suggested we pair up. Thankfully, I'd already asked to take the only single kayak, so I had the pleasure of saying, "No thanks."

It had been a while since I'd last paddled (having sold my kayak to help pay for my trip) but I soon overtook everyone. Being out in front, I couldn't see anything ahead of me and it felt like I was alone at sea. Checking behind, I saw Vinh point me in the right direction. We paddled towards a beach on one of the rocky islands so people could go swimming. I was clearly enjoying myself, so Vinh told me I could explore alone, as long as he could always see me. I'd paddled three and a half miles by the time we returned to the boat.

After showering, I sat in my usual spot. Viet, Vinh's friend, came over and we talked about travelling. He apologised that Luca and I had been separated. Vinh had apparently tried to jiggle things around so we'd be on the same boat, but he'd been unable to make it work. It was a shame but I appreciated his efforts.

At 6pm, Viet told me to come upstairs for refreshment. We were served ginger tea, prawn crackers and delicious fresh fruit. Everyone was chatting away within their groups, so I took my plate of pineapple and mango and sat alone at a small table on the top deck. I felt lonely: it could be isolating when you were in a big group but nobody was speaking your language. I couldn't wait to get back to my room.

Dinner was at 7pm. I felt awkward sitting there while people chatted and ate around me, so I spent the time writing my blog on my phone. I don't usually approve of phones at the dinner table but it was a useful crutch for me in that situation. Once the oysters and shrimp were eaten (not by me), we were brought sea bass. It was really tasty! I also had egg fried rice and beef, and then enjoyed a *proper* dessert of crème caramel.

Straight after dinner, I escaped to my room, feeling instant relief from my social anxiety. I spent the rest of the evening reading and writing in peace. Before I knew it, it was gone midnight. As I tried to sleep, I could hear the Swedes. They'd been drinking expensive wine with their meals, and ironically, had become loud drunks. Smiling to myself, I wondered whether I should ask them to 'lower their voices'.

Despite the bed being comfortable, I didn't sleep well. The boat's engine was rumbling away and I could *feel* rather than hear it. I was therefore very sleepy when my alarm went off. Breakfast on board was good: I had a morning feast of bacon, pancakes and watermelon.

At 7:45am, we got on the smaller boat. The captain pointed to the seat next to him, knowing I liked to sit away from everyone else. He often looked grumpy but he always had a big smile for me. Our morning stop was at a nondescript cave. I dutifully walked through it and then sat quietly on some rocks, taking photos as the sun broke through the clouds. As I went to return to the boat, Luca approached. She said that the people on her boat were a lot of fun and asked how things were on mine. I told her she'd had a lucky escape - the other guests had been no fun at all. It was soon time for us to depart so we quickly swapped contact details.

Once we were back on board, I returned to my favourite spot, nodding to the captain, who was used to me coming and going. Vinh came to join me and we spoke for a long time about his life in Vietnam. He told me that his job was a dream but that it made it difficult for him to meet women. We were joined by Viet and the conversation about romance, or *lack* of it, continued. They were both single. Vinh complained women didn't take him seriously and Viet said he was too shy. They informed me they'd been friends for seven years. Their affection was clear in the way they teased each other. Vinh joked that maybe they'd turn gay and marry each other but Viet didn't look happy about that idea. As I sat with them, I laughed a lot. I'd developed better relationships with Vinh and the crew than with any of the other passengers.

At 10am, Vinh announced it was time to make spring rolls. He gave a demonstration and then told us to have a go. I went to take some gloves and one of the Swedish people snatched them away from me, making the others laugh. I ignored them. My spring roll turned out well. Vinh, who was collecting up the best ones, said mine was perfect and put it on his plate. At the start of lunch, he anonymously held up each one and asked people to vote for their favourite. Mine won joint-first place so I received a free drink. Once it had been cooked, I ate my spring roll and then enjoyed the chicken curry. Next, we were served white fish: it was so delicious that I asked Vinh if there was any more. He kindly gave me a whole plateful (it paid to be friendly with the guide).

At 11:30am, we were transferred to the port, where we waited for our bus back to the city. I wore my headphones but I didn't turn on my music, because as Karl Pilkington once said, "It's the next best thing to wearing a 'Do Not Disturb' sign." The bus pulled up and as we got on, the Swedes started complaining that people were sitting in *their* seats, meaning their seats from the day before. I shook my head in disbelief, glad I had two seats to myself near the front. We got back to Hanoi just before 5pm. Despite some of the company, I'd loved Halong Bay and the cruise, and I was pleased I'd treated myself.

Vietnam: Hanoi -
Happy Chinese New Year! (Part 2)

I was still full from the huge lunch on board the boat so I didn't feel the need to go out for dinner that night. Instead, I looked through my photos of Halong Bay and then had an early night. It was nice to drift off to sleep without the sound of an engine throbbing away.

The next day, I met up with Luca and we spent hours wandering and talking. More shops were open so life in Hanoi was returning to normal. We didn't go anywhere new to me but we went to the train tracks to wait for the 3:30pm train. With lots of others, we sat at a café, inches from the tracks. When people started sounding warning horns, we knew the train was approaching. Everyone stood, keeping themselves close to the wall. Of course, there were a few idiots who wanted selfies of themselves on the tracks, with the train approaching close behind. Some cut it a little close but everyone was out of the way by the time it sped through.

When the excitement was over, everyone left. Luca and I returned to the old quarter, taking some time to look in the shops and the street market. A stall selling bloody, chopped up fish turned my stomach and I felt sorry for the poor live ones, which awaited a similar fate. Luca and I said our goodbyes and I returned to the hostel. It had been lovely to have someone to walk around with and I was pleased we'd had the opportunity to meet up again.

I felt relieved to be leaving Hanoi. There were lots of lovely parts of the city, like the lakes and the gardens, but for me it was ruined by the sheer number of motorbikes. It was exhausting having to watch every step, which is why I'd mostly hidden myself away in the hostel. I hoped things would be quieter in Dong Hoi but first I would need to survive a night on the sleeper train...

Vietnam: Dong Hoi - Trying Not to Sleep on the Sleeper Train

10TH - 14TH FEBRUARY 2019

The train was to leave Hanoi at 10:20pm. As I waited at the station, I felt nervous but as I looked around, I noticed lots of fellow female travellers: I was confident I'd be in good company. I found Bed 10 in Coach 9 and was mildly impressed: the bed wasn't too uncomfortable and neither was it too short (someone had told me I'd be too tall for them). My good fortune didn't last though...

As people excitedly entered their carriages, I was surprised to find myself alone. I knew I'd taken one of the last tickets so I was sure I wouldn't be lucky enough to have the place entirely to myself. Sure enough, ten minutes before departure, an older man came in, taking the bed opposite. Immediately, I felt on edge. He sat staring at me, and then took his phone out to make a video call, waving it about and showing me off to whomever he was speaking with. Glaring, I put my headphones on and ignored him.

Once the train began moving, he hung up. I climbed into my thin sleeping bag liner, hiding my important possessions inside it with me. Keeping the light on and the door open, we both lay on our beds, facing each other, with less than a meter between us. Putting my head in my liner to block out some light, I tried sleeping. However, knowing I was alone with him, I couldn't relax. As I peeked through the thin fabric, I noticed he was still staring at me. He continued to do so for quite some time. Fed up, I moved so that my head was facing his feet.

Half an hour later, the train stopped and two younger men got on. They closed the door and climbed onto the two top bunks without saying a word. I had a mini meltdown and began crying quietly, sitting as close to the door as I could get. To help me feel better, I wedged it open with my flip flop. The men looked at me awkwardly. The younger ones shrugged it off and went to sleep but the older one kept staring. A few minutes later, he started waving his phone at me. He'd typed a message: 'Vietnam is safe and I am safe'. The sentiment was sweet but it didn't make me feel any better - that would only happen if he stopped staring! Turning out the light, he lay down and began alternating between playing with his phone and watching me. I decided I'd have to stay awake all night - I wouldn't risk dropping my guard. This was easier said than done because I was exhausted.

At 4am, he finally put down his phone and closed his eyes. A few minutes later, he was snoring loudly. Unable to keep my eyes open any longer, I fell into an uneasy sleep. At 7am, the man's alarm sounded. He got up, slapped my arm, and told me, 'Do not worry!' before disappearing.

An hour later, the guard announced that Dong Hoi was the next stop. Yawning, I grabbed the Green Turtle and left the train. As planned, a driver was waiting to take me to the Nam Long Plus Hotel. The kind owners allowed me to immediately go to my room. I drew the curtains and climbed into bed for a few hours.

Later in the day, I explored the quiet city of Dong Hoi. I was pleased to find a good running path along the river and noticed lots of pretty fishing boats on the water. Next to the river were the ruins of an old church, which had been bombed by the US on 11th February 1965: fifty-four years to the day. After researching it, I discovered that the city had almost been destroyed in the war. There were only a handful of original buildings left, including the church, a water tower and a gate. The town hadn't been rebuilt until 1990 but it had grown rapidly ever since.

Realising I hadn't eaten for twenty-four hours, I searched for a restaurant. However the city didn't seem as geared towards tourists as Hanoi so it was difficult to find one (if I'd been less of a fussy fart, I'm sure it would've been easier). Luckily, just as I was giving up, I came across a Korean grill by the river, where I stuffed my face with delicious pork belly and fries.

On Tuesday, I went on a tour of the stunning Phong Nha National Park. Our first stop was at Paradise Cave. We took a golf cart up most of the way and then climbed lots of steps to reach the entrance. Once we were in, there were yet more stairs, this time descending into the cave. It was extraordinary: incredible stalactites and stalagmites of all different shapes and sizes dominated the cave. Our guide let us explore alone, saying she preferred to let people make their own minds up about what each formation resembled. Being dirty-minded, I thought several looked like knobbly willies. I walked around with a man from Israel who had some *very* strange ideas of what each one resembled. I'd squint and turn my head but I still couldn't see what he saw.

Paradise Cave, or Thiên Đường Cave, is over thirty kilometres in length. Its height can reach over seventy metres and at its widest, it is one-hundred and fifty metres across. It was first discovered in 2005 by a local man when he was searching for rare wood to sell. The same man also discovered the biggest cave passage (by volume) in the world, Hang Sơn Đoòng. This cave is also in Phong Nha National Park but it is much more difficult to visit: only one company is allowed to offer tours and visitors are limited to five hundred per year. Oh, and it costs US$3000 per person for a four-day expedition.

After leaving the cave, we had lunch. We were served a large platter between five of us, including chicken, pork, ribs, rice, sticky rice and noodles - it was all amazing. In the afternoon, we drove to Phong Nha Cave. There was a twenty-minute boat ride along the river to reach it. I really enjoyed the journey; it was peaceful floating along the blue-green Song River, watching the fisherman work in their small boats.

As we entered the cave, the boat's engine was switched off and two women began paddling the boat, one at the back and one at the front. We passed through an area where the ceiling was very low, and then it opened up. It looked similar to Paradise Cave but it wasn't quite so spectacular. Phong Nha Cave is over seven kilometres long and has an underground river running through it. Tourists can only go 1500 metres into the cave before the boats have to turn around, so we weren't in there long. By the time we returned to shore, it was time to depart for Dong Hoi.

When I got back, I went running. Curious about what was on the opposite side of the river, I crossed over the bridge and ran to the end of the road. I found myself on a beautiful but deserted beach where I took a welcome little break. However, as it was getting close to sunset, I quickly headed for home. As I passed a group of young school girls, they started clapping, waving and cheering. I had no idea why but I smiled and waved back. Maybe they weren't used to seeing female runners. The only runners I'd seen in Dong Hoi were male and there hadn't even been many of those.

The next day, I took a free bike from the hotel. It wasn't long before I realised *why* it was free. I was halfway over the bridge when the chain completely fell off, landing on the road. Shaking my head, I put it in the basket and walked the bike back. It could've been worse - at least I was only a mile from the hotel.

I took a different bike and tried again. This time, the chain stayed on but the brakes didn't really work. I spent a while at the beach and then continued on. After re-crossing the bridge, I cycled north, past the hotel, and towards a different beach, which was also deserted. When I stopped to take a photo, an angry dog ran at me, barking madly. It got a bit close so I quickly climbed back on the bike. The bloody dog gave chase, running alongside me, growling. Thankfully, I was able to pedal faster than it could run and I managed to lose it. *That* was my signal to go home.

In the late afternoon I walked around town. I kept an eye out for food, but little of interest was on offer. I ended up eating at the hotel as it was easier. While I was there, I began chatting to a lovely retired couple from New Zealand. We sat talking and laughing for a couple of hours, until it was time for bed. The next day I'd be taking the train south to Hue – thankfully I'd be travelling during the day so there would be no repeat of my sleeper train ordeal.

Vietnam: Hue - Enter the Dragon

At 8:40am, a taxi arrived to take me to the train station. Ray and Sylvia, a Canadian couple from the hotel would also be travelling on the same train so we shared a taxi. The journey was very comfortable and the three and a half hours passed quickly.

When we reached Hue, I met up with the Canadians again and we looked for a taxi. We didn't have to look hard. Once we'd informed them of our destination, we were told that it would cost 150,000 dong. This was ridiculous as the journey was just over a mile. Ray said we'd only pay 100,000 and the taxi driver happily agreed. As our luggage was being put in the car, I told Ray that my hostel had told me a taxi should cost *40,000* at the most. Negotiations resumed. We got the driver down to 80,000 but he wouldn't budge any further. Taking our bags out of the boot, we walked off. It took all of ten seconds before a different driver pulled up and said he'd take us for 50,000.

We all got out at the Canadians' hotel and I waved them goodbye. The Bon Ami Hostel was nearby so I was happy to walk the rest of the way. I located the hostel on the map app but the hostel wasn't where it should've been. I was confused - this had never happened before. I was also hot and *really* needed to pee. Hugging the Green Turtle in my arms, I wandered uselessly. Eventually, I popped into a travel agency to ask for help and the lady there kindly called my hostel. A few minutes later, someone came to get me and led me to the right location, which was down a narrow alley. I checked in and was shown to my private room.

Before long, I was walking around town. Hue was bigger than Dong Hoi but not as busy as Hanoi. People seemed to honk their horns more though (it was a sound I would grow weary of). To my relief, cafes, restaurants and grocery stores were plentiful so I had lots of dining choices. After lunch, I walked along the Perfume River to scout out a possible running route. The riverside was beautiful and rammed with gardens, ponds and sculptures. Handily, the whole route was runnable, on scooter-free footpaths, so I decided I'd try it on Saturday.

On Friday morning, I ate my hostel breakfast and then collected my bicycle from a company called Hue Smile. Fed up with crap bikes, I treated myself to a decent mountain bike, complete with helmet. Getting out of the city was tricky as there was so much traffic but I soon turned right onto a quiet side road. From there I followed a narrow road that hugged the river. Happily cycling along, I passed colourful shrines and temples, small markets and lots of old ladies in pointed hats (the traditional Vietnamese kind). I didn't see a single other tourist so I felt like I was seeing the authentic Vietnam.

As usual, locals stared when I passed by. I wasn't sure why. Hue was full of tourists so I couldn't have been *that* unusual a sight. However, even though cycling was supposed to have been a popular thing to do in Hue, I'd only ever seen one other tourist doing it, so maybe I really was a rarity. Lots of people smiled when they saw me though, particularly old people, and I always gave them a big smile in return. I especially liked it when old, toothless men laughed and waved - they reminded me of my dad as he was always happy to see me.

After seven miles of cycling, I reached an ornate bridge. The pretty wooden structure was over two hundred years old and had two railings with balconies. After taking some photos, I got back on the bike and continued on. The paths after the bridge were amazing, taking me past vibrant paddy fields and small streams. It was incredibly beautiful and peaceful.

The peace didn't last long though. Cycling to the Royal Tomb of Khai Dinh, I had to use some main roads. As I came to a busy junction, I stopped, deciding it would be safer to get off the bike to cross. It didn't work out well. As I was getting off, my foot got caught on the high crossbar and I ended up with the bike on me instead of me on the bike. I fell onto the road on my left side, the side of my right knee crashing painfully against the crossbar. People around me gasped. Mortified, I untangled myself from the bike and stood up. Ignoring my pain, I crossed the road, hopped back on the bike and pedalled away as quickly as possible, only stopping when I was alone on a quiet country road again. Luckily, apart from a bruised knee and a few scratches, there was no real damage.

Without further incident, I reached the tomb, which was heaving with tourists. After paying to park my bicycle, I climbed some steps to the top tier of the site. The buildings and statues were quite impressive but they were nothing compared to the views of the surrounding countryside – it was stunning. After a little pause to take it all in, I returned to the bike.

This time I cycled to an abandoned water park. It was only three miles away so it didn't take long to reach the turning. The road leading to it was very scenic, passing through woodland on both sides. It ended at a pink building with a 'security guard' and a sign saying 'No Visitors'. I thought maybe it really was closed, that perhaps it had been demolished. Not wanting to turn back without checking, I approached the guard, hopeful he'd tell me a price and let me in (this is usually how things work when visiting abandoned places). Without me saying a word, he said, "20,000 dong." I paid and he waved me though, signalling for me to lift my bike over the barrier.

Once I was in, I cycled along the road until I reached the lake. I was officially inside the Hồ Thuỷ Tiên Water Park. The park had opened to the public in 2004, when it had only been partially completed, but it had never worked out financially and had closed just a few years later. At the centre of the park, in a large lake, was the main attraction: a giant, three-storey dragon-shaped aquarium. Sharks, fish and crocodiles had once been housed there but when it had closed, the crocodiles had been left behind. They used to roam freely about the site, long after its closure. Visitors had seen them frequently, making it a dangerous place to visit. Eventually, after pressure from the WWF and PETA, the government moved the animals to a proper wildlife park. I didn't risk getting too close to the water though as I couldn't *quite* be sure what was lurking under the surface.

While I was there, I saw a few other backpacker-types coming and going but it was mostly deserted. I preferred it to the crowded tomb, although the park was a tomb in itself: a once great dragon was slowly decomposing, being reclaimed by nature. Crossing the footpath, I entered the dragon. I climbed up the stairs, through the ribcage of the beast, and then sat inside its toothy jaws. I took a few moments to enjoy the view from the dragon's mouth and tried to envision what the place would've looked like when it had been bustling with excited visitors. I then found myself wondering if the whole world would one day look like the derelict park (happy thoughts!). After taking a few selfies with the tripod and remote control that Tom had bought me, I walked around the edge of the lake, finding some mouldy water slides and a derelict amphitheatre to photograph.

By the time I finished exploring, it was 3pm and I was hot, thirsty and hungry. I cycled back to town, stopping for a cold coke along the way, and returned my bike to the shop. In total, I'd cycled over thirty miles. As I walked back to the hostel, I thought about what a fun day I'd had – it made me want to rent a bicycle again the following day.

Bleary-eyed, I went running at 6:30am the next morning. It was hard work and I had no energy, but I managed to plod along for five miles. After breakfast, I picked up another bicycle. Wanting some tranquility, I returned to the river and cycled back along the paddy fields for a couple of hours. I then cycled around the outside of the citadel in the centre of Hue.

I didn't do much that evening. I suddenly felt incredibly lonely. I couldn't even drag myself out to eat. I was often fine during the days but the evenings were sometimes difficult. Few of the places I'd stayed in had been sociable so I'd not met that many people. I guessed it was the price I had to pay for solo travelling but it didn't make things easier. I didn't know it then, but it was the start of a downward spiral…

Vietnam: Hoi An - City of Lanterns

17TH - 22ND FEBRUARY 2019

"Traveling is a brutality. It forces you to trust strangers and to lose sight of all that familiar comfort of home and friends. You are constantly off balance. Nothing is yours except the essential things: air, sleep, dreams, sea, the sky - all things tending towards the eternal or what we imagine of it." (Cesare Pavese)

At 8:30am on Sunday, I was picked up from the hostel by a private car. My driver, Johnny, was to take me to Hoi An, making some scenic stops along the way. At fifty pounds, it hadn't been the cheapest method of transportation, but I'd wanted to enjoy travelling on the twenty-one kilometer Hải Vân Pass, a winding mountain road that connected Hue with Da Nang. The first stop was at a large lake, Lập An Lagoon, famous for oyster farming. It was interesting to watch the people work, using rubber tyres to raise the oysters. Traditionally, they'd use bamboo or wooden stakes but tyres were cheaper. I later read that the millions of tyres in the lake were actually polluting it and causing the oysters to die.

Leaving the lake, we started the twisting climb up the Hải Vân mountain road, providing us with amazing views of Lăng Cô beach below. The pass was very scenic but also crowded with bus-loads of tourists and motorbikes. At the summit, Johnny stopped so I could take photos and explore some ruins. Historically, Hải Vân was the division between the Champa and Dai Viet Kingdoms, and these derelict gate-like structures had once been used as a border crossing.

It didn't take long to wind our way down the mountain again and we were soon at our final stop, Marble Mountain. Johnny showed me the steps up and once I'd paid, I climbed to the top. As well as offering good views, there were some pretty caves, temples and pagodas. However, as there were so many tourists, I soon returned to the car.

At 1pm, we arrived at the Thu Bon Riverside Homestay. Ye, my host, was lovely - she even upgraded me to a bigger room with a large balcony overlooking the river. As I was feeling down, I didn't leave the room for the rest of the day. I wanted to go home and felt worried by how tearful I was feeling. After having chats with Tom and my friends from home, I decided to try and improve things. I would get a good night's sleep (a barking dog had kept me awake a lot in Hue) and the next day, I'd eat three proper meals for a change and take lots of photos (an activity that usually made me very happy).

I stuck with the plan. I had a solid eight hours of sleep and a filling breakfast of eggs, baguette and passion fruit. I then meditated on the balcony before walking into town. The ancient town of Hoi An is a UNESCO world heritage site. To explore the old town, I needed to buy an entrance ticket for 120,000 dong. Hoi An was stunning and full of shops, markets and cafes. Keeping my promise to eat more, I went to the market, where I bought some traditional bread topped with pork, a bland banana pancake, a bag of mangosteens (a delicious fruit) and a strange mango 'cake' which was full of nuts.

As I was taking photos of the colourful boats, a young man asked if I wanted to go for a boat ride along the river. I said no at first, especially when he said it would cost 200,000 dong. However, I told him I'd go for 100,000 and he told me to hop in. It was very peaceful and provided the perfect opportunity to take photos from a different perspective.

Back on dry land, I treated myself to a foot massage. Three ladies had been sat outside so I was surprised when a young man of about eighteen years old came over. As usual, I enjoyed people-watching from my chair. My favourite person to watch was the security guy. The street being closed to vehicles, his job was to prevent cyclists or scooters from using the road. He sat on a child's red plastic chair in the middle of the road, looking bored, but his expression turned to one of delight whenever he got to blow his whistle at a rule-breaker. He made me smile quite a few times.

After my massage, I walked by the river, where I spoke with a German woman. She told me that the Lantern Festival would be held that evening. Wanting to see it, I had dinner and then waited by the river. Once the sun set, vendors began selling small paper lanterns, which were floated downstream. Hoi An was at its most beautiful at night as the lanterns were the only real source of light, giving the place a warm atmosphere. Lots of people bought lanterns and released them into the water. It was a pretty spectacle but I couldn't help wondering where all the lanterns ended up.

By 9pm, I was tired and teary so I walked home: I couldn't be sad if I was sleeping. Along the way, the only thing that made me smile was the warbling cries of karaoke blasting out from several households. It was such a popular pastime in Vietnam but the whole time I was there, I never heard a single person who could carry a tune. Maybe practice doesn't *always* make perfect. Still, it sounded like they were having more fun than me.

On Tuesday morning, I woke up early to run. I followed a path that ran partly next to the river, which was blanketed in a thin veil of fog. Considering the early hour and the lack of sunshine, it was still very humid and the air was filled with smoke from where people were burning their rubbish out in the street. It didn't make for ideal running conditions.

Once I'd showered, I sat outside for breakfast and ate my mangosteens and a banana pancake. Another guest joined me and we talked about our travels. While we were chatting, a loud voice blared out from one of the millions of large speakers around Vietnam. I asked if she knew what they were talking about. She said she'd researched it and had discovered they were government information messages, encouraging people to take action such as getting vaccinations etc. They were usually followed by a jaunty national tune. They'd originally started during the war so that important information could be passed onto people, but once the war was over, the announcements had continued. The older generations apparently enjoyed it as it was a tradition they were used to, and it helped them to feel safe and informed. However, with the internet now commonplace, the need for the announcements may cease entirely in the future.

At 2pm, I was picked up for a trip to the My Son ruins, a group of partially ruined Hindu temples and towers, built by the kings of Champa between the 4th and 14th centuries. There had been some earlier (and cheaper) tour options, but being fussy, I wanted a smaller group and a later time slot so that the crowds would be minimal. The ruins were an hour's drive out of town and when we got there it was pleasantly quiet. The guide told us lots of information about the site, showing us the museum, and then we took a large golf buggy to the ruins. We had time to look around a little before being pulled away to watch a traditional dance. However, I sneakily stayed behind to take some people-free photos.

Once everyone came back, we explored the ruins and then returned to the minivan. However, we didn't drive all the way: halfway back to Hoi An, we boarded a boat. We were supposed to enjoy a sunset cruise but the sun disappeared behind a bank of thick clouds so it was a bit of an anti-climax. While we travelled on the river, we were given a *banh mi* sandwich - a Hoi An speciality. The sandwich, served in a hot, fresh baguette, was full of pork, pate and vegetables. Some of my vegetables accidentally slipped out but I happily ate the rest. The journey ended at a night market. We had the option to stay but I didn't fancy a long walk home in the dark. I returned to the guesthouse with the van instead.

On Wednesday, I woke up feeling depressed. Having felt low on and off for a few weeks, I thought maybe it was time to change my plans and swap my planned month in Sri Lanka for a month at home. The idea made me feel better in some ways but it also made me feel I'd be failing. It wasn't that I was miserable *all* the time, I wasn't. I loved seeing new places, but sometimes I'd be overcome by loneliness. I turned to Facebook for advice and my friend Iain messaged me. We had a good chat, discussing my options, and decided that as I was lonely, perhaps I needed to make the effort to talk more with people at home. It seemed a simple solution and it would be cheaper than flying home.

In town, I made an effort to talk to more people and started randomly chatting with other solo people. It was nice to be reminded that I wasn't the only one who was alone. I also bumped into an older Scottish couple who'd been on my trip the day before, so I had a little chat with them too. Just as I was walking by the river, a man stopped me to ask if one of his Japanese students could practise her English with me. Of course, I said yes. It was a bit embarrassing for both of us, with ten people stood around watching, but she did very well. Afterwards, her friends all clapped proudly.

Once I'd eaten, I cycled to a street of clothes shops. I found myself admiring an eye-catching dress. A lady approached to ask if I wanted to try it on. It was too small around the bust but I liked it. Clothing at the shop was tailor-made within twenty-four hours so she took my measurements and told me to come back the next day to try it on. I was about to head back to my bike when I thought that some trousers would be handy. I could never find trousers of a good fit at home so some tailor-made ones would be perfect. Somehow, she convinced me that I should have *two* pairs, so I left the shop seventy pounds lighter.

In the afternoon, I cycled to the beach. The journey was better than the destination as I took a peaceful route through paddy fields. Not that the beach was horrible, there were just too many people selling tourist tat, so I couldn't get any peace. As I cycled home, I passed lots of locals; I always gave them a big smile and almost all of them smiled back - these brief interactions, no matter how small, always made me feel warmer inside.

At 10:30am the next day, I was due for a fitting at the tailors. I told this to Ye, and she looked horrified that I'd shopped at the *Central Market*, telling me the clothes would be of a bad quality. Her reaction was worrying, so I was nervous as I inspected my new purchases. To me they seemed fine and the stitching looked tidy and secure. A few bits needed adjusting however, so I had to return later. While I was having lunch, I saw the Canadian couple from Hue again. Like me, they were going to Ho Chi Minh City the next day. Sadly we wouldn't be on the same flight; otherwise we could've shared a taxi. By 2pm, everything was ready. When I got back to the accommodation, I nervously showed them to Ye. Thankfully, she was impressed and told me they were of a *good* quality – phew!

Vietnam: Ho Chi Minh City - Finding My Mojo Again

On Friday morning, a taxi came to take me to the airport and I said goodbye to Ye, her lovely family and to Hoi An. In the car, I thought about my idea of going home but it didn't feel like the right thing to do. As my running buddy Emma had told me, my travels were like a marathon and I'd clearly hit the dreaded 'wall'. Therefore I had to power through, even if I was homesick. I would never give up halfway through a marathon so giving up on my travels was not an option.

I reached Ho Chi Minh City at 1pm. My pre-ordered taxi was waiting and just after 2pm, I checked into the City Poshtel Hostel, which unusually, I had to enter via a mini-mart. As I lay in my capsule bed, in a twenty-person dorm, I realised I felt better. Maybe a change of scene had helped. Ho Chi Minh City was different to Hanoi, less hectic. The motorbike situation wasn't *nearly* as bad as I'd expected and crossing roads, although still a challenge, was manageable. Drivers even stopped at red lights! However, I knew I had to be careful with my belongings as theft and bag snatching was common. I'd been warned about it by both other travellers and locals, so I took precautions. I wore my rucksack on my front, carrying as few valuables as possible, and if I needed to use my phone, I made sure my back was against a wall or a building, or even better, that I was inside a shop.

In the evening, hoping to make a connection, I sat in the social area. It wasn't long before eye contact was made. Darting towards me, my new friend licked my ankles and then jumped onto my lap. Before you get too concerned, I should tell you that my new friend was a cute, crazy, kitten. While I was laughing at the excitable ball of fluff, a man came downstairs and began playing guitar. Usually, this would annoy me (bad musicians were plentiful in hostels) but this guy had talent.

A few people were milling about and one woman caught my eye. I smiled, making some inane comment. We got chatting and I discovered that her name was Mariana. She was my age and was from Brazil. Discovering that I'd travelled south, she asked if I had any advice, as she would soon be going north to Hanoi. I told her all about Hoi An and on my recommendation, she booked a room at Ye's place.

Mariana said she was going out for dinner, so feeling brave, I asked if she fancied some company. Thankfully she said yes, so we freshened up and left the hostel. We walked down a famous backpacking street, which was flooded with bars and restaurants, all competing to see who could play the loudest music. Mariana suggested somewhere quieter so we turned a corner and found a small bar where we ordered food and drinks. We were chatting away over cider when a voice asked, "Is that a Surrey accent I hear?" A cheerful guy, Phil, introduced himself - he was from Chertsey of all places (only two miles from my home town). He was very friendly so we went over to sit with him. He told us he worked for a large company, sourcing nuts (a few inappropriate jokes were made about this). Over the next couple of hours, the three of us had a good laugh and I marveled again at how different I felt. Once Phil left, we got talking to a solo German woman, Marion, who we invited to join us. She was also heading north, so we discussed travel plans. By the time we left the bar, it was late. Having had three ciders, I was a little tipsy. I was happy though. An evening out with good company was just what I'd needed.

The next day, I chatted with Mariana over breakfast. It wasn't long before the kitten jumped on me. While Mariana tapped away at her laptop, booking flights and hotels, I played with my furry friend. It seemed comfortable on my lap and we ended up sitting together for a couple of hours. Eventually it woke up and moved behind me, sitting on the back of the sofa. From there, it batted my hair about, tangling its paws in it. The man on reception, whose kitten it was, just laughed, shaking his head.

At midday, Mariana asked if I fancied lunch, so we went to a small vegan restaurant. I wasn't sure what the 'chicken' in my chicken fried rice was, but judging by my tummy ache that evening, it was probably soy-based. Mariana needed a new phone so we visited a couple of mobile phone shops until she found the right one. As I'd be taking a Giant Ibis bus to Cambodia on Monday, I wanted to locate the bus stop. Thankfully it was only around the corner from the hostel so I wouldn't need to lug the Green Turtle too far.

Just before 4pm, we returned to the hostel and Mariana collected her luggage and took a taxi to the airport. I thought I'd feel lonely when she left but I didn't. Her company had been enough to allow my loneliness to dissipate and left me content in my own company once again.

On Sunday morning, my last full day in Vietnam, I considered going for a run, but it was too hot and the only decent routes were a couple of miles away. I decided a few days off running wouldn't hurt. While I ate breakfast, I looked at the list of popular things to do in Ho Chi Minh City. I didn't want to see more temples or go anywhere crowded so I settled on visiting the one place I felt I *should* see - the War Remnants Museum. It was a sobering experience. While I read about vile torture techniques and the effects of Agent Orange, and looked at horrific photographs of deformed children, screaming women and dead bodies, my stomach turned and tears ran down my face. I didn't understand how people could do such terrible things. I made sure I visited all the exhibits but I was glad to leave.

Cambodia: Phnom Penh - Travels on a Tuk Tuk

25TH - 28TH FEBRUARY 2019

Bright and early on Monday morning, I was up and ready to take the 8am bus to Phnom Penh. I was walking to the bus station when I turned my ankle on the uneven pavement. Limping, I cursed my carelessness. While it began to swell, I could only hope that I hadn't damaged it too badly. The Giant Ibis bus wasn't fancy but there was plenty of leg room and my seat was comfortable. Once we were on our way, our passports were collected so they could be prepared for the border crossing into Cambodia. At 10:30am, we arrived at Moc Bai, a land border of Vietnam. Leaving the bus, we entered the main building, where we were called up one by one. The process was easy: I handed over a copy of my e-visa and my passport was stamped. Once everyone was through, we returned to the bus.

We drove for all of thirty seconds and then got out again to go through the Cambodian border at Bavet. Clutching my passport and e-visa, I approached the desk. The Cambodian immigration officer didn't say a word as he was too preoccupied with cleaning out his ear wax with a cotton bud. Sixty-eight awkward seconds later (I counted), he finally acknowledged my presence with a grunt. I wasn't sure how I managed to suppress a snigger. Once his ear was clean, he carefully inspected the cotton bud and put it in the bin. Silently, he then took my visa, stamped my passport and looking bored, waved me away.

At 3pm, we reached Phnom Penh. I hopped off the bus (literally, as my ankle was hurting) and was soon swamped with tuk tuk drivers. The guy who spoke to me first told me a taxi would cost five dollars. The hostel had told me to only pay two (which is all I had) so I just laughed and shook my head. He unsuccessfully tried four, and then three. I told him I was happy to walk (I wasn't) but thankfully, he quickly agreed to two dollars.

The hostel was only a mile away so we were at the SLA Boutique Hostel within a couple of minutes. I checked in and then collapsed on the bed. However, I couldn't rest for long as I needed to leave the hostel to find an ATM. As I walked round, I didn't know what to make of Phnom Penh. It was dirtier and dustier than the Vietnamese cities I'd been to and tuk tuks ruled the roads. I couldn't say I hated it; I was simply ambivalent towards it.

Hungry, I went over to a restaurant with helpfully labelled pictures on the window. A surprised woman handed me a menu, and that's when I noticed the other 'diners'. I'd clearly gate-crashed some sort of prostitution establishment. Older white men sat with their arms around young Cambodian women, a couple winking at me sleazily. One guy approached the bar yelling, "Daddy's home - who wants me?" It made me feel sick. Too self-conscious to walk away, I sat at a table facing the street, far away from the creepy men. Needless to say, I ate *very* quickly and got the hell out of there. The experience left a bad taste in my mouth and although I'm sure they wouldn't want my pity, I felt sorry for the women who were in such a position.

When I returned to the hostel, I put my name on the board to go to the killing fields the next day. I then had a shower and slapped on a cold patch, hoping it would help my swollen and painful ankle. Unfortunately, I hadn't been able to find ice in the local shops, so the patch and some ibuprofen would have to do.

The next morning, my ankle was less swollen and a little less painful, but it still made me jump in pain whenever I moved it in the wrong way. It would probably take a couple of weeks to heal but at least I was able to walk on it - it could've been worse. By the time I went downstairs for my complimentary French toast, there were other names on the board. I was relieved I'd be having some company. At

9:30am, I went to reception and met Meik (from Amsterdam) and Fabian (from Berlin). The hostel organised us a tuk tuk, which between us, cost eighteen dollars for the day.

Our first stop was at the Tuol Sleng Genocide Museum (also known at S-21). Between 12,000 and 20,000 people (including doctors, teachers, ministers, engineers, foreigners and monks) had been imprisoned there during the rule of the Khmer Rouge. Khmer Rouge was a Cambodian communist party which ruled between 1975 and 1979: its leader was Pol Pot. The party destroyed anything to do with religion, education and the arts, and made fellow Cambodians give up their land and homes. The regime especially hated intelligent people as they were worried they'd question the party's political ideology and lead a rebellion. These were therefore some of the first people to be imprisoned. During their reign, Khmer Rouge killed almost a quarter of Cambodia's population. It was almost unbelievable that it had happened so recently - the killings had been going on for the first two years of my life. Then again, terrible things are always happening somewhere in the world so I shouldn't have been too surprised.

There were only twelve confirmed survivors from the prison and I was able to speak with one of them briefly. He'd been a child when the Khmer Rouge regime had ended and had survived along with his brother. Their mother had been killed. Other survivors included painters, who'd only stayed alive as they'd been able to draw accurate portraits of Pol Pots. Unfortunately for them, their skills had been discovered later on, *after* they'd suffered cruelly at the hands of the torturers.

The list of rules for prisoners alone upset me; I couldn't begin to imagine how terrified people (men, women and even children) would've been when they'd been brought here to be 'smashed' (a popular phrase used by the Khmer Rouge to describe how they'd torture and kill their enemies). Inhabitants of the prison were beaten and tortured on a daily basis. Blood stains were still visible on the floor and walls. What really got to me were the scratch marks on the walls where desperate prisoners had clawed away at the paint. Inhumane torture methods were described in detail, complete with illustrations. Once enough information (often false, and given only to escape the endless torture) had been extracted from the prisoners, they were of no further use to the Khmer Rouge and were sent to the killing fields, where they were executed and buried in mass graves.

After two hours, we left the museum and the tuk tuk took us fifteen kilometres south of the city. We had lunch and then entered the Choeung Ek Killing Field (one of about three hundred such sites throughout Cambodia). We were provided with an audio guide. I was glad that it wasn't too crowded with tourists, as it meant there were plenty of quiet places to sit and listen to the stories. A large stupa stood in the centre of the site, housing the skulls and bones of the poor souls who'd been executed. As expected, it was a harrowing place. Khmer Rouge had transported prisoners there by truck and they were immediately killed. The regime didn't want to pay for expensive bullets, so people were often killed by being smashed over the head. The victims, sometimes still half-alive, were then pushed into the mass grave and burned.

Coming to a large tree, the audio guide explained that a speaker had once been placed there. Loud music was played to disguise the screams of the executions so that when people arrived, they wouldn't suspect what was about to happen and start fighting. The audio guide played an example of the music, overlapped with the sound of a generator (used to power the lights). I was informed me that this would've been the final thing people heard before they were killed.

A different tree's story was even more dreadful: babies of prisoners had been killed there, having been smashed against the trunk until they were dead. The rationale was that if they were dead, children could not take revenge for the death of their parents when they grew up. In the words of the Khmer Rouge, 'To dig up the grass, one must also dig up the roots'. The tree was decorated with messages of sorrow and hundreds of colourful bracelets, so I added one of mine to it in remembrance. Once I'd listened to every audio track, I met up again with Meik and Fabian and we returned to the hostel. Knowing more about its history, I found myself developing a deeper appreciation for Cambodia and its people.

On Wednesday, I took a tuk tuk to the Moha Montrei Pagoda. I enjoyed travelling by tuk tuk and found it interesting how nobody ever seemed to get road rage, despite the terrible driving. Moha Montrei was a small complex with a few streets running through it and a temple. Once I'd seen the main buildings and taken some photos, there was little else to do, so I walked back to the hostel.

After a short break, I decided to visit Wat Phnom Park. I was just walking through reception when I bumped into Fabian, who asked if I fancied some company. I did, so we took a tuk tuk with the same driver who'd taken me out earlier. The park, surrounding a small hill, was very pretty and had a temple at the summit. We walked around taking photos and then entered the temple where a group of men were playing cheerful traditional music. We enjoyed some fresh mango as we walked along the river and then ate pork and rice at a small restaurant filled with locals.

A little later, Fabian asked if I wanted ice cream. Of course, my answer was yes, so we walked to a nearby shopping centre to buy some at a little kiosk. While we were there, we also ordered fries from a deserted fast food restaurant and ate them while enjoying the views from the fifth floor. After a trip to the market, we returned to the hostel, where I started packing up the Green Turtle. Fabian had decided to join me in Siem Reap and would meet me at the hostel there the following day – I was so excited to have someone to tour Angkor Wat with!

Cambodia: Siem Reap - Angkor What?

28TH FEBRUARY - 4TH MARCH 2019

At 9am on Thursday, I was collected from the hostel in Phnom Penh and taken by shuttle bus to the Giant Ibis station. My ankle felt a little better and I could even see some ankle bone through the swelling.

The bus journey to Siem Reap was to take just over six hours: six very *long* hours. An American man sat next to me and his Thai wife sat behind us. The bus moved off at 9:45am so I put my music on and gazed out of the window (I always booked a window seat where possible). Ten minutes out of the city, Captain America took out his phone and leaned over me to take a photo out of the window. Expecting it to be a one-off, I didn't think much of it, but no, he wanted to film the *whole* trip. I wasn't sure why he felt the need to document the journey so thoroughly, as the scenery wasn't exactly pretty: Cambodia had a big litter problem and it was *all over* the roadside, sometimes in huge piles. He didn't get the message when I coughed and raised an eyebrow, so when he started his fifth video, I said, "Don't mind me." Narrowing his eyes, he carried on. By this point, I was getting frustrated: having his arm in front of my face for long periods of time was too much. I asked him to stop invading my personal space and keep his arms to himself. He didn't like this and started ranting at me. I had no idea what he was saying as I had my headphones on but he did stop recording.

At 4pm, we arrived in Siem Reap. My friend Janine had told me about a lovely tuk tuk driver (Nhik Sophea) and via Facebook, I'd arranged for him to pick me up. As promised, he was waiting. Our first stop was at the 1953 Siem Reap Hostel. I checked in and asked if Fabian had arrived. They told me he had and pointed up to where he was just leaving his room. Once we'd swapped bus journey stories, Nhik took

Fabian and me to the Angkor Wat ticket office, where after 5pm, we could buy tickets for the following day. Angkor Wat is a sprawling temple complex, built in the 12th century: it's one of the largest religious monuments in the world. Originally built as a Hindu temple, it was gradually converted to a Buddhist temple at the end of the 12th century.

At the ticket office, we purchased one-day tickets for Friday. As it was close to the end of the day, we were allowed in to watch the sunset. Nhik took us to the Pre Rup temple and we climbed to the top (not easily done with a dodgy ankle) where there were lots of other tourists. We managed to find a suitable place to stand but the sunset was a little underwhelming. The journey back into town was wonderful though: I loved feeling the cool breeze on my skin and listening to the song of the crickets and cicadas. People were so friendly and smiled as we drove past. If we waved at kids, they always smiled and waved back. We felt very welcome.

The next morning, Nhik picked us up at 4:30am. It was chilly as the tuk tuk raced through the dark streets. We made it to the main Angkor Wat temple early so we could find a suitable place to sit. The moat's water was somewhat depleted from the dry weather so I sat at the water's edge on the damp mud. Fabian chose to sit further back where it was cleaner and more comfortable (he was less bothered about getting good photos and joked that he'd just steal some nice ones from the internet). I sat next to a friendly chemistry professor named Juan. We passed the time by talking about our travels and careers. As we spoke, the night sky grew progressively lighter, until it was a very pale pink. The sunrise was not as spectacular as we'd hoped for so I said goodbye to Juan, who hurried off to climb the largest of Angkor Wat's towers, and rejoined Fabian.

We were eager to see the famous temple (Ta Prohm) from the Tomb Raider movie (only because I liked the look of the trees at that one), so we didn't hang about at Angkor Wat. Nhik pulled up at the Banteay

Kdei temple and we crossed the road to watch the sun continue rising from a lake opposite. It had been above the horizon for a while but the pale sky had turned golden. It was much more beautiful than what we'd seen earlier. Once we'd taken a few photos, we explored the quiet temple for a while, enjoying having the place to ourselves. However, we were eager to visit Ta Prohm so we quickly moved on.

Ta Phrom was busy but not nearly as chaotic as it would become in an hour's time. We found the main sites, including the rooty trees growing out of the crumbling buildings and took lots of pictures. It was great to have someone to share the experience with and of course, take some silly photos with.

We spent the next few hours looking around different temples. We took breaks when we could, once in the shade at the top of a temple and once on a forest path, where we stopped to enjoy the sound of cicadas. The temples were *all* amazing but after a while, they began to blur into one. As we walked along the path to yet *another* temple, looking up at *another* set of steep steps, we shook our heads. We were templed out. The heat didn't help - once midday arrived, the temperature soared uncomfortably. At our request, Nhik returned us to the hostel and we said our goodbyes. We then relaxed in the pool.

In the evening, Fabian bought a bus ticket to Bangkok and then we explored Pub Street and the night market. We saw some crispy fried tarantulas and scorpions for sale but neither of us fancied them - we went for the more pedestrian pork on a stick instead, from a popular BBQ stall, and then some rolled ice cream. Afterwards, we sat at the hostel, sharing photos and chatting. We also enjoyed the company of a young boy whose parents ran the hostel. He was energetic and completely bonkers. Cambodian kids were great: the boys in particular were generally lively and cheeky.

On Saturday morning, we sat by the pool to eat Nutella and bread, and then looked around the city. There wasn't a great deal to see so we walked by the river and then sat at the park. I was surprised to see that the trees there were full of squeaking, hanging bats - it was an interesting sight. As we sat on a marble bench, we watched a gardener watering the grass and trees. He seemed to mostly water himself though, laughing crazily. For the rest of the afternoon, we relaxed at the pool while Fabian plotted his next move and I booked myself onto a bicycle tour for the following day. In the evening, we visited Pub Street again for dinner and then walked around, stopping to buy some rolled ice cream. Before disappearing to our rooms, we went to a bar for a goodbye drink. I was sad we'd be going our separate ways as I'd had so much fun with Fabian; he'd made me laugh so much. Siem Reap wouldn't have been the same without him.

At 7am on Sunday, I hugged Fabian goodbye. I then walked to the Grasshopper Adventures shop. The countryside tour was very low on numbers: including the guide, there were only three of us. Over the course of the next four hours, we cycled fifteen miles on dirt tracks, sand, tarmac and gravel. It was hard work. Along the way we visited a market, where lots of fresh fruit, vegetables, fish and meat were sold. We then went to a mushroom farm where we learned about how mushrooms were cultivated. Whilst we were there, I met two of the cutest kids. I took a few photos of them and they were eager to see the results. Other stops included paddy fields, a Buddhist monastery and a lotus flower farm. It was all beautiful and interesting and I felt I was seeing the 'proper' Cambodia, not just the touristic parts.

I relaxed for the remainder of the day, only going out for dinner, where I sat talking to a newly-retired couple from Newcastle. It was weird being there without Fabian. I missed his company and I struggled to find the cheap rolled ice cream without him there to lead the way! The next day, I would return to Phnom Penh for one night, before flying to Singapore and then on to Australia. Although I was sad to be leaving Cambodia, I was excited at the thought of seeing Katie again.

Phnom Penh & Singapore - Fleeting Visits

4TH – 6TH MARCH 2019

I returned to Phnom Penh on the 9:45am Giant Ibis bus. For once, there were no dramas: the bus was half-empty and nobody sat next to me. At 3:30pm, I arrived at the bus station and a tuk tuk returned me to the SLA Boutique Hostel. Feeling tired, I did little else that day. I ate at the hostel, edited and uploaded my photos and then had an early night.

On Tuesday morning, with my belly full of banana pancakes, I was taken through a sea of traffic to the airport. My flight to Singapore arrived thirty early. I collected the Green Turtle and took the MRT to Kallang station. I'd chosen to stay at the funky Spacepod@SG Hostel. With the blue lighting, futuristic design and various buttons and controls, it was like going to bed on a spaceship.

After my free hostel breakfast, I met Juan (who I'd met at Angkor Wat). He and I walked by the river and through some lovely peaceful parks. We talked a lot about our careers and travel, and I encouraged him to try hostels and guest houses instead of always staying in expensive hotels. He seemed surprised by how cheap my nice accommodation had been in Cambodia and wanted to try it. It was great to catch up and I hoped we'd meet again, when Juan came to lecture in the UK (we did).

At 11am, Juan left to teach, so I went in search of a cheap hawker market. I couldn't to find one so I tried my luck at the shopping mall instead, but I could only find expensive restaurants and crowded fast food chains. Neither option was appealing. However, as I passed the Raffles Hospital, I saw a poster for a food court in the basement. I took the escalator down and was delighted to find myself surrounded by cheap food kiosks. I ordered chicken and rice and the cheerful lady serving even gave me discount.

In the late afternoon, I lugged the Green Turtle back to the MRT station and returned to the airport, ready for my flight to Melbourne. Although I would miss many things about Asia (the banana pancakes, the fresh mango, the satay chicken and the lovely people), I was more than ready to swap them for some adventures in Australia.

Australia: Melbourne - Melbored

7TH - 10TH MARCH 2019

I'd booked a night flight to Melbourne to save me paying for accommodation for one night. However, it turned out to be a terrible idea because I never slept on planes. We landed at 6:30am and after a bit of a wait, I broke through the throng of passengers to drag the Green Turtle off the conveyor belt. I scanned my passport at a machine and was given a ticket. I then put the ticket into a different machine and my photo was taken. That was that as far as immigration was concerned. I hadn't needed to interact with a single human. With my declaration form in one hand and the Green Turtle in the other, I approached the final hurdle: customs. That's when I remembered I had a half-opened packet of peppermint tea in my bag. I wasn't sure if tea was on the list of prohibited items to bring into Australia and had visions of ending up on the next episode of Border Security. Scared of being fined, I blurted it out as soon as I saw the customs officer but he just shrugged and waved me through - he didn't give a toss about my tea.

As I waited for the bus, a strange feeling crept over me: cold. It was the first time I'd felt cold in months - it was therefore lucky I had a hoodie stowed away in the Green Turtle. Buses came roughly every ten minutes so I was soon on my way into the city. The bus terminated at Southern Cross train station. I knew I had to take a tram to get to the hostel so I asked for assistance at the kiosk. An older gentleman helped me, or at least tried to. He successfully sold me a Myki card (like an Oyster card) and loaded it with enough money to get me to my stop but he had to explain the journey five times. Thanks to my tiredness, his instructions kept going in one ear and out of the other. He must've thought me a simpleton.

Despite a couple of small hiccups, I found my way to the Hub Hostel. I banged on the door and another guest let me in. Nobody was at reception so I sat and waited in the lounge area. After a few minutes, the receptionist turned up and told me I couldn't check in until 3pm. I had no idea what to do. I couldn't keep my eyes open. How would I spend the next six hours if I couldn't sleep? Deciding some fresh air would be helpful, I left the Green Turtle at the hostel and went outside. I tried to find somewhere to eat but it was slim pickings in the local area and I soon found myself back by the hostel, looking for inspiration. That was when I spotted a children's hospital over the road. For the second day in a row, I bought lunch at a hospital. While eating at a nearby park, I decided it would be a good place to hang out. I curled up on a wooden bench and dozed. With my unwashed hair and crumpled travelling clothes, I must've looked like a vagrant - I was surprised nobody tried to give me money.

Before I knew it, it was 3pm so I returned to the hostel to check in. I wasn't impressed with my two-bed dorm: it was grubby, with a suspiciously stained carpet. However, my roommate, a young French man, was thankfully very quiet so I was happy about that at least. I chatted with him for an hour and then unable to stay awake any longer, I crawled under the duvet and slept for ten hours straight.

I was still sleepy when I woke but not as zombified as the day before. Once I felt more alert, I had a pastry for breakfast and then walked into the city. I soon came across the wonderful Victoria Market, which sold fruit, vegetables, food, clothes and all sorts. I resisted making any unnecessary purchases but it took a lot of will power.

While I was there, I noticed how different people in Melbourne were compared to in Asia. In Asia, people had smiled a lot, but in Melbourne, everyone looked stressed and hardly anyone smiled. It was like being back in London. I spent the rest of the day exploring but I wasn't really in the mood so I had another early night.

The next day, I got up early for the Parkville parkrun. Usually, I'd smile and talk to people but when I smiled at this parkrun, people didn't seem to want to know. The run itself was fun. I took it easy and got around in just over twenty-eight minutes. Weirdly my ankle didn't hurt at all, not even a tiny twinge: bodies are strange sometimes. Once I'd had a little rest and a free pancake at the hostel, I walked to the CBD (Central Business District) to find the famous street art. There were some interesting murals but I didn't enjoy them as much as usual, maybe because it was overcrowded with tourists. My next stop was at the State Library of Victoria: it was huge, with an impressive glass dome ceiling and obviously lots and lots of books. I could've sat there for days, or even weeks, reading in the beautiful silence.

When I returned to the hostel, I was sad to find my French roommate had moved on. Knowing I had to get up at 5am, I went to bed early. I didn't sleep for long though as my new roommate turned up at midnight and began banging around noisily. After a few minutes, he left the room and I went back to sleep, but an hour later he was back, waking me before leaving again. I didn't get back to sleep this time, partly because the drunks outside were singing along (badly) to someone playing guitar (equally badly). When my noisy neighbour returned again and *still* wasn't quiet, I moaned at him. Without an apology, he disappeared again, and at around 2am, I finally got back to sleep.

My alarm went off at 5am. Still annoyed with my roommate, I let the alarm sound loudly for much longer than was necessary. I then proceeded to pack as noisily as possible, slamming the door whenever I left the room. I opened the curtains so it would be nice and light for him when the sun came up, and then I left to catch the bus to the airport – Tasmania was waiting...

Australia: Tasmania - Sleepless Beauty

10TH - 16TH MARCH 2019

My 8:30am flight arrived dead on time and I was at baggage claim in just a couple of minutes. Having left most of my stuff at the Melbourne hostel, the Green Turtle was looking somewhat emaciated, but being so light, it was a pleasure to carry. Regardless, I didn't have to carry it far as the car hire counter was mere footsteps away. I'd been worried about driving after such a long break, but as I took control of the compact white Hyundai, I realised I hadn't forgotten how. Maybe because it was a Sunday, the roads were deserted. As I wanted to spend the day in Hobart, I went straight to the Nook Backpackers Hostel. Thankfully, they let me check in three hours early.

Once I'd made my bed, Mr. Canon and I went out to explore. Hobart was charming. With all the old-fashioned buildings, it was like stepping back in time. The pace of life was slower too; people weren't in a hurry and were more relaxed: more people smiled at me in one hour there than they had in three whole days in Melbourne. I loved sitting by the harbour, watching the boats. It reminded me of being at home, somewhere like Portsmouth. Already, I wished I could stay in Hobart longer. There were so many places to visit within a drivable distance and I felt sorry that I'd miss out on seeing some of the popular sights. However, I reminded myself that I wanted to explore as much of the island as possible as there were so many beautiful places to see.

On Monday morning, I drove from Hobart to Coles Bay, 120 miles east. It was sunny and the journey was absolutely stunning. I went slowly so I could take in the scenery - almost everyone overtook me but I didn't care. Not wanting a fine, I was careful not to go over the speed limit but sometimes I wasn't quite sure what the limit *was*. On one stretch of road, I saw some signs stating sixty-five kilometres per hour, with a

253 |

picture of a kangaroo, so that's what I did. I was therefore confused when everyone overtook me. That's when I noticed the signs said 'Dusk to Dawn'. For some reason, I'd read them as 'Dawn until Dusk'. What a muppet. To the relief of the other road users, I sped up.

When I reached Coles Bay, I had a toasted sandwich at the bakery and then bought ice cream, which I enjoyed on the small beach overlooking the mountains. After a little walk around, I got back in the car and drove to the Swansea Backpackers Lodge. Once I'd parked up and checked in, I went for a walk around the stunning headland at Swansea. I tried sitting on a bench for a while but due to the wind, it was too chilly. As I enjoyed the scenery, an intense feeling of joy came over me. I saw a small house overlooking the beach and was reminded that I hoped to move somewhere close to the ocean one day. I'd make it happen, even if it took me a while.

On Tuesday, I set off at 10am. The weather was gorgeous again, despite the poor forecast. I was about to pull away when I noticed a young man sitting by the side of the road. I went over to ask where he was going and he told me Launceston. He didn't seem like an axe murderer so I offered to take him as far as Scamander, sixty miles away. Quentin was French, and weirdly enough, had once stayed with a friend in my home town of Shepperton. We talked a lot on the journey - it was nice to have some company. He may have regretted getting in the car with me though as I stopped so often to take photos. When we reached Scamander, I dropped Quentin off at the side of the road and continued on.

After stopping at St. Helen's for lunch, where I had the best doughnut I've ever tasted, I continued on to the Bay of Fires (so-called because the aboriginals used to set fire to the bush there to make it easier to hunt). The quiet road was flanked by pristine white beaches on one side and either water or forest on the other. I took a lot of photos and enjoyed the sea air, stopping at every beach along the way. Returning to Scamander, I checked in at the Scamander Tourist Park, where I'd booked a small studio cabin. After settling in, I went for a walk. Scamander was amazing in terms of scenery: I particularly liked its long stretch of deserted beach, where thunderous waves crashed against the shore. I got to enjoy even more of the place on my twilight run by the forest.

I was exhausted by 10pm, so I curled up in bed. However, even though it was perfectly dark and silent, I couldn't sleep. I wasn't sure what was going on. I'd had disturbed sleep for the previous few nights but that had been because of noisy hostel roommates. I had a feeling my insomnia was gearing up again. It had been a problem almost exactly a year before. I'd solved it that time with herbal tablets (5HTP) but I wasn't sure if they were available in Australia. I really hoped so.

Once the sun rose, I gave up on sleep and had breakfast. It was so cold that I had to turn on the heating. Yawning, I decided I'd search for my supplements when I reached Launceston, which would have a greater range of shops. After a quick walk to the beach, I was back in the car. It was a ninety mile journey inland to Launceston and it started on a six kilometre winding mountain pass. Of course, as with everything in Tasmania, it was spectacular.

Driving enabled me to see a lot of wildlife. Unfortunately, it was all dead (road-kill). I'd grimace every time I drove over a dismembered animal carcass with its guts spread across the road - it was not the ideal way to appreciate the animals of Tasmania.

I arrived at my destination at lunchtime and parked up at the hostel, the Launceston Backpackers. From there, I walked into town. I popped into the first chemist I saw, where a slow-speaking pharmacist told me he didn't stock what I wanted. He suggested a different chemist up the road. As it turned out, that one didn't sell them either but the helpful pharmacist knew where would. He sent me to the main city chemist which sold them to me for twenty pounds. The tablets had solved my issue last time so I hoped they'd work their magic once again.

Hopeful about my purchase, I bought some rotisserie chicken from Woolworths and then walked to Cataract Gorge. The path on the first leg of the journey was easy, but the return path was much steeper and rockier, with lots of steps. The great views definitely made it worth it though. For the rest of the day, I sat on my bed in the dorm, chatting on the phone to Tom and my mum, sorting through my photos and resting. The next day was going to involve driving on mountainous roads so I really hoped the tablets would help.

They did, and I left Launceston feeling refreshed. I was on the road to Cradle Mountain just after 9am. Yet again, I was lucky with the weather. Considering the forecast had been dire before leaving for Tasmania, I'd enjoyed endless sunshine. One of the first towns I drove through was Railton, described on the signs as the 'Town of Topiary'. I saw little evidence of this to be honest - most of the resident's bushes were pitifully overgrown!

It took a while, as it was a one hundred mile drive and I kept pulling over to take photos, but by midday, I reached Cradle Mountain. I wanted to visit Dove Lake so I used the compulsory free shuttle bus to get there. The comedic bus driver was just telling us how he'd rarely seen any snakes at the park when we saw a snake at the park. He stopped the bus to allow the graceful reptile to pass and informed us that it was a tiger snake. Laughingly, he told us not to waste energy worrying about *which* snakes at the park were venomous, as they *all* were (good to know).

It took fifteen minutes to get to Dove Lake, where Cradle Mountain stood guard. The six kilometre route around it seemed simple enough so I set off straight away. Apart from some few steps and loose rocks, the walk was predominantly on wooden boardwalks. The lake was a striking shade of deep blue and the water looked very inviting; however, it was a bit nippy so I didn't bother taking a dip (the bus driver had also mentioned something about leeches).

Still tired from my bout of insomnia, some negative thinking about my life started creeping in. It didn't seem right to be thinking miserable thoughts in such an amazing place, so I tried to shut it down. I decided that whenever I began getting anxious, I'd imagine a printer printing out all the crap going through my head. If a real printer started expelling rubbish, I'd turn it off - that's what I needed to do with my brain. After all, I didn't want to waste 'ink'. Weirdly enough, it worked and I found myself enjoying the present moment. Well, until some kid stabbed me in the arse cheek with a pointy wooden stick he was wielding. I had a moan and smiled smugly when his parents told him off.

The lake walk wasn't particularly exciting. It was pretty, but the lake looked almost the same from every angle, so by mile two I was wishing I was at the end (mostly because I *really* needed to pee). As I still had seventy miles to drive, I couldn't stay at the park to do a different walk so I hopped back on the bus to the visitor centre. However, as the bus pulled up at Ronny Creek, I saw some furry lumps on a hill: wombats. I couldn't help myself. I jumped off the bus to watch them - they were so cute!

Once I was back in the car, I drove straight towards Queenstown. For an hour, I didn't see a single other vehicle. Driving into Queenstown felt like going back in time a hundred years. It was even quainter than Hobart. The town was pretty small so I easily located the petrol station to fill up and then parked outside the Empire Hotel.

Walking into the hotel was like a slap in the face. Not in a bad way, it just smelled *exactly* like the pub my dad would take me to when I was little. It was a welcome memory but I wondered how two places, so far apart in both distance and time, could smell identical. The hotel had been built in 1901, so it was rather old-fashioned and creaky. My room even had one of the heaters I used to have when I was little, the slim metal ones that went near the ceiling and glowed red when they were hot. It didn't work sadly so I had to keep warm by putting on a jumper instead.

I had a quick wander around town before it got dark, enjoying the old buildings. Most shops were closed but I managed to buy some rotisserie chicken from the small supermarket. I went to bed, looking forward to a long sleep but it didn't happen, even with the tablets. I had no idea why I'd been hit with the sudden bout of insomnia but it was bloody annoying.

Bleary-eyed, I drank a couple of cups of morning tea to wake myself up: I had my longest drive (170 miles) to do on twisting roads that would require my full focus. *And* it had rained in the night so the roads were wet - marvellous. Clouds clung to the mountaintops as I set off and I hoped the weather wouldn't turn on me like my traitorous body.

I was only in the car for five minutes when I saw a turning for the Iron Blow Lookout. Curious, I investigated and found it was an open-cut mine filled with emerald water. A viewing platform jutted out to afford visitors a good view so I took a few photos. After that, I crossed the road to walk along a pathway screwed into the side of a mountain, which offered views of the distant Horsetail Falls. I climbed all the way to the top before deciding the view had been better at the bottom (an opinion I shared with some older people struggling up).

As I got back into the car, the clouds began to clear and the sunshine made a welcome return. I spent the next few hours driving on twisting roads with hairpin bends. It was mentally exhausting, especially when I was so tired, but it was also enthralling. The views were so varied: forests, lakes, streams, canals, green fields and golden fields. I certainly never grew bored. The number of road-kill seemed to increase though and I felt sad as I passed by, or sometimes over, the splattered carcasses of Tasmania's wildlife. I was thankful that despite taking out numerous butterflies, I hadn't hit anything with my car.

I finally arrived back in Hobart at 4pm. The roads were much busier than when I'd arrived the previous Sunday, as were the streets, which were full of people. The weekend I'd arrived had been a holiday weekend, Labor Day, which probably explained why it had been like a ghost town. Once I'd checked in at the Montacute Boutique Bunkhouse, I walked into town for more rotisserie chicken. As I was shattered, I didn't feel like doing too much so I returned to the cosy hostel and sat on the balcony in the warm sun.

I liked the hostel. It was in an old house (built in 1895) but it was modern inside and the beds even had little privacy curtains which I always preferred. The girls in my room were very chatty so we spent an hour talking about our travels and adventures in Tasmania. Everyone went to bed early but I waited until I was extra tired in the hope that I'd fall asleep more easily. Despite waking up briefly a couple of times, I slept well - I was so relieved.

At 8am on Saturday, I checked out of the hostel and drove to the Bellerive parkrun, ten miles away. Unlike when I'd been at the Melbourne parkrun, everyone was friendly and chatty. As I was walking to the start point, I heard a couple saying, "Surely it can't be *our* Shepperton?" I smiled and they asked if I was from Shepperton in the UK. After I'd confirmed I was, we had a chat and I found out that Rob and Rachel were from East Molesey, the town where I worked - what a small world. Out of the different Hobart parkruns, I'd chosen Bellerive because it was by the beach. It was a pretty route and although it was cold, it was also sunny.

My flight wasn't until 3pm, so I wasn't sure what to do for the next couple of hours. I looked at my map and saw that the airport was close to Seven Mile Beach. It sounded the perfect place for a walk. The beach was wonderfully deserted. Well, apart from the tiny crabs. There were thousands of them. I wasn't sure what they were up to but they were scurrying about everywhere. Whenever I got close to one, it would bury itself in the sand to hide. It made me very mindful as I had to carefully judge every step, making sure I didn't squash any. I got about two and a half miles along the beach before I had to turn back. Focused, I carefully navigated my way back through the sea of crustaceans. I was about a mile away from the car when I heard a loud roar. Looking up, I saw an airplane coming in to land. I wasn't quick enough to get a good photo but the plane got really close to the beach as it flew over my head.

The time passed quickly and before I knew it, I was back in the car. I had to return it with a full tank of petrol so I'd filled it up just after leaving parkrun. As I drove to the airport, I kept an eye on the petrol gauge, willing it to still read as full by the time I parked up. If it dropped one notch, I would have to find a petrol station to fill it again. Luckily it held out.

Even though I was completely covered by insurance, I was glad the car didn't have any kangaroo-shaped dents in it when I returned it, just a lot of dead insects and a bit of dirt: not bad considering I'd driven 1150.4km.

My time in Tasmania had been a beautiful dream (even if I'd barely slept). According to some locals, I'd come at the best time, when it was quiet and had more stable weather. Without a doubt, it had been my favourite part of the trip so far: people were friendly; the roads were quiet; every journey was stunningly beautiful; the weather was lovely; the bakeries were fantastic; and I hadn't once had to pay for parking! I didn't want to leave and I definitely did *not* want to return to Melbourne.

Australia: Melbourne - Hostelling Hell

Once the plane landed, I grabbed the Green Turtle and hopped on the Skybus to the city. From there, I walked the two miles back to the Hub Hostel. I collected the bag of stuff I'd left behind and went to my room, claiming the bottom bunk. Thankfully, it was a little less grim than the last room I'd stayed in. However, what it lacked in carpet stains, it made up for in noise. My room was right by the outside area where people went to drink and smoke weed. I was not hopeful about sleeping. I no longer cared for hostel dorms. Some were better than others but in general, I hated being dependent on the quietness of others for sleep. Don't get me wrong, hostels definitely have their benefits - they are cheap and can be a great way to meet people, but when you find yourself in a crap one, they can be hellish.

Even though reception had told me a Japanese girl had already checked into my two-bed dorm, there was no sign of her. I went out for pizza and came back at 8pm and she still wasn't there. Reception said three of them had checked in together and thought maybe they were going to squeeze into one room. It sounded too good to be true. It was. Forty-five minutes after I'd gone to bed, in blasted my roommate, who thought that 1am would be the perfect time to make her bed. Needless to say, I barely slept.

The next morning, I went to reception and asked about the possibility of a refund, so I could treat myself to a quiet hotel. Emma, who was working at the front desk, was very apologetic and offered a refund or a change of rooms. I opted for the lazy, cheaper option.

Having moved rooms, I put on my trainers and went for a walk. After eating an Asian-style lunch at the Victoria Market food court, I found myself at the Royal Botanical Gardens, which were pretty but nothing spectacular (maybe it hadn't been the best time of year to visit). I considered sitting on the grass to relax but then I remembered a pink lake I'd seen online. My app told me it was a five and a half mile walk away. Despite being tired, I went for it. As I trudged along quiet residential streets lined with cute little houses, I heard a deafening roar from above. It sounded like an airplane but I couldn't see anything in the sky. An old lady saw my confusion and told me it was a jet flying because of the Grand Prix. I'm not really into planes but it was fun to watch, or at least listen to. Lots of residents came out to watch the spectacle too.

After what felt like a long time, I reached Westgate Park. I'd read that the salt lake only turned vivid pink in hot weather. The sun had come out by lunchtime and it was very warm, so I kept my fingers crossed. The hordes of tourists were a good sign - they must have been there for a reason. I was in luck! The lake was *very* pink! Avoiding the crowds, I found a quiet area and took some photos.

By the time I finished, it was late afternoon. I had a six mile walk ahead of me so I unenthusiastically plodded on. It took a couple of hours but I finally reached the hostel, where I ate a dinner of yoghurt before retiring to my room. My roommate (Mario) was nowhere to be seen. Knowing my luck, he'd probably come back just after I'd fallen asleep. I'd come to learn that many people staying at the Hub Hostel were inconsiderate: they were loud, obnoxious and rarely cleaned up after themselves. Most seemed to live at the hostel while they worked nearby, which was probably why it had been so difficult to meet any other conventional travellers there. Walking past open doorways, I noticed that some of the rooms were very untidy with clothes and 'stuff' scattered everywhere. I missed being in normal hostels, where I shared with girls who were normally in bed by midnight, after a busy day of exploring. In those situations, at least I was guaranteed a few hours of quiet between midnight and 6am.

By 10pm, I was shattered. I knew I'd probably get woken up but I needed to try to sleep a little. As expected, Mario rocked up just after 2am, waking me. Once he was asleep, I dozed off again. I felt like I was awake a lot but every time I checked my watch, a couple of hours had passed, so I must've slept more than I thought.

Monday was my last day in Melbourne and I was *very* pleased about it. Not that it was a horrible city, it wasn't. Melbourne was clean, with lots of green areas and great places to run. I imagined it would be a lovely place to live. My main issue was that I hated the dirty, noisy hostel. If I'd stayed somewhere else, I probably would've had a very different experience.

Wanting to see the beach, I walked a couple of miles to Southern Cross station, and then took the tram to St. Kilda Beach. I was a little disappointed as it was nowhere near as pretty as other Australian beaches I'd seen. Still, I got comfortable and napped in the sun. By 2pm, I was hungry, so I went into town for pizza.

Walking back towards the beach, I cut through a pretty palm tree-lined park. I considered hanging out there but something put me off...In the shade of a tree lay a man wrapped in a black sleeping bag. His head was on a pillow, tipped back, with his mouth wide open. At first I thought he was sleeping, but then I saw the movement of his hand inside his cocoon. He was clearly giving himself a jolly. I was shocked that he was doing it so openly. A man walked past and also did a double-take; making eye contact, we pulled disgusted faces at each other. I decided *against* remaining in the park.

That night, I was ready for bed by 10:30pm. A loud American, who clearly liked the sound of his own voice, was shouting his mouth off in the lounge outside my room and I could hear every word, even through my ear plugs. Two equally loud Italians were also talking. The hostel 'quiet time' was from 10pm but I waited until 11pm before going out and politely asking them to keep their voices down. The obnoxious American had the nerve to ask if I'd tried closing my door. I wanted to reply, "Have you heard *you*?" He was clearly unaware of his own volume. I closed the door and he instantly started shouting, "NO, NO, NO!" As I grabbed the door knob, I heard the quieter American say, "She won't like that!" He was right, I didn't. I yanked open the door and shouted, "Seriously?" He then proceeded to keep talking, even louder than before.

Mario was in and out all night so I was still wide awake at 2am when he finally went to bed. While I was sobbing quietly in frustration, he went straight to sleep, fully clothed, and began snoring. After half an hour of listening to it, and not feeling particularly polite, I got up and prodded him until he woke up. It shut him up for a while, but after ten minutes, the snoring was back. This time I kicked my feet up onto the underside of his mattress. He obviously got the message as he moved and the snoring quietened. I was too awake to sleep so I just lay in bed crying. It was not a good night.

At 4am, Mario's alarm sounded and he left. I must've finally relaxed then, as I managed to claw back a few of hours of sleep. By 8am, I was an exhausted and angry mess. If I'd seen the obnoxious American, I would've struggled not to slap his smug face. I made sure to slam all the doors as loudly and as frequently as possible and ignored the Italians when they said good morning. Someone had hilariously left some ear plugs on the table by my door, so I flicked them onto the carpet (my rage knew no bounds). I had a cry on the phone to Tom, ate breakfast and then packed as quickly as possible. I couldn't wait to leave, even if it meant arriving at the airport a couple of hours early. If anyone were to ask me what the best thing about the Hub Hostel was, I'd have to tell them it was *leaving* it.

Australia: The Great Ocean Road-Trip

19TH - 22ND MARCH 2019

The Green Turtle and I returned to the airport via the tram and the Skybus so I could pick up a rental car and begin my road trip on the Great Ocean Road. It was great: greatly wet, greatly foggy and greatly meandering; but most importantly, it was *greatly* spectacular.

Between my trying time in Melbourne and my ongoing insomnia, I was exhausted by the time I arrived at the airport to pick up my hire car. All I wanted to do was curl up somewhere and close my droopy eyes. I soon discovered that there was no desk inside the airport for Bargain Car Rentals: I had to call them to send a shuttle bus. This would have been fine if I'd been able to make calls, but to save money, my phone was permanently in flight mode and I survived only on free WiFi.

Within five minutes, an older couple sat next to me. I listened as they talked with someone from an airline. Apparently the Russian-sounding woman had taken the wrong bag from the carousel earlier in the day and was there to do a swap. Her husband had an Australian accent, so when they were alone, I asked to borrow his phone to call a local number. He happily passed it to me and I dialed; however, nobody answered. The couple asked where I was going and kindly offered to drop me off.

Finding their car was a bit of a mission. I had to laugh as they bickered over where they'd left it. Thankfully, I found a trolley to carry the Green Turtle around the vast car park as we traipsed back and forth. Finally, they located their car and we all got in. They then squabbled over how to use the satnav. Once they worked that out and we were on our way, they argued when he accidentally took a wrong turn. It was quite funny but I felt bad for having caused them further hassle.

Once we reached the car rental office, I said goodbye and hopped out, telling them I how much I appreciated their help.

Luckily the woman at the desk didn't mind that I was early and released the car to me straight away. Taking the keys to another Hyundai, I located my new vehicle: a bright yellow monstrosity which I was embarrassed to get into. My plan was to drive to Apollo Bay, which was over one hundred miles away. I got started immediately, eager to put as much distance as possible between me and Melbourne.

It was roughly sixty miles to the start of the Great Ocean Road in Torquay, but the roads were quiet and although it was cloudy, it was dry. The journey, as expected, was very scenic but I couldn't help wondering how much more beautiful it would have been if it were sunny.

I reached my destination by late afternoon. I checked in at the quiet Apollo Bay Eco YHA hostel, hoping I could get some rest there. Despite feeling exhausted, I walked to a nearby beach and sat in the dunes, watching a couple of young women learning to surf. The ocean had its usual effect on me and my mood brightened instantly. It was good to feel the sand between my toes and listen to the ocean.

When it began to grow dark, I stopped to eat at a diner and then returned to the hostel. Two German girls were in my room. They weren't very chatty but that suited me. I spent the rest of the evening in the common area. It was peaceful until four loud British girls came in and started blasting out music which they 'sung' along too while drinking vast amounts of gin. They had some choice catchphrases, like 'Bitches who slash together, stay together'. I really wasn't in the mood for their noise so I returned to the room. The girls were already in their beds, reading, which delighted me. By 10pm, we were all in our beds with the lights out. Thankfully, I slept.

By 10am, I was back on the road. It was rainy and foggy so I was worried I'd be unable to see the main sight of the day: the Twelve Apostles. A couple of miles from Apollo Bay, the road took me inland, through a beautiful rainforest. The tall trees looked very atmospheric through the fog and I kept pulling over to take photographs.

Around midday, I reached the Twelve Apostles, rock formations in the ocean that have been eroded by the forces of nature. Even though it was still cloudy, it had stopped raining, so I parked up and walked a couple of miles to see them. I was grateful that it wasn't too foggy; at least I could see the Twelve Apostles clearly. After my walk, I returned to the car and drove on.

At 3pm, I checked into the Discovery Parks Warrnambool and entered my spacious studio cabin. I felt like getting into bed straight away but I'd read that Port Fairy was nice, so I got back in the car and drove twenty miles further on to see it. However, I was too tired to investigate on foot so I just drove through the town, turned around and returned to my accommodation.

Ignoring the tempting double bed, I decided to see some of the local area. Noticing a sign for Thunder Point, I walked there first, intrigued. It wasn't as thunderous as the name implied but it was so cold that I couldn't sit still, so I carried on exploring, finding little paths, deserted beaches, sand dunes, wooden bridges, rocky outcrops and various other nooks and crannies.

I felt simultaneously happy and sad. Even though I'd barely spoken to anyone for days, I'd really enjoyed my solitude. I loved discovering new places: it always gave me a sense of freedom and adventure, and reminded me of being a child. I especially loved Warrnambool because it reminded me of home. Looking around, I could easily have mistaken it for Cornwall or Devon: nothing particularly jumped out as being obviously Australian.

My sadness came from a longing for the past. My wonderful dad had died a few years before. Being by the sea always reminded me of family holidays, of spending time with my parents. I missed them both.

By 7pm, it was starting to get dark, so I reluctantly headed for home. As I walked past the pool area, I was surprised to see it was open and empty. I immediately dashed to my cabin, put on my bikini and ran back. Stepping into the warm jacuzzi was bliss but I kept my hat on as the wind was cold. As I relaxed, I felt grateful I'd ventured out - it had been the best part of my day. I went to bed at 10pm, shattered, but was wide awake by 1am. It was very frustrating.

The next morning, I decided that Thursday's route would be dictated by the weather. If it was sunny, I'd go the long way to Geelong, doing the entire Great Ocean Road once again. If it was cloudy, I'd take the short cut inland. With my running gear on, I opened the curtains to find dull, grey clouds. At least I had sixty less miles to drive. The cool weather was perfect for running and I went along the undulating coastal path for six miles, the furthest I'd run in a while.

Once I'd showered and eaten, my long journey began. The road was straight and tedious. I found it a struggle to stay awake and started wondering whether I'd made the best decision. Two thirds of the way, I stopped to look at my map app and noticed I could head south-east, back to seaside town of Lorne. I could then do the last few miles of the Great Ocean Road. The sun breaking through the clouds cemented my decision. I turned right at the next junction and found myself on a quiet, narrow road, which took me through hills and fields. It was a bit of an adventure and much more fun than the road I'd been on previously.

After a while, I found myself encased in fog, weaving through the rainforest on wet, curving roads. It was stunning and the mist added an exciting, eerie atmosphere. The man driving in the opposite direction must have thought so too, as he was suddenly on *my* side of the road. I'm not sure whether his attention was diverted by the views, but my heart jumped into my mouth when I saw his car. I didn't think he was going to correct himself in time so I swerved. Thankfully he saw me at the last second and we missed each other by inches. I couldn't blame him for being distracted as it was so beautiful. I stopped in the pull-outs to take photos whenever it was safe to do so. The best part was the smell: whenever I stepped out of the car, a wonderful, strong, fresh pine fragrance would hit me.

When I reached Lorne, I had lunch: a bacon and egg roll, and an apple and cinnamon muffin. Then I continued on towards Geelong. Along the way, I stopped at a couple of beaches where I walked and stroked some dogs. I also stopped at Split Point Lighthouse and did a short walk there. In the car park, I came across a bird sitting on a bin. I expected it to fly away as I approached with my camera but it didn't move. Just after I pressed the button to take the photo, it fluffed up and screeched at me in warning. I was a bit scared so I ran back to the car in case it flew at me.

At 4pm, I reached the Kismet B&B in Geelong. I couldn't check in until 5pm so I walked to the local shopping centre and had a small pizza for dinner. The B&B wasn't great as there was dog and cat hair all over the bed. However, the lady was very friendly and the bed was extremely comfortable. That night, I sat in my room, busily editing photos and writing my blog. I was shattered by 8pm and unable to focus on writing, played games on my laptop until I couldn't keep my eyes open.

It was the best night's sleep I'd had in a couple of weeks and I didn't wake up until after 9am. The landlady wasn't in a hurry for me to leave, so we sat in the kitchen chatting over breakfast. She recommended that I stop at Geelong waterfront, so that's what I did. It was a pleasant place with an outdoor swimming pool, a ferris wheel and loads of sculptures of people fashioned from the old timbers of a demolished pier.

From Geelong, it was a sixty mile drive to Melbourne to drop off the car. By 12:30pm, I was on the shuttle bus to the airport. Despite the weather, I'd really enjoyed the 770km road trip. I was also grateful I'd finally had a decent night's sleep and could only hope it wasn't a one-off. I would be staying with my friend Katie again when I arrived in Adelaide and I was really looking forward to catching up with her and her family.

Australia: Adelaide - An Unexpected Decision

22ND MARCH - 4TH APRIL 2019

Returning to the farm felt like coming home. As I got out of the car with bags of food shopping, I shed a few happy tears. It was a sign that I needed normality and was probably why I'd find myself making an unexpected decision only a few days later...

My flight to Adelaide only took an hour but it felt like longer due to all the turbulence. It wasn't terrible but it had been bad enough to keep things interesting. The people next to me and behind me had been petrified and seemed certain they were going to die. I just looked out of the window and enjoyed flying through the towering, fluffy clouds. Once we landed, I went to pick up my car (another Hyundai) from Alamo. As Katie would be working for the majority of my visit, I'd decided that a car would be useful.

Blackwood, where Katie lived, was only thirteen miles from the airport. Despite the Friday night traffic, I was soon at the supermarket near her house. I was excited to go to Woolworths and buy *proper* food to put into a *clean* fridge. I didn't even need to label anything with my name! As I got out of the car at the orchard, the familiarity and comfort of being 'home' hit me. Katie was working so I let myself in, put the shopping away and then made myself comfortable in my room. It was silent and I hoped that it would help me overcome my bout of insomnia, which had left me feeling exhausted.

That evening, Katie came home and whisked me away to a family meal at her sister Michelle's house. It was lovely to see everyone again. I didn't get to talk to Katie but it was nice to talk with her sister, Sarah. Thankfully, I slept well that night. However, while I'd been dreaming, the mosquitoes had been feeding. I got more bites in twelve hours on the orchard than in an entire month in Vietnam and Cambodia.

On Saturday morning, I did the parkrun on the Brighton seafront. I was disappointed with my time. On the way home, I wound down the window for some fresh air. That was when I heard a weird, flapping sound - something was wrong with the car. When I parked up, the problem was obvious. There were deep scratches on the bottom of the bumper and a large part of the mud guard on the inside of the wheel arch was broken and hanging off. I hadn't gone over so much as a speed bump so I knew it hadn't been something *I* had done.

The scratches had been marked on the car's paperwork as previous damage so I called Alamo. The man who answered apologetically promised to swap it over if I returned the car to the airport. It was a slow journey, as the more I drove the car, the louder the sound became. The plastic was clearly flapping against the tyres and sounded terrible. I was worried they'd blame me for the damage but they didn't bat an eyelid and gave me the keys to a new car straight away. To apologise, they even upgraded me to an I30, which had in-built satnav and was even smoother to drive - my belief that things worked out well for me was strengthened.

As it was Luke's birthday we all went out to the Belair Hotel for dinner that night. All the family were there and I ate a particularly good chicken schnitzel. This time I mostly spoke with Katie's eldest sister, Amy. As I was still tired, I went home early and had an early night. Again, I slept like a log - it seemed like my insomnia really was over but I still had a *lot* of catching up to do.

On Sunday, I was supposed to start planning my month in Sri Lanka, but I had no enthusiasm. Instead, I did laundry and edited my previous blog posts for spelling, tense and punctuation errors (I was clearly missing my day job). Katie was busy with family so I didn't see her all day. It felt like she was avoiding me – I wasn't sure why.

I awoke to the sound of heavy rain on Monday. I considered planning Sri Lanka but again, I wasn't interested. I'd felt that way for a long time and wished I'd never booked flights there. I didn't have anything against the place but I'd read a few stories by other solo female travellers that had put me off going alone. These had mostly involved unwanted attention or touching from local men. I'd experienced it myself in parts of Malaysia and it had made me *very* uncomfortable. Another issue was that nothing about Sri Lanka excited me: I was templed out; I'd seen elephants in Chiang Mai; the safaris were too expensive for my budget; and I'd have my fill of beaches when I returned to Bali. What was left?

My thoughts were soon interrupted by the arrival of the sun, so I put on my running gear, grabbed the car keys and took myself to the seafront at Brighton. As I hadn't run more than five miles for months, I pushed myself to do eight. It felt good to realise that I could do it, even if it was a slow slog at times.

After my run, I visited the Harbour Front outlet centre for some new trainers. Before I'd left home, I'd been certain that as I'd be running less, my new trainers would last the year. But I'd forgotten to take into account all the miles I'd also *walk* in them: sometimes up to twenty miles a day. I was particular about the brand and model of trainer I used but luckily the sports shop manager was able to order a pair for me and even gave me discount.

On Tuesday, I woke up with a mission: to finally sort out my Sri Lanka trip. I felt uneasy about it but I started going through my previous research, sorting out destinations, their order and how to get between them. I even got as far as booking a popular train trip. After four hours of research, I had a plan and was ready to start booking accommodation, but something held me back. I found myself looking up something else instead: the cost of a flight home. This signaled to me that I might need a break from my break. Why carry on if my heart wasn't in it?

My decision was made. I spent an hour searching for flights and then booked one with Thai Airways for the third of May. Next, I booked an Easyjet flight between the UK and Paris for the 24th May, from where my booked flight to Albania would depart. I'd have three weeks at home and I couldn't wait. I felt such a sense of relief about skipping Sri Lanka that I knew it was the right decision.

Ecstatic, I called Tom to tell him the good news. He was as surprised and excited as I was that we'd get to see each other again so soon. The next most exciting thing (apart from seeing my friends and family, getting to see the new season of Game of Thrones and eating Cathedral City cheese) was the thought of re-packing my bag and choosing some new clothes for my European trip.

I went to bed happy but I awoke on Wednesday feeling odd. I was sure going home was the right thing to do but it was hard to get my head around such a big change of plan. To take my mind off things, I drove to the little German town of Hahndorf. I popped into an art gallery as its aboriginal art was very eye-catching: I loved the colours and repeated patterns. The woman who ran the gallery was kind enough to show me around and explain the meaning behind some of the paintings. If I'd had the money, I would've bought one. Instead, I settled for eating a posh hot dog at a little restaurant and bought myself a new dress, which was on sale.

Leaving Hahndorf behind, I drove around the scenic roads, enjoying the views, until I saw a sign for Mount Lofty. I followed the signs to the summit, where I parked up and walked to the visitor centre. The views over Adelaide were amazing - I could see all the way to the coast. I sat there for a couple of hours, enjoying the sunshine and the scenery. Just as I was walking back to the car, I saw two people looking up at a tree. Sitting in its branches were two sleeping koalas: an adult and a cute baby. I took a few photos and went to move away when a couple approached. They talked to me about the koalas and then told me where I could see some kangaroos. They explained that they were big but not scary and assured me that I'd be ok to take photos. The kangaroos were where the couple had told me they'd be. Without blinking, the bigger one stared at me. I was a little intimidated. I took a couple of photos and then nervously backed away. The kangaroo immediately returned to its business and I returned to the car.

On Thursday, I drove through the beautiful McLaren Vale wine region. It was stunning but the ground looked a little dry after such a hot summer. The curving, tree-lined roads reminded me of driving around Tasmania. My destination, Maslin Beach, was thirty kilometres away. I was the only person there apart from a few nudists hanging about in the 'unclad' section at the far end of the beach. I walked along the water's edge for a couple of miles, but I avoided *that* area.

After stopping for an egg and bacon roll at a grocery store, I continued on to the beautiful Aldinga Beach, which had gorgeous white sands. I was too lazy to do any more walking, so I sat on the beach and read for a couple of hours. By 5pm, it started to turn chilly. I wasn't sure what to do for another two hours but I was determined to wait for the sun to set. There was a bench up on the verge, so I sat there, writing my blog to pass the time. Mother Nature didn't let me down. The sky, enhanced by the clouds, was set ablaze. It was truly magnificent and I took photos for a good hour before driving home.

As I'd spent most of my time in Adelaide alone, I'd had a lot of time to reflect on my trip. Although I'd enjoyed most of it and had *loved* some parts, I couldn't say it had been life-changing, but then I'd never expected it to be. It had never been my intention to *find myself* and being away only confirmed that I knew myself pretty well. I could sometimes be impatient and grumpy; I liked to be in control; and I had an aversion to *other* people. None of that had changed. It wasn't all bad though - I had good characteristics too: the most important being that if I wanted to do something, even if it was scary, I'd go for it.

I'd enjoyed my first week of exploring Adelaide and the surrounding areas in my hired car but I still had a whole other week to go. With autumn fast approaching, the weather took a turn for the worse. I woke up on Friday to wind and rain, but I didn't mind because it was nice to feel cold - it reminded me of home. It also meant that the mosquitoes went away. That afternoon, I went to the shopping centre to pick up my new trainers. By the time I'd finished, the rain had stopped and there were even patches of blue sky. This led me to drive a little further north to Henley Beach, hoping for another beautiful sunset.

The beach was empty. It wasn't surprising as it was blowing a gale. As I parked up, I could feel the car rocking in the wind. Sand whipped my face as I walked to the pier, or at least tried to - it felt like I was in a wind tunnel. As I struggled along the pier, I watched a couple of surfers enjoying the waves that were crashing against its wooden supports. One of them paddled back to land and then came running up the pier. Holding his surfboard in one hand, he jumped off the side and back into the sea. I supposed it was easier than struggling against the big waves.

I took lots of photos but it wasn't long before my hands and face were numb with cold. I really wished I had a jacket. Seeing a small rainbow and some menacing storm clouds in the distance, I sought shelter in the warm car while I ate a bag of fries and waited for sunset. However, the clouds regrouped and blocked out the sun entirely, so I drove home.

On Saturday morning, I was up early to volunteer at parkrun. It wasn't a good day for it though as it was so cold and windy. Two of us were in charge of manning the boat ramp and would need to stop the runners if a boat was brought down to the beach. With the weather as bad as it was though, none went out, so it was an easy role. My fellow marshal and I had a good laugh cheering the runners on and she enthusiastically gave many of them high fives, whether they wanted them or not. The rain held off until the last participant crossed the finish line - it was excellent timing.

After enjoying a free hot chocolate at the sailing club (a perk of the job), it was *my* turn to run. The weather had improved but it was still windy. I did four miles along the seafront and then drove to Woolworths to do a little food shopping. I was in the car park, eating a healthy post-run snack (definitely *not* a cream cake), when I bumped into Sarah. She told me she was coming for dinner at the house that evening so we shopped together.

When I got back, Katie came to sit with me and we had a brief chat. Sarah then joined us. Once we'd eaten, Katie and Sarah went to a family event and I spent the rest of the afternoon in bed, writing my blog. In the evening, once Sarah and Katie arrived home, we ate tacos and watched a bad movie. Afterwards, Katie went to bed, while Sarah and I had a giggle decorating cupcakes in the kitchen.

I'd planned Sunday to be a lazy day so it started off with a lay in. Once I was fully awake, my hungry tummy led me to the kitchen, where I found Sarah and Katie. Katie went to church so I sat talking to Sarah for an hour. The sisters (and the cupcakes) were all going to a hen afternoon, so once Katie returned home, they left for the McLaren Vale.

Despite my lazy plans, I soon found myself in my running gear and driving to the beach. Fancying a change of scenery, I ran up onto the cliffs. The views were great but it was hard to run on the coastal trail as there were so many steps. Someone at parkrun had told me about the Sea to Vines trail which ran adjacent to some train tracks, so I cut inland until I found it. The paved path was easier but no less hilly. After two and a half miles, I'd had enough, so I turned around and ran back to the car. Thankfully, the return journey was easier as it was mostly downhill. Back in the car, I calculated I'd run seventeen miles that week - the most I'd done for a long time.

After a late lunch at home, I walked around the reservation by Katie's house and also visited Blackwood Forest. It was so different to when I'd last visited in the spring, but it was no less peaceful and beautiful. The lush spring carpet of green grass had merely been replaced by tall, dry, golden grass.

The weather was warm and sunny on Tuesday, so I drove back to Aldinga. Being a creature of habit, I returned to exactly the same stretch of beach as before, which I discovered was actually called Silver Sands Beach. To get my daily exercise, I walked five miles along the beach, enjoying the feel of the cool sea water on my feet. Along the way, I found myself reflecting on my travels. Before I'd left, I'd thought that travelling would make me happier, but it hadn't. This was probably because I was able to find an endless list of things to worry about no matter *where* I was. Don't get me wrong, I had no regrets: I'd had plenty of happy moments, seen so many amazing places and met a lot of lovely people.

I'd discovered that although I wasn't a *people person* and often preferred solitude, I did need people, *my* people, and seeing them was one of the main reasons I was so excited to be going home. I'd also found that I enjoyed free time more when I had less of it. This *hadn't* surprised me, as I've always enjoyed having a purpose. Finally, I remembered that it was the simple things in life that made me happy and *those* were things I could get almost anywhere in the world: sunsets, cloud-porn, thunderstorms and the sea. I just needed to make more of an effort to seek them out.

Nothing made me happier than walking on a deserted beach so I switched off my busy brain and enjoyed the moment, aware that my travels in Australia were coming to an end. I wasn't too down about it though, as I'd had a wonderful time and I was so grateful for having had the opportunity to visit not just once, but twice. There was barely a cloud in the sky, so knowing there wouldn't be a particularly exciting sunset, I drove home. I was eager to see if a parcel from Tom had finally arrived and was delighted to find it had! It was some ear plugs and a new buff to keep me warm in the cooler weather (not the most romantic of gifts but they were very practical). At my request, Katie and I watched Macleod's Daughters and ate fish and chips. Sarah joined us a little later and the two of us made arrangements to meet the following evening.

Late on Wednesday afternoon, Sarah picked me up in her Jeep and showed me where she lived, just up the road. Once she got changed, she took us to Carrick Hill, sometimes known as One Tree Hill (which we would come to refer to as 'our hill'). The path up was very steep but luckily it wasn't too long, so we made it in time for sunset. It was a cloudy but beautiful evening and I loved spending more time with Sarah. As I've said before, we have a lot in common: we both like adventure, exercising and nature, and share a sarcastic, dirty sense of humour. She'd made me smile a lot during my last few days in Australia.

Once we finished at the hill, we met Katie for a schnitzel dinner at the Duck Inn. We also shared an ice cream sundae, topped with what looked like Santa's pubes (white cotton candy strands). It was the perfect way to end my time in Australia. I would miss the orchard, and Sarah in particular, but I would never forget my precious time there.

Indonesia: Bali: Seminyak - Rain Rain Go Away (Part 1)

I drove away from the orchard feeling cheerful. I'd had some incredible travels in Australia but I was okay with leaving as I knew it would take me that little bit closer to home. I dropped off the Hyundai at the airport and looked for someone to hand the keys to. A man came over and said I could give them to him. He didn't have a uniform or any obvious identification so I was a little hesitant, but I did it anyway. As I walked into the terminal, I started worrying. Had I just given some random bloke the car? I hurried to the car rental desk to check and they reassured me I'd done the right thing - phew!

Once I'd checked in, I went through security, where I was swabbed for explosives *again*. They seemed to pick on me on every internal flight within Australia and it annoyed me more every time. Did I have the aura of a terrorist? I tried to find my gate but to get there, I had to pass through *another* security station. Yet again, I was asked to step aside for an explosives test. I must've noticeably bristled because laughingly, they asked if I was having a bad day. I rolled my eyes without answering and was soon sent on my way.

The five hour flight to Bali was boring but it landed on time. A driver was waiting for me and he whisked me away to the Kosta Hostel, the same place I'd stayed at before: they even put me in exactly the same bed. I was overjoyed to be back in Bali. I loved the smell of incense in the air and it was very chilled out. The only let down was the almost constant rain.

My weekend passed in traditional Bali fashion as I fell back into my old patterns. It mostly involved reading by the pool, massages and eating.

I met some nice girls in my dorm though and I ended up spending Saturday evening with Lisa, from France. We had massages, watched a disappointing sunset from a beach bar and had dinner. It was nice to have some company, although I wouldn't be alone for long as my niece was due to arrive on Sunday.

At 3pm the next day, I took a taxi to the Amerta Seminyak Hotel. Needing some fresh air, I went for a long walk on the beach. I was lucky enough to enjoy a half-decent sunset (the only one I'd see all week). Kerry messaged at 6pm to say she'd landed and she arrived at the hotel a couple of hours later. It was so lovely to see her again. We were both hungry, so we went straight out for food, walking along the eerily deserted beach to the Cedana Restaurant, my favourite place to eat. Over dinner, Kerry told me about her exciting plans to go to Australia for a year.

We had an early start the next day, so we were soon walking back to the hotel. As the beach had been creepy, we went along road, but it was even darker and spookier than the beach had been. We were almost back at the hotel when I heard a yelp. I turned around to find Kerry had disappeared. Looking down, I found her in a dirty hole in the side of the road. Bali had a problem with random holes and Kerry had fallen victim to one on her first evening. Thankfully, she wasn't seriously hurt and just had a few scratches. The incident scared the crap out of me but I was relieved she hadn't fallen into one of the bigger holes as she could've really done herself some damage. Once we got back to the room, she washed herself off and applied some antiseptic to her scratches, and then we went straight to sleep. We had an early start on Monday as we were going on a two-day tour of Nusa Penida Island.

Indonesia: Bali: Nusa Penida Island - Finding Paradise

8TH - 9TH APRIL 2019

At 6:30am on Monday morning, we were whisked away by private car to the ferry port at Sanur. Wanting to travel light, we only took small bags and left the rest of our stuff at the hotel. Just after 8am, we boarded the fast boat to Nusa Penida. There was little leg room but the journey was enjoyable as we crashed through the waves. The island became increasingly visible through the morning haze while Bali faded into the distance, leaving a behind a faint outline of Mount Agung, an active volcano. The boat slowed as we approached our destination and when it came to a stop, we all stepped off the boat and into the ocean, wading to the beach. This would've been fine, except that the sea floor was covered in spiky pieces of broken coral, making it a somewhat painful experience. Despite our sore feet, we couldn't help but admire the striking turquoise water - it was really beautiful.

On shore, we were met by Eddy, our guide. He took us to his car and we began the bumpy journey to our first stop: Thousand Islands lookout. Nestled in the feisty azure water below were several small rocky islands. We didn't get to admire the view for long though as we were soon escorted down a flight of seemingly endless steps in the towering cliff face. The steps led to a small rocky outcrop where we were able to take photos. A couple of idyllic tree houses were there and people queued to have their photo taken on their wonky, wooden steps. We decided to join the queue and our guide helpfully took photos of us. The ascent back to the car was tiring and more than a little sweaty, but it wasn't as bad as I'd expected (Kerry disagreed).

Once we were back in car and happily being cooled by the air conditioning, Eddy drove us to our next stop: Diamond Beach and Atuh Beach. We were worried that we'd have to do *both* sets of steps but thankfully Diamond Beach was just a photo stop from the top. We were led down a large set of steps, which were even more challenging than the last lot. Halfway down, we stopped to admire the view. The valley was covered in a lush green blanket which hugged the picture perfect beach. At the bottom, we were relieved to find that we were allowed to relax for a couple of hours. We grabbed a couple of sun loungers and enjoyed some well-earned fries and pancakes. The pull of the sea was irresistible so we both took a dip. However, as the waves were unpredictable and sometimes violent, neither of us ventured too far in. We were right to be cautious. Eddy told us that two people had been killed the previous day at a nearby beach when they'd been swept away by freak waves.

Once our relaxation time was over, we climbed back up the steep steps to Eddy's car, stopping numerous times to 'take photos' (meaning we needed to take some deep breaths). The journey to our final stop was even bumpier. The roads on Nusa Penida were not easy for several reasons: they were narrow, winding and full of giant pot holes or sometimes just not paved at all. Often, there were more holes than there was road. It was clear why it was not recommended for tourists to ride scooters on the island unless they were experienced. More than once, I gasped out loud when we met a car coming around a hairpin bend in the opposite direction or when we got too close to hitting a dog or a chicken that was crossing the road.

Our last stop was at the aptly named 'Tellytubby Hill'. Visiting tourists had nicknamed the area as the rounded green hills resembled the setting of the famous children's TV show. After, we were taken to the Wani Bali Resort, our accommodation for the night. The grounds and huts were lovely although the room lacked a couple of simple basics: toilet paper being one of them. However, it was clean and had a pool, so we were happy enough. We swam, and then ate at the resort restaurant before returning to our room to watch movies.

It wasn't easy to relax. Loud singing blared through the resort and our hut had little in the way of sound-proofing. At first we thought it was another call to prayer, as we'd heard that earlier, but it went on for too long and sounded different. We spent the evening wishing it would stop. Eventually, by the time we settled down to sleep, the warbling came to an end. Our peace wasn't to last all night though, as at 5am we were woken by the call to prayer. We managed to go back to sleep, only to be woken again an hour later by what our driver called the 'Balinese mantra'. Although the main religion of Indonesia is Islam, on the Indonesian island of Bali, almost 85% of people follow Balinese Hinduism, a mix of local beliefs and Hinduism. The mantra, a kind of call to prayer, was part of this. I'd never heard it on Bali, but we heard it twice on Nusa Penida. It even played on the TV and radio stations, dead on 6 o'clock, morning and night. It was interesting to hear but why did religions have to be so loud?

Our driver picked us up at 8am and we were taken to our first stop. The journey was long and tortuous as the roads were even worse than they'd been the day before. With all the craters, I joked it was like driving on the moon. Although Eddy drove as slowly as possible, we were jolted about so much that my head hurt and Kerry felt sick. We were therefore glad to get out of the car and even more pleased that we didn't need to deal with any challenging steps, only a steep slope.

We'd come to Angel's Billabong, a natural infinity pool in the cliffs, created by the destructive seas of Nusa Penida. When we first arrived, it was a haven of quiet serenity, but a few minutes later it was struck by a sudden swell. Vicious waves poured over the ten metre high ledge and into the once calm pool, which instantly became turbulent and treacherous. It was easy to see how several people had died there. The irresistible siren song of Angel's Billabong called to bathers and Instagrammers alike, lulling them into a false sense of security before powerful waves dragged them out to sea. I'd read several news stories of near misses, where people had *nearly* been washed away or had escaped with awful injuries from being thrown against the jagged, volcanic rocks. The need for adventurous tourists to take the perfect selfie has greatly contributed to the rising death toll.

Next, we walked to Broken Beach. The beach itself is only accessible by boat as it is encircled by steep cliffs, the only entrance being through a large natural arch. It was stunning, just like most of Nusa Penida's coastline.

After exploring, we had another journey in the washing machine on wheels. This time we stopped at Paluang Cliff, where our driver took more photos of us posing with views of Kelingking Beach in the background. It was so beautiful it seemed unreal. With its crystal clear, turquoise oceans, Nusa Penida had stolen my heart: it was paradise. Eddy took us to the Kelingking Beach lookout and queued up while we sat in the shade watching monkeys. When it was our turn, he took photos of us in the popular spot, looking down on the beach. He tried to lead us down the steps to the beach but we didn't fancy it. I'd read about the steep, perilous path, and looking at the sweaty, red-faced people coming back, we decided we'd be best off staying at the top. I enjoyed looking down at the beach and watching the sand swirling in the aqua water though - it was mesmerising.

By midday, it was time to move on. Eddy took us for some cold drinks at his family's restaurant, and then he picked up his young son and drove us towards our very final stop: Crystal Bay Beach. As was normal in Asia, Eddy never wore a seatbelt. However, I felt nervous when his cute son was in the front seat without one, especially when he would stand on the seat to face us. One sudden push of the brake would've sent the poor kid flying through the windscreen. We had to brake often too, as we'd frequently have near misses with cars coming from the opposite direction on the many sharp bends.

Crystal Bay Beach was pretty but not as heavenly as Atuh Beach had been. For the next few hours, we relaxed on sun loungers, enjoying the sunshine and cooling off in the ferocious waves. I fell asleep for a bit, tired from being woken in the early hours. At 5pm, we were back on the ferry. It was a shame to leave but we wouldn't miss being thrown around in Eddy's car.

Indonesia: Bali: Seminyak - Rain Rain Go Away (Part 2)

Wednesday and Thursday were lazy days, although I did fit in a beach run each day. Kerry and I sat by the hotel pool both mornings (while it was sunny) and then went into town in the afternoons (when it started raining). Both days we hoped for a sunset but the Bali weather was *not* playing ball.

On Friday, I booked a driver, Dewa, to take us out for the afternoon (I'd used him when Mel had been with me). Dewa dropped us off at Canggu Beach and we walked along it to Echo Beach, where we lay in the sun and watched the waves. The volcanic sand was black and sparkled like tiny diamonds in the afternoon sun.

At 2:30pm, black clouds closed in on us. We made it to a beachfront BBQ restaurant just ahead of a torrential downpour. We delayed leaving as long as possible but at 4pm we had to walk out into the rain to find Dewa. It took him ages to find us, by which point we were soaked.

Even though the weather was atrocious, we continued with our plan to visit Tanah Lot. I'd been before but I thought Kerry would like to see it. Thankfully, the rain stopped by the time we arrived, but it was clear we wouldn't see a decent sunset. Despite the weather, the temple was as busy as ever. We explored the complex, taking photos of the decorative statues and buildings. As we were passing a large grassy area, Kerry pointed to a large, fake snake. I could see its tummy moving so I informed her that it was real. Horrified, she took a step back. I couldn't help but laugh.

Before we left, we stopped at a cliff-top restaurant and ordered drinks and dessert. We sat at a table overlooking the temple, keeping our fingers crossed for the merest hint of a sunset. Although the clouds blocked our view of the sun's descent, some of the sky turned a little pink - it was as good as we were going to get. It got dark quickly, so carefully avoiding the many monkeys that were gathering, we returned to Dewa's car and he drove us back to the hotel.

Indonesia: Bali: Ubud - Fever & Fire

On Sunday morning, I was awake before my alarm: something wasn't right. I felt sick and my stomach was making weird noises. Within seconds, I found myself in the bathroom, suffering with an unpleasant bout of explosive bowels. The timing couldn't have been worse. We'd hired a driver for the day to take us from Seminyak to Ubud and I'd wanted to show Kerry some of the sights I'd enjoyed on my previous visit. Originally, we'd booked a driver called Edy, who was recommended by a friend, but he'd had to cancel the day before because of the funeral of a distant relative. Dewa wasn't available so we booked the exuberant Danu, a driver whose little kiosk we'd passed regularly. He picked us up at 9am and we left Seminyak. Luckily I didn't feel too sick and Imodium stopped my *other* problem.

After driving through a torrential storm, we arrived at the Tegenungan Waterfall. Halfway down to the falls, we stopped for a photo opportunity at a large bird's nest (set up to help tourists get those all-important Instagram shots). We faced forward and smiled, rejecting the more common 'look at me gazing majestically into the distance' pose.

Upon exiting the nest, I felt queasy so I told Kerry to see the falls without me while I rested in the shade. By the time she returned, I felt better. However, we hadn't climbed a dozen steps before I suddenly felt ill again. I sat on a ledge and the world turned black as I was consumed by overwhelming nausea and saw proverbial stars. My sense of hearing faded, sweat poured from every pore and I felt tingly all over. Somehow I managed not to vomit. Slowly, I began to feel better, although Kerry said the colour had completely drained from my face.

I knew I wouldn't be able to manage our planned day of fun so we asked Danu to take us straight to the rice fields. Monkey Forest was easily reachable from our Ubud accommodation so we could go there another day. It took an hour to reach the Tegalalang rice fields as there was so much traffic. When we arrived, I stayed in the car and Kerry went with Danu to see the lush, green fields. I was gutted as I'd really been looking forward to seeing them again.

Our last stop was at our accommodation, the Vinayaka Ubud. It was very hard to find and the road to it was too narrow for our vehicle. Danu drove as far as he could and then got out, bringing the owner to the car. It was much further out of town than my map had shown – it appeared that we'd be staying in the jungle. Getting around in the daytime would be ok but it would be more difficult after dark.

I climbed straight into bed, feeling simultaneously cold and hot. We'd last eaten in the early afternoon of the previous day so too much time had passed for it to be food poisoning. Kerry went out to explore while I stayed in bed, feeling feverish and nauseated. My whole body ached and I felt like I had the flu. As I drifted off to sleep, I kept my fingers crossed that I hadn't picked up malaria or dengue fever.

I needn't have worried; the next morning, after lots of feverish dreams, I awoke feeling better. I was no longer burning up and I didn't feel nearly as sick. Whatever it was had been full-on but short-lived. Just after 9am, we were brought our complimentary breakfast. I was surprised that I could wolf down my banana pancake easily. The watermelon juice was delicious and some peppermint tea helped to settle my stomach. Feeling revived, we went down to the pool, where we spent the rest of the morning.

By midday, I felt up to moving around so we slowly walked to Monkey Forest, stopping for a panini on the way. As usual, the monkeys were simultaneously scary and entertaining. We loved watching them but we quickly moved away if they got too close. It didn't take long before

I saw two monkeys shagging - I couldn't stop myself from filming it as it was hilarious. The baby monkeys were very cute and we liked watching them interact with their mothers, who went from being caring one second to slapping them round the face the next. We spent a couple of hours in the rainforest, but I had to sit down whenever the heat and humidity overpowered me and caused my nausea to return. As we left, we felt grateful that no monkeys had jumped on us and that we'd escaped with all of our possessions intact.

At 7pm, we went to Paradiso, a small, cosy cinema, to watch the first episode of the final season of Game of Thrones. It was a sell-out and many people were turned away, so I was glad we'd bought our tickets earlier in the day. At 7:15pm, we were allowed upstairs to settle down on the comfy seating. We chose a futon right at the front and I had a pot of amazing, smoky mint tea. As the curtains rolled back, people started clapping and cheering. The episode was good: not an awful lot happened, but people left smiling, excited for the next installment.

Tuesday morning was spent by the pool, reading. At around 2pm, we started getting ready to go into town. That's when another wave of nausea hit me (maybe my germs hadn't been as short-lived as I'd hoped). I lay down for a while, and then when I felt up to it, we walked slowly into town. I managed a small lunch of chicken and rice but that was all I had for the rest of the day. We enjoyed a relaxed afternoon consisting of massages, drinks at a restaurant and buying tickets for a traditional dance show.

At 7pm, we arrived at Pura Batukaru and took our seats for the Women's Kecak and Fire Dance. However, our seats were already occupied by some large red ants. Luckily, people pointed them out to us *before* we sat down, so we swapped our chairs for some less anty ones. My paranoia about the ants didn't leave: I felt itchy and checked the back of my chair every few seconds. The woman next to me was just as bad and kept checking herself throughout the performance. At one point, she flicked one from her arm onto me. I wasn't best pleased.

The show began with a large group of women chanting, setting the stage for the performance: a retelling of the Hindu story of Rama and Sita. There was no speaking but the performers' faces and eyes were incredibly expressive. The dancers were mesmerising, particularly their slow, deliberate hand movements. To be honest, if we hadn't read the story of Rama and Sita at the restaurant beforehand, we would've had no idea what was going on. Regardless, it was fun to watch, even just for the colourful costumes and singing. Once the story of Rama and Sita was over, a Fire Dance was performed, where a man danced on a painful-looking bed of burning coconut husks. According to the leaflet, the dance protects society against evil forces and epidemics.

On Wednesday, we read by the pool and enjoyed the calming sounds of the jungle. I felt better and even managed small meals at both lunch and dinner. Kerry did some sightseeing in the afternoon while I had another massage and did some shopping at the market. The next day, we would be leaving for Nusa Dua, Kerry's last stop in Bali. Her time with me was going too quickly; I'd really miss her when she left. I'd also miss Ubud. It was a shame I hadn't been well enough to enjoy it properly but at least the worst of my illness was over.

Indonesia: Bali: Nusa Dua - The Finer Things Club

18TH - 21ST APRIL 2019

On Thursday afternoon, Kerry and I left Ubud. I felt much better (perhaps due to my daily five-pack of Yakult) and was ready for a new adventure. It took well over ninety minutes, but finally we arrived at the D'Mell Bali in Nusa Dua. We checked in and went straight to the pool where we took it in turns to float on the giant inflatable swan.

A little before sunset, we walked to the main road and found ourselves lured into a restaurant promising discount. The special offer worked a charm as the restaurant quickly filled with hungry customers, while the one over the road remained empty. I ordered a starter of crispy calamari and a Balinese fried rice dish that came with satay chicken, prawn crackers and a fried egg. What they hadn't stated on the menu was that the calamari also came with fries; so basically, I had two main courses to plough through. It was a good job my appetite had returned!

Breakfast at the D'Mell was an improvement on our Ubud breakfasts. They were hot for a start and Kerry's scrambled eggs didn't look like small, yellow marbles. After floating on the semi-flaccid swan for an hour, I got ready for our exciting day out. The D'Mell offered a free shuttle to the beach at 11am and we wanted to take advantage of it.

We hadn't been expecting much so we were surprised when we were stopped at a checkpoint where security guards checked the car. As we proceeded past them, it seemed like we'd entered some sort of luxury gated community. It was Bali, but a sterilised version, which had been put through an Instagram filter. Everything was clean and sparkling with wide, well-paved roads, pristine green lawns and landscaped gardens. There was even a hospital and a shopping mall. On both sides of the road were entrances to fancy resorts - this was how the other half lived. In my head, I nicknamed it The Finer Things Club (an American Office reference).

We were dropped off at a disappointingly pedestrian beachside car park. The beach was pretty and the sea was bluer than we'd seen in other parts of Bali, although not as beautiful as on Nusa Penida. We commandeered some sun loungers from the Inaya Resort and waited for the attendant to approach. Most sun loungers on Bali cost 50,000 rupiah for a day, or were even free if you ate or drank there, but we were told that these ones would set us back 150,000! We balked at the cost but paid anyway, as it wasn't like we had many alternative options. For that price, I expected a butler, complimentary massage and free champagne but all we got was complimentary use of the pool and a towel.

Our time at the beach flew by. The sun was at full force and the pool and sea were natural remedies for the heat. I got up a couple of times to walk along the beach and mused that my life was pretty good. I was still looking forward to going home but I was determined to enjoy my last two weeks in Bali.

As it was Kerry's final night with me, we treated ourselves to a slightly fancier restaurant than usual: Ketut's BBQ Kitchen. The food was great and I couldn't resist ordering a 'welcome cocktail'. They'd given us a free shot as a welcome drink and I'd wanted more, so they'd prepared a large glass of it, which tasted much boozier than the shot had. Kerry had dessert but I was full, so I opted instead for one of my favourite Rainbow Paddle Pops from Circle K on the way home.

At 6:30am the next morning, a taxi whisked Kerry away. I felt a bit lost but I didn't want to mope - I had to make the most of my time in paradise. I couldn't decide whether to go back to the beach or sit by the pool. I didn't want to fork out another 150,000 so I had to find out if there was anything else to do. I was in luck: I discovered that there was a 'Water Blow', a temple and a promenade that would be perfect for a long walk. With that in mind, I made the decision to take the shuttle once again.

I was dropped off at the car park and then walked straight to the Water Blow. Despite numerous signs saying they were charging 50,000 rupiah to see it, the staff told me it was free. I was delighted - I liked 'free' (a rarity in Bali). The Water Blow was a large crevice in the spiky, volcanic rocks, eroded by the waves. It was quite impressive, especially when a large wave hit it and water erupted into the air and flooded the surrounding rocks.

Next, I walked along the 'promenade', a paved path leading through all the resorts for seven kilometres. It was a pleasant walk and it was interesting to see the different playgrounds of the wealthy. Some of them seemed lovely but others were a little crowded, with sun loungers bunched closely together. If I had to choose between a posh resort and a deserted beach, I'd choose the deserted beach any day.

After walking a while, I retraced my route to the car park and went in the opposite direction, heading towards Pura Geger, a cliff-top temple. The temple was closed to tourists so I just took a couple of photos from the entrance and stopped to admire the views and have a cold coke. I then returned to a resort near the car park, where I sat in the shade of some palms trees. I'd walked seven miles so I was pleased with that, especially as I hadn't felt up to running since being ill. On the way back to the D'Mell, I asked to be dropped off at the restaurant where I'd had the calamari. I had the same again before buying another Paddle Pop and going home.

For my final morning in Nusa Dua, I did something that would count as a 'Finer Thing': I had a massage at the D'Mell. But it wasn't just any old massage; it was a 'Four Hands' massage, done by two people at once. I thought it might be weird but it wasn't. However, I found that I could only properly concentrate on what one person was doing. It didn't mean it was a wasted experience though - the massage was amazing and my only complaint was that it was over too quickly.

Feeling relaxed, I sat by the pool until it was time to be driven to Seminyak, my final stop before I went home. I was so excited at the thought of seeing my friends and family again, but I was especially excited (and very nervous) about seeing Tom. We'd talked or messaged every day for months but in just two weeks I would actually *be* with him again. I really hoped things would work out.

Indonesia: Bali:
Seminyak - Wanting Home

At lunchtime on Sunday, I was taken to the Green Palms Hotel in Seminyak. I liked Seminyak: people were friendly and I always felt safe, even when walking alone at night. It wasn't perfect by any means but the good outweighed the bad. The bad consisted of the traffic, terrible roads and the constant stream of 'lady massage?', 'lady taxi?' or 'yes, transport?' It drove me mad, as did the constant beeping of cars and motorbikes. I found a way to stop the noise though: headphones. When I wore them, nobody bothered me and I wouldn't have heard them if they'd tried - it was almost magical.

The Green Palms was a small but charming hotel and my room was spacious with excellent air conditioning. In the afternoon, I walked towards the beach. On the way, I passed my favourite spa, Angelica, and remembered that they offered haircuts too. Before long, I was in front of a mirror with my hair being snipped off. The hairdresser, Bella, did an amazing job. It was a shame I couldn't get *all* my future haircuts done there. The products smelt so good that I sniffed my hair for hours after; the head massage was also amazing. The whole thing cost just five pounds; I was so pleased that I left a big tip.

I proudly strutted down the road with my hair all shiny and bouncy, stopping for dinner at my favourite restaurant before going to the beach. My styled hair didn't last long though and after thirty seconds by the sea, it was blown about in all directions. The weather had improved since I'd been in Seminyak with Kerry, so I was able to enjoy a pretty sunset before returning to the hotel.

That evening, I heard about the terrible bombings in Sri Lanka. If I'd stuck to my original plan, I would've been flying into Colombo just four days later. I was so glad I'd changed my mind as it saved me from having to make a decision about whether to go or not. I'm not sure what I would've done to be honest. I might still have gone but I would've been anxious the whole time and it would've been challenging with the curfew and social media ban in place. Thankfully it was out of my hands. My flight from Sri Lanka to Europe had been cancelled anyway due to Jet Airways going bust. It was clearly not meant to be.

On Monday morning, I was up at 7am to run. I'd decided the previous evening that I would try to run two miles a day while I was still in Bali. Two miles was manageable in the heat, even if my route options were limited. Keeping it simple, I ran along a semi-main road, avoiding the hundreds of scooters that whizzed past and the wonky pavement tiles that tried to trip me up.

By 8am, I was on the back of a motorbike and on my way to the James Cook Sports Bar. You may be wondering why I was at a bar before 9am. I wasn't there to drink, but to watch episode two of Game of Thrones. I was the first person to arrive so I picked a prime viewing spot and ordered a 'Bran's Bacon & Egg Cheeseburger' from the Game of Thrones themed menu. By the time the episode started, there was quite a crowd. It was fun watching with other people and I looked forward to returning the following week for episode three.

As I wasn't under any time constraints, I walked the four miles back to the hotel, enjoying the part of the route that ran along green paddy fields. I passed the place where I'd turned around on my run and realised that I'd been running adjacent to what looked like a prison. I looked it up when I got back to the hotel and discovered it was the infamous Kerobokan Prison, or 'Hotel K'. The jail was home to around 1,300 prisoners, even though it had been built to hold only three hundred.

Most were there on drug offences. Due to the high number of international inmates, it was sometimes referred to as the 'United Nations' of prisons. Strangely, the prison was a popular tourist attraction: people could visit the prisoners. I watched a documentary about it on YouTube. For a prison, it seemed quite relaxed. The guards weren't armed and generally got on well with the inmates. The main issue was overcrowding but foreigners, or anyone with money, could apparently buy themselves some privacy for the right price.

At lunchtime, I had my free hotel breakfast: delicious banana pancakes with bright pink dragon fruit and yoghurt. Throughout my stay, I tried a couple of the other interesting options on the breakfast menu. My favourite was the bright pink smoothie bowl, topped with fresh fruit and granola. Weirdly, it was almost as pink when exiting my body as when I spooned it in (too much information?).

I spent the afternoon by the pool and didn't go out again until my tummy started rumbling. I chose a small restaurant near to the hotel and enjoyed some satay chicken. The owner of the restaurant was very friendly and after I'd eaten, we had a long chat about schools in our countries. He also advised me to run before 7am as school started at 7:15am (which is why the roads had been so busy).

The next week flew past in a blur of lounging by the pool, beach walks, massages and watching Netflix in my hotel room. I didn't have much interest in exploring and was content to switch off. Despite my best intentions, it wasn't long before the early morning runs dried up. This was mostly due to picking up a urine infection. Therefore I bid farewell to my trusty (and worn out) trainers, my travelling companions, which had protected my feet while running and walking in over a dozen new countries, up mountains, on beaches, through forests and even up an active volcano.

My 'issue' had first struck on Saturday, a week before I was due to go home. I'd ignored it for a couple of days but by the Tuesday I knew it wasn't going anywhere and would only worsen. Knowing I probably needed antibiotics, I asked the hotel's owner to recommend a local doctor. Luckily there was one just around the corner, Doctor Arie, who was friendly and spoke perfect English. He confirmed that I had an infection and gave me painkillers and antibiotics - the whole thing cost less than ten pounds.

Once I'd seen the doctor, I took a taxi to the Ibis Styles Bali Petitenget. It was where I'd spend my final nights in Bali. The bed was extremely comfortable but I couldn't help wishing I'd stayed at the Green Palms as it was much more cosy and quiet. The hotel had one unexpected benefit though: HBO. While I was feeling crappy, at least I could watch reruns of Game of Thrones. I'd been back to watch the third episode at the James Cook Sports Bar the day before but it was great to re-watch it.

On Wednesday, I woke up feeling a little better and spent the morning at the pool. Whilst I was there, I met a woman in her late forties called KJ, who was once a presenter for The Discovery Channel. Although she was sweet, she only talked about herself. She'd obviously led an interesting and glamorous life so I was happy to listen and nod at the right moments.

By the afternoon, my stomach was starting to rumble in an unsettling manner. It wasn't long before I was in the bathroom. The first 'episode' was followed quickly by five more. Each time, things got worse, until it was like I peeing out poo (I'm over-sharing again but you need to understand how horrific it was). I had no idea what was wrong with me. Was I having a reaction to the antibiotics?

My anxiety got the better of me and I found myself charging to the local medical centre. They gave me different antibiotics, tablets to help with the diarrhea and probiotics. This time it wasn't so cheap. I spent the rest of the day in bed, drinking water with added electrolytes, and eating small slices of white bread. I really wanted to go home. While I rested, I called Tom for a good cry. I needed a hug and knew it wouldn't be long before I could finally have one.

On Thursday, I woke up feeling ok. My cystitis was still lurking and I had no appetite but I didn't feel like staying in bed was my only option. I skipped breakfast and went straight to the pool, where I was joined by KJ. She had some ice water and crackers sent over (she seemed to have the staff at her beck and call) and we spent a couple of hours chatting (well, I mostly listened).

At lunchtime, I checked Facebook and saw that the Bali Sea Turtle Society (BSTS) were releasing baby sea turtles that day. Sea Turtles regularly lay eggs on Kuta beach and the BSTS collects them and puts them in a safe place to give them the best chance of survival. As soon as possible after hatching, they're released into the ocean by excited tourists.

I took a motorbike to Kuta, and the driver dropped me off at the BSTS. I spent a while watching all the baby sea turtles, which were swimming about in large plastic tubs. Some appeared to be dead which concerned me, but the man working there assured me that they floated without moving when they needed a rest. Sure enough, after a couple of minutes, the 'dead' ones perked up. It was fascinating.

At 3:30pm, I noticed that people were starting to line up by the BSTS building, so I joined the queue. We were told that there were 129 baby sea turtles to release and that we had to collect a token. Families were only allowed tokens for the children, and couples, one token between them. I received my token and waited patiently to be called for the release.

Once the siren was sounded, we all took a plastic tub and swapped our tokens for a baby sea turtle. A lover of alliteration, I called mine Terry. Terry was a quiet fellow until he heard the ocean, and then he became very animated. Like me, he was ready for home. Once everyone had their turtles, we lined up behind the rope and placed our tubs on the sand. When instructed to do so, we tipped the tubs and freed the babies. It was so cute watching Terry scurry and flap his way to the sea; it seemed to take forever, but after a couple of false starts, he was taken by a big wave. I wished him luck (he'd need it, as only one out of a thousand makes it to adulthood). I like to think that Terry was in that 0.1% - he was very special, as was the whole experience.

Waking up on Friday morning, I felt both happy and sad. I wanted to go home and see my friends, family, and Tom, but I hated to say goodbye to Bali. Despite its flaws, I'd fallen in love with it and knew I'd be leaving a piece of my heart there. After eating breakfast, I took a motorbike to my favourite spa where Bella washed and blow-dried my hair, so I could return home looking less scruffy.

At 2pm, I took a taxi to the airport, waving goodbye to some of my favourite places, not knowing if I'd ever be back. It felt strange that my travels in Asia and Australia were over. For so long, time had gone slowly but since the new year it had flown by. Although it felt like the end, it wasn't. I'd only be home for three weeks and then I'd fly to Albania to begin my European adventures.

England: Shepperton -
A Holiday from My Holiday

When I arrived at the airport in Bali, I wasn't feeling particularly exuberant. I had a three hour wait, a four hour flight, a five hour wait, and then finally, a twelve and a half hour flight: it wasn't going to be a fun-filled twenty-four hours. My Thai Airways flight to Bangkok with wasn't too traumatic. I was still suffering a little with the urine infection so I explained my situation to the air stewardess, who passed me a large bottle of water that would see me through the flight. I was very grateful. Unusually, the flight left ahead of time so we arrived thirty minutes early. Normally, this would've been a good thing, but in this situation, it only increased my waiting around time in Bangkok. When I saw my flight had been delayed by an hour, I almost cried. Instead, I went to Burger King and munched down on some fries.

Already bored, I passed a sign that made me smile: MASSAGE. I was straight in there for a ninety minute leg and foot massage. The large room was full of weary travellers lounging on comfy, reclining armchairs. It was overpriced compared to the usual prices in Thailand but it was well worth the money. Apart from messaging Tom a lot, I didn't do much else.

Time weirdly passed quickly and before I knew it, I was boarding the Thai Airways flight to London. It felt strange to be going home after such a long time away but I was ready and eager to see my friends, family and of course, Tom. The flight seemed to take forever. There were no decent movies and I couldn't sleep, so I resorted to playing games on the in-flight entertainment system. Eventually, two hours later than scheduled, we touched down at London Heathrow. The baggage took an age to come through but I was finally reunited with the Green Turtle.

Tom was patiently waiting at arrivals for me. It felt so surreal to finally see him again. Even though we'd spent hours on video calls, he looked different to what I remembered (not in a bad way). For some reason, I felt panicked inside and very overwhelmed – I did my best to hide it though. We just had a long hug and then walked to the car.

Before going home, we had another stop: the Ashford Hospital walk-in centre. I was still feeling some discomfort and wanted to check if my infection had gone. After a two-hour wait and a urine test, I was given the all-clear. Tom then took me home. It was so good to see mum, although within thirty minutes, it felt like I hadn't been away at all and my trip felt like some crazy dream. Tom and I went upstairs and lay on my bed talking for ages. Although I was shattered, I managed to stay awake until 7pm, and then I completely zonked out. I woke up at midnight, wondering where I was, but I fell back to sleep and didn't stir again until morning.

As soon as I woke up, I felt totally overwhelmed again. Being home was a huge emotional adjustment, and coming back to being in a full-blown relationship was scary as I'd been single for so many years. When we went for a walk, I tried to explain how I felt and asked if we could take things slowly. He seemed to understand but I couldn't help feeling guilty, like I was letting him down. We'd been so excited about seeing each other again but it felt like too much, too soon for me.

Adjusting to life back home wasn't easy. I had no appetite and I felt exhausted and depressed. I'd been desperate to get home, and I didn't want to be anywhere else, but I couldn't shake the black cloud that hung over me and I found it hard to get out of bed in the mornings. I felt better when I was busy so I went on daytrips to Swanage and Littlehampton with Tom and also met up with friends: I spent three separate days at Charley and Gareth's house, playing with their toddler, Evan, and my favourite dog in the world, Alfred; met Emilie's beautiful baby for the first time in Windsor; spent a day with Liane; made Mr. Men cake decorations with Ed and Mercia; had Nando's with Andrea; had lunch with Gina (my work mum); went to Thames Court with Rina; ate pizza with Kerry; introduced Tom to my oldest friends, Dawn and Gina, over dinner; caught up with Matt; watched Game of Thrones with Paul; did parkrun with Ed; and obviously spent quite a bit of time with Tom. It was wonderful.

My return to running was somewhat hit and miss. I ran a few times and loved being back at the track with my friends from Shepperton Running Group, but despite the cooler climate, my energy levels were low and I'd always run out of steam. I needed to plough on through my slump though, as I'd signed up to do the Burnham Beeches half marathon with Tom in August.

Over the course of the three weeks, my depression lifted, but it didn't leave me *entirely*. Thankfully my appetite came back so I was able to enjoy copious amounts of Cathedral City cheese on toast. More and more, it felt like the previous nine months hadn't been real. I had to look through my photos to remind myself that it *had*. Seeing the photos often made me cry. I'd been to such beautiful places and looking at my smiling selfies, it was easy to forget I'd ever once felt lonely. Despite my sadness, I felt incredibly proud of myself for having travelled solo for such a long time. I'd met some amazing people, seen some awesome sights and had many unforgettable experiences. I had no regrets.

As my departure date fast approached, I began feeling a little anxious. A small part of me wanted to stay in Shepperton and skip the final leg of my journey, but I had too many flights booked and I didn't want to waste money. By the start of my third week at home, I had to begin preparations for leaving. I packed light and managed to get the weight of the Green Turtle down from seventeen kilograms to less than ten.

This meant I'd be able to wear it to walk longer distances, saving me some money in taxi fares.

The night before I left, Tom took me for dinner at Thames Court and I had a little cry. I remembered how hard it had been to leave him in August, how it had almost pulled me in two. At least this time it wouldn't be for long as he'd be visiting me in Lithuania. I hoped that when I returned properly, the depression wouldn't follow. But for the moment, it wasn't an issue. I had two months of travelling Europe to look forward to...

France: Orly, Paris - An Éclair Affair

24TH - 25TH MAY 2019

At the delightful hour of 5am, Tom drove me to Gatwick airport, where we sadly said goodbye. As the newly-svelte Green Turtle and I stepped into the airport, it was like I'd never been home: it was back to business. The Easyjet flight was very short and an hour later, the plane touched down at Paris Charles de Gaulle (CDG). After a long bus journey around the airport, we were dropped off at the terminal building, where I passed through passport control and picked up the Green Turtle.

As I was flying from Paris (Orly) to Albania the next day, I needed to get from CDG airport to Orly airport. I'd booked a ticket online with *Le Bus Direct* so I followed the signs until I found the correct bus stop. The journey took just over an hour. Once I was at Orly, I called my hotel and they picked me up as part of their free shuttle service. The Hotel Senia was just a few minutes' drive away, quietly nestled in the bosom of a beautiful industrial estate.

By 2pm, I was feeling the urge to wander. Orly airport is quite far from the centre of Paris so I explored the local area instead. Once I escaped the somewhat depressing industrial estate, things began to feel a little more...well, French. Pavements covered in discarded plastic tubing and broken glass gave way to cobbled streets, and utilitarian buildings with cracked windows became little stone houses with pretty gardens. I even saw an elderly woman doing her washing in a large stone trough at the end of a street.

If you were to ask what my favourite thing about Paris was, I might tell you that it was the cafe culture, the incredible architecture or the sea of museums, but it would all be lies; it's the cakes (J'adore les gâteaux). So, as I walked, I had one mission: to purchase a coffee éclair from a patisserie. Before long, I struck gold. Impressing myself with my French, I asked for the object of my desire. I also found myself asking for a chocolate chip baguette. The éclair was scrumptious and I although I wanted more, I made myself walk away.

My appetite sated, I continued exploring. There wasn't much to see really and as I wandered through what looked like a council estate, I felt short-changed. I diverted off the main road and went into a small park. It was quite pretty so it kept me entertained for a while. Once the park came to an end, I saw a sign for a hypermarket. I was incredibly excited. I always enjoyed a trip to a supermarket but hypermarkets were supermarkets on crack.

My exuberance didn't last. A security guard asked to see my bag and then proceeded to secure it closed with a strong cable tie before I could protest. What if I needed a tissue? What if my phone rang? Grumbling, I proceeded straight to the bakery to admire the tempting cakes. Glistening strawberry tarts and elegant pear tarts fought for my attention. However, I didn't want tarts, I wanted éclairs. Before I knew it, my hand was clasped around the soft, creamy body of an éclair au café: in fact, not just one, but *two*. I was powerless to resist. Feeling a little ashamed by my greed, I half-heartedly picked up a packet of cooked chicken breast, some fresh mango and a bottle of Diet Coke. In my head, these healthier foods would make up for eating three éclairs. As everyone knows, if you wash your food down with Diet Coke, you negate the calories - it's simple science.

My eagerness for the éclairs distracted me from exploring the remaining hundred or so aisles of the hypermarket. Once my bag was released from its restraints, I paid, and then walked to a nearby bench to enjoy my feast. The éclairs lasted less than five minutes. Feeling a bit sick, I sat on the bench for an hour and watched the world go by. A few men leered at me from their cars, shouting things I couldn't understand out of the window. Maybe they were telling me I had coffee icing spread over my face?

It had been sunny all day but as I sat alone, a black cloud descended and the first drops of rain began to fall. The absence of the sun caused a dark cloud to form in my mind too and I started longing for home. Before loneliness could swallow me, I called Tom for a long chat. It was so nice to be able to use my phone normally again, as in much of Europe, I could use my phone plan as I would at home.

Still talking on the phone, I moved on, towards the hotel. Along the way, I came across a graveyard. You may think that visiting a graveyard would depress me more but it actually had the opposite effect. I liked graveyards, as anyone who has ever been on holiday with me could attest. It wasn't a great one because it was too well-tended. I liked my graveyards overgrown, with gnarly trees guarding dilapidated tombstones. However, by the time I left, I felt better: unlike the poor souls in the graveyard, *I* was alive, so I should make the most of it.

Albania: Tirana - Party of One

Seeing as I'd woken up at 4:45am for my flight to Paris, I assumed that falling asleep would be easy, but it really wasn't. I offered myself to the sandman at 11pm but my consciousness refused to disengage until well after midnight. I then fell into a series of restless, dream-filled 'naps'. Finally, at around 2am, I slept properly, enjoying all of two and a half hours of oblivion before the alarm thrust me from my slumber. As I dressed, I asked myself why I kept booking early morning flights. It was almost masochistic.

At 5am, the hotel shuttle bus transported me to the airport. The traffic was horrendous considering the early hour and horns sounded wildly with impatience. If the grumpy shuttle bus driver had to wait for more than ten seconds, he'd continually beep until the traffic moved. I don't know what he expected his futile efforts with the horn to achieve.

Once the Green Turtle and I were safely inside the terminal building, I used the bag drop and then reluctantly ate a McDonald's breakfast (there were few options at such an early hour) before passing through security to the gate. I don't remember much about the flight because I spent most of it asleep.

Tirana had a very small airport so it took no time at all to pass through customs. As arranged with the hostel, a taxi driver was waiting at arrivals. I must admit, if you'd asked me to imagine Albania before I'd arrived, I would've pictured it as drab and grey, but that would've been a grave misconception. As we drove out of the airport, I immediately noticed that we were surrounded by mountains and green countryside: Albania was stunning.

After a thirty minute journey, the taxi dropped me off at the Art Hostel and Apartments. Nobody was at reception. I *loved* it when that happened. I waited for twenty minutes, growing increasingly impatient, when finally the housekeeper came to my rescue. She called another member of staff, who explained over the phone that I could move into the room and check in properly when she returned to the hostel. My booking had just said 'female dorm' so I hadn't been sure what to expect. Would there be a huge room of twenty beds? Would I get *any* sleep? Well there *was* a huge room with *sixteen* beds, but it wasn't *my* room. To my relief, mine was a cosy four-bed dorm.

As tempted as I was to climb into bed and sleep, I knew I shouldn't. It was a sunny day and I had to make the most of it. Swapping my t-shirt and jeans for a vest top and shorts, I ventured out without a plan (I like to wander aimlessly when I arrive in a new city). I liked Tirana straight away as it was clean, colourful and had plenty of character. I smiled as I passed groups of old men, who were smartly dressed in suits and hats, playing chess together in the park. I felt safe, though the vest and shorts might not have been the best idea as a few of the men were even more amorous than they'd been in France. It became clear why. Looking around, most women covered their legs and shoulders so I stood out like a sore thumb. It wasn't just the men, everyone eyeballed me; even kids stared, some pointing and laughing, and calling me 'turistik'. I later read that because Albania has relatively few tourists, people notice anyone different: not in an unwelcoming way, although it certainly felt intrusive at times.

I'd read that Albania had fantastic Italian restaurants so I entered the upmarket-looking Kriper, eager to put the claim to the test. Apparently, many Albanians work in restaurants in Italy and when they come home, they bring their new culinary skills along with them. The pepperoni pizza definitely exceeded my expectations - it was even better than some of the pizzas I'd had in Rome and it cost only three pounds.

After paying the bill, I looked around Skanderbeg Square, photographing the Opera House, the old mosque and the National Museum. Tirana has a mix of architecture, which reflects its troubled history. New buildings were in the process of being constructed, including a large new mosque (funded by Turkey). The country's communist history was obvious and could clearly be seen in the buildings surrounding the main square, including the Opera House. Needing a rest, I commandeered a shady bench near the square, where I could watch people watching me, and write my blog.

By 6pm, I was exhausted, so I returned to the hostel. Taking a seat in the second-floor courtyard, which overlooked the mountains, I wondered if anyone had moved into my dorm, which had been empty when I'd checked in. Part of me hoped not as I wanted to sleep, but a bigger part of me wanted some company. I was admiring the view when someone came up the stairs - it was the woman I'd spoken to on the phone, Jesse. She told me that once the large group left the following day, I'd pretty much have the place to myself. It wasn't quite what I wanted to hear, but at least I'd be able to catch up on my sleep. As it turned out, I didn't sleep well at all. The group had a party up on the third floor and I could hear the music blaring all the way down on the ground floor. Despite going to bed at 10pm, I didn't fall asleep properly until the music stopped after midnight.

I woke up on Sunday feeling lethargic and alone, with no desire to do anything: the ominous black cloud had returned. Sitting around moping wouldn't dissipate the cloud, so I knew I had to go out, even if I didn't feel like it. After a quick breakfast, I showered, and then ventured outside. I gave myself a mission: to buy a bus ticket to Skopje in Macedonia.

There was only one bus that would get me into Skopje in the daylight but it went via Kosovo. I'd read that it could be tricky entering Serbia with a Kosovo stamp in your passport so I wanted to avoid going through there if possible. However, all the other buses took much longer and wouldn't arrive until midnight or 4am. I did more research and people seemed to say that a Kosovo stamp wouldn't be an issue unless I was going to travel directly from Kosovo to Serbia: doing this would definitely lead to being denied entry. I'd be going to Serbia via Macedonia so I kept my fingers crossed that I'd be fine. I walked a mile to the Metropol Agency and paid twenty euros for a bus ticket. The bus would leave at 6am on the 29th May and arrive in Skopje by 1pm. That sounded much more civilised than turning up in the middle of the night.

As I left the agency, it started to rain, so I sought shelter in the National Museum, dedicated to the history of Albania. The first few sections helpfully explained everything in English, but after the third century, the translations dried up. Wandering cluelessly, I looked at pictures and artifacts, that without context, made little sense to me. Back outside, the rain stopped, so I walked to the Grand Park of Tirana which featured a large, man-made lake. It was pretty and I liked exploring the surrounding woodland.

Next, I visited the so-called Pyramid of Tirana (not a pyramid). Built during the communist years, it was intended to be a museum dedicated to the dictator, Enver Hoxha. It was completed in 1988 but after communism ended in Albania in 1991, it became a conference centre. At the time of writing, it stands derelict, but there are plans to renovate it in the future. Climbing up the steep slopes of the pyramid is a popular pastime for both Albanians and tourists. I tried it myself but I stopped just over halfway as it was slippery and I was scared of sliding down and hurting myself.

In the evening, I joined a free walking tour. Eri, our guide, was very informative and told us all about Albania's history. I learned more from him than the museum I'd been to. Communism first came to Albania in the 1940s. During those years, the country declared itself an atheist state: all religion was banned and most places of worship were torn down. The country was put on lock-down and nobody could leave the country, or even their city. People were encouraged to spy on one other and if anyone tried to escape, three generations of their family would be made to pay for their crimes. It was a horrendous time.

When communism finally fell in 1991, there were people who had never heard of Jesus, or credit cards, or bananas. All these things rushed at them in a sudden period of change, which must've been very overwhelming. Coca-Cola was one of the first new things to come to Albania. Even during my visit, twenty-seven years after the fall of communism, there were no McDonalds, Starbucks or Pizza Huts, only KFC. Funnily enough, the smiling face of the colonel was reflected in the living room window of the building where the communist dictator (Enver Hoxha) resided up until his death. Maybe it symbolised the stand-off between capitalism and communism.

I returned to the silent hostel at 10pm, where Jesse told me that there was only one other guest, a German man. I met him (Melvin) at breakfast the following morning. We got chatting and discovered we both wanted to do the same thing: visit Bunkart and the Dajti cable car. Even though the two places were only a couple of miles away, Jesse told us that she thought it might be dangerous to walk there, as we'd have go through a dodgy part of the city. However, we decided we'd be safe if we stuck together.

The roads were dirty in places but everyone was friendly. Bus drivers frequently stopped to ask if we needed a ride and the fruit seller insisted on giving us his best produce. We passed small groups of old men sitting together on benches, talking and laughing. I told Melvin that I thought the UK could learn something from the Albanians. In my experience (thinking about my dad), too many older men in England had few friends after retirement and found themselves alone, their health and spirits deteriorating. Maybe if more men maintained good friendships and played board games in the park, they'd live longer, happier lives.

Even though the weather had been wet and miserable when we'd started walking, by the time we reached our destination, it was bright. Wanting to make the most of it, we went to the Dajti Express first. Spanning a distance of nearly five kilometres, the cable car journey is the longest in the Balkans. The views over the forests, farms and mountains were spectacular and I enjoyed every one of the fifteen minutes it took to reach the top. As it was a weekday, it was very quiet and we had the place to ourselves. We hiked on Dajti Mountain, stopping to explore some abandoned buildings, and saw some horses with foals, some giant snails and a large, white bunny in its hutch.

Once we returned to ground level, we walked through a long tunnel to Bunkart, a museum detailing Albania's more recent history, contained inside a converted five-storey underground communist bunker. It reminded me of the Secret Bunker in the UK, with rooms that appeared to be stuck in time and endless corridors.

As we walked back to town, we couldn't resist stopping at a bakery. There were so many tempting options but we limited ourselves to two each. I had no idea what mine were, but one was like a fat, fried doughnut roll, covered in syrup, and the other was a layered dessert consisting of sponge, custard, chocolate mousse and cream. Albania was going to make me fat. In fact, the whole European trip would make me fat as there were too many delicious desserts and cakes to devour.

That evening, I went out to dinner with Melvin. He was so easy to talk to and there was never any awkwardness. Melvin fancied Italian, so I suggested Kriper. We shared a refreshing starter of mozzarella, pear, kiwi and crostini, and both ordered pepperoni pizzas, which washed down with Disaronno. We practised our Albanian while we were there and could clumsily say yes, no and thank you. The waitress seemed genuinely pleased that we made the effort. It wasn't easy though as 'thank you' in Albanian takes five syllables to say: faleminderit (valley-man-deer-it). Saying hello is even harder.

Once we paid the bill, we moved on to a small café bar called Komiteti. Furnished from the communist era, it was cosy and quirky, and we sat there for a couple of hours, talking over raki (a type of 40% alcohol fruit brandy). There were many different flavours available but we were recommended to try the honey and cinnamon version which was sweet yet strong - I certainly wouldn't have wanted to have more than a couple. As I climbed into bed that night, I felt grateful for having met Melvin. Being a party of two for a day had greatly improved my mood.

After saying goodbye to Melvin, who was off to Albania's coast with a friend, I went for a run. I'd felt too self-conscious to run in Albania before but as I took off towards the Grand Park of Tirana, I felt good. People stared more than usual but I was used to that. In total, I ran seven miles, going around the lake and through part of Skanderbeg Square.

Once I'd showered and relaxed, I walked around town, stopping to eat more cakes and drink overpriced mint tea in a French cafe, where I did some writing. When I got back, I packed, ready to move on.

Metropol Bus Trip: Tirana - Pristina - Skopje: Hello, Goodbye

29TH MAY 2019

Bright and early, at 5am, I was at the Metropol Agency, ready for my journey to Macedonia. I sat on the steps of the travel agency with a few others; many were chain smoking so I had to keep moving to escape the fumes. An hour later, a colourful bus arrived and everyone boarded: I seemed to be the only tourist. The woman collecting tickets pointed me out to the bald bus conductor, who nodded and smiled at me reassuringly.

As we drove away from Tirana, the bus stopped a few times to pick up more passengers from the roadside. Behind me sat two old men, both reeking of alcohol and cigarettes. As we travelled north, the scenery grew increasingly beautiful. Forest carpeted the snow-capped mountains and there were endless green lakes, winding rivers and waterfalls to admire.

Shortly after 8am, we reached the Albanian border at Morine. Two immigration officers boarded: one collected in everyone's passports and the other checked some people's bags. We passed through the checkpoint, where I expected us to pull over and wait for the passports to be returned, but instead, the bus turned around and we went back the way we'd come. I was confused, but thankfully, we hadn't been turned away; we were just making a stop at a small restaurant, where people bought coffees. I had some loose change so I bought a couple of soft drinks and enjoyed the views.

Before long, a horn sounded and we all took our seats on the bus again. We returned to the checkpoint and an officer handed the passports to the conductor, who then returned them to us. I thought we'd stop again at the border of Kosovo but we just kept driving and didn't pass another checkpoint. Maybe both countries had checked the passports at the same time? It was a relief to find I didn't have a Kosovo stamp in my passport. It put me at ease about crossing into Serbia later in the trip.

Naturally, Kosovo was similar to Albania in terms of scenery: they both offered an abundance of mountains, forests and green fields. Kosovo did however, have a larger share of the poppies, which flooded the fields with a sea of red. As our journey continued, we made several stops and gradually, the bus emptied. While I ate my lunch of bread and jam, I started to worry that I should have got off too, but I told myself not to be silly: the conductor would've told me if I needed to change buses. My anxiety was needless as by 10am, we reached the capital of Kosovo (Pristina), where the conductor pointed to an empty bus stop and told me and another woman to wait for our bus to Skopje. The frowning Albanian, Ina, took me under her wing and we waited at the bus stop together. Luckily she spoke some English. Within two minutes, a bus pulled up and our previous conductor popped out of nowhere and gave the new conductor some money, pointing at us. We put our luggage on the bus and were told that the bus wouldn't leave for another hour.

Ina, unimpressed, said she needed coffee so we found a cafe at the bus station. Before I could stop her, she ordered one for us both. I explained that I didn't have any cash but she waved away my concern and told me not to worry. Chatting over coffee, I discovered that Ina was a manager of a nightclub and was going to fly from Skopje to Malta to visit her boyfriend. Although she was a little intimidating, she was also very kind and looked after me well.

At 11:30am, our bus left for Skopje. A few more tourists boarded this time. The conductor collected bus fares and looked at me expectantly for a few uncomfortable seconds. I looked helplessly at Ina, who reminded him that he'd been paid by the other conductor, and he moved on. Leaving the city, we once again entered the countryside. Apart from music, I didn't need any other entertainment as the natural beauty was more than enough to keep my attention.

Only an hour after leaving Pristina, we were at border control at Han i Elezit. As an immigration officer boarded and collected up all of the passports, I kept my fingers crossed that my passport wouldn't be stamped upon exit. Luckily it wasn't - hurrah!

We passed through the checkpoint and the bus stopped again. Nobody told us to get off but one by one, people hesitantly left the bus. It soon became evident that we needed to join a small queue to have our passports checked by Macedonian immigration. Within five minutes, we were back on the road. The bus made a few random stops to drop people off, including Ina, who got off and into a taxi without even a backwards glance - charming!

After a long but scenic journey, we arrived in Skopje, where I stepped off the bus and collected the Green Turtle, ready for our next adventure.

North Macedonia: Skopje - Go Big and Go Bust

29TH MAY - 3RD JUNE 2019

I got so drunk last night that I tried to spank a statue...It really hurts when you hit rock bottom.

I arrived at the Lighthouse Hostel at 2pm, and after a little rest, walked along the river into town. As soon I stepped into the centre of Skopje, I noticed the number of statues. I'd never seen anything like it: they were *everywhere*. Sometimes I couldn't see one statue properly because another was standing in its way. There were busts, full figures, lions, horses, even a giant bull (and fittingly for the title of this chapter, there were a fair few casinos too).

Up to eighty percent of Skopje (including its neoclassical buildings) had tragically been destroyed by the 1963 earthquake. Plenty of simple, modern buildings have been erected in their place, but in 2012, the Prime Minister announced a major project named *Skopje 2014*. The project oversaw the construction of numerous classical-style buildings and facades, in the hope that it would restore a sense of national pride. Somewhere along the line, a conversation like this might've occurred:

Tomas: (project manager for Skopje 2014): Morning Stefan. Do you remember when I got *really* drunk after our brainstorming meeting last year and *joked* we should fill Skopje with enough statues to rival the Louvre?

Stefan: (in charge of ordering things): (gulping) Pardon me?

Tomas: You knew I was joking, right? I couldn't get into my parking space just now because it was full of statues.

Stefan: You seemed pretty certain...

Tomas: I was hammered Dave! We'll be in the shit for this; we'll lose our jobs. What are we going to do with five hundred statues?

Stefan: We'll pretend we did it on purpose. Tell everyone the statues will bring in tourists: tourists love statues and tourists bring money. We'll line up statues on the bridges; fill the squares with statues; put statues on the streets, in parks, wherever there's space. We'll build more bridges to put more statues on if we have to. No one will *ever* know...

Tomas: You're a genius!

I did some research and discovered the project had been slated due to the extravagant costs. Some of the statues were marked with graffiti, a clear indication that they were not welcomed by all of Skopje's residents. In 2016, the *Colourful Revolution* saw the city's many statues and monuments hit with colour bombs as a protest against the extreme spending. The paint residue was still visible two years later.

Despite the overwhelming (and amusing) abundance of statues, I loved Skopje. The people were friendly and stared less than they had in Albania; however, the men still smiled and winked a lot. Before heading for home, I visited a supermarket bakery and bought a creamy, sponge dessert topped with thick cherry sauce, which I demolished in the hostel garden. By 10pm, I was in bed in my four-bed dorm, which I was sharing with two young men. To give myself some privacy, I used my towel as a makeshift curtain.

At 8am, I put on my running things and forced myself outside. The hostel was twenty feet from the river's edge, which meant I had a convenient running path right outside the door. Considering it was still early, it was incredibly hot so I only managed a pathetic two miles. I was proud of myself for doing it though. I had a half-marathon coming up in August so I would need to keep up with the training.

Once I'd showered and enjoyed the free breakfast buffet, I hurried out of the door to join the free walking tour of Skopje. Our group, led by a local man, Miha, was small but friendly. We met outside the memorial for Mother Teresa, who had been born in Skopje. There had been such a large group on the Tirana tour that I hadn't actually spoken to anyone; the individuals and small groups had all been rather insular. This time there were only eight of us: four from Spain, a couple from Tunisia, a Russian and me, so we all conversed much more.

Also joining us was a pack of seven stray dogs, including Sam, Alex and Bella. Miha told us that most of the strays in North Macedonia are tagged after being neutered and treated with medicine. They are then collected up annually for check-ups. Not all members of the pack were tagged though as some were apparently too good at evading the dog catchers. It soon became clear that the pack's favourite thing to do was chase bicycles and vans travelling along the pedestrianised streets. Sometimes they'd grab a trouser leg or try to bite a van's bumper - it didn't always go down well. Miha laughed that they acted as good traffic control: the vans had to slow down to avoid hitting the dogs and most cyclists (who were supposed to push their bikes in these areas) quickly jumped off when the dogs came at them.

Apart from hating anything with wheels, our furry friends were very sweet and liked nothing more than to be stroked. I was surprised when we first moved off that the pack followed. Miha said it was a regular occurrence. Sam, who looked to Miha as his master, had only missed five of his daily tours in as many years. The dogs kept us amused throughout the tour and would always be waiting when we returned from visiting a place where they couldn't follow. On one of the newer bridges, three of them climbed into one of the fountains for a bath and a drink of water - it was a funny sight.

Miha told us he was embarrassed by the number and grandiosity of the statues. Apparently they'd run out of subjects to make statues from at one point, and when they'd run out of room for them, they'd begun putting them on top of buildings. He joked that the old Mayor of Skopje suffered from 'copy and paste syndrome'. If he saw something he liked in another city, a copy would soon be made for Skopje, usually bigger than the original. However, Skopje also had some *real* historic treasures, including a bridge that was over five hundred years old.

We discovered that Skopje is a hub of seismic activity. The 1963 earthquake killed 1070 people. The train station clock stopped at the exact moment the earthquake struck: 5:17am. The remnants of the station have been left as a memorial. More recently, in September 2016, Skopje had eleven earthquakes in thirty-six hours. It must've been terrifying.

Halfway through the tour, we stopped at a little restaurant, Serdarot, for some free rakija. Like the Albanian version, it was potent and after two shots, I felt quite tipsy. At the end of the tour, we revisited the restaurant to try some Macedonian dishes that Miha had recommended: warm bread pieces topped with cheese, and rolled meat, stuffed with cheese and covered in bacon. I had the pork which was amazing. While we ate, I spoke with Sara, Murad and Artio and enjoyed hearing all about Russia and Tunisia. It was pleasant to enjoy good company over great food; none of us were in a hurry to leave.

By the time we finally parted, it was late afternoon. I wandered around for a couple of hours, taking photos in the old part of town where the bazaar was. Most of the original buildings had been destroyed in the earthquake and had been rebuilt, but there were a few historic ones which looked like they could fall apart at any moment.

When I got back to the hostel, it was a relief to find I had the room to myself as most people seemed to favour the cheaper, six-bed dorm.

After another good night's sleep, I walked to the bus station and bought a bus card from a stationary yellow bus. I was surprised to see so many red double-decker buses being used - it was almost like being in London. Shortly after 10:30am, the bus left the station. I was glad I'd got on at the first stop, as by the second stop, all the seats had been taken and by the third stop, the bus was jammed full of passengers.

It took over an hour for the bus to reach its final destination: Matka Canyon. The canyon and the Treska River were beautiful. A dam had been built, creating an artificial lake. From the boat house, you could rent a kayak or take a boat ride to the Vrelo Cave. I decided to hike first, while the weather was still good. A path started behind the lone restaurant and led up the side of the canyon, giving spectacular views. I didn't see many other people; it was pleasant to have some peace. The footpath climbed high above the water and I could see where parts of the green railings had been swept away by minor landslides. Sometimes there would be a huge drop down to the water so I had to watch my footing. After two and a half miles, the official footpath ended at a barrier. A local told me that it was possible to carry on for another six kilometres but from what I could see, the path became more dangerous. I therefore turned around.

Opposite the barrier, on the other bank of the river, was the Vrelo Cave. A small group of people were walking up a zig-zagged path to the cave's entrance. As they neared the top, I heard someone shout, "Be careful - there's a big snake!" It wasn't what I wanted to hear: I had to walk back alone, knowing there were *big* snakes around. I wasn't afraid of snakes but I didn't know what type they had in Macedonia. That evening, I read that vipers lived in the canyon, one of the most venomous in Southern Europe...

Luckily I made it back without any unwanted encounters. While I ate my lunch on a bench, I thought about what to do next. That was when a man rushed over, saying I could make the next boat if I hurried. For some reason, I got caught up by his exuberance and found myself boarding a small boat. There were six of us: two couples, me and another solo female. I hoped she and I might start chatting but neither of us even said hello. The boat journey was pleasant but I was disappointed by the Vrelo Cave, which wasn't nearly as impressive as the ones I'd seen in Vietnam.

Back on dry land, I made my way to the bus stop. The next bus wasn't due for an hour so I bought an ice cream and waited. At 4:20pm, the solo woman from the boat came over to ask if she was in the right place to catch the bus. I replied that she was and she disappeared. Time ticked by but the bus didn't arrive. Taxi drivers circled like vultures, telling me there'd be no more buses that day. I knew they were talking rubbish but they kept bothering me. Eventually, I walked away and sat with the other woman on some steps. This time we started talking: her name was Gina and she was Dutch. Time flew as we chatted.

The bus turned up over an hour late. Gina and I sat next to each other and agreed we'd to go for dinner when we reached the city. Being a creature of habit, I took her to the restaurant I'd been to the day before. We ate, talked and laughed until it was dark - it was like we'd known each other for years. We got on so well that we arranged to meet up the next day to go hiking.

We met at 12pm on Saturday and walked to the bus station. It didn't take long to reach the mountain. The bus stopped halfway up and from there we took the cable car to the top. Considering it was the weekend, it was very quiet and we had a gondola to ourselves.

The views from the top were amazing. Skopje was spread out below us on one side and on the other, forests carpeted the hills. At the summit of Vodno Mountain was the sixty-six metre high Millennium Cross, one of the largest crosses in the world. The monument was finished in 2009 and was funded by the Macedonian Orthodox Church to commemorate two thousand years of Christianity in the country.

After a long period of sitting and admiring the beauty, we started the hike. There were no maps showing the routes so we had to rely on my map app. We chose a meandering track called the *Pensioners' Path,* thinking that if it was suitable for the elderly, then we'd have no problems.

It started out well, with gradual slopes, but as our journey continued, the path grew steeper and became littered with loose gravel; we had to go slowly to avoid falling. Thankfully, not all the path was scary. Some sections were almost flat and took us through peaceful woodland and fields. The final part of our descent was the hardest as there was half a mile of path where it was steep and slippery with nothing to hold on to. We stuck together, and despite a few small slips, made it to the road without injury. When we reached the city, we stopped for a well-earned pizza.

Sunday was a day of rest. I had breakfast, ran four miles along the river, did my laundry and as usual, bought lunch from the bakery of the local supermarket. I was addicted to their bread rolls filled with melted cheese and their selection of cakes.

It rained heavily the rest of the day so I stayed at the hostel. Just as I was getting ready for bed, a German man entered my dorm: I was no longer alone. He turned out to be lovely and we had a good chat before turning out the light.

Monday was my last day in Skopje so I decided to walk along the river to the large City Park. With its pretty ponds, streams and bridges, it was the perfect place to escape people, if not statues, which still popped up regularly. As I looked around for a place to stop and eat my lunch, I encountered a Macedonian penis. It wasn't my first rodeo: something similar had happened in Mongolia.

This particular guy was peeing. If he'd put it away quickly, looking a bit embarrassed, it may've been *almost* acceptable (considering it was daytime, he was in a public place, and women and children were around). However, this one proceeded to proudly wave his flaccid member at me with a smirk that presumed I'd find the sight of his penis awe-inspiring. Wanting to make my disgust clear, I stopped dead, looking him in the eye while shaking my head. He at least had the decency to look mildly self-conscious. Turning on my heel, I walked away. I was not impressed.

My disgust was soon replaced by hunger. I sat on a bench in a penis-free area of the park and ate my usual: a cheesy roll and a cake. The bottom of the roll was a little solid, so I tore it off and threw it onto the grass behind me, thinking a stray dog might enjoy it. The bready treasure soon attracted attention, not from a dog but a large bird. Every time I turned around to look at it, it would turn and walk away innocently. It became a little game. From the corner of my eye, I'd watch it move towards the food, then just as it was about to grab it, I'd turn. We did this multiple times, until I eventually felt sorry for it and looked away long enough for it to snatch it.

As I returned through the outskirts of the city, I passed an imposing, brutalist-style building belonging to the Post Office. Being a fan of ugly things, I liked it and found it more interesting than the too-clean, classical architecture of Skopje's main square. There's lots of brutalist architecture to be found in Skopje because when the earthquake flattened the city in the sixties, it was rebuilt in the then-current trend of communist, geometric raw concrete. It's not always obvious but if you know where to look, you can always find it.

After stopping at a bar for a drink, I met Gina for dinner. We went to a fancy restaurant next to the river, which had very grumpy staff. The food was tasty and well-presented though. As usual, we had a good laugh and talked about doing some travelling together in the future. A couple of hours later, it was time to go our separate ways. I was glad we'd met though and really hoped we'd stay in touch (we have).

Serbia: Belgrade - Home From Home

4TH - 10TH JUNE 2019

At 11pm on Monday night, I walked to the bus station. As I navigated my way through the maze of deserted residential streets, I couldn't help but feel nervous - I expected someone to jump from the shadows at any moment. To my relief, I safely made it to the main road, which in contrast, was lined with raucous revelers. A late-night parade was being held because RK Vardar (a local handball club) had won the European Championship the previous day and as a result, the road was temporarily blocked.

Eventually, I was allowed to cross the road and enter the bus station, where at midnight, I boarded a Fudeks bus to Belgrade. Although I had a double seat to myself, I couldn't sleep, so I put my eye mask on and intermittently dozed. At around 1am, we crossed the border into Serbia. It was a simple process which only took ten minutes. The remainder of the trip passed relatively quickly and the bus made it into Belgrade at 5:30am. Ignoring the taxi vultures at the station, I strapped on the Green Turtle and walked through the drizzle to the hostel.

I'd confirmed my booking of a private room the previous day but had been concerned that the photos and information from the hostel's description had disappeared. When I reached the apartment block, I buzzed the bell of the hostel and waited. Nobody answered so I tried pushing the door, which swung open with an ominous creak. Letting myself into the building, I climbed the stairs to the Hostel Olimp 777. I rang the bell, but there was no reply, so I pushed the door open and let myself in. The hostel was deserted, despite having been told that someone would be there to greet me upon arrival. Making myself comfortable, I sat on the sofa to wait.

At 8am, an old Chinese woman came out of the doorway of an almost empty dorm. As she silently stood staring at me, I had a sinking feeling. It didn't seem like a typical hostel. The woman made breakfast and disappeared back into her room, but not before taking one last suspicious glance at me. I napped on the sofa until 10:30am, when an old man prodded me, asking what I was there for. I showed him my reservation details and he went to find the relevant member of staff, who was still sleeping.

Eventually, a middle-aged man arrived at reception, blearily rubbing his eyes. He spoke no English so he used Google Translate to inform me that I couldn't stay there. Confused, I showed him my reservation confirmation and the e-mail I'd received the previous day, but he just shrugged and told me again, "No booking." Crying with frustration, I used the hostel WiFi to book a private room at a different hostel and then left, slamming the door behind me. What a shambles!

The Habitat Hostel was only a mile away so it didn't take long to walk there. Upon my arrival, I was greeted warmly by the Serbian owner, Igor, who said he'd have my room made up as soon as possible. Dante, a huge but incredibly soft dog, which looked perpetually sad, came over to say hello and I gave him a cuddle. The hostel was much different to others I'd stayed in and felt more like a friend's apartment. I immediately liked it.

After a nap, I walked around Belgrade. The city didn't immediately appeal to me, maybe because it was so big and sprawling: I generally preferred smaller cities where I could find my way around easily.

Upon my return to the hostel, I felt deflated so I went straight to my room. I'd noticed a lot of brutalist and modernist architecture in Belgrade and having read about the 'Space Architecture' tour, which featured some interesting brutalist buildings, I tried to book it for the weekend. However, I was told that there was a two-person minimum, and as I was alone, it would cost double. This did not improve my mood.

On Wednesday morning, hoping for a fresh start, I joined a free walking tour. However, as the tour began, so did the rain. It was a bit miserable trudging through the wet city but I found that I liked many of the buildings. Belgrade had been destroyed so many times, that on one crossroads alone there were structures from four different decades and of four different styles. The tour was a little dull and wet but we did get to enjoy some free shots of honey rakija which cheered us all up.

Once the tour ended, I visited the Museum of Contemporary Art with a girl I'd met on the tour. Gia (from Slovenia) and I didn't know what to make of the 'art' and discussed the possibility that we were simply too unimaginative to understand it. I found that I preferred the building itself to anything inside it. The museum predominantly focused on an artist who used robotics to create large pieces of geometric art (like a giant Spirograph). We liked some of his featured work but his other stuff was just weird, like when the artist had people throw hundreds of sharpened pencils at him until he bled. We were glad the museum had been free on Wednesdays as we didn't feel there had been anything in there that had been worth paying to see. I often felt this way about modern art yet I still liked visiting modern art museums: it was like I thrived on feelings of bafflement.

Once we were back in the city centre, Gia and I parted ways. I was pleased to get away from her as she'd continually brought up my least favourite subject - Brexit - and kept telling me that my country was 'fucked'. It may have been true but I didn't need to keep hearing about it. Before heading home, I popped into the National Theatre to buy a ticket to the ballet, Swan Lake. I'd read online that the theatre was cheap and that it was usually easy to get tickets. However, it wasn't meant to be: tickets had sold out. Disappointed, I returned to the hostel.

As soon as I entered the busy lounge, I was passed a shot glass of very strong rakija. Normally rakija is supposed to be sipped and enjoyed slowly but not at the Habitat Hostel - we all downed it together. Chatting with everyone greatly improved my mood (as did the rakija). There was a mix of people from different countries but everyone was easy to talk to. We discovered that one of the young women was a sex therapist and this intrigued us all: it certainly gave us something to gossip about anyway.

A Serbian friend of Igor's (or possibly just a long-term guest), Sacha, began referring to me as his English girlfriend, calling me 'My Love'. Igor would shake his head and tell him to leave me alone but I didn't mind – I found him quite entertaining.

Igor had helped me to plan a running route, so on a hot, sunny Thursday morning, I put on my sports gear and walked towards the river. As usual, things didn't quite go to plan. I found that I had to cross the train tracks to reach the river. My map app showed a couple of possible paths but they both seemed to involve walking directly *onto* the tracks, which didn't seem particularly safe. However, it soon became clear that I'd need to do exactly that. Following an elderly man down a muddy footpath, I crossed over six sets of tracks. I stepped very carefully, not sure if any of them were live. Lots of people seemed to be doing it so I told myself it was *probably* safe.

From there, it was easy to find the water's edge but due to the recent rain, the river was very high. After half a mile of easy running, the path diverted around a small bastion and became submerged under a foot of muddy water. Belgrade was clearly determined to make my route difficult but I persevered. First, I tried walking around the very edge of the path where there was a raised grass verge, but it eventually disappeared under the water and there was no way through without ending up with water-logged trainers.

My second option was to cross the train tracks but it didn't look like I'd be able to get back again. Instead, I took option three: I climbed some broken steps to the top of the bastion. It was a gardener's nightmare up there so there was no way of seeing if there was another set of steps leading down on the other side. Taking a chance, I fought my way through the tangled undergrowth to the other side, where I found more crumbling steps. My run resumed.

The next part of my journey was very pleasant. Well, until I reached the foot of a bridge I needed to cross. As a building site was blocking my way, I couldn't work out how to get onto the bridge. That was when I noticed an elevator. Relieved, I pressed the 'up' button, but it didn't move. Confused, I tried again but still nothing happened. Finally, a grumpy middle-aged man came over and told me I'd have to pay two euros to use it (even though nothing like that was indicated on the sign). I only had enough cash on me for a post-run drink so I explained that I couldn't afford it. Angrily, he stabbed his finger towards a set of stairs on the other side of the active building site.

The site extended out both left and right so my only option was to walk through the centre of it. The site was full of rubble and big piles of sand and as I cautiously picked my way through to the other side, I felt like giving up on the run. However, I continued on, climbing the long flight of stairs on the other side. Thankfully there were no further problems and I was able to enjoy the rest of my run along the beautiful riverside. I did eight miles in total.

That night, we had a BBQ at the hostel. Copious amounts of homemade rakija were drunk: I had four shots of the honey version and three of the much stronger plum variety. I got *very* drunk *very* quickly. Sacha began cooking at 6pm, but three hours later, we were still waiting to eat. Being 'his love' meant I was able to wangle some food early - everyone else was sent away. Eventually, at 10pm, everything was cooked. There were sausages, chicken fillets, chicken wings and pork fillets - it was all delicious and the huge bowl of meat was devoured in minutes. It was a great evening, full of laughter, and Igor and Sacha demonstrated such warm Serbian hospitality.

Just before midnight, Igor turned off the music and told everyone to 'get to bed or fuck off to a bar' - it was quiet time. His directness made me laugh. I liked that he had rules and cared that his guests were able to sleep. Just as I was opening the door to my room, he told me that if the couple next door started having loud sex again, I should bang loudly on the wall to shut them up (I'd had to leave my room earlier in the day when they'd noisily been at it). Igor had no time for romance or sex in his hostel and if he saw anyone kissing and cuddling, he'd tell them to stop. The Habitat Hostel was not the place for PDAs.

On Friday morning, I woke up with a headache. After a slow start, I stepped outside. As I started walking, I realised that there was a direct correlation between my enjoyment of a city and the amount of sun: Belgrade was beautiful in the sunshine. Despite not being one of my favourite cities, I was beginning to feel very at home there. I had a favourite bakery, a favourite pizza kiosk and a favourite drinks kiosk, and in those places, I always received a warm welcome. Alexander, who I always bought my drinks from, was always happy to see me and liked nothing more than to chat. He told me it was good to see British people, particularly *pretty ladies*, visiting his country - what a charmer!

As it was such a gorgeous day, I made it my mission to capture Belgrade's beauty. With that in mind, my first stop was the fortress. I'd been there briefly on the walking tour but the bad weather had ruined the views. In the sunshine, it was amazing. I sat high up on the fortress wall, eating breakfast, with my legs dangling over the edge. From there I could see the wide confluence of the two major rivers: the Danube and the Sava. There was quite a drop to the ground below and the height made my legs feel wobbly.

In between eating my pastry and yoghurts, I took out my camera to take some snaps of the river. Before I could stop it, my lens cap plummeted to the ground! Most people would've left it where it was and simply bought a new one, but not me - I hated to lose *anything*. I finished my breakfast and then made my way down, hopeful I could find my way to the lower level and retrieve my lost property. Climbing down some steps and over a small wall, I found myself in the right area. Lizards scurried about in the long grass: I hoped they were *all* I had to worry about. Unfortunately they weren't as I was soon attacked by hungry mosquitoes. After quickly covering myself in insect repellent, I searched for my lens cap, much to the curiosity of the people above. Just as I was about to give up, I found it - my itchy bites hadn't been in vain.

In the afternoon, I visited the 'Palace of Serbia' (an unofficial name), in what is known as Novi Beograd (New Belgrade). Completed in 1959, it's a modernist building used by several ministries of the Serbian government. It is so vast, that by area covered, it's the largest building in Serbia. The palace was one of the few stops of the brutalist/space-age/modernist building tour I'd wanted to go on that was within an easy walking distance. It was an impressive structure and I was fascinated by it, especially the huge fountain at the front. Luckily for me, it wasn't the only building from the tour I'd get to see. Igor had arranged for a young friend of his, Luca, to drive me around the following day to visit the others.

Our first stop was in New Belgrade, at the brutalist Ganex Tower (also known as the Western City Gate). It's an imposing thirty-six floor structure, formed of two towers, which are connected by a bridge and what looks like a spaceship, (which was once, or may still be, a revolving restaurant). Despite its worn appearance, many residents live inside the concrete monster. Some find it interesting but many call it the ugliest building in Belgrade. As a fan of brutalism, I found it so ugly that it was interesting.

As we drove to our next stop, Luca and I chatted about life. We kept it simple as he didn't speak much English (though it was better than my Serbian).

Leaving the city, we weaved our way up Mount Avala, passing through some lush forest. We stopped at the Avala Tower, a 205 metre, tripod-based telecommunications tower. The original was destroyed in the NATO bombings of 1999 but reconstruction of a slightly taller replica finished in 2009. After taking a few photos, I paid for a ticket and took the elevator to the observation deck. The outstanding panoramic views over the countryside, villages, and in the distance, the city, were well worth the money.

Once back at ground level, I found Luca and we drove to our final stop, the Rudo Towers, also known as the Eastern City Gate. The brutalist-style complex, which is formed of three residential towers, is apparently one of the symbols of the city. Three triangular towers, which looked almost like steps from the side, were arranged in a circle. Even though they were very much lived-in, it was clear that the buildings, especially the facades, were in a state of disrepair and could do with a *lot* of TLC. After I'd taken some photos, we returned to the hostel, where I paid Luca for his services.

By 2pm I was hungry so I asked Igor for a recommendation for food. He suggested a grill he knew and we, with Dante, Tayfun and Marcos went to a popular little kiosk, a ten-minute walk away. We all had a delicious pork or chicken fillet stuffed with cheese and ham, enveloped inside a soft bread roll. It was so filling that I didn't need to eat for the rest of the day.

I'd been planning to relax that evening, but when I popped out to the bathroom, I was asked if I wanted to join some others to watch the sunset. I couldn't think of a reason not to, so I grabbed my bag and off we went. As it took so long to walk to the fortress, we ended up missing the best part of the sunset. However, we sat on the wall for an hour, enjoying the view until it grew dark. While we sat, mosquitoes feasted on us. This continued when we moved on to the fancy Boho Bar, where we sat outside on bean bag chairs - I ended up with ten bites and couldn't wait to return to the safety of my room.

As I readied myself for bed, I felt grateful my first hostel booking had gone wrong. I was so pleased I'd stayed at the Habitat Hostel as it had been like living with friends and family. There was always someone to talk to and Igor was like a strict but charming 'mother' looking after us all. Even Sacha amused me, especially when he'd call out, "Welcome my love," in a strong Serbian accent whenever I came home or came out of my room. He'd tell every new guest that I'd agreed to be his wife, and smiling, I'd have to shake my head to let them know it wasn't true.

On Sunday morning, I joined the crowds at Sava Lake. This was where Belgrade's residents came to enjoy the 'beach' on a hot day. The water's edge was packed with people in swimsuits and there were lots of busy cafes and bars. I ran five miles around the lake but in such hot weather and with so many people around, it was tough. Thankfully the path on one side of the lake took me into the woods - the shade and lack of people was a definite improvement. Feeling sweaty and tired, I took the bus back to town.

In the afternoon, I wandered aimlessly through the busy city. I stopped for lunch at a Chinese restaurant and returned to the fortress for the views. As it was so hot, and my feet were aching from all the walking and running, I was home by 4pm. I started packing, ready to leave for Bosnia for next day. I was really sad to be leaving my Serbian 'home' and hoped that one day, I would return.

Bosnia & Herzegovina:
Sarajevo & Mostar - War & Roses

10TH - 15TH JUNE 2019

"For the dead and the living, we must bear witness."
Elie Wiesel (Holocaust survivor)

Just like the start of my time in Belgrade, the end was more trying than necessary. On Monday afternoon, I left the comfort of the Habitat Hostel and walked to the bus station. Stations in the Balkans often have random charges to get in or out and luggage was sometimes included and sometimes not. Bearing this in mind, I arrived for my 4pm bus to Sarajevo early, armed with a couple of spare euros. I tried to reach my platform but was told that I needed to purchase an entrance ticket. Dutifully, I went over to the small kiosk and passed a surly woman two euros. Shaking her head, she refused to accept them. Panicking, I hurried outside to find an exchange office. There was one five minutes away, where an elderly lady was serving. I explained that I would like to swap my euros for 190 dinar, but she shook her head as if she thought I was mad. I pleaded but she adamantly refused to help me. There was only one thing left to do: cry. I'm not proud of myself but tears worked. Presumably to make me go away, she swapped the money with a scowl.

Re-entering the station, I returned to the kiosk. I bought my entrance ticket and gave the woman a self-satisfied smirk before passing through the barrier. As I waited at the platform, I suddenly realised I didn't have any dinar left to pay for luggage, just a solitary euro. For fifteen minutes, I stood worrying. Would I have to run to the ATM for the sake of less than a pound? Would I miss the bus?

As the Centrotrans bus pulled up, I nervously waited in the small queue. The first passenger, a young man, put his luggage in the hold and handed over money. Then it was my turn. I cautiously passed the attendant my luggage, waiting for him to hold out his hand for payment, but he simply smiled and waved me towards the door. Once the bus moved off, the attendant walked down the aisle, collecting tickets. When it was my turn, he sat next to me so he could check my ticket. While he did this, he pressed his thigh tight against mine and moved his arm so that it was almost touching my boob. It made me very uncomfortable. When he finally moved away, I put my rucksack on the seat next to me so it couldn't happen again.

The rest of the journey passed without further interaction with the creepy attendant and three hours later, after a quick border crossing, we passed into Bosnia. The scenery along the River Drina was stunning: hills and mountains were draped with woodland and poppies grew in clusters. The light faded as we drew nearer to Sarajevo but I still enjoyed staring out of the window and watching the world go by.

At 10:30pm, we arrived at the small central station. For the first time in a while, I wasn't staying at a hostel but in a private apartment. The owner, Rasim, kindly came to the station to collect me and took me to Apartment Touch, which was in a grand apartment block, dated 1910. As we entered the building, he reminded me I'd booked the *small* apartment. He wasn't exaggerating: it was teeny tiny. I barely had room to bend over to wash my face in the bathroom sink.

On Tuesday morning, I slept in and then went exploring. Sarajevo was compact, and lying in a valley, was surrounded by forested mountains - I liked it straight away. There was a mix of architecture, ranging from utilitarian communist to classic Austro-Hungarian. Many of the buildings still bared gunshot and shrapnel scars from the Bosnian war, which had ended in 1995.

Before long, I crossed the river and lost myself in Baščaršija, the old part of town. I loved the narrow streets, which were lined with cafes selling burek (a type of pie) and cevapi (a type of sausage served with bread and onion). There were also several small shops selling handicrafts and souvenirs. While mooching around the bazaar, I couldn't resist buying a pretty embroidered purse.

Crossing the river once again, I visited the melancholy War Childhood Museum. Inside were housed various childhood artifacts, paired with written memories of people who'd been children in the war. Many of the memories were of people born in the same year as me, which really struck a chord. I was grateful I hadn't grown up with a war raging around me. Not all the memories were sad though: a few were about things that had made people smile, despite their terror and hardships. For example, a soldier returning from the front line found a plastic ball in the garden of a derelict house and gave it to his child. As it was the only ball to be found in the *whole* street, all the other children lined up to play with it. It was humbling to think that this one faded old toy had given so much joy to so many.

As well as childhood memories from the war in Sarajevo, there were more recent memories from children displaced from the Syrian war. Knowing that such terrible things were still going on in our 'modern' world was heart-breaking. No matter where they were from, a common thread was that many children missed school. During the war in Bosnia, children had been taught for an hour or two a day in their basements, by teachers who would move between buildings. Lots of Syrian children however, had little opportunity to receive any education. Sweetly, many stated that they wanted to make the world a better place. I hoped they'd get that chance.

As I went to leave, I bumped into Marcos, who I'd met in Belgrade. He told me he was going to Mostar the next day. I also wanted to visit so we agreed to meet at the station and travel together.

Continuing the theme of warfare, I joined a 'War Scars' walking tour, about the Bosnian War, or the 'Siege of Sarajevo'. After a brief introduction, we were shown one of the many Sarajevo Roses, markers where bombs had exploded and killed people. The gouges in the ground had been filled with dark red resin, making them look like blood stains. This particular rose was inside a fresh food market. Apparently people had presumed they'd be safe there as it was surrounded by tall buildings on all sides, but one day a mortar bomb landed while people were shopping, killing nearly seventy people and injuring many more.

Our guide, who had been a child during the war, claimed that as she'd been so young, she hadn't been too affected by it, but as she recounted personal stories, I found it hard to believe. She told us that many older people have a much tougher time: some suffered unimaginable loss and heartache and have never been the same. During the war, people were trapped in the city, surrounded by the Chetnik enemy, who hid in the mountains. Over almost four years, more than 11,000 citizens were killed, either by bombs or snipers.

There was no food, water or electricity, and medical assistance was only received by the worst casualties. Indiscriminate snipers would ruthlessly aim their weapons at Muslim targets and shoot men, women and children. With over three hundred bombs dropping per day, people could only hide in their basements and avoid going outside as much as possible. Not everyone hid though. The guide showed us a photo of an elegantly-dressed lady strutting confidently down the street. The woman, who had survived the war, had refused to hide away. She wanted to show the enemy that she would continue to live her life. I had to admire her courage.

On the tour, we were shown many places, including the glass children's memorial, which commemorated the hundreds of children killed, and the 'Romeo and Juliet Bridge', where a young couple was shot by snipers as they tried to escape the city in 1993. They'd held each other as they'd died. It was too dangerous to recover their bodies so they lay that way for four days.

With heavy hearts, we moved onto our final stop: a defaced statue of a tin can. The UN provided food to the trapped citizens during the war: the most memorable being tins of 'beef', which had apparently been more like jelly, similar to cat food. Apparently people had been so hungry that they thought it was delicious. It was only after the war, when they could eat good food again, that they realised how truly awful it had been. Tongue in cheek, a statue was erected, to say *thank you* to the United Nations. As we stood there, a man shouted to us that it was the best statue in the Balkans.

By the time I got back to the apartment, I was shattered. However, I couldn't rest as I needed to do my long run for the week. Thankfully, it had clouded over, which made the heat more bearable. Looking down as I ran, I couldn't help but notice several indents and craters from gunfire and bombings on the path. It felt surreal to be jogging on the same streets where not so long ago, people had been running for their lives. I managed seven miles along the river before heading home.

At 5:30am the next day, my alarm sounded. Yawning, I dressed and walked a mile and a half to the train station, where I met Marcos. As there were only two trains per day, it wasn't a challenge to find the correct platform. The train left promptly at 7:15am. We passed through many tunnels and enjoyed spectacular views of the mountains. It made the early start worthwhile.

Once we arrived in Mostar, Marcos went off to do an organised tour. After getting my ticket validated for the return journey, I hurried in the direction of the city centre as I was hoping to join the free 10am walking tour. I made it with a few minutes to spare.

As we walked around, we were given lots of information by our young guide, Ivan. I hadn't realised that Mostar had also been heavily bombed in the war: it was littered with the pock-marked skeletons of once-grand buildings.

Our group was large, so I don't think anyone noticed when I accidentally-on-purpose got lost. I felt a little bad about it (for five minutes) but it was too hot to stand about listening for long periods of time and I found myself distracted by the views - I was eager to get photographing. I started at the famous bridge, Stari Most, which was a beauty. Destroyed during the war, the 427 year old bridge was rebuilt in 1993 and reopened in 2004. As you might expect, it was close to collapsing under the weight of all the tourists, so I wandered to the next bridge along. From there, I had uninterrupted views and could escape the crowds.

The old part of town was crammed with cafes, restaurants and shops selling a range of local handicrafts. Since I'd only had yoghurt for dinner the previous evening, I found myself in a restaurant eating a chicken schnitzel. I then spent the afternoon exploring and taking photos. I found many abandoned buildings but I didn't enter them as I was aware that there may still be unexploded devices inside. I may have been curious but I wasn't stupid.

By 3pm, I was tired out. The temperature was thirty-five degrees and I couldn't stand being out in the sun any longer, so I found a bench in a park and hid in the shade. I thought about how much I was enjoying my European trip. I felt relaxed and loved visiting the different cities - and I still had more to go! When the 5pm train came, Marcos, who had returned from his tour, and I boarded. Someone from my walking tour sat near us and we recognised each other. Lying, I told him I'd got lost and hadn't been able to find them again.

Once I'd walked home from the station, I relaxed in my very hot apartment. I messaged Masim to ask if there was a fan I could use. He couldn't find one so he allowed me to sleep in the cooler (and much larger), unoccupied apartment next door. In fact, until I checked out, I was able to use it as often as I liked - it was certainly useful to have access to a fridge and a washing machine.

After a lazy Thursday morning, I stopped at a restaurant to try a traditional dish, cevapi. On the cobbled streets of the old town, it seemed that *everyone* was eating it, even a pair of young nuns were eagerly tucking in. Personally, I didn't love the sausages but the hot, fresh bread was delicious.

At 1pm, I met Marcos at the entrance to the Mount Trebević cable car. It was more expensive than the ones in Tirana and Skopje but the views were fantastic. Seas of green forest faded into the horizon, hiding a dark past: snipers had once concealed themselves within the trees, snuffing out the lives of ordinary people from afar. As I found out later in the day, the whole area was peppered with unexploded landmines. I'd known enough to keep me from entering any abandoned buildings but I was blissfully naive as to the dangers of the forest, especially as the cable car was clearly a popular tourist spot.

From the observation point, we followed a paved track down to the derelict 1984 Winter Olympic bobsleigh track. There were few people about, most preferring to take photos at the top and then hop straight back into the cable car. I was therefore glad to have Marcos with me. The heavily-graffitied concrete snake twisted and turned its way through the unkempt forest. It was hard to imagine that once upon a time, it was full of excited spectators and television camera crews. In the mid-nineties of course, it was occupied in a very different way. From the Olympic buildings, sentry posts and bunkers were created. The solid concrete bobsleigh track itself was used as a base to rain deadly weapons down on the city.

Without a care, we walked along the one kilometre track as it wound its way down the mountain. I'm glad we didn't stray from it, as later in the day I saw photos of unexploded mines only a few feet away. Over five hundred people, including a couple of tourists, had been killed by landmines since the war ended in February 1996. It was claimed that if you were to wander from the path and into the forest, you'd be dead within five minutes.

Where the bobsleigh track ended, a paved, zig-zagged path began, which continued to the foot of the mountain. There were also some wrecked, abandoned buildings, covered in graffiti. Marcos suggested entering one but I warned him that it could be dangerous. The grassy track continued downwards. We discussed whether we should take this more scenic route or use the paved path. Sensibly, we chose the safer option. Even though the other path looked well-trodden, it wasn't worth the potential risk: Marcos joked that he liked having legs and I agreed.

As we descended, Marcos explained the Yugoslavia situation to me. I'd heard snippets from my numerous tours in the Balkans but the intricacies confused me. He suggested I watch a six-hour documentary called *The Death of Yugoslavia* and I promised I would. At the bottom, we bought cold drinks and downed them. This prepared us for our steep upward journey to the 'Yellow Fortress', an old defence fortification. From there we had more wonderful views so we rested on the wall for a while before returning to town and sitting at a restaurant for a couple of hours.

I was supposed to meet Marcos for dinner that evening, but I ended up having an argument with Tom, which quickly escalated. He didn't seem impressed by my dinner plans with Marcos and it almost felt like he was making the situation worse than it was to hinder my plans. Tom was supposed to meet me in Slovenia a couple of days later and began saying he wasn't going to come. We managed to sort things out but by that point, it was too late for dinner - Marcos had given up on me. I was disappointed I wouldn't get the chance to say goodbye.

My last full day in Sarajevo began with a five kilometre run and then I joined a walking tour with Neno. It was very interesting and I learned a lot about Sarajevo's five hundred year history. I discovered that Franz Ferdinand, the heir to the Austro-Hungarian throne, was assassinated on a bridge I'd crossed several times, the Latin Bridge. This event had been one of the triggers for World War One.

After the tour, I went to Gallery 11/07/95, a memorial gallery about the Srebrenica genocide of the Bosnian War, the worst in Europe since World War Two. Eight thousand Muslim men and boys were killed over just a few days: most were shot in the back and thrown into mass graves. One of the videos interviewed women who'd had their sons and husbands ripped away from them, never to be seen again. It's said that a picture is worth a thousand words and it's true. The photographs depicted blurred images of people running for their lives, dead bodies, grieving citizens and terrified children. They were horrific and showed the true nature of war.

Despite the depressing focus on war, I enjoyed my time in Bosnia very much and would love to return one day. Many Bosnians I've met have told me the same thing: life goes on and they will keep moving forward. I truly wish them well. I hope humanity learns from history, yet I worry that so many atrocities continue to happen around the world. As I read somewhere, 'history doesn't repeat itself but it often rhymes'.

Slovenia: Ljubljana & Bled - The Sad Death of Mr. Canon

15TH - 21ST JUNE 2019

I'd been planning on taking the bus from Sarajevo city centre to the airport for my 4:45pm flight but I couldn't find a definitive timetable: there were two online but each showed different times. To be on the safe side, I arrived at the bus stop for 1pm, even though the bus wasn't due for an hour. At 1:30pm, an airport bus whizzed past with no sign of slowing down, even though I waved my arms emphatically. I was confused; neither timetable had scheduled a bus for that time.

Nervously, I waited in the sweltering heat. When a bus hadn't arrived by 2:20pm, I knew I needed a Plan B. This became taking a taxi, but first I needed an ATM. The first three I tried either wouldn't let me take out only twenty marks (about ten pounds) or tried to charge a five pound fee. Finally I got lucky with a fee-free ATM and hurried back to the main road. Clutching my cash, I flagged down a taxi. The airport was close to the city so it only took fifteen minutes to get there.

The hour-long flight to Ljubljana was great. There were less than twenty of us on the plane so I had three rows entirely to myself: it was every traveller's dream! At Ljubljana airport, I met up with Tom, whose flight had landed shortly before mine. We had a long hug and brushed over our recent argument. We were ninety minutes early for the 7pm bus into the city, so we sat outside to wait. A bus turned up at 6pm, which Tom pointed out was labelled 'airport' but I didn't think much of it. It was only when I looked at the timetable properly that I realised I'd been reading the timetable for buses *to* the airport: the next one wasn't until 8pm. I was not having a successful day with public transport.

Seeing us standing around uselessly, a man from a nearby shuttle bus company approached and offered his services – we readily accepted. He dropped us off at the door of our accommodation instead of at the main bus station, so it worked out well. Our private apartment was in a quiet residential area, two kilometres out of the city centre. We checked in, stocked up on food at the local supermarket, and then had a quiet night in watching *The Death of Yugoslavia* on YouTube.

On Sunday morning, I woke up to that same sense of panic I'd felt on my first morning at home. It was difficult for me to transition from being entirely alone to being with someone twenty-four hours a day. As we prepared to go out, I tried to ignore it, hoping the feeling would go away.

As we walked into the city, I brought up the argument and told Tom how I sometimes felt he didn't listen to me (he would often just nod and make a 'hmm-hmm' sound). He told me it was just how he was and that it would be hard for him to change (it didn't bode well for our future). I began to think how our relationship had been easier when we were separated by thousands of miles.

Putting our differences to one side, we explored the city. The Austro-Hungarian architecture was beautiful but it was the castle on the hill, in the heart of the pedestrianised city centre, which dominated the cityscape. We spent a while looking in the shops, walking around the castle grounds and seeing the famous Ljubljana Dragon Bridge (the dragon is an icon of the city and appears on the city's flag, coat of arms and even on the drain covers).

Marcos had recommended the lesser-known Metelkova area, so after lunch at an Italian restaurant, we walked there. It was indeed quiet (by day at least) but judging by the number of bars and clubs, it would come alive after dark. Metelkova, an alternative, artistic area, covered with graffiti, was originally an Austro-Hungarian army barracks. During World War Two, it was occupied by Nazi soldiers and later, it was used by the Yugoslavian army. After the volatile breakup of Yugoslavia, it was left abandoned. Squatters soon claimed it and now it's a self-claimed haven of tolerance and creativity. With its numerous strange sculptures, art galleries and clubs, it was certainly interesting to explore.

On Monday afternoon, we rented bicycles from the Tourist Information Centre: the brakes barely worked and neither had gears (this would later become an issue). We decided to cycle part of the 'POT' route, a thirty-four kilometre path of remembrance, which follows where barbed wire was used (during World War Two) to surround Ljubljana and prevent any contact between the city and the countryside during the war.

From the tourist centre, we cycled two miles south until we connected with the trail. Unwisely, we chose to go anti-clockwise: this meant we were essentially going *backwards*, so the signs weren't pointing in the right direction. It wasn't a big deal though as the trail was clearly marked on my map app.

After some pleasant riding through flat parkland, we came to the foot of a steep hill. Without gears, we couldn't even try to cycle up the gravel path, so we had to push the bikes up. It wasn't any easier on the way down. As an experienced mountain biker, Tom was fine, happily skidding away (and scaring the hell out of me in the process), but I was nervous. The descent was steep and my tyres kept slipping on the loose gravel so I decided it would be safer to just walk my bike down.

From then on, things became easier. As much as possible, we followed the green POT signs or the metal POT markers on the tarmac. I enjoyed looking out for them and it became a bit of a game, like a treasure hunt. We cycled through pretty parks and over the river, where we saw a lone river otter swimming. Our time on the trail ended at Žale Cemetery but we didn't have time to explore as we needed to return to the apartment.

Having changed into our running gear, we walked to Tivoli Park, where we met up with the LJ Tekači running group. Tom and I were both members of Shepperton Running Group so we thought it would be fun. Instead of a sea of purple (SRG's colour), there was a sea of lime. Many people turned up but we had no idea how the run would work. Would people split into different groups? How would we know which one to join? After standing about confused for a while, we were pointed in the direction of the group leader, who explained that there would be three groups going at different speeds and distances. We decided on the middle group and at 6:30pm, ten of us set off.

I was surprised when we stopped after five minutes to do some warm up exercises. Once these were completed, we carried on with the run, going uphill, but just as we were finding our stride, we stopped for *more* exercises. This happened a few times over the course of five miles. As it was sometimes hilly, I was grateful for the short breathers but it seemed an unusual way of doing things. Throughout the run, an older guy explained the terrain and informed us when hills were coming up. It was sweet of him to look after us and it helped us to feel part of the group. Once we finished, we gave our thanks and then ran home so we could round our distance up to ten kilometres.

As we'd enjoyed the POT trail so much on Monday, we hired bicycles again on Tuesday to cycle the other half of it. It took ages to find two half-decent bikes and even then Tom had to pump up the tyres and do some adjustments. We began by cycling south, to where we'd started the day before, but this time we turned right instead of left. As we were now going in the 'right' direction, we hoped the POT signs would be easier to follow. They weren't, but I got better at spotting them.

Even though my arse hurt from the previous day's cycle, I really enjoyed the route. There were no big hills, just a few steps with a helpful bike slope. As before, we finished at the Žale Cemetery, but this time we had time to explore: it was huge and very well-maintained. There were many memorials, including a striking one with barbs and skeletal figures; we presumed it was linked with the Holocaust. We used Google Translate for some of the memorial inscriptions but it wasn't very helpful. For example, I'm not sure this is a well known Shakespeare quote:

"Transfer the time you put into it tell what you cutis
and no more or less"

After sixteen miles on the bikes, we sat at a bar by the river to enjoy a couple of drinks and a pizza. Tourists and locals streamed past, all enjoying the cool evening breeze. As the sun began to set, we walked home through Tivoli Park. It had been a lovely day and I was starting to relax back into the idea of being in a relationship.

On Wednesday morning, we took the bus to Lake Bled. In the centre of the turquoise water lay a small island with a castle perched on top. Mr. Canon and I couldn't have asked for a more picturesque view and we immediately got down to business. As usual it was a hot, sunny day. I'd forgotten my swimsuit so we settled for sitting on a wooden jetty with our feet in the water. On the opposite jetty, two teenage boys were back-flipping into the water - we suspected they were trying to impress a nearby group of girls. We could've sat there all day, but instead we walked four miles around the lake's perimeter, only stopping to eat our packed lunch at the water's edge.

From the lake, we began walking the three miles to Vintgar Gorge. However, it wasn't long before thunder rumbled and the sun hid behind the clouds. Unwisely, we hadn't prepared for rain: neither of us had jackets. As the rain started to fall, I wrapped Mr. Canon in a cloth bag and put it away in my tatty rucksack. We took shelter under some trees and waited for the worst to pass, but it was obvious the weather wasn't going to improve by much, so we continued on.

Soon, the rain got so heavy that we had to take shelter under some large umbrellas at a restaurant. We sat at a picnic bench and a waiter rudely shouted to us that we shouldn't expect *convenient* table service. Feeling obliged to make a purchase, we ordered drinks from a sour-faced woman at the counter.

By the time we finished our drinks, the rain had stopped so we gladly left. We reached the entrance to the gorge a little soggy and paid to get in. With blue water rushing through it and lit by a newly-returned sun, Vintgar Gorge was incredible. A handy wooden platform was attached to the rock wall of the canyon, making it easy to navigate. The path twisted and turned as we crossed numerous bridges and passed under rocky overhangs. Mr. Canon and I resumed our business as we walked the mile to Šum Waterfall, but by the time we reached it, the rain had returned. I took a quick photo, and then quickly put the camera away.

Retracing our steps to the entrance, thunder became our constant companion and heavy raindrops soaked us to the bone. We were so wet that it seemed pointless to take shelter, but the arrival of hail soon changed our minds. As we hid under a tree, we were pelted with large chunks of ice. I held an abandoned traffic cone above my head but it didn't help to protect the rest of me. Noticing a car port on the other side of the bridge, we ran for it and stood there shivering until the sun came back out. There was some pretty scenery on our return to Bled, so I took out my damp camera. I switched it on but nothing happened. Assuming the battery had died, I put it away again. Back in Bled, we stopped at a cafe to warm up before taking the bus back to Ljubljana.

When we got home, I immediately thought of Mr. Canon and changed the battery. Hopeful, I switched it on, but it was dead. We spent the next hour researching things to try and giving them a go but my camera remained immune to our efforts. With a heavy heart and a few tears, I had only one option: to let it dry out overnight and hope it would turn on in the morning. Thankfully, the memory card was fine so I was at least able to download the day's photos.

I didn't sleep well that night; I loved my camera and couldn't imagine continuing my travels without it. £900 of 'spare' money was available to me but that was for emergencies and to live off when I got home (I wouldn't be paid again until the end of September). With my fingers crossed, I crept out of bed and returned to the patient. I put in the battery and switched it on but it did not come back to life. Mr. Canon had done so well but our journey together was over.

Needing a plan, Tom and I pursued several ideas: buying a camera on zero percent finance from the UK was my favoured option but I had no way of getting it to me. I even looked into flights home so I could pick it up in person but that would've been expensive and a huge hassle.

By midday, we decided that the only realistic option was for me to buy one in Slovenia, so we found a local camera shop: Foto Beseničar. Mr. Canon had been a 70D and it seemed the current version was an 80D. I only needed the body and luckily they had one in stock. The camera was discounted at €959, which was still cheaper than Amazon. As I went to pay, I realised I'd left my credit card at the apartment so we had to catch the bus back to pick it up and then return to the shop. The female sales assistant was very sympathetic as I showed her my poor dead friend and explained what had happened. Sweetly, she asked the manager if she could give me more discount. He agreed to twenty euros, which was better than nothing.

Cringing, I handed over my credit card and paid the £840. My emergency funds were down to only sixty pounds. I would need a loan from my kind brother, Graham, when I got home, but at least I had a lovely new camera. I was so happy when I held it – Tom said it was the first time he'd seen me smile in hours. To prevent further disasters, Tom kindly bought me a proper case for Mr. Canon II and offered to take my old one back home for me.

For the rest of the day, we wandered the city aimlessly while I nervously began using my new camera. I was scared of damaging it at first but the feeling soon passed. In the evening, we stopped for drinks and pizza at our favourite riverside bar and then walked home.

RIP Mr. Canon. Together we saw the mysterious Northern Lights, the impressive Great Wall of China, the wonders of Petra and so, so many others.

I will always remember our precious moments together.

Dawn x

Slovenia: Maribor -
Feeling Sleepy in a Sleepy City

On Friday afternoon, Tom and I went our separate ways. I shed a few tears but I wasn't too worried as I'd see him again in a couple of weeks. The two hour journey was so peaceful that it was hard not to fall asleep (this would become a theme during my stay in Maribor).

When I arrived, I found it was calmer and quieter than Ljubljana. I walked a mile to Anna House, my accommodation for the next five nights, which was set in the ground floor of a grand building. My room was large, comfortable and cool, despite the humidity outside.

Feeling lazy, I spent the rest of the day in bed, only leaving to visit the supermarket. As I walked through the city centre, it was clear from the several stages that there was a big event on. My host informed me that it was Lent - an annual music and arts festival. He was keen that I attend the various concerts but I didn't have the heart to tell him that I couldn't afford it, so I just nodded politely. I got to see snippets of some free ones as I walked around town though.

On Saturday morning, I woke to the sound of heavy rain and thunder, which continued for a couple of hours. I found myself feeling relieved, as it gave me an excuse to stay in bed. When the rain finally stopped, I took the opportunity to go for a five mile run along the riverside. Luckily the storm caused the temperature to drop so although it was sunny, it was still pleasantly cool.

By Sunday morning, the thunder and rain had returned so I ate breakfast and then returned to bed. When it seemed safe to venture outside, I took Mr. Canon II and hiked up the famous (in Maribor at least) Piramida Hill. From the top, I enjoyed great views of the city and the pretty surrounding countryside and vineyards. The summit is now marked by a small white chapel, but up until 1784, a castle sat atop the hill, the foundations of which can still be seen today.

Next, I visited the extensive Mestni Park. I was taking photos of the small lake there when I noticed the angry storm clouds. Within seconds, the weather changed - it was like someone had flipped a switch as thunderous rain began pouring. Immediately, I whipped out my umbrella and took shelter under a large tree.

Eventually things calmed down and I was able to put the umbrella away and walk back to the city. I felt like going straight to my room to dry off but I thought I should probably explore a little more first. Unlike in Ljubljana, most of the shops in Maribor closed on Sundays, so between that and the weather, there was barely anyone around. I took a few photos of the prettier buildings but I didn't feel particularly inspired, so I ate a slice of pizza and then returned to Anna House.

More storms were forecast for Monday, so I decided that's when I'd do my long run for the week (rain being preferable to oppressive heat). However, I was disappointed to wake up to blue skies. Having slept in, I didn't leave until 10:30am, by which time the temperature had shot up. Grasping my bottle of water, I ran along the river. There was little shade and no breeze, so I struggled to keep going. It didn't help when the paved path disappeared and I had to run on an uneven grass verge. I was nervous about twisting my ankle again so I took things slowly, just to be on the safe side.

Four miles into my run, I stopped at a small bridge. Rather than run on the grass again, I went along the road, enjoying the pretty views of the surrounding countryside. After six miles, I'd drunk all of my water and was parched. Luckily a supermarket was only half a kilometre away so I popped in and bought two bottles of iced tea. I downed both on a bench before running back to the guest house - my eight miles were complete. I was knackered though and wondered how I'd managed a fifty kilometre race only a year before.

On Tuesday, I walked into town to do some food shopping. I was therefore confused to find everything closed again. I soon discovered it was a public holiday, Statehood Day, marking Slovenia's declaration of independence from Yugoslavia in 1991. Finding one open bakery, I bought something for lunch and then I walked to Stražun Forest, a couple of miles away. When I got there, I found I was quite tired, so I sat on a bench in the shade of the trees and enjoyed the peace and quiet.

That evening, my host told me the forest had a dark history: a bloody battle had taken place there between local partisans and those who fought with the Nazis during World War Two. I found it a little depressing: it seemed that everywhere I went in Europe had a sad history in some form or other.

That night I packed, ready to make my way to Slovakia the following day. I wasn't sad to be leaving Maribor but I would miss my quiet single room and the uninterrupted sleep it provided.

Slovakia: Bratislava - UFO Spotting (Part 1)

26TH - 27TH JUNE 2019

On Wednesday morning, my host kindly drove me to the bus station. It was less than a mile away but the heat had crept up to the mid-thirties and with the Green Turtle on my back, it would've been an incredibly sweaty journey. The bright green, double-decker Flixbus left at 10:50am. The air conditioning was most welcome and the three hour journey was comfortable. I had to swap buses at Vienna, which meant a ninety minute wait, but luckily there was a cool waiting room to hide in.

A little later than scheduled, the bus arrived in Bratislava. There was no direct route so I had to walk over a mile on tricky cobbled streets in the humid heat. My four-bed dorm was satisfactory but I dreaded having to share a room again. I was too tired to explore the city properly so I just popped to Tesco for food and ate it in the hostel's kitchen.

As expected, I didn't sleep well. I went to bed at 11pm but I couldn't settle as I suspected other people would turn up late. I didn't have to wait long: an older man came in and started unpacking at midnight. *He* just got settled when a younger guy turned up. Finally, once they were *both* in bed, I slept.

At 9am, I was the first to wake up but by the time I'd eaten breakfast, both men had checked out. Fed up with hostels, I changed a couple of future bookings to private accommodation. It meant spending more money but it was worth it to get a good night's sleep.

Grabbing my camera, I walked out into the oppressive heat to take photos of the main sights: the castle, St. Michael's Gate, Cumil the

Sewer Worker, the 'UFO' Bridge and the blue church. Bratislava was very photogenic: I particularly appreciated the mix of classical architecture and imposing brutalist, communist style buildings. The old part of the town was also beautiful with its cobbled streets and narrow alleys.

The heat was draining so I ducked inside a fancy ice cream shop called Arthur to treat myself (the white chocolate and the mascarpone ice creams were so creamy and delicious that I became a regular customer). Next, I sat outside a small restaurant near the main square. It was a good spot to watch the world go by and it made a nice change to treat myself to a *real* meal at a *real* restaurant. Keeping it cheap, I ordered a cheese-covered chicken breast with potatoes and a jug of ice-cold mango lemonade. The lemonade, with its huge chunks of fresh mango, ended up being better than the meal.

After lunch, I walked over the bridge to take a closer look at the brutalist UFO, but the footpath was *underneath* the main road so I couldn't see the structure. I tried walking along the river for a sideways angle but trees blocked my view. I was tempted to take the elevator to the observation deck of the UFO but I couldn't afford it and being *inside* the UFO wouldn't help me to take good photos of it. Defeated, I returned to the hostel.

Once in my dorm, I cooled down and spent some time editing the day's photos. While I was at it, a couple about my age moved into the room. The woman seemed angry and the man looked like a snorer. They didn't say hello and neither did I. A little after they went out, a younger Polish man checked in. This meant the room was full and nobody would turn up in the middle of the night – result!

At 7pm, I went for a four mile run. I crossed the UFO Bridge, turned right onto a paved path through some woodland next to the river, turned right again over another bridge and then right once more, back along the riverside to the start of the UFO Bridge, making a wonky rectangle. I returned to the hostel via the shop, where I bought a much needed bottle of iced tea. Then I showered and sat in front of the room's fan for the rest of the evening. Everyone came back just before midnight, so we all went to bed at the same time. As I'd suspected, the man snored but my ear plugs blocked out the worst of it.

Austria: Vienna - Day Tripping

28TH JUNE 2019

I'd originally wanted to stay in Vienna for a couple of nights, but having looked at the accommodation prices, I'd discovered it was much cheaper to stay in Bratislava and arrange a day trip instead. Flixbus sold return tickets for only eight pounds and buses left Bratislava almost hourly.

Not wanting an early start, I took the 9:35am bus, which got me into Vienna an hour later. Erdberg Station was a couple of miles from the city centre, so I took the underground and was there in minutes. As soon as I exited the subway, I was swamped with crowds of tourists: large tour groups swarmed the city like locusts. I tried not to let it bother me but I only lasted twenty minutes before ducking down a quiet side street.

Vienna was very grand but a little too fancy for me. After wandering aimlessly for a while, I hid on a shady park bench to look through my photos. Thirty seconds later, I was soaked when a sprinkler suddenly erupted (luckily no harm was done to the camera).

Feeling damp but refreshed, I moved on. I treated myself to chicken schnitzel and chips from a fast food kiosk and sat down to plot my next move. I hadn't come to Vienna with a plan and that was a mistake. The city was too big to just *happen* upon the main sights accidentally so I plotted a couple of key attractions on my map app.

I read that the popular Ankeruhr clock was 'one of the most outstanding works of art nouveau', so I went there first. When I arrived, people were crowded underneath the impressive clock with their cameras and mobile phones, waiting for it to strike twelve.

Thinking something very exciting was about to occur, I switched Mr. Canon II to video mode, ready to capture the action.

A bit behind schedule, five minutes after midday, the clock finally started moving. I pressed *record* and filmed the most underwhelming forty seconds of my life. I don't know what I'd been expecting, maybe some sort of punchy cuckoo clock effect, but all that happened was that the large characters moved very slowly past the clock face while music played. After one minute, I stopped filming, deleted the file and walked away.

My next stop was Karlskirche, considered the greatest baroque church in all of Vienna. With its two large columns, it was certainly a spectacular sight. I took a few photos and walked around the grounds, trying to avoid the spurting water erupting from several nearby sprinklers. Not wanting to return to the chaos of the city centre, I chose to walk the tree-lined ring road which encircled it. Apart from some hurried cyclists, it was pleasantly quiet.

Eventually, I reached the narrow Vienna River, where people were making the most of the good weather, many choosing to sunbathe on the grass in their swimsuits or run through the sprinklers. I followed this to where it converged with the wider Donaukanal River. This area, with lots of street art lining the walls, felt more my style and I enjoyed walking along the graffitied riverside.

Needing some peace, I crossed the river into the extensive Pratar Park. It was a haven of tranquility and I barely saw another human. I spent three hours there before returning to the station. Although I'd had a nice time, I was glad to be leaving Vienna – it just wasn't my cup of tea.

Slovakia: Bratislava - UFO Spotting (Part 2)

28TH JUNE - 2ND JULY 2019

Late on Saturday morning, I set off towards my favourite attraction: the UFO. I'd decided that I'd been *too* careful with my money, which was making my trip a little less fun, so I would pay the entrance fee to go to the observation deck. As I crossed the Nový Most Bridge, the 'love locks' attached to a small metal grid (to cement a couple's 'forever' love) vibrated with the movement of the traffic above. I thought how lovers seemed to stick locks on any old bridge - personally, I find it a tacky form of littering (I'm such a romantic).

On the other side of the bridge, I entered a little cabin and paid for my ticket. As we ascended in the lift, it sounded like we were on a fast-moving train. It took seconds to reach the flying saucer at the top of the eighty-five metre pylon, where there was a bar and restaurant. However the observation deck was slightly above the UFO, which meant climbing up a couple of flights of stairs. The views of the city were great, especially of the castle opposite. I could even see my running path through the woods. I wasn't sure it was worth the seven pound entrance fee but I didn't regret going; after all, it's not every day that you can claim to have been inside a flying saucer (and without getting anally probed).

Next, I walked through the nearby Sad Janka Král'a, a public park established in 1774, full of ancient trees. Ephemeral dandelion seeds danced in the air: it was quite pretty until one flew into my eye and temporarily blinded me. In one corner of the park is a random gothic tower. It was once a 15th century church tower but it was damaged during an earthquake in 1897 and placed inside the park. As I took photos of it, a nearby violinist played the Superman theme tune - it was a surreal moment.

Leaving the park, I walked to the huge Petržalka area, where over 100,000 people live in panelaks (tower blocks), built during the communist-ruled seventies. Brightly-coloured facades were added to the buildings in the late eighties and I found them quite attractive. In the spaces between the apartments were play areas. Considering it was a Saturday, I was surprised not to see a single child using them, even though I could hear their laughter and cries from open windows.

As I crossed the bridge, back to the old town, I considered going straight home, but there was another building I wanted to see: the Slovak Radio Building. Heading north, I came across the palace, where I passed through its attractive, well-maintained gardens. Almost immediately after, I passed through another park, Námestie Slobody (Freedom Square). Once the pride and joy of communist Bratislava, it was now completely deserted. In the park's centre is a large square where you can find the biggest fountain in Bratislava (and apparently the whole of Slovakia). The main focus of the fountain is a giant metal sculpture of a linden flower. After the fall of communism, the fountain fell into disrepair and it hasn't worked since 2007. It is now covered in graffiti and grass grows out of cracks in the concrete. There are currently no plans to repair it as it would cost a million euros to do so. I preferred it as it was anyway - an abandoned reminder of the past.

Moving on, I reached my stop: the mesmerising Slovak Radio Building, which is shaped like an inverted pyramid. Built in 1983, it has apparently featured on the 'Ugliest Buildings in the World' list. However, with its unusual angles, I thought it was incredibly innovative. The architecture I'd seen throughout the day only served to make me fall in love with Bratislava even more and I was pleased I'd explored some new, less touristic areas.

That evening, I ran my rectangular route again. It was one of my favourite runs from the whole of my travels, maybe because it was quite varied in terms of scenery and was also quiet and flat. By the time I got back, the dorm was fully occupied. Although two people woke me when they came in from drinking, I soon went back to sleep and didn't stir again until my alarm woke me.

Late on Sunday morning, I took the bus to Devin so I could visit the castle there. It was only a twenty minute journey and it cost less than a euro. The ruins of Devin Castle, set on a rocky hill, were as impressive as the confluence of the two rivers there, the fast-moving minty Danube and the calmer but darker Morava. I liked how the colours of the two rivers swirled together like paint as they merged.

Devin Castle is one of the oldest in Slovakia, original parts of it dating back to as long ago as 864. It was destroyed in 1809 by the retreating forces of Napoleon but some parts were reconstructed in the 20th century. More recently, the castle witnessed a darker history: standing on the border of Austria, the Iron Curtain of communism ran alongside the river, just in front of the castle. Although the castle had remained open to visitors until 1989, the area had also been a heavily-fortified military zone with a barbed wire fence and watchtowers. Over four hundred people were shot there trying to escape. There are now various memorials, including a large heart constructed from the barbed wire.

After the castle, I walked along the river for a while, stopping for a hot dog and a jar of delicious raspberry and rose homemade lemonade from a small cafe. It felt good to sit back and relax by the river; I was in no hurry to leave.

At 3pm, I took the bus back to town. The city felt much hotter than Devin and after grabbing something to eat, I began walking back to the hostel. On the way, I noticed two brass stumbling stones, commemorating a Jewish couple who had been deported to a concentration camp in 1944. I'd seen stumbling stones frequently on my travels over the years: in Berlin, Budapest and Krakow, and they always made me stop and think. The stones, actually brass cubes, were installed outside the last place of residence of someone who'd been a victim of Nazi persecution or execution. These particular stones marked the residence of Jonas and Regina Unreich, who died at Auschwitz concentration camp. Their son, David, who managed to flee the Nazis, was a Slovakian wrestling champion, as written on a nearby sign.

On my last day in Bratislava, I wanted to visit the Slavin Memorial but having been busy with budgeting and planning, I made the mistake of leaving at midday. Upon stepping out of the hostel, I was hit by a wall of thirty-eight degree heat. I stuck to the shade where possible as that made it a little more bearable.

On the way, I passed a shady cemetery and couldn't resist taking a peek inside. Most of the gravestones were very old, some so old that the writing had worn away, and there were no other people, only squirrels and birds. Some of the older graves were overgrown: perhaps nobody was left in their family to tend them. It was a little sad to see but I also liked that nature had reclaimed the area.

Turning left out of the cemetery, I began climbing the hill. The route grew steeper and steeper and offered little shade, so by the time I reached the memorial, I was soaked with sweat. The views from the top were good though and I enjoyed seeing the UFO from a new perspective.

Slavin is a military cemetery and memorial, which opened in 1960 to remember the Soviet soldiers who died whilst liberating Bratislava from the Nazis in April 1945. 6,845 soldiers are buried there, some in individual graves, but most lay in one of the six grass-covered mass graves. The monument itself is a forty-two metre high obelisk, set upon an imposing concrete hall, with a soldier at the very top, crushing a swastika with his foot. It reminded me of a similar monument I'd visited in Berlin. I thought it might be busy with tourists but for a while I was there alone. When a couple of girls did turn up, they spent ages taking selfies of them laughing and posing on the monument. I found it quite disrespectful, just as I had when I'd seen people do it at Auschwitz.

I spent the rest of the day on my bed with the fan on. It's a good job I did, as an hour after getting back to the hostel, a much-needed thunderstorm began; it was still raining torrentially when I went to bed in my empty dorm, just after 9pm. Near to midnight, a new guy came in, turning on the lights and loudly rummaging in his bag. I wasn't pleased. I was even less impressed when his phone went off and he started chatting away like I wasn't there. Unable to bite my tongue, I grumpily told him off and he hung up with a scowl. After that, I slept well, until my alarm went off at 4:30am anyway. Seeing as my new roomie lacked basic manners, I didn't overly concern myself with being quiet.

At 5am, with the remnants of a red dawn fading in the sky, I walked to the bus station. It was much cooler and I enjoyed the novelty of the empty streets. My Flixbus to Vienna airport departed on time and I waved goodbye to the UFO as we drove past. As one of my favourite structures from my travels, I'd miss it. I'd actually miss Bratislava in general as it had become one of my favourite places in Europe. Considering I'd heard it described as a 'one-day city', I'd found plenty to keep me occupied.

As my flight to Vilnius (via Riga) wasn't until 9:35am, I wasn't initially concerned when we hit traffic, but as time progressed, and we stood stationary for longer periods of time than we moved, I began to worry. Nervously, I used my map app to tell me the distance to the airport every time we stopped. It wasn't good: we'd only move a fraction and then we'd have to sit and wait for five minutes. If it carried on at that rate, I'd miss my flight.

Gradually, sleeping passengers began waking up, and noticed our journey time had doubled. People huffed and puffed, and we pulled worried faces at each other while shrugging, sharing our frustration. Finally, four miles from the airport, we passed some roadworks; the traffic vanished and we began moving. In total, a forty minute journey had taken two hours and ten minutes.

Lithuania: Vilnius - Baltic Ways

2ND - 6TH JULY 2019

Rather than take a direct flight to Vilnius, I flew via Riga (a cheaper option). A six hour layover was required but writing my blog made time fly. With two hours to go, I moved to the gate. Being so early, the information screen was blank, so I sat with my back to it and tried to stay awake. I was blissfully unaware that I'd made a grave error...

At 6:10pm, I turned to check the gate's screen and was confused when it said *Tallin*. Realising my mistake, I ran to the departures board in panic: my flight was at 6:15pm, not 6:45pm and it said **CLOSED**. How could I have been so stupid? Cursing my idiocy, I ran to the correct gate. I could've cried with relief when I saw the attendant (who was busy with an elderly priest) and the open doorway. Grinning, she waved me through. As I took my seat, my hands were shaking: travelling could be so stressful.

Being such a small airport, within fifteen minutes of landing I was on the bus to the city centre. After six nights in a hostel, I couldn't wait to get to the Hot Spot Apartments, where I would have a private room. My apartment was new and modern; I knew I'd be happy there. Feeling tense from my long day of travel, I went for a run. I did a three mile loop, partly next to the river, and then went back along the main road. Exhausted, I showered and then climbed into the comfortable double bed with a smile - sometimes there was nothing better than the possibility of uninterrupted sleep.

I slept soundly and didn't wake up until late on Wednesday. Knowing that I only had three full days to see the city, I quickly ate breakfast and ran out of the door. There were two particular buildings I wanted to see and as the sun was out (meaning better lighting for photography), those were my first priority. The first was the Lithuanian National Opera and Ballet Theatre, built in 1974. It was a fine example of Soviet-era modernism and I loved it (the architecture, not the communism). Through the glass, I could see numerous cascading chandeliers hanging inside - it looked very grand.

Next, I visited the abandoned Vilnius Palace of Concerts and Sports, another communist modernist structure, which opened in 1971. With its mix of curves and sharp angles, the raw concrete arena was striking. Deemed unsafe in 2004, it has been standing derelict ever since. It seemed a shame that such an interesting building was being left to decay but I discovered that there was a reason: the site was once the Piramónt Jewish Cemetery, dating back to the 15th century. The Soviets destroyed it to build a large stadium (the palace was added later).

As I left the grounds, I came across a pile of broken gravestones. A small sign reminded people to show respect as they were at the site of desecrated Jewish graves. There had been plans to turn the arena into a convention centre but a petition against it had collected 38,000 signatures. For now at least, it seemed the area would be left alone.

Moving on, I wandered through the city. There were many beautiful buildings and churches: the cathedral was particularly stunning. Just outside the cathedral, on the large square, was the 'Miracle Tile'. Apparently, to make my wish come true, I had to stand on it and turn 360° three times with my eyes closed. I gave it a go, even if I felt a little ridiculous.

After lunch, I visited the Museum of Occupations and Freedom Fights. Based in the building of what was once the KGB headquarters, interrogation centre and prison, it was a sobering experience. I learned about Lithuania's troubled recent history. It was occupied by the Soviet Union from 1940-1941, with large numbers of Lithuanians being arrested and deported to hard labour camps (many dying in the process). Then, in 1941, Nazi Germany invaded and murdered almost 95% of the Jews living there. Once the war ended, Lithuania was retaken by the Soviets. Over the course of these occupations, many lives were lost. Partisans fought for years for the country's independence but it took until 1991 for it to become a reality. In the basement of the museum was the old prison. I felt sick when I saw the solitary confinement cells, water torture rooms, execution chamber and padded cell. I could only imagine the horrors that people suffered.

Needing some fresh air, I left the museum. Soon, I came across the Choral Synagogue, the only one in the city. There had once been over a hundred synagogues in Vilnius but all the others had been destroyed, either by the Nazis or Soviets. It seemed that little remained of the city's Jewish heritage.

Later, I crossed the River Vilnia to meet my Lithuanian friend (Ruta) in the bohemian 'republic' of Užupis. As agreed, I waited at the Angel Statue, next to the beer pump, which delivers free beer annually during April Fool's Day (Užupis' 'founding' day). Once the Jewish quarter, Užupis was left empty after the Holocaust. Eventually it became home to prostitutes, drug addicts, writers and artists.

The artists soon began livening up the abandoned buildings with graffiti and in 1997, Užupis declared itself (with tongue firmly in cheek) a republic. Ironically, it's now one of the most expensive areas in the city to live. There were many sculptures, including the mermaid and a backpacking Jesus. Ruta explained that Užupis had even created its own constitution and took me to where it was displayed in different languages on a wall. The forty-one rules revolve around peace, equality and acceptance for all (including animals).

It was lovely to have a personal tour guide. I'd met Ruta on a tour of northern Montenegro a couple of years before. She told me lots of stories and showed me some of her favourite places, including the Park of Hills, with its underwhelming singing and dancing fountain, and the gothic-style St. Anne's Church. Time flew as we spoke about Lithuania, our travels and our lives, and before we knew it, it was almost dark. Finally, we went our separate ways, agreeing to meet again on Friday.

I woke on Thursday ready to run. The weather was perfect: bright but cool. I ran five miles along the riverside, passing graffitied walls and derelict buildings but few other people. I then turned around and ran five miles back again. It was my longest of the year.

Once I'd showered, I hurried back out to join the *Alternative Walking Tour*. Our leader, a friendly young woman named Violeta, was waiting at the square near the cathedral. First, she showed us the Miracle Tile and then a tile I hadn't noticed before, with a pair of footprints embedded in it. She explained that it marked the end of the Baltic Way, or the Chain of Freedom, a peaceful protest that had occurred on 23rd August 1989. The citizens of the three Baltic countries wanted freedom from Soviet rule and the protest made a powerful statement, gaining global attention. Seven months later, Lithuania gained its independence, with Estonia and Latvia following soon after. During the event, approximately two million people from the three countries joined hands in solidarity, creating an unbroken human chain (the longest in history). Starting in Tallin (Estonia), the Baltic Way spanned over 370 miles, stretching through Riga (Latvia) and ending at the square in Vilnius (Lithuania). It must've been incredible to witness.

Violeta told us a few other stories about Vilnius landmarks. A common theme seemed to be that locals hated new things at first, be it a statue, a building or an idea, but eventually came to embrace them. Funnily enough, Ruta had said the same thing. Taking the bus to the suburb of Šnipiškės, which is protected as cultural heritage, we visited the traditional village there, which was situated next to several modern skyscrapers. Some of the wooden houses were beautiful and others were in various stages of dilapidation. Violeta explained that some residents still live very traditionally, using an outhouse for a toilet and have no electricity or running water.

Next, we entered one of skyscrapers and took the elevator to the thirty-first floor. The views over the city were great but it was so windy that we could barely hear what our guide was telling us. Back on the ground, Violeta showed us some communist-era buildings and then we took the bus to a popular prostitution zone near the train station. Although illegal, it's apparently 'overlooked'. Close by was some popular political street art: Trump and Putin in an embrace, and a large golden sculpture of Stalin's head, complete with a pig's nose.

Once the tour ended, I took another stroll through the old town, taking a few photos, before stopping to buy something to eat. As usual, the young blonde woman serving at the supermarket was rude. When she threw my change at me, I couldn't resist thanking her for the *fantastic* customer service. She merely glared in reply. To be fair, it wasn't just her: every time I visited a supermarket in Vilnius, the young women at the counters were generally unpleasant to deal with. I think their training must go something like this...

How to Deal With a Customer:

1. Without looking up, convey your disgust at the customer's presence.
2. Scan the customer's groceries quickly, smashing each item down hard on the counter.
3. Show you have finished processing the customer's items by looking bored and/or angry.
4. Wait for the customer to look at the till's screen so they see the total cost of the goods.
5. If the customer stands there dumb, stab your finger at the screen while rolling your eyes.
6. Huff impatiently until the customer produces cash or card.

7. If the customer does not give the *exact* amount of cash, exhale loudly and shout, "Small money!"
8. Throw receipt and/or change at the customer.
9. If the customer does not leave immediately, start serving the next customer regardless.

The following day, I woke up to the sound of heavy rain. Grateful for an excuse to be lazy, I ate breakfast in bed and caught up with writing my blog. I'd agreed to meet Ruta in the afternoon but as 1pm approached, the rain showed no sign of stopping. We began making an alternative plan but by the time we'd decided on one, the rain had stopped so we went back to the original plan.

Ruta picked me up from outside the Turkish Embassy and drove me through a few districts on the outskirts of the city, including Fabijoniškes, which had some interesting communist-era buildings. From there, we drove to the Green Lakes. They certainly lived up to their name and as the weather was so cool, it was perfectly quiet (everywhere was far more beautiful when humans weren't there to ruin it). After a quick look around, we drove to a quiet residential area, where Ruta had once lived with her mother. We looked at her lovely old house and then walked along the riverside.

To finish our trip, we visited Ruta's mother. She was warm and welcoming, and I loved her cute springer spaniel, Luna. Kindly, Ruta's mum made traditional fruit dumplings, which we ate warm with sour cream. They were amazing, especially the cherry ones, and I demolished a plateful in minutes: it was such a treat to eat something homemade.

Returning to the city, Ruta and I realised we hadn't taken a photo of us together. We'd had so many opportunities but had simply forgotten. We looked around for a suitable background and settled on a house with pretty flower boxes. As we said goodbye, I hoped we'd meet again: we had a lot in common and I enjoyed her lively personality.

At 10:30am on Saturday, I left my cosy apartment and walked to the bus stop. It was a shame to be leaving, as it was a state day celebrating King Mindaugas' coronation: there would be several events in the city and most museums would be free to visit. However, it wasn't all bad news: the buses were also free.

I boarded the bus to the main station but I felt anxious without a ticket. This was because I'd seen the gangs of ticket enforcers in action. On my first full day, when I'd sat on a bench to enjoy some iced tea, a group of four older men in bright yellow jackets had been waiting at the bus stop opposite. When the bus had pulled in, they'd all jumped aboard, two blocking the exits while two checked people's tickets. They'd been quite intimidating and more than one person had received a fine. Ruta and Violeta had both said that it didn't matter whether a person was old, young, disabled or pregnant; if they didn't have a validated ticket, they'd get fined, and if they made a fuss, the police would be called.

From the bus stop, I walked to the bus station and took the Eurolines coach to the coastal city of Klaipeda (also in Lithuania). Ruta had told me the people there were supposed to be the friendliest in the country, so perhaps the customer service would be better? (I wouldn't hold my breath.)

Lithuania: Klaipeda - Spitting Distance

My first impression of Klaipeda wasn't promising - there wasn't much of interest around. Once I arrived at the Linterp Guesthouse, things didn't get any better. I entered the code to the outside safe and picked up an envelope with my keys inside. After some trouble with the gate and the main door (requiring two phone calls for help), I was able to enter my single room. In the description, it had been described as *basic* and basic it was. Most furnishings were on their last legs: the wicker blind; the chest of drawers; and the coat stand. Also, the bed was lumpy and the room was just generally pokey and depressing.

Although I had a private room, I had to share a bathroom with one other room. *I* was used to sharing bathrooms but the other guests clearly weren't. It soon became apparent that I was the only one who knew how to change a toilet roll or use a toilet brush. However, the worst aspect wasn't the bathroom; it was the gate attached to my room's exterior wall. Whenever anyone shut it, the wall would reverberate loudly (the gate had to be slammed to shut properly).

By the time I'd settled in and bought food at the supermarket, it was getting late. Sunset wasn't until 10:30pm and I wanted to stretch my legs, so I walked down to the waterside to find the beach. I was really excited as I hadn't been to the seaside since I'd been home. However, my mood soured when I discovered Klaipeda was just a port - there was no beach. I soon made an exciting discovery though – there was a passenger ferry that took people to the narrow, ninety-eight kilometre long Curonian Spit, just five minutes away. *There*, I'd find my beach. The knowledge turned my frown upside down and I felt excited again, even if I had to wait another day.

On Sunday, I didn't wake up until 11am. The gate had been suspiciously quiet. I later discovered that some naughty (but amazing) person had left it open, which meant people came and went in exquisite silence (sleep was better than security, right?). I wanted to do a three mile run but I didn't know which route to take. From the previous day's exploration, I knew I could easily run next to the Dane River for a bit, so that was a good start. I set off in sunshine, but five minutes after leaving the guesthouse, a rainstorm came out of nowhere and I had to hide under some trees. Once it stopped, I continued by a small river, diverting into a couple of small parks. Next, I followed a pleasant paved path by a wider river until I crossed over a bridge and returned to my accommodation via the main road. I loved running new routes - I never knew what was coming next and my curiosity often led me to do longer distances. By the time I'd finished, I'd run seven miles.

After a shower and lunch, I readied myself to explore the *wonders* of Klaipeda. I stepped out of the door and that was when heavy rain started again. I made the wise decision to wait it out indoors. This time, it didn't stop so quickly and it was well over an hour before I felt able to go outside without contracting trench foot. Once it felt safe to do so, I left the guesthouse with my trusty umbrella. First, I visited the beautiful Sculpture Park, where a hundred sculptures hid amongst the trees. I later discovered that the site was once a graveyard but the Soviets had demolished it to build the park and the poor citizens had to rebury their loved ones elsewhere. Many of the sculptures captured my imagination but I particularly liked the really weird ones. I didn't know what they represented, so I made up my own little stories.

From there, I wandered through the less entertaining Danes Park and some quiet streets. Nothing was grabbing my attention so I returned to the ferry port - the beach was calling. I paid one euro for a return ticket (not bad considering it cost fifty cents just to use a public loo) and took the ferry to Smiltynė. With a few others, I walked to the northern part of the spit and then I went off alone, taking a footpath which led to a low, narrow sea wall. I could hear the waves before I saw them and felt instantly happy. The sea wall was a kilometre long and I walked almost to the end. Thunderous waves crashed into the piles of massive tetrapods (funny-shaped concrete things). As tempting as it was to climb on one to get a better photo, I stayed safely on the path, not wishing to be washed away.

Afterwards, I walked along the deserted beach, watching the waves of the Baltic Sea and enjoyed some time relaxing in the dunes. It was lovely to be alone: I didn't want to leave. Unfortunately, an hour later, I was chased off by more rain. I'd known it was coming for a while but I'd optimistically kept my fingers crossed that the angry black clouds would pass me by. When the full fury of the storm was unleashed, I only had seconds to hide under my umbrella, which I broke in my haste. Still, it did a good enough job and allowed me to keep my camera dry, if not myself. Once the clouds rolled past, the sun came back out. Nevertheless, I decided to head back towards the ferry. Cutting inland, I took a barely-there path through a stunning pine forest. It was so quiet: I didn't see another human the whole time I was there. Once the sun hid away again however, it wasn't long before my solitude became an issue...

The deeper I ventured into the forest, the darker and denser it became. I started to imagine all sorts of scenarios and scared myself good and proper: there were too many spots to hide a dead body. Hurrying along, I escaped the forest just as the rain began again. Thankfully I had perfect timing as the ferry was just about to set off. The rain didn't stop so by the time I got back to the guesthouse, I was very soggy. I had to resort to turning on the heater to dry out my clothes. It seemed strange to think that a few days before, I'd been struggling in the unbearable heat of Slovakia.

I wasn't sure if someone had left it open, or if everyone was just in bed early because of the weather, but between 11pm and 8am, the gate didn't clang once. As a result, I slept soundly.

At 11am, I took the ferry back to the spit and then hopped on one of the hourly buses to Nida, which was a small town thirty miles south and close to the Russian border (a Russian exclave). As I was the first person aboard, I sat on the top deck of the bus, right at the very front so I could enjoy the great views. A mother with two children sat in the pair of seats on the opposite side: one of the kids didn't stop chattering the whole hour-long journey. She barely drew breath between relentless 'whys'. Why is the bus going so fast mummy? Why are we slowing down mummy? Why are we overtaking that car mummy? Why is the road so long mummy? I felt sorry for *mummy* as she could rarely offer sufficiently satisfying answers. To be fair, the poor woman remained calm and always *tried* to give reasons. If it had been my child, I would've lost my sanity after ten minutes (it was therefore a good job I'd chosen not to procreate).

Just after 11am, the bus arrived in Nida. The weather was better than expected so I was pleased I'd not allowed the rainy forecast to put me off. One of the main sights in Nida is the Parnidis Dune, an eastward-drifting sand dune. To reach it, I had a short but pleasant uphill trek through a sandy forest. The first thing I saw was the fourteen-metre tall sundial. Ample information can be obtained from it, including seasons, and the length of daylight hours in any day of the year. Apparently the spit is the only viable place in Lithuania for such a complex sundial as the sun both rises and sets into the water.

From the viewpoint at the top, the dune looked spectacular - it was much bigger than I'd expected. I took a few photos and then walked around the edge of the dunes, following the partially-covered footsteps of previous walkers. When the sun came out, the white sand was blinding. Small purple flowers grew sporadically which added a touch of colour.

It was hard work walking on the dunes and before long, my trainers ran out of room for my feet as they were so full of sand. As I checked my map app, I saw I was in 'Death Valley'. It made me laugh - I'd been to the real Death Valley and that really had been deadly. This was more like *Discomfort* Valley, due to the grass and weeds whipping my lower legs and being a bit 'ouchy'. Once I'd circled back to the sundial, I walked down to the water's edge and enjoyed the subtle beauty of the grassy meadows. A large wooden throne looked out to sea, so I sat there for a while to watch the gentle waves.

Reaching the main town again, I wasn't sure what to do – should I walk some more or take the next bus? The onset of rain made my decision for me: I took the 4pm bus. I sat in the same place as before (after checking that my curious travel companion wasn't lurking nearby). I'd just settled into my seat when I heard a familiar voice, "Mummy, why is someone sat in *our* seat? I couldn't believe it. They sat behind me but luckily the kids were so tired that they fell asleep. Torrential rain continued for the whole of the bus journey, the ferry ride *and* the walk home. In fact it was still going strong when I went to bed after midnight. I kept my fingers crossed that it would improve by morning, as until the bus left the next evening, I'd be homeless.

Just before 7am, I was jolted awake by the sound of the gate slamming shut. I'd purposely left it open the night before so at least I'd been able to get a few hours of uninterrupted sleep. To my relief, the sun was shining, so after checking out, I took the Green Turtle to a luggage locker at the station. My bus wasn't until 6:10pm, so I had a day of aimless wandering. I considered returning to the spit but it was very windy and I was worried that the ferry back might not run and I'd be stranded. Instead, I treated myself to a pizza. It tasted *so* good after days on end of butter-less cheese sandwiches, yoghurts and granola.

Latvia: Liepaja - Making My Heart 'Liep'

9TH - 12TH JULY 2019

The bus from Klaipeda arrived in Liepaja just before 8pm. As it was threatening to rain, I took the city's one and only tram (the oldest in the Baltics) to my accommodation, the Medainie Apartments. My kind host had left the key in the door to my room, and when I arrived, I found she'd left a welcome note and a pot of fresh honey in the kitchen, produced by her own bees. I had the whole top floor to myself with no neighbours to disturb me: the space and silence were glorious. After a walk to buy food from the supermarket (where I bought some delicious cinnamon buns) and a long chat with Tom, I fell fast asleep.

On Wednesday, I awoke to the sound of rain. Not wanting to get wet, I waited until it stopped before venturing out. Over seven hours and fourteen miles, I wandered through the city, barely stopping as there was so much to see: Liepaja made my heart *liep*. Liepaja is known as the *City of Wind*: when I arrived at the captivating white sand beach, I could see why – I sat on a dune to watch the waves and immediately ended up with sand blown in my eyes. With my eyes watering and sand whipping my bare legs, I walked along the beach until I came to a deteriorating sea wall. I followed it until it ended - I didn't see a soul and enjoyed feeling the sea spray on my face.

Eventually, I moved inland to explore the tree-lined Seaside Park, which as well as a running track, had several paths and cafes. Turning towards the city centre, I noticed that Liepaja had a mix of architecture on its cobbled streets, including several grand Art Nouveau buildings; however, it was the faded wooden houses that really captured my heart. They had a huge amount of character and some looked *so* old and dilapidated that I was surprised that people still lived in them.

In the late afternoon, I walked to Liepaja Lake, the fifth largest in Latvia. There were some wooden boardwalks across the wetlands and a kilometre-long concrete pier featuring a wooden watchtower. I climbed to the top to enjoy the view but even though the sun was out, the wind was so cold that I didn't hang around long.

After such a tiring day of sightseeing, I was glad to get back to my quiet apartment, have some food and take a long, hot shower. I edited my photos until I could no longer keep my eyes open, and then I fell into a deep sleep.

I woke on Thursday to cloudless skies. Although it was sunny, the wind was chilly, so I didn't overheat on my ten mile run. My route took me south, through Seaside Park and down to a cemetery, where I turned around. On the way back, I popped into an overgrown park to investigate some derelict forts. I was tempted to go inside but the interiors were littered with broken glass and despite the sunshine, the darkness and my solitude put me off.

An hour after finishing my run, I ventured out again. Locking my door, I turned the key and it snapped clean in two. Why did these things always happen to me? Using my fingernails, I was able to retrieve the other half of the key from the lock. I went downstairs and apologetically gave both parts to my host, who provided me with a new one. She also gave me the keys to the bicycle I'd hired.

I hadn't had much luck with previous hired bikes, and this was no different. Cycling to the end of the alley, I braked upon reaching the main road. However, I didn't stop, and nearly crashed into three young Latvians. They laughed as I yelped and desperately put my feet down to stop myself. Kindly, they looked at the bike and in broken English, told me the brakes on the handlebars were broken but pedalling backwards should stop me. It worked to a degree but I wasn't happy. Backpedalling *slowed* the bike down but it didn't *stop* it - I'd be in trouble if I needed to brake suddenly.

For the first couple of miles, I cycled slower than my running speed but I soon gained confidence. I was just grateful for the fantastic cycle paths. I'd hired a bike so I could visit the distant district of Karosta, in the north of Liepaja. Karosta (meaning *War Port*), a city within a city, was constructed in 1890 as a Russian naval base, later serving the Soviet Baltic Fleet. It had full infrastructure: its own sewage system, schools, railways, church and a power plant.

During the Soviet years, the base was made into a secret area and shut off to the public. However, it was abandoned after the Soviets left Latvia. Many of the buildings fell into disrepair and it became a ghost town. Slowly, people moved in but not the *most desirable* of people. In the nineties, with drugs and crime rife, it earned a reputation for being a dangerous neighbourhood. With an improving economy, things have improved in recent years and even though people still live in some of the crumbling communist-era apartment blocks, the area is now growing more popular with tourists.

It was an odd place. There were many large buildings that would've been beautiful in their heyday, but were now just broken, empty shells with boarded or bricked up windows. Some areas had a few residents walking about but others were utterly deserted - it was eerie and I could never lose the feeling that I was trespassing. I cycled the lonely streets, taking photos of interesting buildings such as the shell of the Manege, which once had an impressive glass roof. It was used for indoor exercises and festive celebrations and would've been beautiful in its prime. I also visited the St. Nicholas Orthodox Maritime Cathedral. Built in 1903, this was a stunning gem, hidden away behind some particularly ugly concrete housing blocks. During the Soviet occupation, it was turned into a Sailors' club, but after the fall of the USSR, it was returned to its original purpose.

Next, I went to the ex-military Karosta Prison, where I joined an escorted tour. Originally built to be a hospital, it became a detention centre instead, and operated as such between 1905 and 1997. It's now a popular tourist spot - you can even spend the night in one of the cells. I enjoyed looking around but with the interior walls painted black, it was a bit spooky. There was a lot of donated Soviet memorabilia to see and we also got locked in the pitch-black solitary confinement room for a while which was rather disconcerting.

After the tour, I cycled on a few miles to the Northern Forts. Part of the Liepaja Fortress, these forts lined the coast. They'd been difficult to destroy by man-made means but over the years, the ocean has done an effective job: many now lie ruined, half in the sea. I loved exploring them and especially appreciated some of the street art on the deteriorating walls.

On my way back from the forts, I made a final stop at the Karosta Breakwater, which jutted far out into sea. I followed this as far as it was safe to do so, but after the protective tetrapods ended, the wall became crumbled and dangerous. Treading carefully, I continued for a while but when it became too slippery, I turned around.

By the time I returned to central Liepaja, I'd cycled twenty-five miles on the deathtrap. Feeling I deserved it, I treated myself to another pizza before cycling home. Before bed, I packed, ready to leave for Riga the following day.

Latvia: Riga - Humble Heroics

12TH - 17TH JULY 2019

My bus from Liepaja arrived in Riga a little before 7pm. My accommodation, the Wicked Weasel Hostel, was just a short walk from the station. Clean and new-looking, I immediately liked it. That evening, I stayed in my room to write my blog, only popping out to the supermarket and to enjoy a free cider at the hostel's quiet bar.

I was in a four-bed female dorm with two others. When they hadn't come back by midnight, I turned out the light and went to sleep, hopeful that they would return quietly. They did *not* return quietly. Two young women waltzed in at 1:30am, chatting away, and turned on the lights. When I pointed out their inconsiderateness, they looked insulted, as if shocked I was cross. Ignoring me, they began packing. I mumbled the 'f' word a couple of times and gave them a good glaring at until they reluctantly returned the room to darkness. However, at 4am, they woke me *again*, this time with their alarm, but at least they had the decency to leave the main light off while they got ready. Once they left, I slept soundly, and with no more disturbances, I didn't wake until 11am.

After breakfast, I began exploring the city but my heart wasn't really in it: I was just going through the motions. However, that changed when I came across the ruins of the Great Choral Synagogue. From the memorial, I learned that on 4th July 1941, along with other synagogues in Riga, it had been set alight by the Latvian Auxiliary Police (a paramilitary force created from willing local volunteers by the Nazis). Any Jews inside had been prevented from leaving and were burned alive. I couldn't imagine their terror. Not for the first time, I wondered how one human being could do such a terrible thing to another.

| 384

Next to the ruins was a monument, this one praising the selfless acts of several Latvians who'd saved Jews during the war. Their names were engraved on columns and a symbolic leaning wall of marble pressed down on them, as if trying to crush them under its force (symbolising Nazi oppression). The central column of the monument featured the image of an old man, Žanis Lipke, who had saved around sixty Jews. He had a warm smile and twinkling eyes and I immediately wanted to know more about him. Despite a promise I'd made to myself not to focus on any horrible history when I came to Riga, I found myself drawn into the atrocities of the Holocaust, but Lipke's story would show me that kindness, hope and courage can endure, even in the darkest of times.

I discovered that over two days (30th November and 8th December 1941), 25,000 Jews were killed in, or on the way to Rumbula Forest. Strong men were taken away to be used for forced labour, while the remaining people, the elderly, the sick, the women and children, were taken from the Riga ghetto and marched twelve kilometres to the forest. Those who refused to leave or couldn't keep up with the cruelly fast pace, were immediately shot: the road was soon laden with dead bodies, blood blooming on the crisp white snow.

When the Jews arrived at the freezing forest, they were organised into small groups (by Einstzgruppe A and the Latvian Auxiliary Police), forced to strip naked and lay in one of the large pits (dug by three hundred Soviet prisoners of war, who became the first to die in them). Once in the pit, they were shot in the head. After a while, people had to climb on top of piles of dead bodies to await their turn to be shot. According to witnesses, the Jews were generally resigned to their fate and calmly did as they were told. Families tried to stay together as much as possible so they could at least choose to die together.

However, not everyone died instantly; some weren't even mortally wounded but were crushed under the weight of the other bodies. Moans could be heard until late into the night. Any poor souls who managed to successfully crawl out were soon shot dead by waiting guards. Fewer than five people escaped and lived to tell their stories. One of these was the young Frida Michelson, who threw herself onto the ground and feigned death. She lay motionless, face down in the snow for hours. When it was fully dark, she fled and went into hiding. Years later, she wrote a book called *I Survived Rumbula*.

Witnessing the Jews being forced from the ghetto, and the murders of those too weak to survive the march, Žanis, along with his wife Johanna, became determined to rescue as many as possible from certain death. To do this, he purposely sought a job at a German Luftwaffe, an air force warehouse where Jews worked under forced labour. Žanis quickly impressed his superiors as he was a reliable worker, who unlike many, didn't drink. Before long, he was trusted enough to be put in charge of transporting Jews between the ghetto and the warehouse. This provided the perfect opportunity for him to fulfill his mission.

Gradually, Žanis began sneaking Jews out instead of returning them to the ghetto, falsifying numbers. Some were hidden with friends or others who wanted to help, and the Lipkes hid several in their own house. When this became too risky, they dug a three by three metre cellar under their woodshed. The secret cellar had two exits, one covered by a kennel and one leading to a ravine, so the inhabitants could escape if one exit was discovered. Žanis also installed electric lights, which would be switched off if a stranger approached: this warned them to be on the alert. To lessen their feelings of isolation, the Jews were provided with weapons, food, books, clothes, newspapers and even a radio.

As the war progressed, and the Nazi noose pulled ever tighter, Žanis' task became much more difficult. He would sometimes have to bribe officials with cigarettes and alcohol but he never lost his nerve. Despite some close calls, including a Nazi bullet skimming his head during a rescue mission, he was never found out and lived to the ripe old age of 87. I found his story incredibly uplifting and I couldn't stop reading about him. When I discovered there was a museum dedicated to him, I knew I had to visit.

Leaving the synagogue behind, I crossed the bridge to the peaceful Zakusala Island. From the overgrown meadows, I was able to take a few photos of the 368-metre high, tripod-based Radio and TV Tower. It reminded me of a spaceship and I half expected it to take off.

Returning to the city centre, I visited the popular tourist attractions: the Old Town, the Three Brothers (three very old houses), the House of the Blackheads, the Freedom Monument etc. There were also several fancy Art Nouveau buildings in an array of colours. By late afternoon, I was tired so I returned to the hostel for a well-earned rest. I was delighted to find my room was still empty and made a wish to the universe that it would stay that way.

Later on, I went for a run around a nearby park. It was becoming harder to force running into my days. I was often walking many miles sightseeing and adding running miles into the mix was getting exhausting. So, as I only had ten days of travelling left, I decided that it didn't matter if the running dropped off a little. Once I was home, I could pick it up again properly. When I got back to the hostel, the other beds in my room were still unoccupied: my wish had come true and I had a great night's sleep.

My alarm went off at 7:30am. Leaving my luggage at reception, I took the train to Kemeri where I met the lovely Annette, who offered free tours of the national park on Sundays. We walked eleven miles through fragrant pine forests, eating sweet wild blueberries while we talked about life in Latvia. Annette took me to Green Dune Hill, some swamps, a pretty lake and on a picturesque wooden boardwalk to some stinky sulphur ponds. It was fascinating to hear her talk about the wildlife and plants - she certainly knew her stuff.

Towards the end of the tour, she showed me around the old park, which once very popular, had become derelict and overgrown. Annette showed me photos of her grandparents there before the war; it looked very different. The park featured a huge, white hotel: it was very grand but it sadly stood empty. May be one day it will get a new lease of life. At 2:45pm, I tipped Annette for her time and we said goodbye. It had been a wonderful day and although my legs were tired, I felt mentally refreshed by my time in the forest.

Back in the city, I stopped to pick up the Green Turtle from the hostel and then walked to the Hotel Saida. It was such a relief to have my own room again and the bed was *so* comfortable. The best part was the huge jar of dried peppermint leaves - it made the best mint tea and was much better than any teabag.

On Tuesday, I took the train to Jurmala. On the way to the station, I came across a small plaque on the ground, stating: *Here, people of Latvia sheltered Jews from certain death during Nazi occupation.* Marked as a Žanis Lipkes memorial, it made me look forward to visiting the museum about him the following day.

Jurmala Beach was pleasant but I couldn't relax as it was so crowded with young families and couples. For this reason, I only stayed an hour. Moving inland, I walked up and down the pedestrianised main street. Apart from cafes, restaurants and souvenir stalls, I didn't find much of interest so I took the next train back to Riga.

Instead of going straight home, I took a train to Rumbula, so I could pay my respects at the Jewish memorial. On the way, I passed through Šķirotava station. This was where the first 942 Jews from Germany had arrived by train from Berlin in November 1941 (Hitler wanted Germany to be entirely free of Jews so deported them). As they'd arrived the day before the massacre, there was no room for them in the Riga ghetto. Therefore the poor people, mostly the weak and elderly, had been made to walk to Rumbula and were shot in the same pits where thousands of Latvian Jews would also be murdered.

Rumbula didn't have much of a station building, just a rickety wooden shack next to the tracks with RUMBULA written on it in large white letters. Tall grass flanked the tracks but little else was around. I was the only person to leave the train and it felt like I was in the middle of nowhere. The memorial was located in the forest, between the train tracks and the main road. According to my map, it wasn't far from where I was standing, but I couldn't see how to get to it. I resigned myself to going the long way round, which would take twenty minutes (this wasn't ideal when I had less than an hour until the last train home). Turning right onto a narrow path next to an industrial estate, I then turned right again, onto the busy main road. Cars tore past me as I cautiously walked along the edge of the road.

I knew I was in the right place when I saw the twisted metal sculpture of what looked like a branch containing lumps of broken stone at a turning. The sculpture is said to represent the unyielding force of the Nazis. From there, I turned right onto a smaller road, where a memorial stone informed me that I was walking the same road that thousands of Jews had taken on those two fateful days.

As I entered the strangely silent forest, I found myself utterly alone. Swaying in the wind, the trees sometimes creaked, as if trying to whisper their story. I didn't want to imagine the terrible scenes they'd been witness to. The road led to a path, where there were more memorial stones. Several concrete pillars marked the way, simply engraved with the Star of David and *1941-1944*. People had placed small rocks on top of them in memory of the dead. The centrepiece of the memorial was a twisted steel tree, 'growing' out of a large cluster of jagged stones, each engraved with the name of a victim. The street names of the Riga ghetto were marked on the surrounding paving stones and the tree's branches were shaped into a Jewish menorah – it was an incredibly poignant tribute.

Around the site were large, raised rectangular mounds. These were the six mass graves, each topped with a single boulder. While I looked at them, I my blood ran cold; it wasn't due to the weather. At the end of the memorial path, I found steps leading down to the railway. I wasn't sure it was safe but it seemed better than taking my chances along the main road again. Turning right, I walked alongside the tracks. Luckily no trains passed and after a short walk, I made it to the platform. It had been a fleeting visit but I was glad I'd seen the memorial. I believe it's important to remember the terrible things that happened during the Holocaust so we can learn from them and try to prevent them from happening again.

Due to Soviet censorship, the Latvian massacre was overlooked for a long time. The Soviets consciously ignored the events at Rumbula and prohibited anyone from publishing information about it. However, in 1961, a group of Riga Jews began tending the site, erecting a memorial. This was removed by the state but the Jews didn't give up their battle to make Rumbula a place of remembrance. Eventually, in 1964, the Soviets relented and allowed a small monument, dedicated simply to *Victims of Fascism*, to be erected. This still stands today, and is referred to by some as the 'Aryan Compromise'. It felt like the site was *still* being hidden away, as except for the sculpture, there were no signposts on the main road directing people to the memorial. Perhaps it's for the best though, so the dead can rest in peace.

Continuing the haunting theme of the Holocaust, I spent my last full day in Riga visiting two museums: the Jews in Latvia Museum and the Žanis Lipke Museum. The first was hidden away on the second floor of the Jewish Cultural Centre. I spent two hours there listening to the detailed audio guide, which led me through the history of the Latvian Jews, and ended with an account of the Holocaust. It was some of the details that struck me the hardest: wanting an 'easy' job, the executioners told mothers to hold their children above their heads so a clear shot of them could be taken. How could anyone be so inhumane? Particularly touching was the diary of a teenage girl. I felt deep sadness as I listened to her recount of the terrifying days after the Nazis first entered Latvia. She'd said that she almost wanted death, as waiting for it was worse. She was murdered within a month.

The final exhibit showed a map of Latvia's mass graves, but more positively, it also showed where Jews had been concealed by those who'd wanted to help, people who were willing to risk their own lives to save others. Some hid friends and neighbours but most helped complete strangers. One couple hid a young Jewish girl who'd lost both parents - she went on to have kids of her own and live a happy life. Out of the 729 hidden Jews, 544 survived the war. The others were discovered and killed, usually along with their would-be saviours.

The second museum was across the river, on the island of Ķīpsala, next to the Lipkes' old home. Close to the site of the original woodshed, I entered what appeared to be a large wooden structure through a darkened corridor, where bright sunlight shone between the black slats. The whole museum, although surprisingly spacious, was designed to give people the feeling of living in the cellar under the woodshed. It was shrouded in darkness and featured a cellar in the basement that could be looked down upon, the exact same size as the one the Lipkes had built. It contained nine bunks, as the original had, and at the bottom played a video interview with an elderly Johanna Lipke.

Helpfully, I was provided with a free audio guide, which informed me that the museum was created to honour not only the Lipkes but all of the Latvians that had saved Jews. According to the book, *Like a Star in the Darkness* (written about Žanis Lipke), Latvia wanted to bring local and international attention to the *good* deeds of Latvians and regain some of the respect it had lost because of the disgraceful acts done by some of its own people (participating in the Nazi firing squads).

"If they survive, we survive."

This was said by Johanna Lipke after she and Žanis saw scores of Jews murdered with their own eyes. Disgusted by what they'd witnessed, they'd vowed to save as many as possible: they couldn't have lived with themselves if they'd just stood by and allowed it to happen.

Although Žanis was said to be quietly pleased to be remembered, the couple didn't like to talk openly about their selfless deeds after the war. Apparently, Žanis felt like he hadn't done enough: he was haunted by the memory of those he was unable to save. However, to every person he *did* save, he was a true hero. Many of those people, and their friends and relatives, visited him often. He received gifts and letters of gratitude right up until his death in 1987 (an impressive funeral was arranged by the Jews of Riga, to whom he was adored).

In 1977, the Lipkes were honoured as *Righteous Among the Nations*, a title given to non-Jews who saved persecuted Jews in World War Two. They were invited to Israel to receive the title but the Soviets (Latvia still being behind the 'iron curtain') wouldn't let them leave. They went anyway (as always, Žanis had his ways). After a lot of pressure from the Lipkes' widespread friends, they secured permission to visit their son, who they hadn't seen for thirty years, in Australia. From there, a flight to Israel was arranged.

As is traditional for those given the Righteous title, Žanis planted a tree at Israel's Holocaust memorial with his own hands. A reflective panel in the museum asked me to take a good look at myself and ask if I would have done the same. Would I have risked my life to save others? I like to think I would but I can't be certain: fear can quickly snuff out good intentions.

When I reached the end of the audio guide, I walked into the basement to see a small art exhibition. The artist, Velta Emīlja Platupe, had created some powerfully vivid pieces of work based on the Holocaust. Her argument was that forgiveness is impossible: by forgiving someone, you are wronged twice and the other person wins twice. I wasn't sure how I felt about that; it felt right (especially in terms of something as horrendous as the Holocaust) and wrong. I understand that forgiveness can sometimes be hard but by harbouring hate, you only hurt yourself. It was something that I thought about a long time after leaving the museum.

On the way home, I passed another of the footprint tiles marking the Baltic Way. I'd seen the first in Vilnius and now I needed to complete the set by finding the final one in Tallinn. My time in Riga had come to an end. Although I'd broken my promise, I was very glad I did. It reminded me that no matter how much darkness and hatred there is in humanity, there is also light and goodness. There are real heroes in the world, extraordinary people in ordinary clothes, people like Žanis and Johanna Lipke.

Estonia: Tallinn - Hipster Heaven

17TH - 22ND JULY 2019

It was noticeable upon arrival that Tallinn differed from the other Baltic capitals: along with more traditional wooden houses, there was a large amount of buildings that could've featured in an IKEA catalogue and there were lots of blonde-haired people. It felt very Scandinavian and the people seemed friendly. Ok, maybe 'friendly' was pushing it. Nobody smiled at me or anything. In fact, most people were too aloof to even notice me. I wasn't sure if people were *trying* to look hipster but as I walked from the bus station to my accommodation, there was an abundance of beards and moustaches, pretty tattoos, multi-coloured hair, unusual shoes and *artsy* clothing. There also seemed to be more than the usual amount of drunks.

For my five nights in Tallinn, I stayed at the Uue Maailma Apartment, just outside of the city centre. My host met me at the door, showed me around and then left me to it. I loved the apartment: it was cosy, quiet and had everything I needed (even a bicycle).

I spent a lot of my time there just relaxing and thinking. My trip was coming to an end and I didn't know how I felt about it. Part of me was pleased to be going home but another part felt lost. Including planning, the trip had consumed two years of my life and I couldn't help but wonder what was next. Being in the apartment made it clear I craved my own living space. I'd have to continue living with my mum while I restocked my bank account but should I start saving for a mortgage deposit, or should I move out sooner and rent? I had no idea. It wasn't just where to live that bothered me, I didn't know if I wanted to teach anymore as the stress wasn't good for my mental health. Would I need to find a new career too?

Before I'd left, I'd hoped that travelling would provide the answers to these questions but all it had given me was an empty bank account - I was still clueless about my future. I had to ask myself if it had all been worth it. Did I waste twenty thousand pounds on a whim? Did I regret my decision to travel? In all honesty, no, it wasn't wasted and no, I didn't regret it. The trip definitely wasn't what I'd expected but I had a huge amount of memories to look back on. I'd learned a couple of things about myself too, a key one being that I hurried too much in almost *everything* I did: driving, eating, walking and even reading. This only occurred to me on the way to Tallinn, so while I was there, I tried to take my time more. For example, at breakfast, I poured juice into a glass and drank it at the table instead of chugging it from the carton while standing at the fridge.

On my first full day in Tallinn, I didn't go out until midday. Instead of hurrying to see the main sights, I pottered around on the bike, taking photos of anything I found interesting. I really liked Telliskivi, an industrial complex and creative centre, consisting of artsy shops and cafes - it was hipster heaven and everyone there looked suitably fashionable and indifferent. I especially enjoyed the huge amount of creative street art.

For lunch, I stopped at the nearby Depoo, a trendy but slightly overpriced street food market. It was a fun place to people-watch and relax, and the chicken and pineapple pizza was delicious.

On my travels, I came across the seemingly derelict Linnahall, once the Lenin Palace of Culture and Sport (built in 1980). Although slightly crumbling, it was a good example of brutalist architecture. The final place I stopped at was a memorial park, a couple of miles along the seafront. Close to the monument for those killed by communism was a creepy sculpture. It reminded me of a nightmarish alien invading the city walls.

By the time I returned to the apartment, I'd cycled sixteen miles and my bottom hurt from the rather uncomfortable saddle. I'd enjoyed my unhurried explorations though and already felt more relaxed. After showering and eating, it was well after 11pm. I was surprised by the time as it was still so light outside. Sunset was at 10:20pm but as Tallinn was so far north it took ages to get properly dark, and then not for long. This was where my trusty eye mask proved useful.

I slept straight through until 11am. Getting up so late wasn't good though as I had a twelve mile run to do and would have to do it during the hottest part of the day. From the moment I stepped outside, I hated it. I don't know why but my body fought me every step of the way. The route didn't help, as it was mostly along busy main roads: there was little shade and nowhere to stop for a drink. I managed six miles and then found a handy little rock to perch on for a while. I didn't want to move, but I was thirsty and knew I had to make the return journey at some point (although the bus was a tempting alternative). Eventually, I made it back to the apartment. I was knackered but pleased I'd done it.

For the rest of my time in Tallinn, I took it easy. I slept a lot, ate at Depoo a couple more times, cycled to a small beach to sit by the sea and cycled to the peaceful Harku Forest for a hike. The chain came off my bike on the way home from the forest but thankfully I was able to fix it (after a little helpful advice from Tom) and save myself from a three mile walk home pushing a bike. The most touristy thing I did was venture into the Old Town, which was as crowded as it was beautiful. I managed to take a few photos in the less popular spots but within an hour, I found myself escaping back to my usual haunts.

On my last morning, I woke up to rain for the first time in days but luckily it stopped for an hour while the Green Turtle and I trudged the two miles to the port. From there, I would take the ferry (the biggest I'd been on in many years) to Helsinki. I'd enjoyed my time in the Baltics and had learned a lot about the countries' histories, the most memorable being the powerful Žanis Lipke story and the inspiring Baltic Way event (after much searching, I finally found the final marker in Tallinn's Old Town).

Finland: Helsinki - Final Port of Call

The 12pm Eckerö ferry from Tallinn arrived in Helsinki a couple of hours later. As with flights, everybody swarmed to the exit so they could be the first to disembark, most laden with crates of alcohol. After seeing the prices in Finland, I could understand why the route was used as a booze cruise. Even a small bottle of iced tea cost three euros (a big bottle in Tallinn only cost one euro).

Upon exiting the terminal, one of the first things I saw was a huge fountain/sculpture of a man peeing on the street. It was strange but it made me smile. My hostel was two miles away from the port. Having already walked two miles between the Tallinn apartment and the port, the Green Turtle and I were certainly putting in some miles.

The Diana Park Hostel was in a swish building but the hostel itself wasn't anything special. Annoyingly, a large school group of noisy young teenagers had taken over the place: I was so glad I was staying just the one night.

Because it was raining, I stayed in my dorm for the next couple of hours. I was almost glad as it gave me an excuse to be lazy. I'd temporarily reached my limit for appreciating new places and didn't have much interest in surrounding myself with tourists - my tolerance for idiocy was at an all time low. When I finally did venture out, the weather was gloomy, much like my mood. I dutifully took some photos but I felt sad and just wanted to be home, in my own bed. More than anything, I wanted to hug my mum, see Tom and eat a baked potato with cheese and beans.

I didn't have time to explore Helsinki properly but there were lots of people with dogs so that was a good start. There seemed to be a much bigger mix of cultures than in the other cities I'd been to and nobody gave me a second glance. Even the people in the shops were friendly - thumbs up for Finland!

By 9pm, I was back at the hostel in my six-bed dorm. Three German girls had already told the rest of us they'd be leaving at 3am so I was mentally prepared to be woken in the middle of the night. It didn't bother me as I knew I could sleep properly at home the following night. A young French girl in the room, a newly-trained teacher, was very friendly and we had a long chat about travelling, and the similarities and differences of teaching in our countries. She asked if I was sad to be going home but I told her no. If someone offered me the chance to extend my trip, I wouldn't have taken it. I didn't have the energy to keep moving around and needed to rest my weary feet.

I woke up to a bright sunny day. I was gutted as I found myself suddenly eager to explore the city. Instead, I packed up the Green Turtle and made my way to the train station. The train to the airport took just over thirty minutes. Everything went smoothly at the airport. Finland has the friendliest airport staff and even the people at security and passport control were chatty.

When I got home, Tom was there, waiting to take me home. My adventure was over. It was done. I must admit to feeling very sad about it in the end. However, my travels weren't over for good; I was already thinking about where to go next, possibly with Gina, who I'd met in Macedonia.

Writing the blog consumed a huge amount of my time (and was all written on my phone) while I was away but it surprised me how much I loved the act of writing. When I re-read old posts, I realise there's so much I would've forgotten if I hadn't recorded it so I'm grateful that I made the effort. A few people suggested turning my blog into a book and that's what I did: it will be a lovely memento. I hope you've enjoyed reading about it - maybe it will inspire you to have your own adventure?

England: Shepperton - Changes

My blog, as written on the day:

Since I came home two weeks ago, things have been somewhat difficult. When I first chose to go away, I thought it was because I needed the excitement of travel but I've come to understand that it wasn't that at all - I simply longed for change.

A friend kindly collected me and the Green Turtle from Heathrow Airport on Tuesday 23rd July. Despite finding out that Boris Johnson was about to become Prime Minister, I felt happy to be back on British soil. I would be able to see my friends and family and enjoy home-cooked food. To celebrate my first night back, I drunk the best part of a bottle of Disaronno. As I hadn't eaten for hours, I got <u>very</u> drunk <u>very</u> quickly. I was sick the next morning. It wasn't a great start to home life.

Over the next few days, I happily caught up with friends while cycling, kayaking, hiking, swimming and running. I was soon exhausted though and seemed to need far more sleep than usual. My happiness dissipated like a fart in the wind when I moved my stuff back into school that Friday. It dawned on me that my life hadn't really changed. I was back at the same school, still living at home with my mum and had already slipped back into my old routines: I felt like I'd never been away.

Not for the first time, I wondered if it had all been worth it. Had I wasted thousands of pounds? I didn't want to end my travels on such a negative note so I asked myself what the trip had taught me and how I'd changed. I came up with the following list:

1. I'm less bothered by how I look. I rarely wear make-up these days and no longer feel self-conscious when I go out bare-faced.

2. I discovered a love of writing. The blog has been such a huge part of my life for the past year and I'm now busy turning it into a book. Something might happen with it and it might not, but that doesn't matter at all - it will always be something that I can proudly look back on. I've never spent much time writing before, except with the kids at school but it gives me a lot of joy and satisfaction.

3. I know I want to live by the sea one day: maybe not for a few years, but at some point in the future.

4. I want to move out and have my own place. Ironically, if I hadn't gone travelling, I probably would've had a mortgage by now. The key thing is that I didn't _know_ I wanted my own place for certain back then. Now I do.

5. There's no place like home. I discovered that for all its faults, I like living in England and there's nowhere I'd rather be (but maybe ask me again after Brexit).

6. I am adventurous and brave. I travelled for almost a year by myself and despite some homesickness, I coped well and came home in one piece. Apart from breaking my nose, nothing bad happened to me.

7. I no longer feel the need to watch television. Before I went away, I wasted too much time in front of the TV. When travelling, I rarely turned it on when I had one, and apart from catching up with Poldark, I haven't had it on since I came home.

8. I now like babies (_some_ babies). I still don't want my own but I like my friends' ones.

9. I'm more positive. It's a work in progress but I'm getting better at shutting out the negative voices in my head.

10. I've learned that I do things too quickly. I need to slow down and not be in such a hurry all the time.

Individually, these things might not seem particularly significant, but together, they prove that my trip wasn't wasted and that I shouldn't regret my decision to go.

On my way to have some blood tests done this morning (to see if there's a reason for my tiredness), I realised that the key pull of travelling wasn't the travel itself but change. I'd probably been feeling down because I saw myself as being back to square one, but I know now that I'm not. Although I'm ready to return to work, the thought of returning to teaching depresses me. I enjoy aspects of the job but I hate the stress and how miserable it makes me at times. Switching to a new year group could help but it's possible I will need a career change. After all, nobody is making me teach; if I'm not happy, then I will need to change it.

In terms of living arrangements, I will stay with my mum while I start saving again. I don't know whether I will try to buy somewhere or decide to rent but I'm not going to overthink it as I can't do anything until I have money again.

In the spirit of keeping busy and exploring new avenues, I have booked onto an eight-week happiness course, which starts in September, and a free, two-day life coaching course in London. I'm really excited about both. I have four weeks left before I go back to school, and even though I have no money, I am determined to enjoy every minute of my free time. Today, I discovered that my local library has a lovely garden, so I sat there for a couple of hours reading some inspiring books. I might be hanging out there quite a lot this month.

Travel will always be important to me but I've realised that I don't always need to fly far away to see new places - there are plenty to appreciate closer to home. Whether it's a museum, a town or a forest, I'd like to try to visit at least one new place a month and keep feeding my adventurous spirit. In total, I travelled almost 50,000 miles in twenty-seven countries. People often ask what my favourite place was but it's hard to choose. I often say Tasmania for its natural beauty but they were all special in one way or another.

I would like to thank my unofficial sponsors: Snickers (the only chocolate bar that was available in every country I visited and <u>always</u> tasted the same), Pocari Sweat (a delicious Asian sports drink with electrolytes) and 7-11 stores (where I bought many of my meals in Asia). Without you, I would never have survived.

This is it, my final blog entry (at least about this trip anyway). I'm really enjoying turning my blogs into a book and reliving the ups and downs of the journey. In hindsight, I wish I'd appreciated it a little more while it lasted but I can't change that now.

As always, thank you for reading and remember, if you aren't happy with something in your life, then make a change. XxX

Final Thoughts - One Year Later

You might be wondering what's happening one year on. Well, like the rest of the world, I am slap-bang in the middle of a dreadful pandemic. I can only be grateful that it didn't happen a year earlier; otherwise my trip would've been a very different (and shorter) experience. Home took a long time to adapt to. In fact, I don't think I have adapted. I've felt unsettled ever since returning and I'm desperate to have a place of my own. I have therefore decided to move to Somerset: it's not the seaside but the countryside is just as lovely. I've spent a lot of time in Somerset since coming home and I love it. Rent is cheaper than in Surrey and I should be able to afford a small house rather than a flat.

I'm thinking of leaving teaching so I'm considering other possible avenues. The life coaching course led me to do a full diploma with the Coaching Academy. I'm currently halfway through my studies but I'm hoping it might eventually lead to a job where I can link coaching with my education background (or perhaps I might start my own small business).

My relationship with Tom only lasted three months. He's a lovely guy, but unfortunately, it just wasn't the right time for me - I had a lot of thinking to do and some big decisions to make and I couldn't balance that with a full-on relationship.

My blood tests came back fine and I've been in good health, if a little depressed at times. That's where the Action For Happiness course has been a sanity-saver. I met some wonderful people, who lift me up when I'm feeling down. We share ideas and experiences and are always there for each other when things get difficult. Several people in the group have kindly been my coaching guinea pigs too, for which I am very grateful. I now even lead a new group with my friend Mandy.

So one year on, not a lot has changed (on the surface at least) but it's going to and I can't wait to see what happens...

My Travel Questions Answered

What kind of luggage should I buy?

The Green Turtle is an Osprey Fairview 70 litre rucksack (which cost about £150), including a smaller rucksack that zips onto the front: it's comfortable, strong and will last for years. I also took a lightweight, foldable rucksack for when I needed extra space - mine was surprisingly strong and just about lasted until I got home. The most useful items were packing cubes: I had a large one for clothes (which I rolled up), a medium one for 'stuff', and a small one for underwear. They kept my bag neat and tidy (I never had to rummage around to find what I needed) and simplified the constant packing/repacking process.

What travel insurance should I get?

I used World Nomads, which cost almost £500 for the year. I only needed to use it once (when I broke my nose) and although I had to upload seemingly endless documents to their website as proof (*and* chase them up a couple of times by phone), I received the money back reasonably quickly.

How will I prevent theft of my belongings?

I had a panic about this in the preparation stages and investigated all sorts of safety devices; however, all I needed was some common sense and a little luck. I took three padlocks (with four-digit combination locks) so every bag was always secure. I also had a lock with a large metal loop to use on hostel lockers. When I was on the move, my valuables were kept in the small rucksack, which I wore on my front, and my *really* important belongings (passport, phone, cash and bank cards) were kept in a neck pouch, which I wore under my clothing. When I travelled between destinations, I kept a cash card, credit card and some emergency cash in a secret pouch that hooked onto my bra. My bank cards and passport were always kept inside RFID sleeves so they couldn't be used contactlessly without my knowledge.

When I went out for the day, I rarely took my passport (although I always carried a photocopy) or more cash than was necessary and would lock them inside my bag, locked inside a locker. I never once used hotel safes. Whenever I went out, I *always* locked my important belongings away. I never relaxed this rule and as a result, I never had anything stolen.

What credit and debit cards should I take to avoid international fees?

I opened up a Starling Bank account before I left (a mobile phone only bank). They had no foreign transaction fees and my account was easy to manage within the app. All of my savings were kept in a savings account and I transferred roughly £1200 per month into my main bank account. When I needed cash, I transferred money from there into my Starling account and then withdrew it from the ATM. This saved me from ever using my main debit card while I was away (limiting the chances of fraud). The Starling app was great because I could turn off ATM withdrawals or internet transactions, which made me feel more in control. It would also notify me straight away (as long as I had internet) whenever a transaction was made, so if anything untoward did happen, I would immediately be aware.

I took a Halifax Clarity MasterCard, which again, had no fees for foreign transactions. I used this for travel bookings so my money was always protected (for example, I had £350 returned to me when an airline I'd booked with went bust). I never had to use my main credit card as it was just a back-up.

Even though the cards I used did not charge fees (saving me a fortune), some of the individual ATM machines did (particularly in

Thailand). I generally did my research first (into which banks were cheapest to use), but I got caught out a couple of times. I also tried to use ATMs attached to banks rather than stand-alone machines or those inside mini-markets, which were more likely to have skimming devices on them.

How will I manage my budget?

I'd booked and paid for most of my flights (up until Christmas), the Australian West Coast tour and the Russia-Mongolia-China train tour before leaving England. I then divided my money up and gave myself a strict budget of £1200 per month: this worked out at roughly forty pounds a day. In Asia and Eastern Europe, this was fine but in some countries (especially Australia), it made life challenging. I also had a couple of thousand pounds of 'spare funds', which I used for flights, trains, buses, trips and occasional treats - it was also useful for emergencies although thankfully these were few and far between.

My money lasted well because I was careful, even when friends came to see me. The lack of funds sometimes made life a little depressing though, particularly when I had to miss out on seeing fun places or going out with friends for nice meals. Staying with friends in Australia saved me a lot of money on accommodation, for which I was very grateful.

I always booked accommodation with Booking.com, choosing places that offered free cancellation as I was prone to changing plans (usually when I was being paranoid about bed bugs or decided I was desperate for privacy). This meant I always knew how much my accommodation would cost at the start of a new month. I would then subtract this from my £1200 and see what I was left with as a daily budget. I must admit I spent quite a lot of time checking my money but the last thing I wanted was to overspend and have to go home because I was broke.

What visas will I need in advance?

Before I left, the only countries where I needed visas in advance were Russia, Mongolia and China. I used the same company I booked my train tour trip with. Even though it was more expensive (the three visas cost around £450), they made the process much more user-friendly than it would have been to do it independently via each country's website. Once I'd completed the online forms and uploaded my photos, Real Russia handled the rest and safely ferried my passport between embassies at the appropriate times. All I needed to do was take a trip to London to have my fingerprints taken as part of the application for the Russian visa. When my passport was ready, with all my visas inside, it was posted back to me.

The countries for which I applied for e-visas before arrival were Vietnam and Cambodia. These were done online and the process was simple. Also, I had to complete an online tourist e-visa application for Australia, which was fast and free. I always kept up-to-date with the current visa and passport requirements for the different countries I was visiting as I didn't want to get caught out.

Will I get homesick or lonely?

Yes. Staying with friends or making new friends always helped, especially when I'd get to meet up with them more than once. Talking to friends and family was also lovely as it helped me to feel connected. I was lucky that so many people came out to visit me as this meant I was never alone for too long.

How will I chat to friends and family?

Easily - I called people on the phone on the rare days I paid to use my data and used Facebook Messenger or WhatsApp the rest of the time.

As a fussy eater, what will I eat?

This was tricky in some places but I rarely went hungry. I ate a lot of chicken, rice and banana pancakes.

Will I get food poisoning?

No. I was always careful and made sure I visited busy restaurants or food stalls where the locals ate. I always made sure meat was properly cooked before I ate it and either washed my hands or used hand sanitiser before eating. I also regularly drank Yakult, to keep my good bacteria topped up.

Will I get a horrible parasite or disease?

No. I was always careful about the food I ate and tried to minimise insect bites by using repellent. If I had any cuts or scrapes, I would avoid going in fresh water (lakes, rivers etc.), use antiseptic and keep them covered. I only drank bottled water in countries where tap water was unsafe (I always checked this online and also checked with individual accommodations as some offered safe filtered water).

What immunisations will I need and how will I prevent malaria?

Apart from the standard jabs, I also had Rabies and Japanese Encephalitis (JE) immunisations. They were both quite expensive: the rabies jabs cost fifty pounds each (I needed three) and the JE ones cost ninety pounds each (I needed two). I didn't have any side effects apart from a sore arm luckily. I didn't take Malaria tablets as I looked at the Malaria maps for each country and saw that I would only be visiting low-risk areas. I therefore just used insect repellent (with at least fifty percent DEET) where it was necessary and took the usual sensible precautions.

Will I lose my running ability and how will I track my runs?

My running certainly slowed down (especially in very hot countries) and sometimes I took a break from it for a week or two but I kept at it. To track my runs, I used a Garmin Forerunner 30 watch with GPS. It was reliable and as it didn't look expensive, it didn't attract unwanted attention.

Should I take my heavy Canon camera or buy something smaller?

A few months before I left, I bought a compact camera, knowing it would be lighter and less bulky than my DSLR. However, after using it for a couple of months, I decided that Mr. Canon took much better photos. I wanted to take the best pictures I could, so I sold the new camera. I didn't regret it: Mr. Canon was old and battered so he wasn't appealing for thieves anyway.

How will I edit and back up my photos?

I bought a small, lightweight Lenovo laptop and downloaded PhotoScape (free photo editing software) onto it. Every couple of days, I downloaded the photos from my memory card using an SD card reader and edited them. Once I was happy with them, I uploaded them to the cloud (Google Drive) over WiFi (which sometimes took forever). This always worked well and I knew my photos (including any mobile phone photos) were always safe.

How about toiletries and sanitary products?

Toiletries were easier to find than I thought; L'Oreal hair dye was available in every country I visited, although sometimes only in larger chemists in the capital cities. Many of the accommodations offered free toiletries so that saved me some money. I took bar shampoo and conditioner from Lush to save me carrying heavy bottles around - they were great and I still use them now I'm home. I used liquid soap by Dr. Bronner as only a tiny amount is needed.

How will I do my washing?

In many South-East Asian countries, laundry was so cheap that I could afford to have it done whenever it was needed (and it always came back smelling beautiful). In other places it was relatively expensive (especially on a tight budget) so I did it by hand in the sink. I used liquid detergent when I could find small bottles of it but otherwise shampoo or shower gel did the job.

What will I do about my mobile phone?

I took my Samsung S6, which was a couple of years old. I had a cheap SIM-only plan and could use my data/phone plan as normal for five pounds a day in most countries. I barely ever did this though and just used free WiFi. I could have gone down the route of getting new SIM cards in every country but I was too lazy. Things were easier in EU countries where I could use my plan as normal.

What should I pack?

General	Clothes & Shoes	Toiletries/Medical
Cards & cash	Walking sandals & trainers	Sanitary towels & tampons
Passport & driving licence	Flip-flops (plain & fancy pairs)	Make-Up (minimal)
Photocopies of passport/visas	Underwear x7	Dr. Bronner's soap/body wash
Phone, spare phone & charger	Trainer socks x3	Bar shampoo/conditioner
Camera, batteries & charger	Bras x2	Flannel
Memory cards & USB reader	Bikini x2	Body oil moisturiser
Laptop, case & charger	Running bra	Eye make-up remover pads
MP3 Player & headphones	Running leggings & shorts	Toothbrush & toothpaste
Battery pack & spare cables	SRG running vest	Interdental brushes and floss
USB sticks	Running t-shirt	Sudocrem (small)
GPS watch and charger	Shorts x2	Deodorant
International adapter	Skirts x2 (1 long & 1 short)	Razor & blades
Head torch	Light scarf	Sun lotion
Sleeping bag liner	Trousers	Insect repellent
Sunglasses	Dress	Dry shampoo
Travel towel	Baseball cap & beanie hat	Plasters
Cutlery set	Short-sleeved tops x3	Antiseptic cream
Zip-lock bags	Long-sleeve tops x2	Vitamin D supplements
Padlocks & cable ties	Fleece	Ibuprofen & paracetamol
Notebook & pen	Sarong	Antihistamines

Door stop	Vests x5	Diarrhea tablets
Metal water bottle	Leggings x2	Hydration sachets
Running belt	Denim shirt	Tweezers
Bra security purse	Jeans (Europe)	Hairbrush
Neck pouch	Rain jacket (Europe)	Nail clippers, file & scissors
Packing cubes		Pumice
Ear plugs	**Train**	Lip balm
Eye mask	Metal cup	Wet wipes
Foldaway rucksack	Tea bags	Coldsore patches
Rucksack!	Lilo	Hand-washing liquid
Across-body canvas bag	Toilet roll	Toiletry bag
Make-up bags (for storage)	Food (porridge, cereal bars etc.)	Tissues

Printed in Great Britain
by Amazon